The
Mac OS® X
Panther™ Book

The
Mac OS® X
Panther™ Book

Andy Ihnatko
with Jan L. Harrington

WILEY

Wiley Publishing, Inc.

The Mac OS® X Panther™ Book
Published by
Wiley Publishing, Inc.
111 River Street
Hoboken, NJ 07030
www.wiley.com

Copyright © 2004 by Wiley Publishing, Inc.

Published by Wiley Publishing, Inc., Indianapolis, Indiana
Published simultaneously in Canada

Library of Congress Control Number: 2004102360

ISBN: 0-7645-6794-2

Manufactured in the United States of America

10 9 8 7 6 5 4 3 2 1

1V/RV/QX/QU/IN

For general information on our other products and services or to obtain technical support, please contact our Customer Care Department within the U.S. at (800) 762-2974, outside the U.S. at (317) 572-3993 or fax (317) 572-4002.

Wiley also publishes its books in a variety of electronic formats. Some content that appears in print may be available in electronic books.

This book is dedicated to:

My mother, out of love and respect as well as in anticipation of her maybe finally cutting me a little slack about the ponytail already.

Credits

Acquisitions Editor
Michael Roney

Project Editor
Maureen Spears

Technical Editors
Debbie Gates, Steve Arany

Copy Editor
Kim Heusel

Editorial Manager
Robyn Siesky

Vice President and Executive Group Publisher
Richard Swadley

Vice President and Publisher
Barry Pruett

Project Coordinator
Maridee Ennis

Layout and Graphics
Beth Brooks, Amanda Carter,
Carrie Foster, Lauren Goddard,
Joyce Haughey, Kristin McMullan,
Lynsey Osborn, Heather Pope

Quality Control Technicians
Susan Moritz, Angel Perez

Book Designer
Marie Kristine Parial-Leonardo

Proofreading
Linda Quigley

Indexing
Joan Griffitts

Cover Image
Anthony Bunyan

Special Help
Adrienne Porter, Tim Borek,
Cricket Krengel

Foreword

As a Close Personal Friend of Andy Ihnatko, it has fallen to me to write the foreword to this book. If you doubt my credentials beyond my belief that we can each spell each other's last names without help, consider the fact that Andy and I were born on the exact same day (November 18th, 1967, if you wish to send chocolate). Also, when I was talking to him not long ago about visiting his hometown of Boston, he said that he would have offered me a place to crash for the night but it wouldn't work out because, as he said, "I know that I have a carpet and a sofa, but chiefly because I have a good memory." And if anecdotal evidence is not sufficient and you require proof in cold, hard, electrons, I could show you the actual email message I recently received from him that opened with "Greetings, Close Personal Friend Of Andy Ihnatko!"

For the purposes of argument then, let's assume that Andy and I are like this. (Note to production: please insert complicated hand gesture.) That implies a deep and abiding bond for which either of us would risk bodily injury, if not an actual PowerBook, to defend the honor of the other. That means of course, that I'm going to say nice things about Andy and his book, even if I've just maligned his housekeeping. You want a tough, probing foreword? Okay, I really can't finish that sentence with a straight face.

So here goes. You will enjoy this book. In fact, you will enjoy this book more than any other book about Mac OS X Panther you have read, or will ever read, with the possible exception of that one Pogue did with all the naughty pictures of his Broadway celebrity clients. I base that on the years I've spent, as a Close Personal Friend of Andy Ihnatko, reading Andy's columns in *Macworld* and the *Chicago Sun-Times*. I have even read *Playboy* for Andy's articles (or at least that's my story, and I'm sticking to it). Simply put, and I say this not just because I haven't actually seen the book I am so lavishly praising, Andy Ihnatko is the funniest man in the Mac world. We Macintosh journalists are bitterly jealous of the pop-culture references that Andy can so easily weave into reviews of Microsoft Office, and that jealousy just gets worse when we hear him speak to a crowd and find out that he's not just funny on paper. In fact, but for being a Close Personal Friend and my position well above Andy on the MDJ Power 25 list of who wields the most influence in the Macintosh industry, I'd probably be so put out by his talents that I'd refuse to write a foreword for his lousy book.

But I'm not, so read his book. I will too, if he sends me a copy.

Adam C. Engst, *TidBITS* publisher, May 2004

Preface

Not easy things to write, these prefaces. I've been pulling books off my shelves and reading a few prefaces just to warm up. The one for *The Jeeves Omnibus* is pretty hot stuff, as is the piece that kicks off *Real Alaskan Bear Tales*. But they're not much help. I'm not P. G. Wodehouse, a tragedy that I don't think I'll ever recover from, and I've never been attacked by a bear, which is a lifestyle choice that has really worked out well for me over the years.

But as an experienced, professional writer, I suppose that all works begin with the question "What is your audience?" It soon pauses with the question "I suppose it's too early to knock off for lunch, then?" but before more than three hours have passed, you're back at the keyboard and pondering that first question again. I suppose the readers of this preface fall into exactly two groups, and for the sake of making sure that no one feels slighted, I'll address both of you individually:

Thank You, Book Purchaser!

I mean, honestly. Other authors forget what a miserable experience it is to have to wake up every morning at 6 A.M. and put on a name badge and a paper hat. But not me; I'm grateful for every book I sell and for every day that ends without me reeking of frying medium and pity.

Actually, I feel as though I ought to give you a little something to show my appreciation. How about this: when you're making scrambled eggs, keep testing the skillet by flicking water onto it from your fingertips. The temperature is perfect when the water immediately boils away. Then pour in the eggs and *let them sit*. Resist the urge to keep stirring them around; letting them sit is the difference between moist, fluffy clouds of eggs and dried, rubbery squibs. Don't start moving the mixture around until it starts getting a little dry at the very edges. Then slowly scrape the bottom of the pan — you're turning the eggs over more than stirring them up — and prevent overcooking by occasionally removing the pan from the heat from time to time. When the surface goes from glossy to moist, the eggs are ready to plate and serve.

This will be one of the 10 best pieces of advice you'll ever get in your life. Love often dies with the first forkful of hard, bland scrambled eggs, and if you can master the above procedure you'll be well on your way to attracting and keeping your perfect mate.

Oh, and it occurs to me that many of you might have paid full price for the book. Extra thanks to you. Don't get the tops of your ears pierced because that's cartilage and it hurts like bloody *hell*. On the whole that information is probably even more valuable than the egg thing.

Preface

If you *haven't* bought this book yet:

Welcome, Mall Megabookstore Browser!

If you don't own this book, then you're probably reading this preface while standing in whatever aisle of the bookstore that they're shelving Mac books these days, and you're trying to decide whether or not to pull the trigger and buy the thing.

Good for you. Can't be too careful with a dollar these days. Why don't you move to one of those comfy club chairs down by the Biography section? As the backbone of the American publishing industry, you *deserve* to be pampered!

Comfy? Good. You probably want to know what I had in mind when I put this book together. To teach everything there is to know about any operating system requires at least two or three thousand pages. That's way too much to cram into one book, and besides, in this economy I'm hoping to touch you for another three volumes further on down the line. So if you're looking for a book that explains how to use Unix's "cron" command to adjust the scheduling of automated system maintenance tasks and to ensure that your own scripts and functions are performed on a regular basis...you're going to be desperately disappointed with this book.

But if you've just bought or been given your first Macintosh, or if you've just upgraded to Panther from a previous version of the Mac OS, or if you've been using Panther for a while but are only just now realizing that you're just not exploiting it fully, well sir or madam, you're precisely the sort of person I was thinking about when I dove headfirst into this project.

And if a happy accident with an airport metal-detector fried that implant at the base of your brain-stem and as a result you suddenly found yourself thinking that you could do *better* than Windows...oooh, baby, let me show you Paris the way no one's ever shown you Paris.

Read on. Get yourself a coffee and a Cinnabun to enjoy while you browse through this book. Take your time. Check out the Bonus Chapters at the end of the book, which are easy to get through without having a keyboard in front of you.

I'm confident that you'll like what you see. But if you decide to postpone your purchase for another day, throw me a bone and smudge up the pages with frosting and stuff. It'll convince future browsers that this book is worth thumbing through from start to finish, perhaps even suggesting that you had read some stuff that caused you to howl with laughter. It'll also make the bookseller feel funny about returning the book unsold, which can only help to boost the book's numbers.

Icons Used in This Book

So, how get you started? First, let's introduce you to the unique structure of the book that you hold in your hands. There are a couple of book elements that you need to know about.

Sidebars

You'll notice these sidebars scattered here and there throughout the pages of the book. Sidebars are where I take the opportunity to digress. I share information that might enhance your understanding of the topic at hand, that add new perspective, or that I Just Plain Find Interesting.

> **A BOOK YOU SHOULD BUY AFTER BUYING THIS ONE**
>
> Actually, I got the idea from Martin Gardner's *The Annotated Alice*, in which the complete text of Lewis Carroll's classic is accompanied by sidebars that explain just exactly what the guy was talking about. You know, on the off-chance that you're *not* aware that mercurous nitrate was a key chemical used in the manufacture of felt, and hatmakers often suffered from mercury poisoning and exhibited psychotic behavior.
>
> The book's still in print and led to a whole line of "annotated" classics. Definitely worth a look.

Ideally, the effect of these footnotes will be like the "commentary track" you'd find on a good DVD of a great movie. Possibly it's like having some idiot in the audience yelling at the screen while you're trying to enjoy *Vertigo*. Hard to tell. My hopes are high, and frankly you might as well just grin and bear it because there really isn't much you can do about it at this point.

Though I suppose you *could* just put this book back on the shelf and spend the dough on Roger Ebert's *Movie Yearbook* instead. Hmm. That honestly never occurred to me. Well, okay, the man has a Pulitzer and everything, but did he ever teach you how to network two computers via Firewire? Just don't do anything rash; that's all I ask.

Notes

And then there are those comments that I inserted because I'm undisciplined and uncontrollable — and I need to comment on the discussion at hand. Right now. With sidebars, there's sort of an implied warranty. If you read the sidebar, you'll probably learn something useful but not essential. But notes are mostly here because I have a hard time controlling my impulses. All I can promise is that each note certainly seemed like a good idea at the time, and my heart was in the right place, absolutely.

Preface

▼ Note

See, as a writer, the most difficult part of the job is figuring out just how much Coke you need to drink before sitting down at the keyboard, and how often to redose over the course of the day. Some people need the assistance of university medical facilities and complex nuclear imaging devices to monitor the seratonin levels of their brains. All I have to do is read back the stuff I've written over the past hour or so. I'm on an HMO so it's a real time and money saver.

Book Organization

The book's chopped up into three major sections:

Part I: Using Panther

The bulk of it's dedicated to the nuts-and-bolts details of installing and using Panther. This book is ecumenical, embracing geeks of all skill levels. If you already know what the yellow button in a window's title bar does, feel free to skip around until you find something that provokes that not unpleasant sensation of mild confusion.

Part II: The Technical Bits

There are two areas that few users of Mac OS X seem to bother with: Unix and AppleScript. That's because you really don't *have* to. Unix is the OS that lurks underneath Panther's slick façade, and AppleScript is a resource for automating your Mac's functions and writing your own software.

"Unix?" "Writing your own software?" From way over here (in Boston, several months in the past) I can hear some of you getting up, misshelving this book somewhere convenient, and then stalking off to the Cartoons and Humor section to see if there's a new *Peanuts* anthology. Well, that's why these chapters were quarantined. But you really ought to read about this stuff. There's a difference between a User and a Power User, and it's the difference between knowing Unix and AppleScript...and, only having heard of those things. It's also often the difference between leaving the office at 4:30 and still being stuck working when Letterman's starting his monologue.

Part III: Bonus Material

"The Professor and Mary-Anne" of the book. Here are items that are interesting and informative but don't necessarily fit in with the other two sections. Think of these as the bonus materials that come on a decent DVD.

Acknowledgments

Andy Ihnatko

Many thanks are owed and many thanks shall be given:

First and foremost to my editors, Mike Roney and Maureen Spears, for consistently going above and beyond the call of whatsit and offering me as much support as an author could hope for;

My agent, Carole McClendon, for explaining all the fine print;

Keri and Nichole at Apple, always there with needed resources;

The makers of the Fluke Ukulele, whose portability and playability kept this project on its feet by keeping me at my desk;

Bob LeVitus, for making an offhanded comment to me while we sipped cocktails on a ship near Christmas Island...a comment that directly led to this and the other books in this series;

HB, the only author I like as much as P. G. Wodehouse, Douglas Adams, or myself (this is my way of saying "So send me your latest book already, for Heaven's sake!");

The folks, the sisters, their husbands, and their children;

The cooks and waitstaff at The Fifties Diner in Dedham, Massachusetts, for impeccable grilled-chicken club sandwiches when they counted most;

My Aunt Mary, who would be my real-life Aunt Estelle if not for the fact that she's not at all annoying and is more like Cher (only without the plastic surgery and boytoys (as far as I know — just kidding Auntie — again, as far as I know);

And You, the Reader, without whom I probably would have just blown the past few months dating girls and stuff.

Jan Harrington

I would like to thank the following people, who have helped me along the way: Gib Henry (iChat partner), Steve Glickman (iChat partner), Jim Weir (AirPort screen shots), and Gene Leeb (CD-burning screen shots). A big thanks to Maureen Spears, Kim Heusel, Mike Roney, and the rest of the Wiley folks.

About the Authors

Andy Ihnatko describes himself as "the world's 42nd most-beloved industry personality" because "it's vaguely credible but utterly impossible to prove or disprove, and thus precisely the sort of tagline I was looking for."

An unabashed geek ("The bashings ended when I left high school for Rensselaer Polytechnic, thank God"), Andy's been writing about tech since 1989. In the past, he's written for every single magazine or website with the word "Mac" in it, highlighted by 10 years as MacUser and then Macworld's back-page opinion columnist. He's currently the *Chicago Sun-Times'* technology columnist.

In his pursuit of "heroically stupid applications of technology," Andy has built an animatronic Darth Vader doll that could be controlled over the Internet via telepresence to hassle his room-mate's cats and written and published a complete set of plans and instructions for converting any Classic-style Macintosh into a fully functional 2.5-gallon aquarium. "The Original MacQuarium" was one of the Internet's first e-Books and can be downloaded from several sites after a quick Google search.

This is Andy's fourth book. Andy lives in Boston with his two goldfish, Click and Drag. He invites you to visit his aptly named "Colossal Waste Of Bandwidth" at www.andyi.com.

Dr. Jan L. Harrington has been working with and writing about the Macintosh since March 1984. In her day job, she is Associate Professor and Chair of the Department of CS/IS/IT at Marist College, where she carries the torch for Macintosh users with great enthusiasm. Her 30+ published books include more than a dozen Macintosh-specific titles, including several on various flavors of the Macintosh OS.

Contents

Contents

Contents

Contents

Contents

PART I

Using Panther

Why Having Chosen Mac OS X Was by No Means a Dopey Idea

In This Chapter

If Mac OS 9 Were Really Your Friend, It Wouldn't Crash On You So Often • Panther Is Non-Crashy *and* Faster
Panther Is Non-Crashy *and* Faster *and* Easier To Use • In Most States, Your Spouse Owns Half of That $2,000 Mac
The Lord of the Rings Soundtrack Isn't Coming Out On 8-track • You Can Still Run Your Old Apps
Panther's Got a Creamy Nougat Center of Thick, Rich Unix • Because I *Said* So, Young Man/Missy!

I suppose I should start off by stressing that I am totally on your side. I'm your pal, I'm your friend. I don't think I'm willing to co-sign a car loan for you or anything like that, but on the whole, when you picture Andy Ihnatko in your mind, just take a stock mental image of St. Francis of Assissi and add a hat and a downright stupid quantity of personal electronics, and you'll have me down to a T. Two reasons for this visualization: first, because I really *do* want you to be a happy, capable, and proud user of Mac OS X Panther; and secondly, I'm spending all this time writing a chapter telling you why Panther is a great OS.

Look at it this way: I already *have* your money. And yet, here I am, sitting in a hotel room in Kauai, reassuring you about the wisdom of Mac OS X, when I'm *supposed* to be at the beach competing in the XBOX Pipeline Masters Tournament, a surf contest that I was heavily favored to win. Plus, there were going to be girls there, probably. So why am I doing this? Exactly. Selfless dedication to the needs of *you,* the reader. No, don't thank me; honestly, I just don't know any other way.

At this writing, Mac OS X has been out for three years and yet (according to Mr. Steve Jobs' most recent Mac OS X keynote) it's been installed on just 40 percent of the world's Macs. We need to reaffirm why Mac OS X is the best thing to happen to Macs specifically and even computers in general.

HELP YOUR FRIEND, HELP YOUR AUTHOR

Here's some advice: You can tear this chapter out for handy, discreet reference in a variety of social situations. Such as, you're at a library and spot someone with a Power-Book who's still running Mac OS 9; or you strike up a conversation with a fellow ahead of you in line at the DMV and learn that he's a Windows user who's right on the edge of switching; or as a distraction for your spouse during parties, who is about to tell that interminable story about the water damage to his or her record collection unless someone heroically changes the subject. Another reason for you to tear out this chapter is that there's an excellent chance that you'll ruin the book and will have to go out and buy another copy. It's called Smart Marketing, people.

No question about it, one day you'll look back on your decision to upgrade from Mac OS 9 to Mac OS X and regard it as that pivotal moment when your entire life changed for the better. Why?

IF MAC OS 9 WERE REALLY YOUR FRIEND, IT WOULDN'T CRASH ON YOU SO OFTEN

We all like to have a little variety thrown into our workday. But when your computer freezes up on you 20 minutes before deadline of a critical project and you know that you had plenty of unsaved changes...well, you long for the stable, reliable, hour-to-hour routine of a federal prisoner.

Mac OS 9 was a steady evolution of the same OS that shipped with the original Macintosh 128K in 1984, which means it uses the same methods of managing programs and memory that were in vogue during the Reagan Administration. Sure, it made sense back then; with the ever-present threat of an intercontinental thermonuclear holocaust hanging over our heads, all of a computer's programs crashing at once really didn't seem like such a big problem, all things considered.

Thankfully, times have changed. New ideas about OS architecture and memory management were inspired and perfected and started to appear in Windows and other operating systems, while the Macintosh OS was stuck in the early 1980s. Before too long, the Mac got a bad reputation: It was known as that one operating system that always crashes, taking all of your work down with it — and for moving like a three-legged pig.

Such slings and arrows are a thing of the past with Mac OS X, thanks to Protected Memory and Preemptive Multitasking. *Protected Memory* is a memory-management scheme in which the operating system isolates every piece of running software, assigning it a private, walled-off little box of memory. Under the old scheme, the OS used one big memory space for all software. When one app trashed its space, it also trashed the space that every other app used. Result: Boom. One app might accidentally write data to a bit of memory that another app is using. Again: boom. The difference between protected memory and the way the Mac OS *used* to do things is like the difference between roommates living in a two-bedroom apartment and sharing an open loft space. Oscar Madison can decorate his bedroom with day-old newspapers and week-old pizzas, and it won't affect Felix Unger in the slightest.

Preemptive Multitasking is a bit more complicated. Essentially it's the way that the OS juggles multiple tasks. The old OS could run multiple apps, sure, but it used an unsophisticated scheme called *cooperative multitasking*. Those of you who've ever worked with Humans before see the flaw in this scheme right away: It only works if all of the running apps cooperate with each other, and because software is an ego-driven tangle of selfish personal interests, the "cooperation" was marginal at best. When a running app needed to perform a function, it would seize complete control of the CPU and only relinquished it to other running apps when its immediate task was complete. It all usually happened so fast the user barely noticed, but still, cooperative multitasting is fake multitasking.

Note

For a flawless demo of the limits of cooperative multitasking, just pull down a menu in Mac OS 9. Every other function comes to a dead stop; the snippet of code that handles the menu bar owns the Mac, and nothing else can happen until you let go of the mouse button. If you don't have Mac OS 9 handy, you can try to brush your teeth while your significant other is exfoliating. You can try as best you can, but you can't get around the fact that there's just one sink and one mirror.

The old Mac OS fakes real multitasking well, but X is better. The OS prioritizes all of the apps' ongoing tasks so that no one app can tie up the CPU.

As a result, Mac OS X is way more stable and feels way more responsive. Applications can indeed freeze up, but each piece of software, including the OS itself, runs in its own little bunker of protected memory. One malcontented piece of code can't bring down the entire Mac.

Under Mac OS 9, you're probably forced to restart your Mac once a day. As a longtime Mac OS X user, I can tell you that the only times I ever restart my Mac are when I've installed new software that requires me to do so. *This way is better.*

Note

Let's not pooh-pooh the advantages of using a computer that can crash at any given moment with the slightest provocation and take all of your open documents down with it. When I upgraded to Mac OS X, my only big disappointment with it was that I suddenly couldn't use "My Mac crashed and ate all my work" as an excuse any more. It was almost as bad as when I replaced my 12-year-old Pontiac with my first brand-new car. All of a sudden, people started expecting me to show up at work on *time* and stuff. It was a very stressful turn of events.

PANTHER IS NON-CRASHY *AND* FASTER

Mac OS X was written from the ground up, recycling little. Along the way, all of its basic code was enhanced and covered with Teflon to make it slicker and more aerodynamic.

If that weren't enough, it's optimized to take full advantage of modern Mac hardware, such as the G4's Velocity Engine coprocessor, the absurdly advanced architecture of the G5, machines with multiple microprocessors, and even new technologies for sharing the processing power of several Macs across a network.

Thanks to X's support of multiprocessing, any time Apple wants to make a faster Mac, all it needs to do is add more processors. Figure 1-1 is a graph of how hard a two-processor Mac works while playing music, building a DVD, *and* emulating a Windows PC all at once!

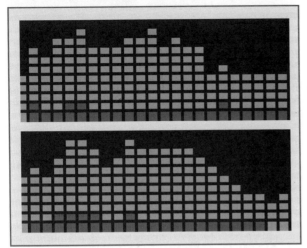

Figure 1-1
The Activity Monitor is the Mac's "dashboard" for examining performance

Bottom line: the first time you boot your old computer with Mac OS X, you'll feel as though you've taken the stock engine out of your Volkswagen and replaced it with something you pulled out of a Porsche while its owner was off in Vail.

PANTHER IS NON-CRASHY *AND* FASTER *AND* EASIER TO USE

I've been focusing on technical advances that have been made in the field of OS architecture since 1984. But Apple spent a fair amount of time reconsidering how Humans interact with computers and (by extension) how computers can be encouraged *not* to be such truculent nincompoops.

From the Dock to the new Aqua interface and beyond, Mac OS X's elegance and ease is as big an improvement over Mac OS 9 as Mac OS 9 is over any version of Windows. Check out Chapter 6, which is all about the universal and holistic of The Dock (Figure 1-2), Mac OS X's biggest and best basic improvement to the Mac interface.

▼ Note

Gosh, you're *still* reading this chapter? I'm terribly flattered. I think that Mac OS X already made a smashing case for itself at this point in the proceedings and if you're reading the rest of this, it can only mean that you're enjoying the writing. It's an overwhelming vote of confidence and I shall endeavor to be worthy of it.

IN MOST STATES, YOUR SPOUSE LEGALLY OWNS HALF OF THAT $2,000 MAC

Funny, isn't it, that when you come home after blowing thousands of dollars of the household budget on a new toy, other members of the house actually insist on getting a turn at the keyboard, too! I mean, *really.*

The petty demands of your spouse and kids will still sting, but at least they can't mess around with your personal files and customized settings. Mac OS X is a true multi-user operating system. If you set up the Mac with separate accounts for Mom, Dad, and little D'Artagnian, it's like owning three different Macs. Mom and Dad don't have to look at their kid's Sailor Moon desktop picture, and the kid

Figure 1-2
The Dock. The glorious, wonderful, funderful Dock is just one of the Mac's many X-only user-interface innovations

will never pore through Mom and Dad's copy of Quicken and learn that they spent all of his college money on that new Cadillac Escalade parked outside. Chapter 15 is all about sharing your Mac and its resources with other people.

THE LORD OF THE RINGS SOUNDTRACK ISN'T COMING OUT ON 8-TRACK

Mac OS X is the present, and it's the future. There is no serious ongoing development of Mac OS 9 software. Every important app, every utility that shaves an hour of work out of your day, every incredible new piece of hardware, every revolutionary Internet resource, every component of iLife that awakens talents in you that you've only hitherto-fore envied in others, and every efficient mechanism for locating and viewing pictures of scantily clad people will be available solely and exclusively for Macs running OS X. Not Mac OS 9.

YOU CAN STILL RUN YOUR OLD APPS

God knows why you'd want to, but you can. Mac OS X can bamboozle all of your old OS 9 software into thinking it *isn't* running on the most advanced OS on the planet. It's sort of like when aliens abduct Amish people and make their spaceship look like it's made out of pine lumber and hay, just to keep them from freaking out. Read Chapter 14 to see me heap additional derisive abuse upon the idea of running old apps, and parenthetically I also talk about how to actually do that.

PANTHER'S GOT A CREAMY NOUGAT CENTER OF THICK, RICH UNIX

And this is the point in the pitch when the car salesman talks about how this model has a Hanley-style fuel-injection

system instead of an old-fashioned venturi carburetor. You haven't the foggiest idea what *either* term means but so long as it makes the car go faster, that's all you're interested in.

Unix makes the Mac go better. No question. It means that your Mac is more stable; it's more secure from attacks by viruses and Trojan horses and evil, egg-sucking weasel system crackers trying to sneak in through its connections to the rest of the world. It also works with almost any network up to and including the one that controls the group-consciousness of the hyperintelligent race of cyborgs that shall surely enslave us all some day.

With Unix at the heart of X, the Macintosh community gets a lot of things for "free." That's literally true; open-source software (in which the apps are copyrighted but they're authored by the entire developer community and can be freely distributed) is a big deal in Unix, and every-thing from games to audio-recording apps to a complete suite of Microsoft Office–compatible apps are available for pennies (see Figure 1-3).

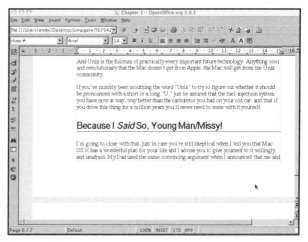

Figure 1-3
Open Office, a Microsoft Office–compatible suite of apps, is free for the downloading

Note

> Plus, there are a lot of bars and clubs near the Massachusetts Institute of Technology where you won't get anywhere with anybody unless you're wearing a wristwatch with more than 2 megabytes of flash storage and can honestly claim to be running some sort of Unix at home. Word to the wise.

But it's also *metaphorically* true. Apple tried twice to create its own next-generation operating system from the ground up and both times they quickly got bogged down in the infinite and stubborn details of forging revolution. Ten seconds after they decided to base Mac OS X around Unix, the new OS inherited all of Unix's advantages. It's aggressively a network-friendly OS: It's secure; it's extensible; it's based on international standards; it's supported and maintained by uncountable developers, which means that when something very basic breaks, chances are excellent that the problem is already well understood and the fix is easy for Apple to implement.

And Unix is the fulcrum of practically every important future technology. Anything cool and revolutionary that the Mac doesn't get from Apple, the Mac will inherit from the Unix community.

So I've sold you on the Unix and given you the technical reasons why it's a Very Good Thing for the Mac. But if you've numbly been mouthing the word *Unix* to try to figure out whether it should be pronounced with a short or a long *U*, just be assured that the fuel-injection system you have now is way, way better than the carburetor you had on your old car; and that if you drive this thing for a million years, you'll never need to mess with it yourself. If you *do* care to learn a little about Unix, however, and you want to take that giant leap forward towards Enlightenment and Productivity, be sure to check out Chapter 18, taking a deep breath first if necessary.

BECAUSE I *SAID* SO, YOUNG MAN/MISSY!

I'm going to close with that, just in case you're still skeptical when I tell you that Mac OS X has a wonderful plan for your life, and I advise you to give yourself to it willingly and unafraid. My Dad used the same argument when I announced that a couple of friends and I were going to drive to Rhode Island and get the cover art from R.E.M.'s *Automatic for the People* tattooed across our backs. It was *very* effective, and I avoided making the worst mistake of my life.

Instead, I got Weird Al Yankovic's *Dare to be Stupid* cover and have gotten nothing but compliments on it ever since.

Installing, Saying Hello, Saying Goodbye

In This Chapter

Rehab versus Scorched Earth: Updating • The Questions You Should Ask Yourself Before Installing
Part I: Installing Basic Files • Part II: Configuring a New Installation • Installing Applications
Getting Software Updates • Chunnngggg! Welcome to Macintosh: Startup and Login
Shutdown and Restart • Sleep and Energy Saver

Ah! A fresh, new copy of the operating system. Such a feeling of...what am I looking for? As though the first cool dew of Spring has broken. The announcement that pitchers and catchers are reporting to training camps. The unexpected and delightful appearance of shorts on your UPS guy.

Oh, and the dread, the crushingly cold feeling that you are atoning for the bad karma accumulated from every past life in one fell swoop as you gamely try to upgrade from Mac OS X 10.2 to Panther and, because your toddler chose a rather critically bad moment to yank out your Mac's power cord, your hitherto friendly and complacent computer is about to turn into Linda Blair, ejectile pea soup and all.

Well, chin up. Unless you bought a new Mac with Panther preinstalled, installing a Panther upgrade is just Something You'll Have To Do, and even if Panther *was* up and running the moment you unpacked your new Mac, you have to update it from time to time. Plus, remember that back during one of your previous incarnations you just blithely went ahead and pulled the lever to guillotine Marie Antoinette, just because an angry mob told you to? Well, *I* sure do. She was my favorite auntie! Never forgot a single birthday, she did. And she wouldn't just fob me off with a gift-certificate, either. So there's time to atone for past sins. Never lose your fear that one day, the Universe will finally turn its attention to you and cause a system crash of such profound and divine thoroughness that your only recourse is to reinstall from scratch.

REHAB VERSUS SCORCHED EARTH: UPDATING

Exactly what happens when you install OS X depends on what OS you currently have installed on your computer:

- **Mac OS 8 or earlier:** Before installing OS X, you must upgrade to OS 9, preferably version 9.2. Then you can perform a complete OS X install.

- **Mac OS 9:** You must perform a complete OS X install.

- **An earlier version of OS X:** You have three choices:

  - Upgrade your existing system software, preserving as much of your current system as possible.

  - Perform a *clean install*, which preserves your existing OS files in a folder named Previous System. When you select this option, you can also decide whether to keep your user accounts or create new ones.

> ▼ **Note**
> You create one administrator-level user account automatically when you install OS X. To learn how to create others after installing the software, see Chapter 15.

  - Reformat the disk on which you plan to install OS X. This is the equivalent of installing the software from scratch.

If you plan to perform a new installation or a Clean Install, you should also gather information about your Internet connection. If you use a dial-up connection to reach the Internet, you need your account name, password, and at least one telephone number to dial to reach your Internet Service Provider (ISP).

For all types of connections, know how your computer gets its Internet Protocol (IP) address. If you have a dial-up connection, the IP address is almost certainly *dynamic*, which means that your ISP assigns the address each time you dial in; for all other types of connections, you may have either a dynamic or a *static* connect, which is assigned permanently to your computer. A dynamic IP address may be assigned through Dynamic Host Configuration Protocol (DHCP), which is the most common scheme; Point-to-Point Protocol over Ethernet (PPPoE), which is used by some digital subscriber line (DSL) providers; or BootP, which you rarely encounter these days, but is still in use here and there. Your ISP or network administrator assigns a static IP address.

> ▼ **Note**
> Static IP addresses are relatively rare. Given today's network security concerns, most static IP addresses are assigned to network routers, which then take care of handling the addresses for other machines on the router's network. For more information, see Chapter 11 (for networking) and Chapter 16 (for security).

THE QUESTIONS YOU SHOULD ASK YOURSELF BEFORE INSTALLING

There are three big questions to ask yourself before installing a new OS.

The first one is "Do you feel lucky? Well, do ya, punk?" And yes, that's a serious question. You should always be a bit timid about installing newly released software. Apple voraciously tests all of its code before it's shipped, but even if 1,000 people have tested the new OS, it may still ship with bugs that won't be discovered until 1,000,000 million people start using it 7 days a week in real-world situations.

Fortunately, Panther has been out for a good while, so it's not a serious issue. But it's something you should always keep in mind. If a piece of software is absolutely critical to

EXPERIMENT ON ANIMALS BEFORE UPGRADING THE ONE YOU LOVE

I'm lucky; I have a big collection of guinea pigs here in the office. First, I install the new OS on a tower Mac that I rarely use. I test it out for a few days, and if it appears stable and seems to work with my accessories and software, I install it on the big tower where I do a lot of real, actual work. I install it on my PowerBook only after it's proven to work stable and happily on both towers.

You see, my PowerBook, Lilith (I've owned seven PowerBooks, each with the same name), is the most important piece of hardware I own. If Lilith gets messed up, I can't do my business. I can't write, I can't get at my email store or my address book, I can't access my manuscripts...on and on. So I don't perform any upgrade on Lilith that hasn't already been road tested.

Um, except for Panther, because the day after it was released I did something incredibly clever (read: stupid) to Lilith's System directory that caused it to stop working. And this was 24 hours before I had to go away on business. Fortunately, in this and all past lives I have lived a clean and pure life and so Karma was more than pleased to upgrade it from Jaguar to Panther without any Linda Blair-age. Just another reason why you should give blood, be kind to animals, and return your library books on time.

your life — and gosh, your operating system sure is — you might consider waiting a couple of weeks before updating it. By then, Apple will have discovered and fixed any obscure bugs that cause, say, all of your files to become unrecoverable mincemeat.

The second question is, "Should I perform a Clean Install?" Upgrading the OS is a lot like remodeling a house. Not everything changed since the last version; many components and subsystems are the same as they always were.

Normally, the Installer just replaces individual subcomponents, keeping the bits and pieces that Apple's programmers didn't rewrite. This makes the installation go a lot faster, and all of your Mac's old settings will persist. The third question is "Should I perform an Easy Install or a Custom Install?"

Should you perform a Clean Install?

Think about the Clean Install option. In a Clean Install, the Installer replaces the entire OS from top to bottom.

It takes longer, and afterward, you might have to change your Internet settings, your desktop, etc., back to the way they were before the upgrade. And sure, it's a lot of hassle. So why bother? Because an OS is an incredibly complicated piece of software, and over months and years of use, *teensy-tiny* things can go wrong with it. A word processor crashes, and it doesn't close one of the OS's critical files. You tried a piece of software that messed something up in a tiny way. Et cetera.

These tiny things add up. If they caused your Mac to stop working, you'd have fixed it, but they didn't; they just made it a little less reliable and stable. Performing a Clean Install whenever you buy a new OS is just one of those little things you can do to keep your Mac healthy. It's sort of like the difference between replacing a couple of rotted floorboards and replacing the whole floor. You're fixing the bits that are visibly wrong and you're also ensuring that there isn't a *hidden* problem remaining to send your 500-gallon aquarium crashing through to the basement at an inopportune moment during your Christmas party.

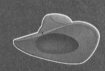
Should you perform an Easy or Custom Install?

The last big decision in this particular passion play is whether to do an Easy Install or a Custom Install. Easy Install is truth in advertising: Click a button and the Installer puts all of Panther's features and components on your hard drive. In a Custom Install, you get a chance to pick and choose.

- **Easy Install:** Honestly, you should just do the Easy Install. You rarely look back on the decision to do a Custom Install and think "You know, that's the best choice I ever made."

- **Custom Install:** If you choose Custom you're likely to — I want to say you will *inevitably* — leave out a component that you're going to need later, such as printer definitions. You have an Epson printer, you're installing Epson drivers, why would you want to install the drivers for the Monongahela 1200-Q? And then a year later you're in a strange town with your Power-Book and you *desperately* need to print something,

and thank *God* you found a copy shop that's open late — and the only printers it has are Monongahelas. Custom Install is good if you're desperate to save hard drive space (but drives are so cheap they're practically giving them away these days) or if one component of the OS has gone bad and you just want to replace that one component (but how do you know that it's just this *one* part that's gone wonky? You're better off reinstalling the whole thing). So actually, Custom Install is nearly always a bad deal.

Human factors to consider when installing

All the issues discussed thus far in this chapter are related to the Installer. There are a couple more things to consider, and they're both Human factors.

Before you upgrade, you should visit the Network portion of System Preferences. You should take snapshots of your customized network settings before doing a big update, just in case you're struck by the slings and arrows of outrageous whatever and need to reconfigure your access to the Net.

Just jot down your TCP settings and your Proxy settings (if they're not set to the automatic defaults). For speed, you can just click on the tabs to display the settings and then press ⌘+Shift+3 to take a screen shot of them.

Finally, make sure you've set aside enough time for the job. An OS upgrade is nearly completely automatic (the only thing the Human has to do is switch CDs when commanded; honestly, a monkey could do it), but it can take half an afternoon. You should only install the upgrade when you're sure you won't need your Mac for the rest of the day.

PART I: INSTALLING BASIC FILES

Because there are a myriad of installer options, walking you through each one of them would require a separate book! The following steps present you with the most common choices you can make and give you enough information to handle the less common options.

1. **Insert OS X install disc 1.**

2. **Double-click on the Install OS X icon** (Figure 2-1). The installation process begins, the launcher runs, and a window appears letting you know that it needs to restart the computer.

3. **Click the Restart button** (Figure 2-2). If you are currently running a version of OS X, the launcher asks you to supply an administrator password.

4. **If you are upgrading OS X, type your administrator password and click OK.** The launcher forces all running programs to quit and restarts the computer, booting from disc 1 rather than the computer's

hard drive. The launcher restarts itself and begins by displaying several windows that configure the installation.

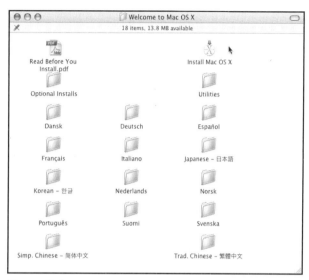

Figure 2-1
Launching the installer

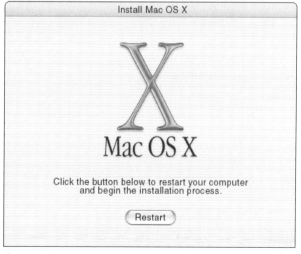

Figure 2-2
Getting ready to restart

HOW IMPORTANT IS THE IMPORTANT INFORMATION AND SOFTWARE LICENSE MATERIAL?

Yes, you do need to read all this stuff. The last thing the Apple people do before finalizing the CD is fill this screen with last-minute information. If hypothetically they knew a month ago that even *looking* at the Escape key kind of funny during installation causes the destruction of the entire contents of your Documents folder, they'd have fixed the problem. But they only discovered the bug three hours before mastering the final CD so the only thing they could do was include a note saying, "For God's sake, don't even *look* at the Escape key kind of funny while Panther is being installed."

But the software license? *This* you can just blow off. It'll only scare you. You have to read and approve more legalese to install Panther than you do to become a Navy SEAL. And Apple isn't Microsoft. Do you know that Microsoft released an absolutely critical safety and security upgrade to Windows, and snuck a clause into its installer license that said, "And oh, yeah, one other thing: by installing this software you also give Microsoft the right to track all of the digital music you listen to and sell the information to marketers."?

I mean, when the guy at Microsoft who added this clause reincarnates, that's one marmoset that will never catch a lucky break its whole life, believe you me. Clean living, kids; I can't recommend it highly enough.

5. **Select the language you want to use for the rest of the installation and click Continue.** An introduction window appears.

6. **Click Continue.** An important information window appears (Figure 2-3).

7. **Click Continue.** The software license window appears.

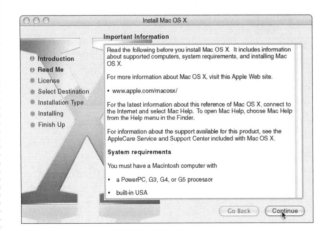

Figure 2-3
Reading additional installation information

8. **Click Continue.** The installer displays a window to confirm that you agree to the terms of the software license.

9. **Click Agree.** The installer looks for hard disks on which it can install OS X and asks for a destination to install.

10. **Click the icon that represents the hard disk on which you want to install OS X** (Figure 2-4). The installer begins installing OS X on your system.

11. **If you are upgrading from a previous version of OS X, click the options button to select the type of upgrade you want to perform and click OK** (see Figure 2-5):

   ▪ If you want to replace only essential files, leave the Upgrade Mac OS X option checked, and click OK.

   ▪ If you want to perform a Clean Install, preserving existing OS X files, click the Archive and Install option. To keep users and network settings during a clean install, click the Preserve Users and Network Settings option.

▣ If you want to erase the target disk and then install OS X, click the Erase and Install option.

Figure 2-4
Choosing a target disk for OS X

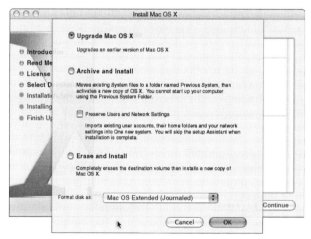

Figure 2-5
Choosing installation options

 Note

For more on these options and determining which is best for you, see the section "The Questions You Should Ask Yourself Before Installing."

WHEN USING THE ERASE AND INSTALL OPTION ISN'T AN EMBARRASSING SIGN OF OCD.

Even *I'm* not such a sadomasochistic freak that I'll erase my whole hard drive before installing. There's "Clean Install" and then there's "Obsessive-Compulsive Disorder Clean Install," where you can't sleep until you've scrubbed every platter of the hard drive with a brand-new Neutrogena soap bar.

Still, you should use this option if you're about to sell or give away your Mac. Your Mac contains loads of personal information plus thousands of dollars of commercial software. You're going to want to wipe it clean before you let it out of your hands. There are utilities that wipe the drive in a far more secure fashion but at bare minimum you should perform a reformat.

12. **Click Continue in the Select a Destination window.** The Easy Install window appears.

13. **Read the information in this window.** If you proceed with an Easy Install, the installer uses all the default settings to configure your OS X installation. Unless you want to use non-English fonts (especially Asian language fonts), this probably isn't the best choice.

14. **If you hate me so much that you're willing to do a Custom Install simply because you know it'll anger and irritate me, click Customize.** See the section "The Questions You Should Ask Yourself Before Installing" for why clicking Customize annoys me.

15. **Click the check boxes next to the items you don't want to install** (Figure 2-6). And make sure you know what you're doing because, man oh man, the *moment* you realize that you should have taken my advice, I'm going to be over at your place pointing and laughing.

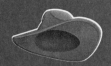

APPLE'S MIRACULOUS FOURTH DISC OF ETERNAL MYSTERIES

Three CDs? But what about that fourth one, the one that isn't all black and chrome and claims to contain XCode and developers' tools?

Um...it's packing material. Just there to keep the three install discs from bumping around and getting scratched. Pay no attention to the man behind the curtain. You don't need to see his papers. These aren't the droids you're looking for. *Move along.*

Okay. This fourth disc contains all the tools that real, big-time professional software developers need to write Mac software. But! Just as my new car didn't include detailed instructions on how to bore out the Flayven and remove the Boysenheimer Valve Winkel Drive for its quarterly pointing (for fear that I'd emit a dignified, ladylike scream and then go off and see what a 10-speed bike would cost me), Apple has isolated all that stuff into its own separate install CD.

It's cool beans. Really. At some point, you'll probably want to investigate that disc. But for now, you should seal it inside a manila envelope, write the word UNCLEAN on it in big, fat marker, and then tape it to the underside of the least-used piece of furniture in the least-used room of your house.

Inside that envelope contains your first steps into a larger and more exciting world, but it is not wise to tip the vessel of wisdom, young apprentice.

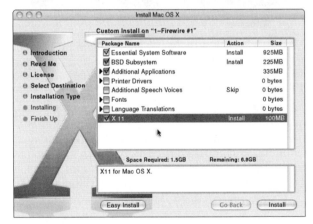

Figure 2-6
Choosing customization options

16. **Click Install.** The Installer begins by verifying the integrity of installation disc 1. Assuming that the disc media passes the verification, the Installer installs the software. First, it prepares various parts of the

software; then it copies files to the target disk. In each step, a moving bar appears to let you know that the installation is making progress.

Depending on the complexity of the installation, the Installer goes through either two or three of the Install CDs that came with Panther. Keep an eye peeled for the satisfying *shhffff-K-KLUNK* of the drive door opening and the CD being ejected. It's time for the monkey to take out Install 1 and put in Install 2, as bidden.

PART II: CONFIGURING A NEW INSTALLATION

If you are upgrading from OS 9 or doing a Clean Install without preserving users and network settings, your Mac has essentially been born again and needs to get reacquainted with you. The setup application launches automatically after the computer restarts (Figure 2-7):

Figure 2-7
Panther OS X welcomes you

1. **Select the country for which you want to configure OS X, and click Continue.**

2. **Select the type of keyboard layout you want to use, and click Continue.**

▼ Note

The options that you see throughout this configuration process depend in large part on choices that you have made. For example, the language that you select for the installation determines the countries presented in Step 1; the country you select determines the options in the keyboard layout list.

3. **Create an ID and password for an account at Apple.com**. If you have a .Mac account, you can use that as your ID; otherwise, you can create a new account:

   ◻ If you have an existing Apple.com account, enter your user name and password. You can also use a .Mac account name and password.

   ◻ If you don't have an Apple.com account and want one, click the Create an Apple IS for me option.

   ◻ If you don't want an Apple.com account, click the Don't create an Apple ID for me option.

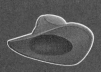

BUT WHY GET AN APPLE ACCOUNT?

Well, it's one of those things that costs you nothing, incurs no liabilities, and might pay off in some *small* way in the future. Essentially, every time you deal with Apple (when you need service, when you want to buy something, when you want to access certain parts of the website), Apple will already know who you are, and you'll be whisked straight in.

Bottom line: you'll probably set up an Apple.com account for yourself someday. Might as well make it today.

▼ Cross-Reference

For more information on .Mac accounts, see Chapter 12.

4. **Click Continue.** A screen appears asking for your software registration information.

5. **Type the software registration information, and click Continue.** The installer asks you some survey questions, and the answers are sent to Apple along with your registration information.

6. **Type the information for creating your account** (Figure 2-8). This is the name by which your Mac will know you and the password it will use to verify your identity.

7. **Click Continue.**

8. **Select options to set up your Internet connection.** Do you want to set up Panther's Internet connection right now? If so, tell the Installer what you want it to do. If you don't have an account with an ISP, you can set up a trial account with Earthlink (either by using the free trial you get with Panther, or by taking

advantage of a different trial offer you might have received). If you already have an ISP, you can click the third option. If your head is spinning and you'd rather just get on with using Panther, click the last option on the list.

Figure 2-8
Setting up your user account on this Mac

9. **Select how you are connected.** If you are connecting to the Internet right now, the Installer asks how you are connecting (Figure 2-9):

   ◻ If you are using a modem for a dial-up account, leave the first option selected.

   ◻ Click the second option if you are using a cable modem connected directly to your computer.

   ◻ Click the third option if a DSL is connected to your computer.

   ◻ Click the fourth option if you are using a shared Internet connection through a network connected through your computer's Ethernet port. In a home, you will typically have a router to which either a cable or DSL modem is attached. There is a wide variety of shared Internet technologies used in business, but typically you will have an Ethernet jack on the office wall from which you can run a cable to your computer.

Figure 2-9
Choosing a method for connecting to the Internet

Which screens appear next depend on the Internet option you selected. Because the installer has many screens, which depend significantly on your specific situation, it's impossible to show you all the possibilities. Make sure that you have your networking information with you and follow the instructions on the screen. For example, assume that you are sharing an Internet connection over an Ethernet network. The Installer checks the network for a device known as a router. If it finds a router that assigns network addresses, it asks if you want to use that configuration.

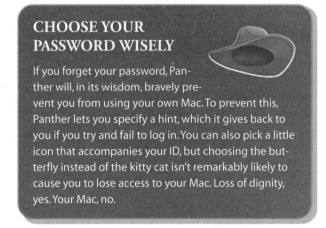

CHOOSE YOUR PASSWORD WISELY

If you forget your password, Panther will, in its wisdom, bravely prevent you from using your own Mac. To prevent this, Panther lets you specify a hint, which it gives back to you if you try and fail to log in. You can also pick a little icon that accompanies your ID, but choosing the butterfly instead of the kitty cat isn't remarkably likely to cause you to lose access to your Mac. Loss of dignity, yes. Your Mac, no.

10. **Click Continue.** The Installer asks if you want to sign up for a .Mac account (Figure 2-10).

Figure 2-10
Deciding whether to establish a .Mac account

11. **Click the option that corresponds to your choice, and then click Continue.** The Installer is now ready to connect to the Internet.

12. **Click Continue.** The Installer gives you the choice of sending your registration information now or sending it later.

13. **Click the option that corresponds to your choice.** If you choose to register, the Installer uses your Internet connection to send the data. The installer lets you set up the OS X Mail application (Figure 2-11). The information you need to type in the text boxes in this window comes from your ISP. When you are done, click Continue.

▼ Note

If you are using a different email client, such as AOL or Eudora, leave this window blank, and just click Continue.

---

14. **Set your time zone.** You do this by choosing a city in your time zone from the Closest City pop-up menu.

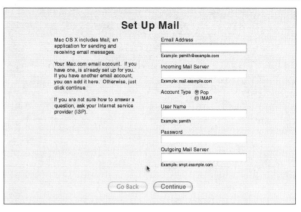

Figure 2-11
Configuring Mail

15. **Click Continue.** If you have a working Internet connection, the installer sets the correct date and the precise time automatically from a clock on the Net. Otherwise, set the date and time manually.

16. **Click Continue.** At this point, the basic installation is finished. The Installer either transmits your registration information, or reminds you to register later (see Figure 2-12).

Figure 2-12
Finish the basic installation

17. Click Done. You can now move on to installing applications.

INSTALLING APPLICATIONS

Naturally, we've been focused on installing Panther. So how do you install individual apps? It varies. Every software publisher has its own scheme for installing its software, but it usually comes down to one of three ways:

- **Using Apple's standard application installer kit.** Apple was nice enough to create a standardized mechanism for installing software and make it available to developers. So the process of installing most apps is the same as installing Panther: Chuck in a CD, launch the installer app, and then follow the familiar interface step-by-step until done. Some apps require that you restart your computer immediately; others wouldn't dream of harshing your mellow like that.

- **Drag the application from the CD into your Applications folder.** And honestly, that's all you need to do. Some publishers are even helpful enough to put a note next the file, visible right in the Finder: *Copy this to your Applications folder.* It's the easiest $300 a documentation author ever made.

- **And then there's everything else.** Many publishers (a) pooh-pooh Apple's installer, and (b) know that their software is too complicated for a user just to drag it into the Applications folder. So they create their own custom Installer app. Most of these are very easy to use, but overall, Godspeed, John Glenn.

GETTING SOFTWARE UPDATES

Apple is continuously updating OS X and its applications. Sometimes whole new features are added — some are esoteric performance enhancements, and some fix bugs. And then there are SECURITY UPDATES. These are extremely important because they repair security vulnerabilities that OS X has identified.

And the best part is that you don't really have to do anything to receive any of these updates. Thanks to a feature known as Software Update, Panther connects to the Internet at regular intervals to check for updated software. If it finds some, the Software Update window pops up and invites you to download and install them.

OS X has the Software Update feature turned on by default. Through System Preferences you can tell your Mac how frequently to check for updates, tell it to look for updates right now, or turn the automatic feature off entirely using these steps:

1. **Connect to the Internet.**

2. **Click on the System Preferences icon in the Dock.** Unless you've moved things around in the Dock, the

System Preference icon is the second or third icon from the left. The System Preference dialog appears.

▼ Note

If you find the Dock mysterious, take a quick peek at Chapter 6.

3. **Click the Software Update icon.** The Software Update dialog appears.

4. **Click the Check for updates option:** If you want OS X to check for updated software automatically, keep the Check for updates option checked (Figure 2-13). To change the frequency with which OS X should check for updates, click the pop-up menu arrows (Daily, Weekly, or Monthly). If you want to check for updates immediately regardless of the schedule, click Check Now. OS X uses your Internet connection to check Apple's servers for updated software. The results appear in a list (Figure 2-14).

5. **Click a check box to remove the check and prevent installation.** Click an empty check box to enable installation. Software Update places checks in check boxes next to the updates it thinks you will want to install.

6. **Click Install 5 Items.** In this example, five items have been selected for installation. The number of items will vary depending on the number of downloads that you select. Software Update downloads the update files and installs them on your hard disk.

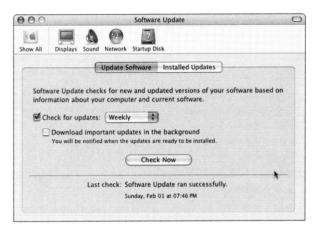

Figure 2-13
Selecting automatic software updating

WHY *WOULDN'T* YOU WANT PANTHER TO CHECK FOR UPDATES AUTOMATICALLY?

Well, if you use a dial-up connection, it's annoying to have your Mac suddenly dial out to connect to Apple's servers, even if it only happens once a week. Otherwise, the only people who turn it off are those who were taught that life is naught but a vale of tears and that it's the hardships that we suffer for that temper our souls to greatness.

If Panther is set up to check for updates automatically, why click Check Now on your own? Because Apple often *does* add cool new features to the OS and the iApps, and maybe you don't want to wait a week for them.

One caveat, though: Apple wouldn't release an update unless it was confident that it was safe and stable, but if Software Update offers you a major upgrade to Panther or an important app, you might want to wait a few days. Hit the Mac-oriented news sites just to make sure that those who've installed it haven't become intimately familiar with that "life is naught but a vale of tears and hardship" business I mentioned earlier. There was one rather legendary major update that actually wiped out a few users' hard drives. The update was quickly withdrawn and fixed, but man alive, an incident like that has an effect on your future decisions, you know?

Figure 2-14
Viewing a list of available software updates

Once Software Update has installed and optimized the updates, you may be asked to restart your Mac. You'll have plenty of opportunity to finish your work with other apps before restarting, so chin up.

 Note

> And I should tell you that chances are 50-50 that one of your running applications will refuse to quit and will cancel the automatic restart. Chin up. There is beauty and grandeur in the world. You are the sum total of the universe's desire to improve itself. Thus emboldened, quit those remaining apps manually and restart your Mac.

APPLE'S PARANOID SO YOU DON'T HAVE TO BE

Download the security updates, but don't worry about what might have happened during the time the security problem went unfixed. In Chapter 1, when I told you that we all inherit the benefits of Mac OS X's Unix foundations. One of them is that hordes of benevolent, white-hatted geeks are constantly poring through Unix to look for weaknesses that might even *theoretically* be exploited. And when one is found, someone immediately comes up with a way to eliminate it.

So usually, a Security Update is like adding a coat of phaser-proof paint to your front door. Nobody's ever produced a phaser gun, but the guys at Home Depot came up with an additive that costs nothing, so why not use it?

CHUNNNGGGG! WELCOME TO MACINTOSH: STARTUP AND LOGIN

When you start your Macintosh, OS X goes through a series of initialization steps to initialize the computer. As the initialization progresses, you see a sequence of messages telling you what OS X is doing (for example, Figure 2-15).

 Note

> The messages are extremely nerdy and aren't nearly as fun to watch as the stately progression of icons that you used to get in Mac OS 9. Though if you're over the age of 21, great sport can be had by lining up 20 or 30 shots of tequila on the bar, getting five or six friends together, and then when your Mac restarts, someone has to take a shot in turn whenever the word *loader* or *system* flashes by.

Figure 2-15
A sample startup progress message

You get a chance to log in at the completion of that process.

If you have just installed OS X, you will have only one user account — the one you created during the installation. OS X logs you in to that account automatically and takes you directly to the Desktop. However, after you create additional accounts (see Chapter 15 for details), you have three choices:

- You can have one account logged in automatically each time the computer starts.

- You can display accounts as a list from which users can pick (Figure 2-16). The user picks the account name and then types a password.

- You can require users to type a user name (Figure 2-17). The user must type both the account name and a password.

▼ Cross-Reference

For details on how to set these options, which have major security repercussions, see Chapter 16.

Figure 2-16
Logging in from a list of users

Figure 2-17
Typing a user name and password to log in

Startup Keys

Before the Mac even starts up, it looks at the keyboard to see if you're pressing any special keys that trigger all kinds of alternative behaviors. A sampling:

- **C** forces the Mac to bypass the normal drive and boot from a CD.

- **T** is for FireWire Target Mode. If (after shutting your Mac down) you plugged a FireWire cable from it to another Mac, pressing this key during boot makes the cable act like an external hard drive to the other Mac.

- **Shift** starts the Mac in Safe mode. If your Mac is experiencing problems, this runs a few quick disk checks and then loads the bare-minimum amount of code it needs to run Panther.

- **⌘+V** starts the Mac in Verbose mode, reporting on every last detail of the startup process as it happens.

▼ Note

⌘+V is a wonderful thing to scare less-savvy users with. Many startup keys are like that. Once I needed to make sure nobody used a specific Mac while I worked on the other side of the room. I restarted in single-user mode (⌘+s), which means that the Mac boots into a text-only, incredibly gnarly looking Unix command line. Believe me, nobody came near it. Which was good because in single-user mode someone who knows Unix can wreak havoc with the whole system. "He who lives by the sword" and whatnot.

And there are plenty more where that came from; go to the Help menu and do a search for "Shortcuts for starting up" to get a complete list. To use a startup key, press the key(s) right before you turn on your Mac (or right after the screen goes dark, if you're doing a Restart), and don't release the key until you see their effect.

Chiefly you use a startup key when you're diagnosing a problem with your Mac.

▼ Cross-reference

See Chapter 21 for more about troubleshooting.

Specifying Startup Items

There are probably some programs that you *always* use (like your word processor or the apps you keep your schedule and addresses in). Your Mac can automatically launch that stuff every time it starts up through its Startup Items panel. It's a timesaver. Remember, it's better to have the computer waste its time by launching apps you'll never use than to have it waste *your* time making you sit and wait for an app to launch when you're sitting at your desk, as opposed to off somewhere getting coffee and a Pop-Tart and stalling before you start work. Still, don't abuse this. Having more apps running at once means the Mac has to manage more resources to keep them running, which means reduced overall performance.

You can specify Startup Items using the following steps:

1. **Click System Preferences in the Dock.** The System Preference dialog appears.

2. **Click the Accounts icon.** This opens the Accounts preferences panel (Figure 2-18).

3. **Click the account for which you want to set startup items in the list of accounts.** This is located at the left of the window.

4. **Click the Startup Items button at the top right of the window.**

5. **Click the plus (+) sign below the list of startup applications** (Figure 2-19). This adds a new startup item.

6. **Use the Open File dialog to locate the application.**

Figure 2-18
The Accounts preferences panel

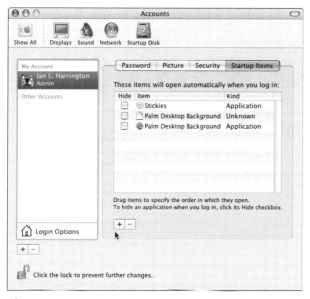

Figure 2-19
Adding a startup item

▼ **Note**

If you aren't familiar with the Mac OS's Open File dialog box, see Chapter 8.

7. **Click the Add (+) button.** OS X adds the application to the list of startup applications. The new application launches automatically the next time you start up the computer.

SHUTDOWN AND RESTART

When you're done with your computer, you shouldn't just cut the power. That's like ending a party by turning the indoor sprinklers on. It isn't polite. Your guests need a few moments to collect their things and make an orderly and safe exit. Though Lord knows, sometimes your guests don't deserve your patience and indulgence. I want to give you advice in life, not just in Panther, so I'll tell you that sometimes a fully charged fire extinguisher is the only thing that'll prevent Uncle Ike from climbing onto the bandstand and doing the risqué version of *Gentlemen Prefer Blondes* that he learned in the merchant marine. He'll sputter back to his Honda Prelude looking like the ghost of Jacob Marley, but your party will be saved.

A computer is no different. The OS uses scads of little invisible programs and files to manage all of its processes, and unless Panther properly closes them down, all kinds of gremlins and instabilities can crop up later on.

▼ **Tip**

OS X can have so many problems resulting from a "dirty" shutdown, you may consider getting an uninterruptible power supply. If there's a sudden blackout, big batteries inside the UPS take over and provide enough juice to close your files and shut down your Mac like a civilized member of society. That's a lot of peace of mind for less than a hundred bucks.

RESTART: DEFROSTING THE GREAT FRIDGE OF YOUR MAC'S MEMORY

The reason why restarting improves performance is a bit technical, but it's like totally emptying out the contents of your freezer and repacking it. After weeks of taking things out and putting things in and moving things around as best you can, food is packed terribly inefficiently. Look, the Ben & Jerry's Chunky Monkey is buried behind the warehouse-club sack of frozen peas, and to get at your Eggos this morning you had to pull out three loaves of the homemade bread your Mom made last Thanksgiving!

Things have a natural tendency to get disorganized in your Mac's memory as time passes, and a restart gives Panther a fresh start and helps things run faster and more efficiently. If your Mac is as slow as a truck with wheels made out of old copies of *National Geographic,* try restarting.

Performing a clean shutdown

To perform a clean shutdown, select Apple ➜ Shut Down. OS X closes all open applications, giving you a chance to save all files that have unsaved changes. The shutdown process then logs you out and shuts down all system processes. Finally, the computer powers itself down.

Quitting manually

Sometimes OS can't close an application, and you must quit manually and click Shut Down again.

Restarting does the same thing as Shut Down, except that after your Mac closes all of your apps and shuts down the whole operating system, it starts up again. You really shouldn't have to use this procedure very often. You might

be asked to restart after installing new software, and you might want to do it if your Mac is acting sluggish for no apparent reason.

SLEEP AND ENERGY SAVER

Finally, there's Sleep mode. Shutting down turns off your Mac, which saves power, absolutely, but you have to start up all over again when you're ready to go back to work. Sleep is a compromise. The OS keeps power flowing to every part of your Mac that's responsible for remembering what applications and documents are open and what they're currently doing. It turns off everything else: the display, the hard drive, bits of the motherboard itself. The end result is that when you return to your Mac and touch a key or move the mouse, it springs back to life instantly as though you'd never left it. And yet for the 3 hours you were off seeing *The Lord of the Rings* for the ninth time, your Mac was consuming a fraction of the 250 watts of power it might normally use.

Besides, Panther's built-in Energy Saver feature automatically puts your Mac to sleep when it detects that you haven't touched it in a while.

Setting Automatic Inactivity

You configure Energy Saver through the Energy Saver preferences panel, where you tell OS X how and when your computer should sleep:

1. **Click the System Preferences icon in the Dock.** This launches the System Preferences dialog.

2. **Click the Energy Saver icon.** This displays the Energy Saver preferences panel (Figure 2-20).

3. **Set the computer inactivity option:** Move the top slider to set the period of inactivity before OS X puts the computer to sleep.

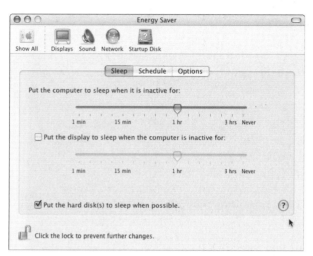

Figure 2-20
The Sleep pane of the Energy Saver preferences panel

4. **Set the display inactivity option:** If you want the monitor to go to sleep before or after the computer, click the "Put the display to sleep when the computer is inactive for" option. Then use the slider below to set the inactivity period.

5. **Leave the "Put the hard disk(s) to sleep when possible" option selected.** This puts hard disks to sleep as well.

▼ Note

Putting hard disks to sleep can significantly extend their lives. However, if you have programs running in the background, such as a file transfer over a network, it may not be possible to stop the hard disk from spinning.

Setting Scheduled startups and shutdowns

Energy Saver can also automatically start up and shut down your computer at times that you specify:

1. **Display the Energy Saver preferences panel.**

2. **Click the Schedule button.** This displays the Schedule pane (Figure 2-21).

3. **Click the Start up the computer option.** This starts the computer at a specific time.

4. **Select the frequency from the pop-up menu.** Your choices are Weekdays, Weekends, Every Day, or a specific day of the week.

5. **Set the startup time.** To do so, click in the hours box. You can either delete the 0 and type the hour or use the up and down arrows to change the hours. Next, click in the minutes box, and set the minutes.

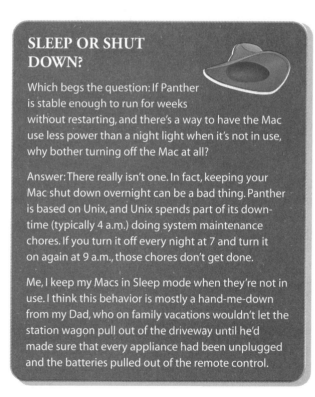

SLEEP OR SHUT DOWN?

Which begs the question: If Panther is stable enough to run for weeks without restarting, and there's a way to have the Mac use less power than a night light when it's not in use, why bother turning off the Mac at all?

Answer: There really isn't one. In fact, keeping your Mac shut down overnight can be a bad thing. Panther is based on Unix, and Unix spends part of its downtime (typically 4 a.m.) doing system maintenance chores. If you turn it off every night at 7 and turn it on again at 9 a.m., those chores don't get done.

Me, I keep my Macs in Sleep mode when they're not in use. I think this behavior is mostly a hand-me-down from my Dad, who on family vacations wouldn't let the station wagon pull out of the driveway until he'd made sure that every appliance had been unplugged and the batteries pulled out of the remote control.

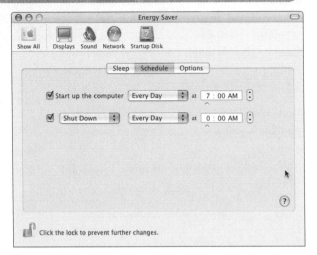

Figure 2-21
The Schedule pane of the Energy Saver preferences panel

The Preferences panel has a pane for a few additional options. There are times when you really don't want your Mac to be asleep at the switch. Like, if someone's sending you a fax, or if the folks who maintain your office network want to update some files. You can tell Energy Saver to always wake up when these events happen by clicking the Options tab and selecting the appropriate options:

- Sleeping the computer by pressing the Power key can be a big convenience, particularly in an office environment. When you get up to use the photocopier, you don't want passers-by to read what's up on your screen. Pressing the Power key dims your computer to black.

- The "Restart automatically after a power failure" option can be a lifesaver in the right hands. Sometimes your Mac isn't just your Mac; it can share its files and even its printers and other hardware with other Macs on the network. By clicking this option, a five-minute power outage won't turn the lights out on your Mac's network services for the rest of the weekend.

POWERBOOK USERS: HAVE YOU HUGGED ENERGY SAVER TODAY?

There are other settings that only appear when you're running Energy Saver on a PowerBook. Obviously, conserving energy is way more important if you're using a machine that relies on batteries. I don't give a pair of dingo's kidneys about whether there'll be enough light, heat, and power for my great-grandchildren. I want to be able to watch *The Magnificent Seven in its entirety* on this flight! The guy in the seat next to me is dressed like an insurance man and he has the hungry, rheumy eyes of a man who's under his monthly quota.

So Energy Saver has specialized, optimized settings that adapt to various operational situations. Longest Battery Life cuts off the hard drive and screen quickly. DVD Playback keeps the screen on but tries to conserve everywhere else. You can also have one setting for battery and another, "hogs greedily slurping at the trough of unlimited energy," setting that goes into effect when you're plugged into AC.

That pretty much covers the topic of installation, starting up, and shutting down. I had a nagging feeling that I'd left some unfinished business, though, and it didn't hit me until I scrolled back and reread this chapter in its entirety.

Just to keep the folks over in Legal happy, I should probably warn you that Karmic precipitation is solely the function of the ineffable and unquestionable universe and that attempts to influence the apportioning of same or project a desirable result into a future incarnation may *not* cause your functional conscious awareness to become elevated into the elusive *all-awareness*.

So, word to the wise on that. Onward!

Getting to First Base with the Mac User Interface

In This Chapter

The Desktop: What Lies Beneath • Menus: Drop (Down) Squad
Apple's Standard Menus • Pointing Devices: Mouse Hunt
Windows: View from The Top • Exposé: Sliding Doors
Keyboard Controls: Key Largo • Monitors: Through A Glass, Darkly
Help!

Whether you upgrade from Mac OS 9 or Windows, your first few hours with X are like your first few hours behind the wheel of a new car. You don't notice how much better everything is ("Hey, look! No duct tape on the windshield!") as much as you try to get used to how different everything is ("This seat hugs my butt in a manner which I publicly disapprove of, but which I silently quite enjoy.").

It's all about fit and function, and X has its own opinions on how users should be mollycoddled, cajoled, supported, urged on, dealt with, tolerated, welcomed, assisted, manipulated, soothed, and otherwise made to think that tearing this thing off the desk and making a sleek, iMac-shaped hole in the nearest exterior window is not a course of action to be advocated.

The hallmark of any decent OS — of which X is one, I assure you — is that you'll spend 95% of your time using the simplest 5% of its features. So once you master the basics of the OS X user interface, you'll be sitting on velvet and prepared to attack the more advanced topics in this book with a certain amount of tra-la in your heart.

When you get down to atoms and molecules, the visual elements of the Macintosh Interface come down to the Desktop, menus, and windows.

THE DESKTOP: WHAT LIES BENEATH

We talk a lot about the Macintosh Desktop (chiefly because we like to hear ourselves talk). It's a real character fault, I know, and we're working on it because it's a basic metaphor that has stuck since 1984. "The Macintosh Desktop" is simply The Thing You're Looking At when you look at a Mac screen. It's your workspace. Take a look at Figure 3-1. Like a real desktop, you're likely to only see something this clean and tidy the very first time you ever use it and then never ever again. Not once. Not until you buy a new desk and have the old one hauled away or are ever lucky enough to do that thing that happens in the movies where your sweetheart, consumed with immediate passion, swats everything off your desk in one fluid motion and then you proceed to smooch away atop it with fierce abandon (warning: unlikely).

Even in its bare-bones appearance, Figure 3-1 shows off three basic Macintosh elements:

- **It has a menu bar.** On Windows and Linux systems, there's a menu bar inside every window. On the Mac, there's just the one, and it changes every time you switch from one application to another. If you have more than one monitor attached to your Mac, it appears on only one of them: the *startup monitor*. You can choose which monitor you want as the startup monitor through the Displays section of System Preferences.

> ### ▼ Note
> Like most things that non-Mac users don't like, Mac users claim that this "one menu bar" idea is actually a feature. "It conserves screen space and it gives you an immediate and obvious visual cue regarding which app is currently in use," they will tell you. And that's actually quite true, but it really just comes down to "that's the way the Mac has always done it."

- **It has a Dock.** This is anchored at the bottom of Figure 3-1, can also appear to the left or the right of the startup monitor. It gives you easy access to applications and documents that you use frequently, as well as all applications that are running at any given time. Do not fear the Dock. The Dock is pure, the Dock is kind, the Dock has a wonderful plan for your life. The Dock is also the subject of Chapter 6.

- **It has icons:** Any external storage devices that the computer can access appear as icons on the Desktop. In Figure 3-1, there is only one storage volume, a hard disk named Macintosh HD.

> ### ▼ Note
> The Macintosh HD is chiefly just a holdover from the old days, included so that longtime Mac users who expect to see hard drives and CDs and such on the Desktop wouldn't wet themselves in fear when they discover that, holy cow, something actually works *differently* in this new edition of the Mac OS!
>
> And if you are indeed an old-school Mac user and you feel a certain creeping dampness because you don't see the Trash Can in its familiar spot in the lower-right corner of the screen, it's in the Dock now. It's also a wire basket instead of a can, but again, there's really no reason to panic.

But again, this Desktop is so clean that presenting it as a working Macintosh is tantamount to fraud. Figure 3-2 presents a more typical view:

Figure 3-1
A bare Desktop

Get a load of:

- **A listing of some of the programs** stored on the computer's hard disk (the window named Applications).

- **The Calculator application.**

- **The Address Book application.**

- **A Chess game** (in which I promise you as a former Eagle scout that I am, like *totally* kicking whatever passes for a butt on a Power Macintosh G5).

- **A file containing an illustration** for this book with the name of 567942fg01-03.tiff.

Yes, things are getting sort of cluttered here, with all the overlapping windows and such. It'll get even more cluttered. Why, the Desktop will get so cluttered that you can't even see the Desktop anymore.

Figure 3-2
The Desktop with open folders and documents

WHAT IS THIS USER DOING?

I apologize. What **is** this user doing? Um, I dunno. I suppose I should guess. He's killing time in his office playing games because he's about to knock off for a long, long meal with a friend he's about to phone, calculating how much he can spend on the entrée without alerting his boss that he's abusing his expense account. As a typical office computer user, he's also opened one or two random windows to cover up his browser window, so his boss won't see that a moment before she walked by, he was looking up naughty words on Dictionary.com. But take it from me, the state of an *actual* working computer is not a helpful illustration of the elements of the Macintosh user interface. It is an illustration that Mankind is a creature of emotion, not of logic.

And here we have to pause and stretch the Desktop metaphor a bit. I stress that the Desktop is indeed modeled on a real, honest-to-God grey Formica desktop. You toss documents and tools on top of it and commence to work, ultimately burying the thing under papers.

When folks refer to the Macintosh Desktop, they are indeed usually referring to the sum total of their workspace. But sometimes you hear people refer to the Desktop as that nice, empty acreage you had before you started opening windows. "The Desktop picture," for example, refers to the artwork that serves as the background to everything else, and that folder icon in Figure 3-2 is said to be "on the Desktop"...i.e., not inside a window.

The Desktop's desktop isn't terribly useful because as you've seen, it tends to get covered up rather quickly. That's why Apple moved the Trash can to the Dock. Sitting on the Desktop, other things quickly cover it up, and you can't drag anything into it until you drag other windows out of the way first.

 Tip

Which is why in Mac OS X, you can access the Desktop's contents via its own folder as well. You find it right inside your user directory. I've dragged mine into the Dock, so if I need to access something on the Desktop, I can simply get to it through the Dock instead of having to hide a huge pile of windows. And you thought I was just blowing bubbles when I told you how hyper-megasuper-useful the Dock is?

MENUS: DROP (DOWN) SQUAD

Let's move on to menus. Again there's just the one; it's at the top of your monitor (the top of your Startup Monitor if you have more than one screen). Menus are the chief mechanism for telling your Mac to do something.

Macintosh menus *drop down*, which means that when you click the mouse on a menu's title, its contents appear. As you can see in Figure 3-3, the title remains highlighted while the contents are visible.

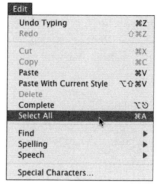

Figure 3-3
Behold, a menu

The menu stays open while you move the mouse over its contents. Click again to select an item.

An item might be dimmed, and won't respond when your mouse passes over it. That's because it represents a feature that you can't use right now for some reason. And it's not because anything's broken. If your word processor has a "Translate selected text into Egg Latin" menu item and you haven't selected any text, it'll be dimmed out. It's an elegant way to avoid having to throw up error messages that begin with the unhelpful phrase, "Hey! Dimwit!"

Some menus have an ellipsis next to it (...).

 Note

It's very, very satisfying to refer to it as an "ellipsis" instead of "a dot-dot-dot." Hey, you **want a** freebie? That tic-tac-toe button on the telephone is technically called an "octothorp." The little rubber footy thing at the bottom of a crutch that keeps it from scratching up the floor? I don't know what that's called. How about "Theodore"? I've always liked that name.

An ellipsis means that the function the menu item represents is complicated enough that the Mac needs to open up a user-interface item called a *dialog box.* A dialog box is the Mac's way of asking for a few details before it can go off and do what you've just told it to do. Before it can print a file, for instance, the Mac needs to know how many copies you want, do you want it collated, which paper tray should it use...that sort of stuff (read all about Printing in Chapter 10). Thus, selecting Print brings up a dialog that *then* creates a printed document when you click its OK button.

Some menu items contain graphical dinguses next to them. They tip you off that an item contains a submenu, or that you can activate it through the keyboard, without picking up the mouse at all.

Submenus

If you look again at Figure 3-3, you'll see that some of the option names have triangles at their right edges. This means that there is another menu — a *submenu* — available. To make the submenu appear, just drag your mouse over the submenu as in Figure 3-4.

Edit	
Undo Typing	⌘Z
Redo	⇧⌘Z
Cut	⌘X
Copy	⌘C
Paste	⌘V
Paste With Current Style	⌥⇧⌘V
Delete	
Complete	⌥⎋
Select All	⌘A
Find ▶	
Spelling ▶	
Speech ▶	
Special Characters...	

Find submenu:

Find...	⌘F
Find Next	⌘G
Find Previous	⇧⌘G
Use Selection for Find	⌘E
Jump to Selection	⌘J

Figure 3-4
A submenu

If you're reasonably sober and are thus capable of using big words (and have a weird idea of what impresses people at dinner parties), you can refer to this whole concept as a

Hierarchical Menu System. You can spot an elegant, well-thought-out app immediately by its paucity of menus. If an app's programmer is clumsy, every time they add a new feature, they'll just keep sticking on more and more menus, and adding more and more submenus.

▼ Note

Sometimes programmers force you to navigate through submenus inside submenus. As a result, changing the background color of a cell of a spreadsheet can make you feel like Indiana Jones, who spends most of his time wondering why the ancient Machapoans couldn't just leave the golden idol of the Kauan Goddess right at the entrance to the tomb instead of jerking him around like this. It's a cold, lonely feeling.

Keyboard shortcuts for menu options

You'll see symbols at the far right edge of some of Figure 3-2's menu items. These are the *keyboard shortcuts* that you can use instead of choosing the item from the menu. Keyboard shortcuts use ⌘, which is colloquially known as the flower key, the fan key, and once while I was speaking at a user-group meeting an older person in the group referred to it as The Rug Beater. It's stuck in my mind ever since and now I pass this meme onward to you. To execute a shortcut, hold down ⌘ and then hit a character key. You'll probably have to cheat at first and pull down the menu to remember that ⌘+Z is the same as going to the Edit menu and clicking Undo, but you don't need to pull down anything to execute a keyboard shortcut.

The keyboard shortcut might contain a whole string of symbols, which means that you'll have to hold down some additional keys, such as the Control, Shift, or Option keys. Even if the keyboard command is Control+Shift+Option+B, you don't have to press the keys in any specific sequence. The Mac is just waiting for that character key. As soon as you tap the B key, OS X checks what other modifier keys you're holding down and you're off to the races.

Tip

If all of these multiple key presses make you feel like your playing a special phalangeal edition of "Twister," turn on the Mac's Sticky Keys feature, which is discussed in Chapter 4. The Mac allows you to tap in a keyboard equivalent one stroke at a time.

APPLE'S STANDARD MENUS

Menu bars vary from application to application, but there are a few that appear in all of them. The Apple Menu, File, Edit, and (way at the end) Help menus are part of the basic Mac user interface, and are 99 and 44/100 percent consistent from app to app.

The Apple Menu

The Apple Menu is always there in the extreme left corner, proudly flying the Apple colors — well, the Apple *color*, anyway — shining out like a beacon of hope over all of your work.

The purpose of the Apple menu has gotten a little vague in Mac OS X, but chiefly it's for dealing with "the big picture" of Macintosh operations. Viz:

- **About This Mac:** Tells you (in broad strokes) what version of Mac OS X you're running, and what sort of hardware you're using (see Figure 3-5). For details, click the More Info button. This launches the System Profiler utility, which outlines everything you could ever know about your Mac's hardware and software in exhaustive, excruciating, "who-is-this-person-and-why-won't-he-stop-explaining-to-me-how-the-designated-hitter-rule-created-an-unfair-advantage-for-left-handed pitchers" detail. But when something goes wrong with your Mac and you phone somebody for help, the first thing they'll do is ask you to read off some of the information therein. So I shouldn't be so snippy.

THE APPLE MENU: A HISTORY

If you want a sign of the Mac's growing pains, look no further. The Apple Menu was once one of the cornerstones of the interface, but in the transition to X, most of its important duties have been given over to other elements, like the Dock. Still, we like the old dear. At first, Apple moved the Apple menu to the middle of the screen, which to Mac purists was like seeing the Queen knighting rock stars and philanthropists while wearing an ermine miniskirt and a tube top. A fuss was (justly) raised and the Apple icon was moved back where it's been since 1984.

Figure 3-5
The About This Mac box

- **Software Update:** Connects to the Internet and checks if newer versions of the OS or any of its components are available. Mac OS X does this automatically (through System Preferences), but using this menu item is a good way to get the latest bug fixes ASAP.

- **Mac OS X Software:** Launches your Web browser and navigates to the Downloads area of Apple's Web site. Here you find offers for commercial software as well as apps you can download and try out. Some of them are free, some of them are shareware (try them and send in some dough if you like them), and some are demonstration software (special test-drive versions of commercial apps).

▼ Note

I use this one a lot. Apple tends to highlight most of the coolest shareware and freeware here. It's not the only place to download software, but it gives you the greatest chance of finding something that's actually *good.*

- **System Preferences:** Takes you straight to the System Preferences panel, where you can adjust basic system settings.

- **Dock:** Lets you make quick adjustments to the behavior of the Dock. Have I mentioned the Dock? Great little item? A million and one uses as you work, play, and worship? Learn all about it in Chapter 6.

- **Location:** You can read more about this in Chapter 11. At the office, you plug into a network through your Mac's built-in Ethernet port. At home, you connect via Airport. When you're in a hotel room in San Francisco, you dial an Earthlink number in the 415 area code, and, incidentally, it's three hours earlier over there. Every time you change locations you don't have to go in and change a million settings to reflect your new reality: Just change to a new location that you've pre-configured.

- **Recent Items:** The Mac OS keeps track of all the apps and documents you've used recently. If you want to get your hands on the report you were writing earlier this morning but you can't remember where you put it, hey, your Mac does. Just look for it here.

▼ Tip

I love Recent Items when it has the document I need. I think it's a cruel tease when it doesn't. It only remembers a limited number of items, so if it keeps letting you down, click System Preferences ➜ Appearance and increase that number via the "Number of Recent Items" popup menu.

- **Force Quit:** When an app acts naughty and refuses to respond to your mouse and keyboard, and you can't quit it the polite way, the Force Quit command gives it a spanking, and terminates it with extreme prejudice. For more information, see Chapter 7.

- **Sleep, Restart, Shut Down:** From left to right it puts your Mac into power-saving Sleep mode, politely closes all open documents and applications and reboots the Mac, closes all open documents and applications, and then turns the Mac off completely. But you already know that, because you've read Chapter 2.

- **Log Out:** Logs you out of the system, closes all of your open documents and apps, and places your private files back under lock and key. It leaves behind a login window so another user can start using this Mac. See Chapter 15 for more information.

Application menu

Next to the Apple menu you find an application menu. Its name is always the same as the application with which you are working. For example, in Figure 3-6 you can see the application menu for Adobe Acrobat.

known. Get a load of Netscape Navigator's preferences in Figure 3-7.

- **Services:** (Back to Figure 3-6) Many apps are friendly, outgoing, salt-of-the-earth types who like to make their features available to you no matter what you're doing with your Mac. Let's say you're in a Web browser and you see a Joke Of The Day that's right up your friend Stanislau's alley. Select the text, go to Services, navigate to Mail, and click on Send Selection. Mac OS X's built-in email app creates a new message containing the joke.

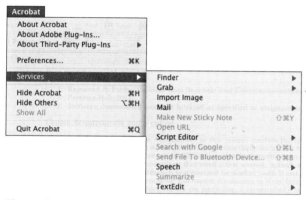

Figure 3-6
An Application menu

Contents will vary from app to app, but there are some consistent items here:

- **About:** Just as it does under the Apple Menu, this tells you what version of the app you're running. Many apps also have an item for registering the software online, looking for updates, and buying add-ons...just like the Apple Menu.

- **Preferences:** For adjusting the app's basic settings. If your app opens a new, empty document when it's launched and you wish that it asked you for a file to open instead, here's where you make your wishes

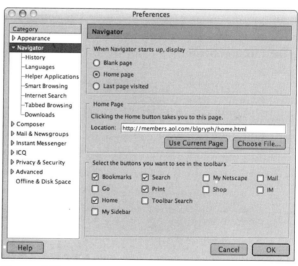

Figure 3-7
A preferences panel

▼ Note

This is probably the most under-used feature of Mac OS X. I know better than to look through the Services menu. If I do, I'll discover that an eleven-step process that I go through once an hour can be done in one mouse click through Services, and then I'll feel pretty bloody dumb. And I assure you that I thought I'd hit the bedrock of that particular foundation years ago.

- **Hide/Show:** Remember in the section "The Desktop: What Lies Beneath" earlier on, when I complained about a jillion windows cluttering up the Desktop? Mac OS X lets you make some of your apps (and their windows) invisible. Select Hide Others while within Word and all other windows will disappear. Those apps are still running and the documents are still open — they've just agreed to make themselves scarce until you switch to them or use the Show command to make them visible again.

- **Quit:** The explanation of this menu item is left empty as an exercise for the student.

The File menu

The File menu (Figure 3-8, for example) always appears to the right of the Application menu. It contains commands that deal with files, such as creating new files, opening files, saving files, and printing files.

Figure 3-8
A File menu

Individual features vary from app to app. Most apps are kind enough to add a Recent File feature in here somewhere, offering quick access to the last ten or so documents that the app opened.

The Edit menu

To the right of the File menu you will find the Edit menu (for example, Figure 3-9). The commands in the Edit menu deal with manipulating text and objects, providing copying and pasting operations.

All Edit menus have Undo commands and Clipboard items. I remember my first day at Driver's Ed and how dumb I felt when the teacher said, "So just go ahead and start the car" as though this information was issued to me at birth, along with a copy of *Breathing For Dummies,* so I'll touch on these ultra-basics.

- **Undo:** Undo undoes. Whatever you last did, Undo makes things as though you never did it — and, good Lord, one of these features should be installed in every hair salon, singles bar, and carnival bungee-jump operation in the country.

  Some apps have "multiple undo," aka Undo Again. This command can step back and back and back through every change you ever made to the document all the way back to the first line, "My Dearest Darling Sweetheart," which, considering that this person clearly just wants money and stability, was indeed your first mistake.

- **Cut, Copy, and Paste:** These commands are for moving elements around. Select a paragraph of text, cut it, click the mouse where you want it to go, and Paste it in. Before you Paste an item into its destination, it occupies an ethereal netherworld known as the Clipboard. It's a state of mind. Pay it no worry.

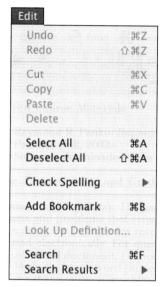

Figure 3-9
An Edit menu

 Tip

As soon as you Copy or Cut another item into the Clipboard, it takes the place of whatever was in there before. Certain Jedi-level Mac users swear by utilities that allow you to have more than one Clipboard. If you're making a bunch of common changes to a big pile of documents, multiple clipboards can be a big time-saver. It's a popular category of software and there are plenty to choose from. My favorite is You Software's You Control at www.yousoftware.com.

The Help and Window menus

At the right of the group of menus at the left of the menu bar, you'll find the Help menu. We'll take an in-depth look at using that menu in the very last section of this chapter, "Help!"

Most applications include a Window menu to the left of the Help menu (see Figure 3-10). The contents of this menu vary from one application to another. However, in most cases the bottom section of the menu contains a list of the application's open windows. You can therefore use this menu to zap straight to windows that are hidden by other items on top of them.

Menulets

At the right of the menu bar you will find a collection of menus whose names are icons or other symbols. Menulets aren't part of the running app; they're system add-ons that typically give you quick access to some of the Mac's hardware settings, like speaker volume, or the dimensions of your screen.

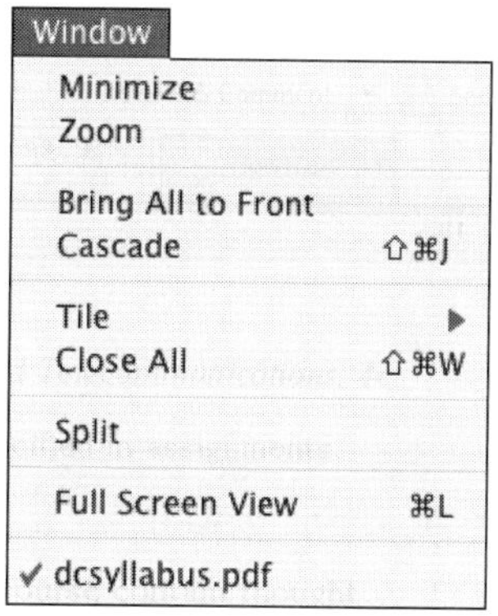

Figure 3-10
A Window menu

In Figure 3-11, you can see four menulets, one of which (the one with the U.S. flag) is a drop down menu. From right to left, the menulets are

- **The menu bar clock.**

- **Sound**, which lets you adjust the volume of your Mac's chosen audio output device.

- **Input**, which lets you choose a local or international keyboard layout and provides access to Keyboard

Viewer, which shows you which characters are produced by which keys in a given font.

- **Keychain**, which provides access to a number of keychain functions. A keychain, as you learn in Chapter 16, is a device to manage all those Internet passwords we seem to accumulate as we surf the Web.

Figure 3-11
Menulets

▼ Note

Keyboard Viewer replaces Key Caps, which also showed which characters were produced by which keys in a given font in earlier versions of the Mac OS.

But, of course, not all menulets are associated with hardware. Because the menu bar is always visible and is never covered by windows, it's often used for little indicators that you'll want to keep an eye on (like the time, the strength of your AirPort connection, or what your iChat status is). You also use it to access features that are handy in all apps. AppleScript can install its own menu in the menu bar so that your favorite automated scripts are always right there when you need them.

Menulets can join your menu bar in three ways:

- **Sometimes an application's installer also installs a menulet.** For example, iChat and iSync do this.

- **Sometimes if you look through an application's Preferences you'll see a check box for a menulet.** You can see an example of this in the Displays pane of System Preferences. You can see many of these menulets explained throughout the book.

- **A few are user-installable.** If you get a menulet on CD or if you download it, you can just drag the menulet file straight into the menu bar.

You can also re-order your menulets by holding down ⌘ and dragging its icon where you want it to go. Figure 3-12 shows an example of this happening.

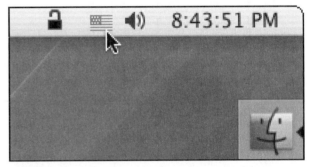

Figure 3-12
Moving a menulet

DOODAD CRAZY

But I know what you're saying: clutter, clutter, *clutter*. Well, you were thinking it, anyway. Apple's actually sort of discouraging companies from releasing new menulets, preferring to reserve that (limited) menu bar real estate for more fundamental things. In fact, Steve Jobs had actually made a formal edict that the menu bar is to be used for hardware-related features *only* — but then one of the AppleScript guys sort of bamboozled the AppleScript menulet up there and Apple realized that there was room for flexibility.

POINTING DEVICES: MOUSE HUNT

Mousing is another one of those basic skills that, with every new birth, is worming its way deeper and deeper into our DNA. But I have been a victim of the sort of sneer that can only come from an eleven-year-old kid who believes that anybody who can't get a simple two-point conversion in John Madden Football 2004 should be put into some sort of home, so let's touch on the basics.

First, you Windows and Linux users, don't let the single mouse button throw you. It doesn't make the Mac less powerful. Remember, the Mac had one mouse button from day one. You don't have a prehensile tail, and yet you seem to do OK for yourself, right?

The mouse button was the source of long and loud arguments among the Mac's designers. Although the only other commercial mouse-based computer had multiple buttons, what would the "extra" buttons *mean?* How would the second button's functionality remain consistent from app to app to app? Sensing that they already had their hands full teaching the world what to do with *one* button, Apple decided to keep things simple.

If you're freaked out about the one-button thing, go to any mall with $20 in your pocket and buy a two-button mouse. It'll work just fine. The Mac OS has supported other mouses since way before Mac OS X. Here in my office I actually have a — let me count — *seven*-button mouse but I never use it.

And while we're just going to talk about the mouse, here, the glorious world of pointing devices also includes trackballs (you twiddle a billiard ball–like thing under your fingertips instead of chasing a mouse around the Desktop; great if your desk is as cluttered as mine), graphics tablets (write on an electronic surface with an electronic pen; great for art and photo editing), knobs, joysticks...never

you mind, there are always plenty of opportunities to spend lots of money accessorizing.

▼ Note

When you're talking about puck-like computer pointing devices, the plural is "mouses," not mice, just as the plural of "Fan Of Scooby-Doo Cartoons" is "Morons."

Clicking and double-clicking

There are two basic operations with a mouse button: click and double-click. A *click* means that you tap the mouse button once. A *double-click* is two single clicks close together in time.

Remember, for every action, there's an equal and opposite reaction:

- **Clicking simply selects an item.** Think of it as simply calling the Mac's attention to an item. When you select Print from the Finder, you're essentially saying, "Remember that document I clicked on before I told you to Print something? That's what I want printed."

- **Double-clicking typically opens an item.** Double-click a folder icon in the Finder and the folder's contents display. Double-click an application icon and it runs. Double-click a document icon and it opens, launching its application first if necessary.

▼ Note

I used the Finder in both examples, but when it comes to big, colorful items that are part of the basic user interface (like icons, or items inside a scrolling list), this scheme works pretty consistently.

And, of course, there's more to it than that. Clicking inside a word-processing document simply zaps the cursor to a new location. Double-clicking on a word selects the entire word. Triple-clicking is rare, but some word processors use it to select the next biggest thing in scale; select the whole paragraph instead of just one word, for instance. Clicking also can do different things if you hold down certain keys while you do it.

Changing the double-click and tracking speed of your mouse

Do you want to zap from one edge of the screen to another with just a nudge, or do you want enough fine control that you can do this in two or three strokes? If you're moving to the Mac from Windows, it probably seems like your mouse pointer is whipping all over the place. And if it seems that you're double-clicking too fast or too slow and you're not open to various electro-shock training tools that can get you right on the ball with only minimal nerve and tissue damage, you'll probably want to adjust the double-click speed, too.

You can control the interval between the two-click with the Keyboard & Mouse preferences panel:

1. **Go to the Apple Menu and open System Preferences.**

2. **Click on the Keyboard & Mouse icon.** The preferences panel displays.

3. **If necessary click on the Mouse button to display the Mouse pane.** See Figure 3-13.

4. **Move the Double-Click Speed slider.** This adjusts the interval between clicks.

5. **Double-click anywhere in the "Double-click here to test" area.** This determines whether the double-click speed is what you want. If the Mac OS interprets

your double-click correctly, then one or more words highlight.

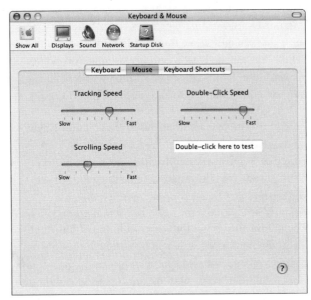

Figure 3-13
The Mouse pane of the Keyboard & Mouse preferences panel

6. **Move the Tracking Speed slider to adjust pointer speed** (seen in Figure 3-13). If you're horsing around with the double-click speed, you might also want to adjust the tracking. The tracking determines the ratio of mousing distance to screen distance. In general, the larger your monitor, the faster you'll want the pointer to move. But twiddle with the settings until it "feels" right.

If you're using a mouse with more than one button, the Mac OS looks for clicks from the button on the left side. Your Mileage May Vary: Most of the freakazoid mouses come with software that lets you define what each one of those 39 buttons and levers and dials do.

Contextual menus

A contextual menu is a little menu of commands that are specifically relevant to the thing you've clicked. For example, holding down the Control key while you click pops up a *contextual menu* under the pointer. Take a look at Figure 3-14, which shows you what happens when you control-click a file in the Finder. All of the things that the Finder can do to an individual file are grouped under the pointer. No muss, no fuss.

immediately. Hmm. That's actually a great use of the second button. Well, if Apple had thought of contextual menus back in 1984, they would have thought of the second button, too. One revolution at a time, I suppose. Even the Fathers of Our Country didn't hit upon the idea of the Right of Free Assembly until they'd taken a few years off and returned to the foundations of democracy after a nap and a hot meal, so we should probably cut Apple some slack here.

Selecting more than one item

Using the Shift key, you can select multiple items, such as file icons in a folder or items in a scrolling list. Click the first item and then Shift-click any additional icons you want to select. This technique is particularly useful for selecting multiple Desktop icons, especially when you have the icons scattered all over your Desktop real estate. Figure 3-15 shows the results. Every thing from the first item through the second item that you clicked will be selected.

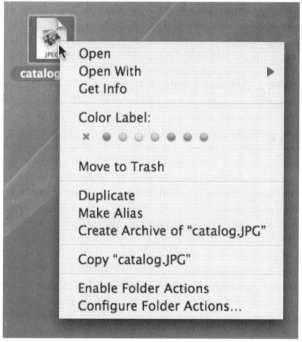

Figure 3-14
A contextual menu

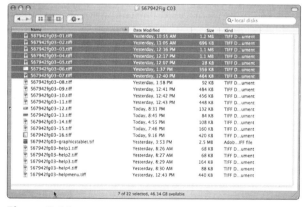

Figure 3-15
Multiple continuous selection in a list

 Tip

And if you're using one of those two-button mouses that I denigrated so cruelly a moment ago, the right-hand button will bring up the contextual menu

If you don't want to select an unbroken continuum of items, you can point-and-shoot multiple items by holding down ⌘ and clicking, clicking, clicking each item one at a time, (see Figure 3-16).

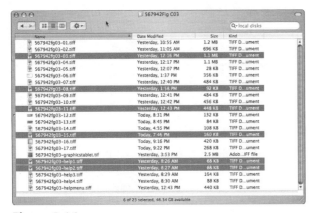

Figure 3-16
Multiple discontinuous selection in a list

Either way you slice it, when you finally give the Mac that verb ("Print!"), Mac will act upon everything that you select.

Dragging

What else can you do with a mouse? You can *drag*. Next to clicking and double-clicking, dragging is probably the mouse action you do the most. To drag, you hold down the mouse button and move the mouse, keeping the mouse button pressed. When you get where you want to go, you release the mouse button.

What good is a drag? There are two major things you can do with it: You can move things (files, folders, windows, and other graphic objects) and you can select text. Typically, when you select an item and then drag it, you're moving it. You'll learn a great deal more about using a drag throughout this book.

 Tip

Bonus points: Hold down the option key while dragging and you'll be moving a *copy* of the selected whatsit, not the original. So if you select a paragraph and option-drag it elsewhere in the document, the document will contain two copies of the paragraph.

Mouse pointer shapes

As you are mousing around, the mouse pointer takes on a variety of shapes to give you a cue that it might be doing something out of the ordinary, viz Table 3.1 for common mouse pointer shapes.

Table 3.1: Mouse Pointer Shapes

Shape	Name	Purpose
	Arrow	Your basic, plain-vanilla pointer.
	Contextual menu	Indicates that you're holding down ⌘ and you're about to activate a contextual menu of functions related to the item you're going to click.
	Copy	Indicates that you're moving a copy of the item, not the original.
	I-beam	Clicking this on text will move the cursor to a new location.
	Pointing hand	Typically indicates that the text the pointer is hovering over is a hyperlink to another page (as in a Web browser).
	Move right and left	Moves a border (like the side of a cell in a spreadsheet, or the edge of a sub-pane in a window).
	Move up and down	Ditto, except up and down.

Shape	Name	Purpose
	Wait	The spinning beach ball appears when the app is busy doing something and can't be bothered with you right now. If this mouse pointer appears for too long, it's likely that the application isn't responding to anything it's receiving. This is also known as the Spinning Pizza Of Death, a term of absolutely zero affection. Usually it's just the current application that's tied up. If you switch to another, you can amuse yourself while the first app gets its head together.
	Wait	The spinning watch and the crash-test-dummy spinning disc are holdovers from older versions of the OS. It means the same thing as the beach ball. If you want to learn something new while you watch it spin (and spin and spin and *spin*), I'll tell you that Mac OS X uses these old-fashioned spinners only when it's running old, pre-X code. These things should appears less and less as more publishers eliminate all the old code from their apps.

WINDOWS: VIEW FROM THE TOP

Windows are the graphical devices your Mac uses to present information, be it the contents of a document or your library of iTunes music.

I've just gotten off the phone with my editor and he confirms that a 4,300-page book explaining every doodad of every Mac window of every Mac app is slightly unrealistic, particularly if I'm committed to color printing. But as with everything else on the Mac, even in endless variety there's reliable consistency.

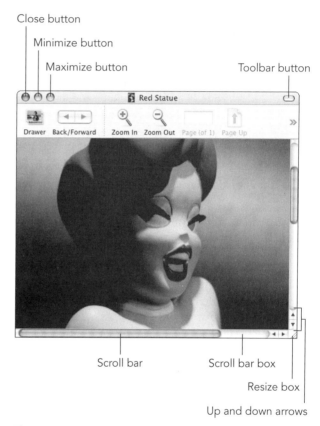

Figure 3-17
An honest, clean, working-class window.

Fanfare for the Common Window

The tippy-top span of the window is its title bar. See? There's the title of the window, which is usually the title of the document it's displaying. You can drag a window by its title bar to move it around on the screen.

Check out that little icon next to the title, too. It's a miniaturized version of the document icon. Partly this is to remind you of what sort of document you're working on; I can look at the top of this window and see that I'm editing a Microsoft Word 10 document (as opposed to using Word to edit a file in a different format).

But it's more useful because it gives you a "handle" to drag around. If you drag the title bar, yes, you're dragging around the window itself. But this mini-icon represents the actual *file*. You can exploit this in all kinds of timesaving ways. When I'm done with this chapter and I need to email this to my editor, I can grab that icon and drag it straight down into the Dock and drop it on top of Mail. Apple's built-in mail client will create a new email with that file as an attachment, just as though I'd gone into the Finder, located the document in its original folder, and dragged it onto Mail directly.

Window controls

The buttons that manipulate windows are known as *controls*. Figure 3-17 shows you the controls that you will see in almost every window:

- **Close button:** The red one is the Close button. Click it to close the window. Bonus points: Pressing ⌘+W almost always closes the front-most window. Option-clicking the Close button almost always closes all of an app's open windows (but it'll ask you if you want to save any changed documents first, of course).

- **Minimize button:** The yellow button minimizes the window. The window slurps down into the Dock. You can call it back by clicking on its minimized version inside the Dock, or simply choosing it from the app's list of open windows, if the app has one. Again, you're not closing the window; it's just hiding it away — yet another way to combat Desktop clutter.

- **Maximize button:** The green button maximizes the window, expanding it to the largest size that'll fill the screen. If the window's already been maximized, clicking the button again will shrink it back down to its original size.

▼ **Note**

Note two things: First, when your mouse pointer hovers over these three buttons, little symbols pop into view, both to remind you what the buttons do and to tell you that, yes, you can indeed close a window even if it's in the background.

Second, Red, Yellow, and Green do not by their natures suggest or even imply the functions with which they're associated. Since when did the universal color for "Caution" mean "Slurp this into the Dock?" I saw a whole safety film on the subject of traffic lights back in Grade 10 and the only slight correlation between a yellow light and Minimizing had to do with what would happen to your body if you ignored the light and cruised straight through a four-way intersection just as an asphalt truck made a left turn. I just like my universe to make a little sense. Is that wrong?

- **Toolbar button:** At the right edge of the title bar you'll see a button that looks like a Tic-Tac. That's the Toolbar button. If the window has a toolbar — a row of icon buttons that represent various features — clicking the Tic-Tac hides the toolbar, giving you a little more room in which to read your document. If you have the toolbar hidden, clicking the button reveals it again.

- **Resize box:** At the bottom-right corner of the window is the Resize box — known as a grow box in the classic Mac OS. Drag the Resize box to change the size of a window. Depending on the program, you may see an outline of the window as it changes size or the window's contents may resize on-the-fly right as you drag.

Scroll bars and scrolling

When the content of a window is larger than the window's viewable area, the window typically has scroll bars that let you bring hidden bits of its contents into view. A window can have both vertical scroll bars and horizontal scroll bars (as in Figure 3-17). Scroll bars have the following parts:

- **Up and down arrows:** Clicking the mouse pointer in an up or down arrow moves the document one "line." If the document doesn't contain text, then how much it scrolls depends on the specific program. In Figure 3-17, the scroll bar arrows are grouped together at the end of the scroll bar, but they don't have to be. They can both be separately located at either end at the bottom of the scroll bar. To change the position of the arrows, launch System Preferences, click on the Appearance icon, and in the Appearance preferences panel that appears click the At top and bottom radio button. This is located in the second section of the panel (see Figure 3-18).

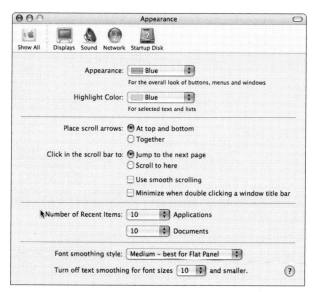

Figure 3-18
Putting scroll arrows in their place

- **The scroll box (or thumb):** Dragging the scroll box moves the document to a position proportional to the scroll box's location in the scroll bar. For example, if you drag the scroll box to the very top of the scroll bar, the beginning of the document appears. If you move the scroll box to the middle of the scroll bar, you come to the middle of the document. Therefore, the amount of scrolling that you get when you drag the scroll box depends on the size of the document.

▼ Note

The size of the scroll box depends on the percentage of the document that is visible in the window. If the document is twice the size of the window, the scroll box fills half the scroll bar. If the document if four times the size of the window, the scroll box fills a quarter of the scroll bar. The larger the document relative to the window, the smaller the scroll box.

- **The scroll bar itself:** By default, clicking above or below the scroll box in the scroll bar moves one "page." Depending on the program and its settings, a page may be the size of the window's viewable area or it may be a printed page. You can change the behavior of a click in the scroll bar so that you scroll to the location proportional to the site of the click. To do so, open System Preferences, click on the Appearance icon, and in the Appearances preferences panel that appears, click the "Scroll to here" radio button. This is located in the second section of the panel.

You can also scroll through a window using just the keyboard. Tapping the up and down arrows on your keyboard is usually the same as clicking the up and down arrows on the scroll bar. Tapping Page Up and Page Down is the same as clicking above or below the scroll box.

Window toolbars

Many Macintosh windows have *toolbars*, areas underneath the window's name that contain icons or menus that provide quick access to some of the program's actions. For example, the toolbar in the Finder window in Figure 3-19 provides (from left to right) navigation arrows, choices to view by icon or a list, access to the window's contextual menu, and a file search capability. Compare this window with Figure 3-20, which has no toolbar.

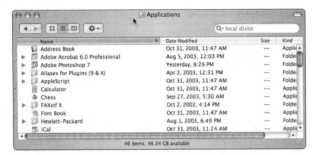

Figure 3-19
A Finder window with its toolbar showing

These toolbars are often configurable (look for a "Configure Toolbar" item under the Edit menu; names and locations vary). You can remove the functions you never use and toss in buttons for functions you want at your fingertips.

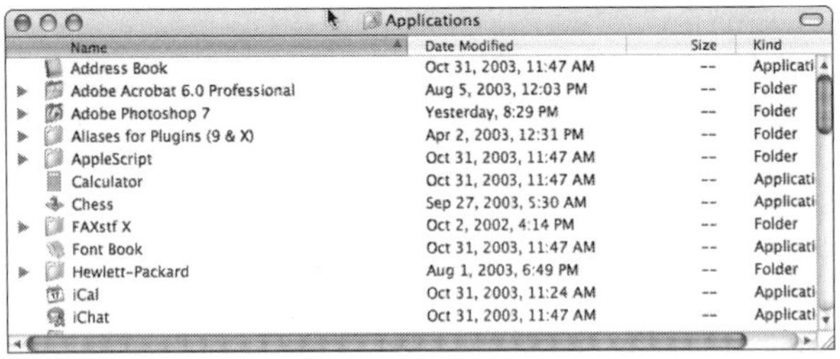

But Mac OS X continues to evolve and it's possible that the era of window toolbars, like the era of clear cola beverages, is waning. I like 'em. They add some extra functionality with a small (and reversible) loss in screen real estate. Every Apple application had a toolbar when X first came out. Now they're starting to disappear.

Windows with panes

Some windows are divided into regions, known as *panes*. This is a big deal with the iApps and most apps that sport Mac OS X's "Brushed Metal" appearance.

For example, the Finder window in Figure 3-21 has a sidebar at the left that contains location icons for easy navigation; the right pane displays the contents of a folder. Other windows with panes that you encounter include the Mail application. The dividing line between the panes is actually a moveable bar that you can drag to adjust the size of the panes to your liking. You can make the Finder window's sidebar so small that it disappears completely.

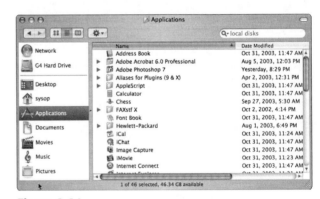

Figure 3-21
A Finder window with a visible sidebar pane

Figure 3-20
A Finder window without its toolbar

The window usually gives you some sort of tip-off that its panes are re-sizeable. Notice, for example, the dimple in the gap between the sidebar and the rest of the window. "Resize me," it says.

Some apps offer older-style window panes. At the top of one of the window's scroll bars you see a bar or a bead. Slide it down and you create two separate, scrolling views of the same document, all in the same window. It is very useful when you're working in spreadsheets, such as when you want to eye the section of the document with last quarter's sales results as you work on a section four pages later, cooking the figures for *next* quarter's sales.

EXPOSÉ: SLIDING DOORS

Desktop clutter has become a recurring theme in this chapter. The clever men and women of Apple Computer did their level best to give us the planet's most powerful and elegant operating system, but no one can see inside the human soul. And therein lurks a demon who resists all attempts at discipline and order.

But Exposé is a powerful weapon in the battle. You're using your word processor and you want to zip to a Web page you opened an hour ago containing your research. And already you're choking back a tear because you've got a dozen apps open and dozens and *dozens* of windows piled up.

Before Panther, you had to switch to your Web browser, locate that one window among the 23 or so, find the info, then switch back to your word processor and repeat the process.

Thanks to Exposé, all you need do in Panther is hit the F9 key on your keyboard.

Every window shrinks down into a tidy mosaic in which nothing overlaps anything else (viz Figure 3-22). It's like being 1,000 feet above a cornfield in a hot-air balloon. The title of each miniaturized window appears as your mouse moves over it, and when you find what you've been seeking, you click it. The windows un-shuffle, and you're left with the Desktop the way it was before — except the selected window is now up front.

Good God, this one feature was worth the whole upgrade fee to me. And I don't just use it to move from window to window, either. I often hit F9 before getting out of the chair. Every miniaturized window is still "live," so whether eight or nine different news sites update their Web pages, an application has thrown up an error message, or I want to keep a bored eye on one of my *West Wing* DVDs, I can see the entire state of my Macintosh from across the room, and quickly zoom back in on an item that's caught my interest.

Exposé can also just show you the windows associated with the current app (F10), or clear away every window entirely and show you the naked Desktop. Pressing the same button on your keyboard again pops you back into reality without switching to another window. And all those keys are configurable. Check out Exposé's pane in System Preferences (Figure 3-23).

You can trigger Exposé by placing the mouse pointer in one of the corners of the screen, by pressing a function key, or by using the right or middle buttons on a two- or three-button mouse.

Figure 3-22
Using Exposé to show all windows

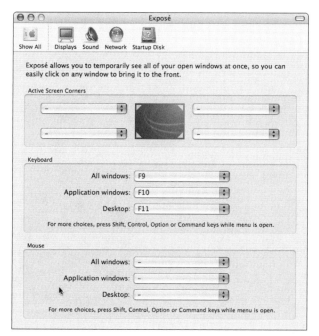

Figure 3-23
The Exposé preferences panel

ANDY IHNATKO, HIS HUMILITY IS JUST PART OF HIS PERFECTION

Well, it takes a big man to admit when he's wrong. Maybe I should recant what I said earlier and start using that 42-button FrankenMouse.

KEYBOARD CONTROLS: KEY LARGO

In science fiction movies, people sit down and talk to computers — and the computer understands, regardless of the person's accent, sentence structure, language, or

vocabulary. That kind of speech recognition is still a dream; today we use the keyboard as our primary method of getting text into a computer.

Special keys

The Macintosh keyboard has lots of special keys that you won't find anywhere else. They include the extra modifier keys we've discussed off and on throughout this chapter as well as some keys that affect hardware settings and actions:

- **The ⌘ key:** We've already talked about using ⌘ (aka cloverleaf, aka fan aka, Apple key, aka the Rug Beater) to trigger menu options, and how it sometimes modifies mousing and clicking actions. You can also use it to navigate dialogs without the mouse. You may not have noticed it, but every button starts with a different letter. Holding down ⌘ while tapping that letter sends a click to that button; ⌘+C hits Cancel, ⌘+D means Don't Save, et cetera. Coooooolllllll.

- **The Option key:** The Option key was originally designed to provide access to an additional set of printing characters. (You have un-Shift characters, Shift characters, Option characters, and Shift-Option characters, meaning that each key on the keyboard can produce up to four distinct characters.) Today the Option key still plays its role in generating characters, but you can also use it in conjunction with ⌘ and Control keys to select menu options.

- **The alt key:** Most of today's keyboards have the characters alt in small letters at the top of the Option key. The Macintosh doesn't use an alt key, but PC software does. The alt is there just to let you know that if you are using PC emulation software, such as Virtual PC, you can use the Option key wherever the PC software expects alt.

- **The Control key:** The Control key dates from the earliest days of computing. Typically it was used to interrupt the hardware; Pressing Control+C would end a program's operation, for example. Today, Control chiefly serves as another modifier key, often used in conjunction with function keys or the Option key to provide menu command access from the keyboard.

What's the difference between the Return and Enter keys? In poorly designed applications, the difference is that Return does what you expect it to do and Enter does something different than "Return," which isn't what you expected it to do at all. So the chief purpose is to confuse people and make them say naughty words. Some programmers really like it when people curse. They can't hear it, but they know it's happening.

- But in dialogs, hitting, Enter is always the same thing as clicking on the default button (the one that's colored-in and pulsating).

Like most computer keyboards today, the Macintosh has *function keys* across the top of its keyboard. Depending on the size of your keyboard, you may have 12 or 15, each labeled with the letter "F" and a number. Function keys have been around since the very beginning of mainframe computing, when they were more or less the user interface to your software.

They're a bit of a holdover today, which is why Apple makes many of the function keys do double-duty. This can get confusing when you use an application that really needs a function key which has been co-opted by Apple's special functions. If you find yourself muting your speakers when trying to access F3, for example, you can hold down the fn key while you tap the key that normally mutes the speaker in order to regain "normal" F-key functionality.

As you've seen elsewhere in the chapter, Apple uses these keys to make certain features (like Exposé) more accessible. Some apps use them for their own little shortcuts, and you can also define function-key actions yourself.

Assigning Function keys

Let's say you use Apple's Preview app to look at artwork. You're always using the Full Screen feature to see the images at the largest possible size, but there's no command-key equivalent in the menu. Here's how to make the F7 key into Preview's Full Screen key (see Figure 3-24):

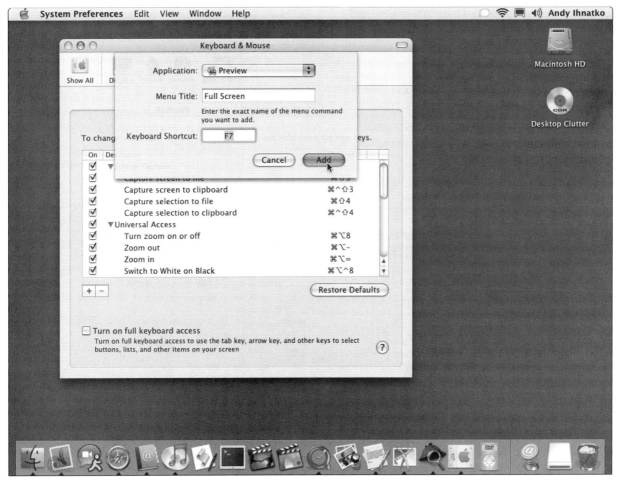

Figure 3-24
Adding a Keyboard Shortcut

1. **Quit Preview if it's already running.** You can't assign function keys to an app while it's running.

2. **Open System Preferences and navigate to the Keyboard & Mouse pane.**

3. **Click on the Keyboard Shortcuts tab.** Notice that every single keyboard shortcut is nicely outlined for you. Convenient!

4. **Scroll down and click on Application Keyboard Shortcuts.**

5. **Click on the plus button (+).** This adds a shortcut and a sheet drops down.

6. **From the pop-up menu, select Preview.** The example uses the Preview application.

7. **In the field marked Menu Title, type in the exact name of the menu you want to activate.** In this case, type Full Screen. Type the menu in exactly as you see it in the menu, including the "..." if you see one.

8. **Click on the Keyboard Shortcut field and then type the function key that should activate.** Here, we're using F7 but it can be anything, even command-option-control-shift-F7, if you're feeling like you need to do something aerobic.

9. **Click the Add button.** Now you can use the short cut to activate the feature.

This is actually a very flexible feature. You can use it to assign any kind of key equivalent to any kind of menu, or even change keyboard equivalents that already exist.

You can also use a bunch of third-party function-key re-mappers that are a bit more ambitious, allowing you to launch apps, open files, and run AppleScripts. CE Software's QuicKeys X (www.cesoft.com) is the 900-pound gorilla of this category.

There are also a bunch of special keys that take the place of mechanical switches to control simple hardware functions like volume (up, down, and mute), screen brightness (up, down), and an Eject button for internal optical drives. Your Mac might have some or all of these buttons.

▼ **Note:**

But don't be bamboozled into thinking that tapping Eject immediately ejects a CD (or CD-ROM, or DVD, or whatever). In Windows, hitting Eject has an immediate effect. On the Mac, it merely requests that any app that's currently using whatever disc is in the drive to please politely close it down and release it. If the app decides that you'll get the disc when it's dashed good and ready to *give* you the disc, you'll have to wait.

Choosing alternative keyboard layouts

In the Menu section of this chapter, we mentioned the Input menulet, which lets you choose keyboard layouts. How cool is this? If you happen to want to use a character set other than U.S. English, it's very cool. Although the keys on the Macintosh keyboard might be labeled for U.S. English typing, you can switch the characters that the keys produce by changing your *keyboard layout* or *input method*. You do this with the International preferences panel:

1. **Launch System Preferences.**

2. **Click International.** This displays the International preferences panel.

3. **Click the Input Menu button**. The Input Menu pane displays (see Figure 3-25).

Figure 3-25
The Input Menu pane

4. **Check the "Show input menu in menu bar" check box.** The Input menulet appears.

5. **Place a check next to each item you want to appear in the Input menu.**

Viewing a character set

The Keyboard Viewer (Figure 3-26) displays the characters that a given font can generate. To make the Keyboard Viewer appear, follow the directions for "Choosing Alternative Layout Options" — the last subsection — and check the box for Keyboard Viewer. It appears under the Input menulet.

Pressing Shift, Option, or Shift-Option shows the modified characters. The Character Palette (Figure 3-27) lets you insert special characters (either graphics or non-Roman) into a document. Click on the character you want and click the Insert button.

Figure 3-26
The Keyboard Viewer for a U.S. English font

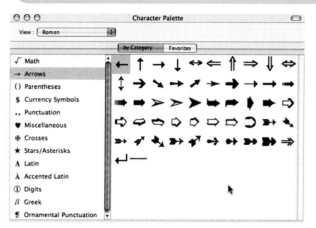

Figure 3-27
The Character Palette for inserting special characters

KEYBOARD VIEWER: LUST FOR GLORY

I have to admit that the only times when I use Keyboard Viewer are (a) when I can't remember how to make a Euro symbol (Option+Shift+2, incidentally) and (b) a counterintelligence agent burst into my office, spilled Dr. Pepper on my keyboard, and then made his escape (yes, it was a secret agent; I would never do something so foolish as to bring a sticky beverage into my office, oh, no), and the onscreen keyboard became the only thing I could use to shut down my Mac politely before taking it in to be repaired.

And (c) It's kind of cool to see all the keycaps flicker insanely when I type. Chicks dig a guy who can type at 108 words per minute. At least that's what my mom kept telling me during countless hours of keyboard practice while all of my little friends were gamboling and romping and playing and taunting me just outside my window.

The remaining items in the Input menu pane are either methods for generating characters for pictographic scripts such as Traditional Chinese, or keyboard layouts. Click all of those that you want to appear in your Input menu. You can then select a layout by choosing it from the Input menu. For example, in Figure 3-28 you can see the Keyboard Viewer for a Dvorak keyboard layout. (Rumor has it that if you learn to type with a Dvorak layout, you can type a lot faster than you can on a QWERTY layout; but once you've learned QWERTY, it's pretty hard to switch.)

Figure 3-28
The Keyboard Viewer for a Dvorak layout

MONITORS: THROUGH A GLASS, DARKLY

Just as the keyboard is your computer's primary input device, the monitor (or display) is its primary output device. For us visual humans, there is little else that could be better. I'm big on second-guessing the decisions of people who are smarter than I am, but even I will grudgingly agree that having some sort of screen on your Mac or built into your PowerBook was a good call with plenty of practical long-lasting rewards for the user. So whoever came up with that idea: Good job; take another twenty bucks out of petty cash and take a long lunch.

Setting display resolution

If you bought your Macintosh recently, you probably have a flat-screen, LCD monitor. Many older desktop Macs, however, are still using CRT monitors. Regardless of which type you have, most Macintosh-compatible monitors support multiple *resolutions*.

On my own Stonehenge-size monitor, I keep flipping between low and high resolution. When I'm writing, I keep it at a somewhat sensible size of 1024 pixels wide by 768 high. The individual dots are big, and so the menus and windows and text are easy to read. But when I'm managing lots of tasks at once, I increase the size to roughly double that. With a Desktop the size of Nebraska, I can have ten windows open without overlapping, or make my iTunes window so big that I can see every song and album title without anything being chopped off for lack of space.

Each different display has different screen resolutions available. You choose between 'em via the Displays panel in System Preferences:

1. **Launch System Preferences.**

2. **Click on the Displays icon.**

3. **If necessary click on the Display button.** The Display pane appears, as in Figure 3-29, showing you the current settings for your monitor and alternative possible resolutions.

4. **Choose the resolution you want from the scrolling list at the left of the preferences pane.**

5. **Choose the number of colors you want the monitor to be able to display from the Colors popup menu.**

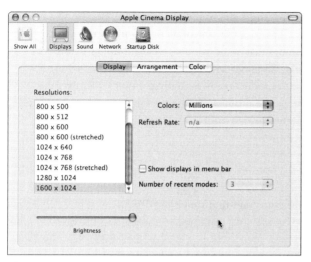

Figure 3-29
The Display preferences pane

Configuring multiple monitors

The Macintosh is still the only personal computer that seamlessly supports multiple monitors. The Mac OS supports up to eight displays — although no current Macintosh has enough expansion slots to handle anywhere near that many video cards — as a single Desktop surface. You control the logical arrangement of the monitors, as well as the startup monitor (the monitor containing the menu bar), from the Displays control panel:

1. **Launch System Preferences.**

2. **Click the Displays icon.** The Apple Cinema Display dialog opens.

3. **Click the Arrangement button.** This displays the Arrangement pane.

4. **Drag the images of the monitors until they are positioned in the layout you want for your Desktop.** The mouse pointer slides from one monitor to the next, based on this arrangement.

5. **Drag the image of the menu bar to the top of the monitor that you want to use as the startup monitor.**

 Tip

If you aren't sure which rectangle in the Arrangement pane's display represents which of your monitors, click a rectangle. The Macintosh flashes a red border around the corresponding monitor.

HELP!

Help? You're using a *Macintosh!* It's flawless! I've got a tea-trolley here that became a competent Mac user after just 3 or 4 days. Everything will run flawlessly and the air will always smell like bacon and/or lilacs, depending on how you feel about the smell of bacon and/or lilacs.

See? Isn't it good to laugh?

Panther has a built-in Help resource, chiefly in the form of a big, smackin' Help menu near the end of the menu bar. Help is context-sensitive; if you're in Safari and you activate help from the menu, OS X steers you straight to the Help Viewer app and Help opens Safari's Help file (Figure 3-30).

There might be a delay, as Help Viewer might connect to the Internet to look for updated information.

The interface is familiar to anyone who's used a browser. Every help file has a *cover*, which like a magazine, steers you towards items of universal interest and vodka ads. You can ask Help a specific question by clicking in the search box in the upper-right corner and hitting "Return." Help searches through all of the information articles to which it has access and returns a list of relevant items. Double-click on whatever looks good.

Figure 3-30
Safari's help home page

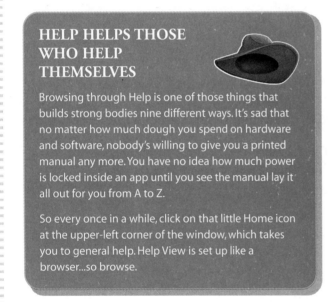

HELP HELPS THOSE WHO HELP THEMSELVES

Browsing through Help is one of those things that builds strong bodies nine different ways. It's sad that no matter how much dough you spend on hardware and software, nobody's willing to give you a printed manual any more. You have no idea how much power is locked inside an app until you see the manual lay it all out for you from A to Z.

So every once in a while, click on that little Home icon at the upper-left corner of the window, which takes you to general help. Help View is set up like a browser...so browse.

So them's the basics of the Mac interface. But everybody learns The Mac the same way: by playing with it. There are things that Windows does well and things that it does poorly. Windows' interface – and I have a beloved niece who uses and enjoys Windows, so it pains me to say this – is clearly the product of a designer who spent much of his childhood with a cardboard refrigerator box as his sole plaything.

But the Mac is different. Chances are, the thing you *think* does what you want actually *does* what you want; and if you're ever about to do anything destructive (like delete a file), Panther asks you if you're *sure* you want to do it.

Learning to drive via the Braille method makes you a menace to life and property, but learning the Macintosh that way quickly makes you into a confident and competent user.

Leopard-Skin Pillbox Mac: Making Your Mac Your Own

In This Chapter

Custom Desktops • Custom Colors • Custom Sounds • Custom Screen Savers
Working with Fonts: The Font Book • Universal Access Options

Communism is a concept that never really took off in this country, but honestly, you have to admit that it had its advantages. For example, as a teenager in Russia, you could be secure in the knowledge that no matter how well you did on tomorrow's exam, or who won the big homecoming game against Vladivostok Middle School, or that you threw up in your balalaika case when Milena Dimitriyeva turned you down for the prom, it didn't change the fact that three years later, you became a worker in a radio factory. So, here's to freedom and democracy, where you, as an individual, can express yourself as you see fit. While the Soviets were busy trying to develop a third shade of brown, we were walking around in paisley bellbottoms.

And the Mac is no less a vector for individuality. All Macs leave Cupertino exactly alike, but over a course of days, weeks, and months, you can alter your Mac's appearance and behavior to make it uniquely your own. Some of these changes simply exist to suit your personal tastes; others make your Mac easier and more comfortable to use. Both kinds are vastly superior to struggling under the iron yoke of faceless totalitarian oppression, as I'm sure you'll agree by the end of this chapter.

CUSTOM DESKTOPS

There are only two situations in which you're likely to see a Mac OS X Desktop that sports the familiar image of translucent blue swirls: in Apple's official PR shots, and after you've booted up a brand-new Mac for the first time. Your cubicle's bare walls have amusing *Family Circus* and *Hi and Lois* cartoons pinned on them; the corner of your desk sports a framed, tasteful photo of you and your sweetie doing something ambitiously silly during your last vacation. So the background of your Mac's desktop needs a far more interesting image.

▼ **Note**

…but not *too* interesting, if you are indeed in an office. An image of a kitten dangling from a clothesline, captioned with an encouraging admonishment to Hang In There: good. A doctored image of Edvard Munch's *The Scream*, with the central figure reacting to the company's last annual report: bad. *Funny*, but bad.

Replacing the default Desktop image

To replace the default Desktop image:

1. **Open the System Preferences Window.** You can either select Apple ➔ System Preferences or click on the application icon in the Dock.

2. **Click on the Desktop & Screen Saver icon.** When you do so, the Desktop & Screen Saver window appears (see Figure 4-1). OS X knows that you want to deal with images, so it assembles a list of all the locations on your hard drive where pictures are stored. The first four in the list are OS X's built-in collections of images, including abstract swooshy things just as dull as the image you started with, photos of creepy insects, and even a palette of flat colors for those whose idea of excitement is wearing black shoes with a brown belt.

   Underneath, you find direct links to common storehouses of imagery. Desktop Pictures is OS X's default directory for Desktops (you can see it in the Finder,

inside your Library folder). Your Pictures folder is listed, too, and if you use iPhoto to manage your photos, you can access your entire library and all albums.

▼ **Note**

What you actually see depends on whether you last worked with the screen saver or the Desktop pattern. If the screen saver panel appears, click on the Desktop button.

Figure 4-1
Choosing a Desktop pattern

3. **Click on the Desktop picture you want.** Your screen changes immediately to show the next background.

   If the image you want is inside a different folder, you can navigate to it directly through the Choose Folder item, which brings up a standard Open Folder sheet. The selected folder takes the place of the Desktop Pictures folder in the list. You can drag the file straight from the Finder into the image directly above the scrolling list.

▼ Tip

You can use nearly any sort of image file as a Desktop image. JPEG, TIFF, PICT, GIF… it's all good. So, be ambitious. I get most of my favorite Desktop images from NASA's Astronomy Picture of the Day site (http://antwrp.gsfc.nasa.gov/apod/). They make your Desktop look like the main viewscreen of the starship *Enterprise*, or ideally the main viewscreen of a spaceship in a much better TV show.

▼ Tip

If you have more than one monitor, you will see a Desktop Picture panel on each monitor. You can, therefore, choose a different Desktop picture for each monitor.

If the image you've selected is larger or smaller than the dimensions of your screen, a pop-up menu appears with some display options:

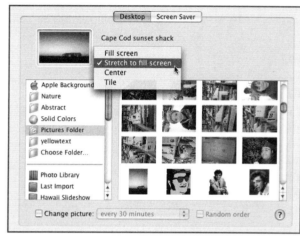

Figure 4-2
Choosing how the image will be displayed

- **Fill screen** scales the image up or down until one of its dimensions matches the height or width of the screen.

- **Stretch to fill screen** scales both dimensions of the image. If the image proportions don't match those of the screen, the image appears squeezed or squashed.

- **Center** simply plops the image in the center of the screen. So what if it isn't a perfect fit? OS X couldn't care less.

- **Tile** repeats a too-small image in a geometric pattern that fills the whole screen.

Multiple Desktop images

So, cool. Now your Desktop image is a photo of your new baby. But what about your three other children, your spouse, and that boat you've so lovingly restored? There's no need to slight any of the loved ones in your life because OS X can change your Desktop image for you automatically at regular timed intervals:

1. **Open the Desktop & Screen Saver panel.**

2. **Click the Change picture check box, as shown in Figure 4-3.**

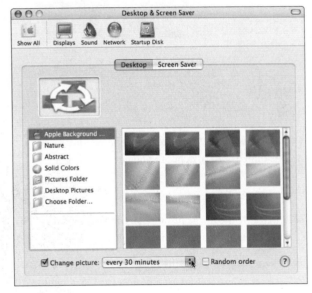

Figure 4-3
Configuring a changing Desktop pattern

3. **Select how often you want the picture to change from the pop-up menu at the bottom of the panel.** Your choices are: when logging in, when waking from sleep, every 5 seconds, every minute, every 5 minutes, every 15 minutes, every 30 minutes, every hour, or every day.

 Note

The transition from one Desktop picture to another is very subtle. Therefore, switching every 5 seconds isn't as schizophrenic as it might sound. Try it; you might like it.

The randomized pictures come from whichever image folder you selected from the list of sources. Thus, if you've selected the Abstract folder, no images pop up from your Pictures folder or anywhere else.

 Tip

Incidentally, do you want to know the easiest way to determine if there are any smutty pictures inside a given folder? Set the Desktop image to Randomize, select the folder, and then wait for your supervisor to walk by. Unless you've spent every single waking moment of your life up to that point accruing positive Karma, that'll cause the naughty picture to pop up the moment the boss is within eyeshot. Powerful forces control the universe, dear reader, and they are very easily amused.

CUSTOM COLORS

When you have to use someone else's Mac for an afternoon, it's subtle things like the differences in how they've set up Appearance colors that'll throw you the most. It just goes to show you what a subtle contribution color makes in the user interface.

You can make bits of the interface that scream out, "I'm clickable; look *here,* right *here,*" (such as window scrollers, dialog buttons, and highlighted menus) either a soothing Blue or a I-Know-This-Is-A-Mac-But-Dagnabbit-All-Those-Colors-Are-Distracting-And-I-Just-Can't-Deal-With-It grayish graphite.

To change from the default blue to graphite:

1. **Launch System Preferences.**

2. **Click on the Appearance icon to display the Appearance panel, as shown in Figure 4-4.** Notice that the panel has four sections. To set custom colors, you only work with the top section.

3. **Select Graphite from the Appearance pop-up menu.** You'll see, for example, that the background of the up and down arrows at the right of the pop-up menu turns gray immediately.

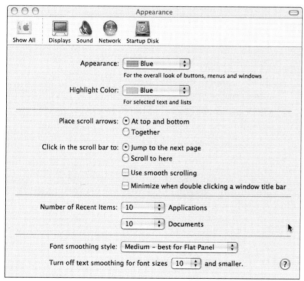

Figure 4-4
The Appearance preferences panel

The text highlight color is actually a more important choice. The highlight color is what you see when you select a bit of text in a word-processing document, or when you select a row of data in a list. Keep in mind that changes in color are what steer your eye through all the text fields in a dialog and keep your hand steady as you try to end a selection between the words *rib-eye* and *vinyl*.

To change the highlight color:

1. **Open the Appearance panel.**

2. **Select the highlight color from the Highlight Color pop-up menu, as shown in Figure 4-5.**

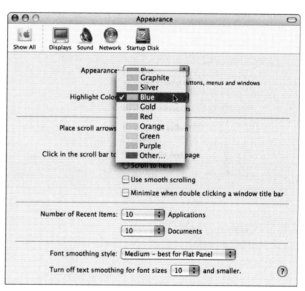

Figure 4-5
Choosing a highlight color

EXTREME MAKEOVER

And previous editions of the Mac operating system show you how much you can muck things up by making not-so-subtle changes. Apple experimented with allowing you to take nothing for granted by letting you change the shapes and colors of menus, windows, buttons, everything, to your liking. But (a) that compromised the power of a clean user interface that's consistent from machine to machine, and (b) all that jewelry and makeup made the Mac look cheap. I mean, is *that* how well we raised you, young lady?

If you really do want to give the user interface an extreme makeover, third-party utilities give you way more power than God intended mere users to have. My favorite is Unsanity's *ShapeShifter* (shareware from www.unsanity.com). With it, your Mac can look just like the computers in the movies: colorful, flashy, unique, and about as useful as a sock full of carpet samples when your ship suddenly encounters an enemy star cruiser.

▼ Note

The change you make to the highlight color *should* affect all applications. Then again drivers *should* heed the Snow Emergency parking signs when a 3-day blizzard is going on, but given that it's Tuesday and I still can't get my car out onto the street, we all know how orderly and sensible the world can be sometimes.

Some rare apps disregard convention. Don't let it get you down. Curse them mightily, and then congratulate yourself for having done so.

▼ Tip

Again, I make the case that it's an important user-interface thing. A mother penguin can recognize her offspring's distress call from way across the ice shelf amongst the cries of thousands of other hatchlings. Granted, when a Mac fails to completely burn a CD, it's not in the same dire situation as the hatchling when it encounters a walrus, tusks glistening and thirsting for gore, heaving itself out of the water. However, it's still good to make your Mac's warning sound, not only clearly audible, but also distinct from all other Macs in the room.

CUSTOM SOUNDS

When you do something that OS X doesn't like — and we all do, regularly — OS X *beeps*. Why is *beep* in italics? Because the alert sound is a *beep* only by default. You can change it to something that better suits your mood and/or personality.

Customizing your sound

To change your custom sound, follow these steps:

1. **Launch System Preferences.**

2. **Click the Sound icon to open the Sound preferences panel.** As you can see in Figure 4-6, the Sound Effects panel lists a variety of alert (beep) sounds and lets you set speaker volume.

3. **Scroll through the list of sounds.** To hear a sound, double-click on its name in the scrolling list.

4. **Select the sound you want to use as your alert sound.**

5. **Move the Alert volume slider.** This sets the alert volume.

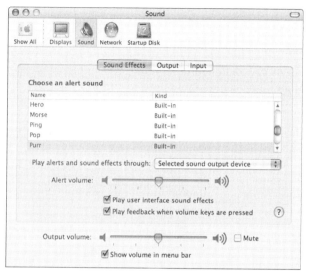

Figure 4-6
Choosing an alert sound

Using your own sounds

You'll notice that the list of sounds has a column labeled Kind. Sounds can either be Built-in (you got 'em when you installed OS X) or Custom (provided by you, the freedom-loving user).

You can use any AIFF sound file as a system beep. You can download AIFFs from sound sites (that's where I got my R2-D2 chirps and flutters) or make them yourself, using sound-recording software. Once you have the AIFF file,

WHY I'LL HAVE A LOT OF EXPLAINING TO DO WHEN I DIE AND GO FOR MY BIG EXIT INTERVIEW (#8229 IN A SERIES)

A longtime standard Apple beep sound was the sound of a water droplet, which you can perfectly duplicate by flicking your finger against your cheek while giving a little whistle. If I thought a friend of mine was working a little too hard, I'd nonchalantly stroll behind him and make the sound.

After a half an hour of hearing his Mac make error beeps for no apparent reason, he'd turn to me in desperation. I'd say, "Why don't we run Disk First Aid on your hard drive, and see if the problem doesn't go away? The diagnostic shouldn't take more than 20 minutes to complete." And then he'd be free to go out for waffles with me.

copy it into the Sounds folder inside your Library folder. It shows up in the list the next time you open the Sound preferences panel.

If you have external speakers, you can choose whether to play sounds through the Mac's internal speaker or the external speakers:

1. **Display the Sound preferences panel.**

2. **Click the Output button.**

3. **Choose the sound output device you want to use.** For example, the selection in Figure 4-7 tells the Mac to send sound through the external speakers.

4. **Move the Balance slider.** This sets the balance between two stereo speakers.

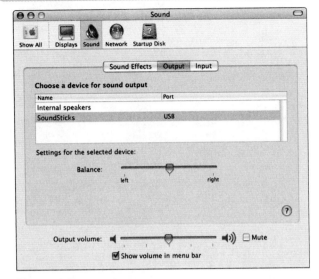

Figure 4-7
Choosing a sound output device

CUSTOM SCREEN SAVERS

The original purpose of a screen saver was to provide an ever-changing image to prevent an image from becoming permanently burned into a monitor. This is much less of an issue with today's CRT monitors, but it is still a concern with newer LCDs. For the most part, screen savers serve an aesthetic purpose; when not in use, your 20-inch iMac shows a slide show of your kids' ski trip, not a pile of Excel spreadsheets. They also help with privacy and security. When you're away from your desk, passersby can't glance at the spreadsheets on your desk and discover that you've been keeping two sets of books to protect your embezzlement scam.

OS X comes with a group of screen savers. Some are animated; others are made up of a collection of still images that transition in and out. There are also boatloads of creative third-party screen savers available on the Web.

Changing the screen saver

You can choose which screen saver you want to use, as well as when it activates:

1. **Launch System Preferences.**

2. **Open the Desktop & Screen Saver panel.**

3. **If necessary click on the Screen Saver button to display the screen saver panel.** In Figure 4-8, the left side of the panel contains a list of available screen savers.

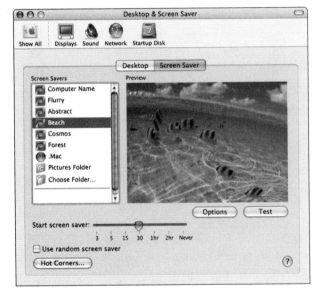

Figure 4-8
Choosing a screen saver

4. **Click on the name of the screen saver you want to use.** A small preview appears to the right of the panel. The Test button lets you sample it in full-screen mode.

5. **Use the Start screen saver slider to determine how much idle time must elapse before the screen saver starts.**

DARNED IF THOSE FOLKS AT APPLE HAVEN'T PROVED THEIR GENIUS AGAIN!

And once again, we see the awesome power of just blindly doing what Apple tells you, and organizing your image files into standard folders. You'll note many of the same folders in the Screen Saver panel that you saw back in the Desktop Images panel (see the section "Custom Desktops"). They work the same way: Selecting an iPhoto album as your screen-saver causes your idle Mac to show off the photos you took when you won the big Dream Getaway to Branson with Yakov Smirnoff contest.

6. **Click the Options button.** Depending on the screen saver, you might be able to customize the look and presentation of the screen saver. Click the Options button to see what you can do.

Using hot corners

If you are going to leave your computer turned on with sensitive or private documents on the screen, you may want to activate the screen saver immediately when you leave your desk. The easiest way to do this is to set *hot corners*. With hot corners, a corner of your monitor triggers the screen saver when you move the mouse pointer to that corner. Hot corners can also prevent the screen saver from coming on.

To set up hot corners:

1. **Display the screen saver panel.**

2. **Click the Hot Corners button in the lower-left corner of the window.**

3. **Select the corner that you want to trigger the screen saver.**

4. **Select Start screen saver from the pop-up menu that corresponds to the chosen corner.**

In Figure 4-9, moving the mouse pointer to the top-left corner of the startup monitor triggers the screen saver.

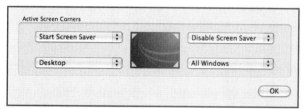

Figure 4-9
Setting hot corners

5. **Select Disable Screen Saver from the pop-up menu that corresponds to the corner that you want to use to prevent the screen saver from appearing.**

▼ Tip

You'll want to set a corner of your screen to Disable Screen Saver. Sometimes your Mac will be munching on a long process, for example, burning an iDVD, which can take an hour or more. Moving the mouse to the Disable hotspot means that you can glance at the screen from across the room and see that things are still proceeding on an even keel.

Of course, he who lives by the hotspot, dies by the hotspot. I didn't know that I had a tendency to give my mouse a little flick when I let it go. That flick tended to send the pointer to the Start Screen Saver hotspot, which meant that every time I let go of the mouse I'd suddenly be looking at 3D animations of X-Wing fighters instead of the paragraph I had just selected. It was like having a small child at your elbow who wouldn't stop telling you knock-knock jokes. I didn't chuck my Mac straight through a closed third-story window only because I have the emotional strength of ten men.

WORKING WITH FONTS: THE FONT BOOK

Customizing fonts isn't directly a part of the Mac interface, but it's another way to make your Mac your own. Things get awfully dull and uniform when everybody on the planet uses the same collection of standard fonts. And I'm not just talking about Humans, or even mammals, here; it's a danged shame when even the lowliest of freshwater bivalves can create a résumé with as much stylistic pizzazz as yours.

If you haven't bought a few custom fonts, download 'em. Just as there are aficionados of classic cars and folk music played on discarded vegetables, there are plenty of font perverts on the Web with immense libraries of typefaces free (or almost free) for the downloading.

One of the best things added to OS X with the release of Panther is the Font Book, an application that helps you install and manage all your font files. And thank heaven for it. For all my guff about wanting to have lots of fonts, they tend to infest your Mac like a devouring fungus. There are the ones your Mac came with; the ones that were installed alongside the applications you bought; freakish foreign faces that are only useful when translating Klingon into the Elven language of *The Lord of the Rings* (but it was part of an Apple System Update last week, so now it's in your Font menu); and others that seem to appear simply by force of collective will.

The Font Book works in conjunction with applications that use a Font panel, such as TextEdit and Stickies. The Font panel in Figure 4-10, for example, comes from the TextEdit application that is part of OS X. The list at the far left of the Font panel displays Collections, groups of fonts that you create. Within each Collection, you have one or more font families, each of which may have multiple typefaces.

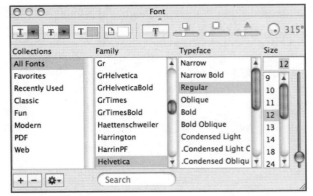

Figure 4-10
A Font panel

▼ Note

A typographer defines a font as a single typeface in a single size. However, most computer users think of an entire font family as a font.

The Font Book lets you create and manage collections of fonts. It also lets you disable fonts so that they don't appear in a Font panel or in the Font menus of applications that haven't been updated to use a Font panel.

Disabling fonts

You can find the Font Book application in the Applications folder on your hard drive. The first thing you probably will want to do with it is disable some fonts:

1. **Launch the Font Book application.** A window like that in Figure 4-11 appears. You see several columns:

    The column at the left lists font collections. All Fonts is exactly what its name implies — all the fonts in your Fonts folder. The others are collections that have been installed with OS X. You can keep them, modify them, delete them, or add your own collections.

- **The middle column lists the fonts in the currently selected collection.** Disabled fonts have the word Off to the right of their names.

- **The right column shows a preview of the font selected in the Font column.** You can adjust the size of the preview by dragging the slider at the far right of the Font Book window or by using the Size pop-up menu at the top right of the preview.

Figure 4-11
The Font Book window

 Tip

If a dot appears at the right of a font name in the middle column, it means that there are duplicate fonts in that font family. To turn off the duplicates for a given font family, select the font name in the Font column, and then select Edit ➜ Resolve Duplicates.

2. **Click on the name of the collection with which you want to work.**

3. **Click on the name of the font you want to disable.**

4. **Click the Disable button at the bottom of the Font column.**

The alert in Figure 4-12 appears.

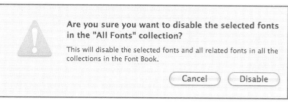

Figure 4-12
The Disable Font alert

5. **Click Disable.** The Font Book places Off to the right of the font name.

To enable a font that you've previously disabled, repeat the preceding process. (When you select the name of a disabled font, the Disable button reads Enable.)

▼ **Note**

When you disable fonts, the changes won't appear in application Font menus or Font panels until you quit and relaunch the application.

WHEN IT COMES TO FONTS, I'M WILLING TO GO IT ALONE

I don't want to create the impression that I'm some sort of isolationist. (I'll have you know that I did the It's A Small World ride at Disneyland twice and consider myself a better person for the experience.) But the first thing I did with Font Book was disable all of the international fonts. I never use them, and they only slow me down on my way from Albertus Black to Xanadu Light Compressed.

Adding new fonts

The next best thing you can do with the Font Book is to simplify the way new fonts are added to your system configuration:

1. **Make sure that the font (font family) you want to install is on a disk that is accessible to your system.** It could be on your hard disk or on a CD, for example.

2. **Launch the Font Book application.**

3. **Select the Collection to which you want to add the font.**

4. **Select File ➡ Add Fonts.** The dialog in Figure 4-13 appears.

5. **Locate and select the font you want to add.**

6. **Select an Install Font option at the bottom of the dialog.** Choose whether you want to add the font for all users on the computer, just for your use, or to the Classic (OS 9) environment.

7. **Click Open.**

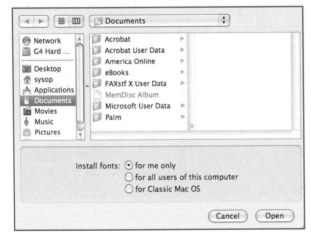

Figure 4-13
Locating a new font to add to OS X

Creating font collections

If you work on projects for which you use specific groups of fonts, you can simplify your font management by creating your own collections of fonts. You can enable and disable entire collections. Disabling a collection shortens that Font menu that seems to scroll on forever and greatly simplifies the display in a Font panel.

▼ Note

Font collections help you, and the people with whom you work, to use typefaces consistently. If you've taken the time to create collections named *For correspondence, For internal reports,* and *For ads and marketing,* it reduces the risk that when your medical division files important paperwork to the FDA for approval of your new arthritis medication, the subheads won't be printed with that font in which each letter is formed out of a clown contorting himself in a different shape.

To create a new collection:

1. **Launch the Font Book application.**

2. **Select File ➡ New Collection.** A space for the name of the new collection appears in the Collection list at the left of the Font Book window, as in Figure 4-14.

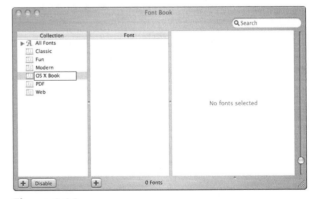

Figure 4-14
Adding a new collection

3. **Type a name for the new collection.**

4. **Press Enter.**

Your new collection won't have any fonts in it. To add fonts, you must first install them in another collection, even if it's only All Fonts. Once you install the font, you can place it in the new collection:

1. **Select the name of the collection containing the font you want to add to another collection.**

2. **Click and drag the name of the font from the high-lighted Font list to the name of the collection to which you want to add it.**

UNIVERSAL ACCESS OPTIONS

Universal Access makes the Mac OS easier to use if you have difficulties seeing, hearing, or using a standard mouse or keyboard. To some users, Universal Access is indispensable.

But even if you're skimming this and thinking, "Okay, this doesn't describe me; I shall move on," you should stick around. Universal Access offers basic changes to the way that standard user-interface elements operate and as such, they can be a treasure trove of shortcuts and streamlined techniques to anyone who takes the time to explore the possibilities.

Zooming in on the screen

Boy, this is useful. I've got an enormous screen, the kind that would have even impressed the apes who encountered the monolith in *2001: A Space Odyssey*. Thanks to Zoom, the monitor sits more than 2 feet away from my seat. The bright screen is far enough away that I can work all day and all night without eyestrain, and by zooming in on the one window I'm actually using I have all the benefits of an aircraft carrier–sized screen without having to peer at teeny-tiny type.

I also use it when my Mac is doing something I need to keep an eye on from afar. With the screen zoomed to the status indicator of a disk utility, I can just glance up from the sofa, see that the process is only halfway complete, and return to my comic books without getting up.

First, you can zoom in on the screen. To turn Zoom on:

1. **Open the Universal Access preferences panel.**

2. **Click the Seeing button to display the seeing pane.** See Figure 4-15.

3. **Click Turn On Zoom.** Zooming is now on. Pressing ⌘+Option+equal sign (=) makes the screen image larger. You can press ⌘+Option+minus sign (-) to make the screen image smaller. You can also toggle zooming on and off by pressing ⌘+Option+8.

Figure 4-15
The Universal Access seeing pane

Contrast and color

If the contrast or color of the screen is a problem, you can change it in several ways:

- **Click Switch to White on Black.** This turns the screen to a negative of itself.

- **Click Set Display to Grayscale.** This replaces colors with shades of gray.

- **Use the Enhance contrast slider.** This increases or decreases the contrast between colors.

Flashing alerts

For those who can't hear the Mac's speaker, OS X can flash the screen when an alert sound is played:

1. **Open the Universal Access preferences panel.**

2. **Click the Hearing button.** This displays the hearing pane (see Figure 4-16).

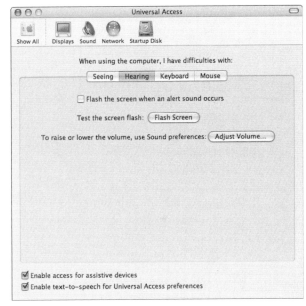

Figure 4-16
The Universal Access hearing pane

3. **Click the check box next to Flash the screen when an alert sounds.**

4. **Test the flashing by clicking Flash Screen.**

Pressing only one key at a time

The Mac was the first computer to extend the normal character set by having an extra modifier key on its keyboard (the Option key). The problem with this arrangement is that if a user has trouble holding down more than one key at a time, these extra characters — and ⌘ key shortcuts for menu commands — are unavailable. OS X provides a solution with Sticky Keys, which lets you press one key at a time:

1. **Open the Universal Access preferences panel.**

2. **Click the Keyboard button.** This displays the keyboard pane (see Figure 4-17).

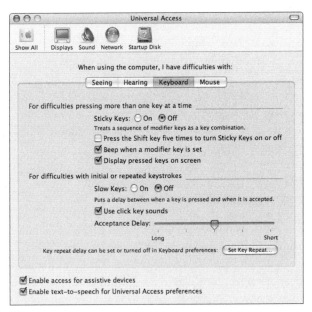

Figure 4-17
The Universal Access keyboard pane

THE TALKIN' MAC SAVIN' MY ENERGY BLUES

The System Preference's Speech panel hides a cool alert feature. You're in the living room watching hour 27 of the big Arbor Day Weekend *Bob Newhart Show* Marathon, when you hear your Mac beep from the other side of the room. You have to take the bowl of Cheetos off your belly, wipe the orange stuff off your fingers, redo the buckle on your trousers...I mean, walking over to the desk to identify the problem is a Herculean labor, and meanwhile, you're missing the bit when Bob has to walk out on a window ledge dressed as Zorro.

But if you activate Speech's Talking Alerts feature, your Mac actually speaks alerts and error messages aloud. "Excuse me: The file server Uncle Mimsy's Public Folder has unexpectedly gone offline," it says in Victoria's soothing tones. And because you just hit Uncle Mimsy's Mac to look at a couple of photos, you shrug and go on with your life.

I want to stress that I don't spend my entire life on the sofa, trying to give my Mac as little attention as possible. But it's good to know that Apple is looking out for the best interests of not only the 20-hour-a-day people, but also those users who want to scorn and neglect their products.

3. **Click the On button next to Sticky Keys.** OS X automatically checks the "Beep when a modifier key is set" and "Display pressed keys on screen" options. Click either or both of the check boxes if you want to disable these options.

▼ Note

Here's another useful feature. When you're struck by the fancy of using your Macintosh in the style of the grand odalisques of old — reclining on a chaise with your head cradled in one arm — you'll be glad that you know how to operate a Mac one-handed.

Using the keyboard instead of a mouse

If you have trouble using a mouse, or if your mouse decides to take a journey to mouse Heaven, you can control the movement of the mouse pointer with your numeric keypad. You do this by turning on Mouse Keys:

1. **Open the Universal Access preferences panel.**

2. **Click the Mouse button to display the mouse pane (see Figure 4-18).**

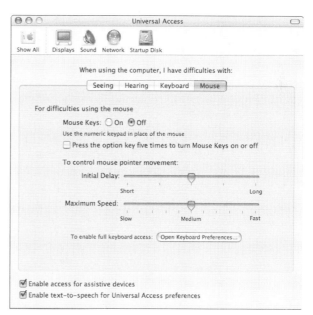

Figure 4-18
The Universal Access mouse pane

3. **Click the Mouse Keys On button.**

4. **Move the Initial Delay slider.** This slide controls how long you need to press a key before the mouse pointer begins to move.

When you have turned on Mouse Keys, you can use the keys on the numeric keypad to move the mouse (see Table 4.1).

Table 4.1: Mouse Keys

Action	Key
Move mouse pointer up	8
Move mouse pointer down	2
Move mouse pointer left	4
Move mouse pointer right	6
Move mouse pointer diagonally	1, 3, 7, and 9
Click the mouse button	5
Hold down the mouse button	0
Release the mouse button	Period (.)

 Tip

If your keyboard doesn't have a numeric keypad, as is the case with iBooks and PowerBooks, press the function (fn) key to make the center keys on the keyboard act like a numeric keypad. To find which keys will work, look for the small numbers on the keys.

"Okay, Mr. Big Shot," you're saying. "I suppose you're going to make up some sort of suspicious phony-baloney Power User thing about *this*, too, right?" Well, not if you're going to be so snotty about it.

But yeah, I use this one a lot, too. There are plenty of dirt-cheap infrared remotes that let you map buttons on the remote to keypresses. They're intended to let you skip from track to track in iTunes and such, but with Mouse Keys enabled you can easily use it to do simple things with your Mac from across the room.

Because of that little snippy reaction some of you had, I won't tell you about the G4 Cube, flat screen, and keyboard that I've screwed into one of the walls in my kitchen. But suffice it to say that Mouse Keys (and Sticky Keys) make a wall-mounted Mac eminently practical and useful.

I Don't Know Why They Call It the Finder, Either

In This Chapter

What's on the Desktop • Finder Window Views • Using the Toolbar • Using the Sidebar
Filenames: More Interesting Than Supposed • Finding Things • Creating Folders
Trashing Things • Moving Things Around • Custom Labels • Getting Information

A medium-sized FedEx box has just arrived. Good news, it's the analogy that I sent away for about 3 weeks ago in anticipation of this chapter. Let's see what they came up with:

"The Finder is like the lobby of a hotel."

Hmm. I see what they were going for, but frankly I was sort of hoping for something better, perhaps a baseball theme. Still, a good, reputable firm, who has been handcrafting analogies and similes since the days of the Harding administration, built this. Plus there's a 40 percent restocking fee on returns — so I'll make the most of it.

Yes, the Finder is like the lobby of a hotel. It's where the Mac deposits you after it's completed the startup process and for good reason: No matter what business you have in the Macintosh, at some point you're probably going to have to pass through the Finder to get there. It's the center of activity. You examine the contents of your folders and volumes. You search for files. You connect to remote file servers. You launch files and applications. You organize and re-organize the things you've stored.

WHY IS IT CALLED "THE FINDER"?

No, I actually *don't* know why it's called the Finder. It's one of those names that made sense in 1981 when the Mac and its OS were still being designed, but as things moved from Goals-And-Ideas into Practical-Actual-Product, the Finder became complicated enough that the original connection between the name and its function blurred beyond recognition.

Those of you who've ever built a house and have seen what became of that place the blueprints identified as "Sunroom" understand this all too well.

Okay, the hotel lobby idea is working. But I'll butter it a little: It's also a little like the hotel's concierge, too. If you're unsure of what you can do on your Mac, how to make adjustments to make your stay more pleasurable, and get information about what's going on with the system in general, your default resource is to click the Finder.

WHAT'S ON THE DESKTOP

Everything you do with OS X's GUI starts at the Finder's Desktop. Whether you're browsing through the contents of a disk, or working with an application window, it all ultimately lies on the Desktop.

As you can see in Figure 5-1, there are numerous visual elements that can appear:

- **The Dock:** Anchored at the bottom or either side of the startup monitor, the Dock provides quick access to programs, folders, and documents. It also contains the Trash Can. The Dock is discussed in depth in Chapter 6; we cover the Trash Can later in this chapter.

- **Disk icons:** All disks (or discs) that OS X can access, either locally (on the same computer) or over a network.

- **Folder icons:** Folders contain other things, like documents, applications, and even other folders.

- **Document and application icons:** Help you access the projects you're working on, or applications, such as iTunes.

- **Aliases to folders and files:** *Aliases* (also known as *shortcuts*) point to a file or folder that is located somewhere on a disk. You can identify an alias by the curved arrow in its lower-left corner. Although the actual file or folder isn't present on the Desktop, you can work with the alias as if it were the original.

- **Finder windows:** Finder windows show you the contents of a disk.

- **Application windows:** Application windows either contain something you are creating, reading, or viewing (documents), or collect information from you.

FINDER WINDOW VIEWS

A Finder window shows you the contents of a folder or a volume. Through one, you can launch applications, open documents, store files, delete files, move files, and copy files. But a Finder window can display its contents in three very different ways, viz:

Icon view

Icon view (for example, Figure 5-2) shows files and folders as icons. Icon view is sort of the classic image people have of the Mac, particularly for people who've acquired most of their education on modern computers from movies. Just once I'd like to see a movie where a computer's

Figure 5-1
A typical OS X Desktop

user-interface doohickeys aren't so big that they could stun a mole rat. But I suspect that I'll be dead before I'm ninety, so fat chance. This view isn't terribly efficient because it can only display a handful of icons at once, so you'll be scrolling around a lot. Most people never use it.

You're free to drag these icons around willy-nilly (or pell-mell, if you prefer), clumping them together in whichever order happens to make sense to you. But that can cause a

mess. The Finder can tidy up those icons for you. When an Icon view is active, you can use View ➔ Cleanup to align the icons to a grid and View ➔ Arrange ➔ *desired order* to sort the icons.

However, in a few cases Icon view is handy because it's so customizable. When you select View ➔ Show View Options, you'll get the tool palette shown in Figure 5-3.

Figure 5-2
A Finder window in Icon view

Figure 5-3
Setting Icon view options

Icon view options include

- **This window only/All windows:** These items let you customize the look of *just* this one window or the look of every window the Finder creates. So you can set things up your Pictures window to make it easy to see your images, but you're not stuck with that sort of view when you've got a window full of spreadsheets. You'll see this feature in the View Options palette of each of the Finder's three different views.

- **Icon size:** You can make the icons huge or tiny, and scale the label text so that it's easier to read, or takes up less room.

- **Snap to grid:** This ensures that icons stay in nice, orderly columns and rows, no matter how you drag 'em around.

- **Show item info/Show icon preview:** The icons can show you more information about the files they represent, too. When you click options, instead of generic JPEG icons the window shows you thumbnails of each JPEG image, along with its dimensions. Obviously this info will vary depending on what sort of file the icon represents.

- **Keep arranged by:** This option lets you arrange your icons by category.

- **Background options:** You can also change the window's background. Normally it's white (clean white, non-distracting white, thank-God-nobody-messed-around-with-the-background-white, but by clicking one of the buttons at the bottom of the View Options window you can change it to a different color, or hang an image back there.

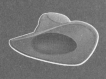

WHEN IT COMES TO BACKGROUNDS, I'VE MELLOWED WITH AGE

Sigh. When I was a younger man, I would have simply mocked anyone and everyone who would even *consider* switching the background away from white, and then moved on. Sample: "Whenever I see a customized window background, I imagine that this is a person who has the sort of good taste that commands them to cover a beautiful oak desk with leopard print contact paper."

But alas, with age comes the burden of Understanding. So with all due mumbling and kicking of the ground, I begrudgingly admit that this feature has its uses. For one, the Finder quickly becomes a maze of overlapping windows and when your Documents window has a red background, it's easy to spot in the scrum. And when you're responsible for keeping other people's Macs running, it's clever to draw a card of instructions as a JPEG image and set that as your users' window backgrounds. For example, "Valued User: Any documents placed inside this window are automatically copied to the server's 'Project' folder. So if you're abusing company hardware and bandwidth to download nude photos of former 'Love Boat' cast members, save them elsewhere...and I'm obviously just talking to Ted, here."

List view

The List view (see Figure 5-4) displays files and folders in an ordered list. You'll use this when you need to see the most information possible. I refer to List view as the "Where the Heck Ramsey did my 40 gigabytes of storage go?!?" I can easily pull up a list of my drive's and folder's contents, sort it by file size, and then see that, oh yeah, I seem to have downloaded roughly 13 gigabytes of music from the iTunes Store.

Figure 5-4
A Finder window in List view

You can sort the list by any column. To sort by file size, click on Size column header. By default, items appear in ascending order. To change it to descending, click the arrow at the right of the highlighted column (the column used for ordering).

You can change the width of a column by dragging the edge of its title left or right (the mouse pointer will change to a vertical bar with left and right arrows). You can also change a column's order by dragging the titles around.

List view has its own custom View Options (see Figure 5-5).

The Size options are familiar. The real meat of these options is choosing what sort of information is presented. By default, the filenames and mini-icons are joined by the date the file was last changed, its size, and its file type, but you can click on others to fill the window with more info, or de-select any info you're not interested in to prevent mental informational overload.

If you believe that the word "Yesterday" is a friendlier thing to see than yesterday's date (and why wouldn't you; it's not as cool as "The Fool On The Hill" or "Helter Skelter," but in this economy you take what you can get), check the Use relative dates option.

Figure 5-5
Setting List view options

Normally, the Finder doesn't calculate the sizes of enclosed folders in the list. That can take a lot of time. If you want that info, though, click on the Calculate all sizes option.

 Tip

If you're trying to bamboozle your spouse into letting you buy a peppier Mac, enable the Calculate all sizes option — particularly if you have lots of folders inside folders inside folders, and your Mac is indeed tragically slow. You'll be off to the Apple store with a co-signed check in no time, unless your spouse likes to watch you suffer, which is something you should have determined before you moved in together. Unless, of course, you're into that. Who am I to judge?

Column view

And here we have the most useful view of them all. You can easily navigate from anywhere within a volume *to* anywhere, all in one window. You can get a good overview of an item's total contents. Yes, from an inarticulate mass of lifeless windows, I bring you a cultured, sophisticated, one-window view of everything inside my hard drive. *Hit it!*

 Note

Um...that was a Mel Brooks reference."Young Frankenstein?" Where Gene Wilder shows off the...yes, that's it. Good. Onward.

Column view contains multiple columns, showing you a portion of the file/folder hierarchy, as in Figure 5-6. Although it doesn't give you as much information as List view, Column view can be easier to use if you need to thread your way through a file system.

Figure 5-6
A Finder window in Column view

You can crawl through the whole hierarchy of a disc. Click on a folder and a new column appears to its right, listing its contents. Click on a folder in that one and *another*

The left button chooses Icon view. The middle button chooses List view and the right button chooses Column view.

Figure 5-7
Setting Column view options

Figure 5-8
A Finder toolbar

column appears. Click on a file and the next column shows you a preview of what that file contains, along with information about that file. Yee...I say, *yee*...haw!

You can change the width of an individual column by dragging the handle at the bottom of its scroll bar. And just like Icon and List views, you can configure the Column view display by using View → Show View Options (Figure 5-7). You can choose a text size, whether icons should appear, and whether the final, rightmost column should include a preview of the contents of a selected document file.

To switch between the three views, you can use the view control in the Finder window's toolbar, which is the second group of tools in Figure 5-8.

USING THE TOOLBAR

If you're migrating up to Panther from Jaguar, you might ask, "Where did the toolbar go?" Well, like Love, it's still inside every one of us and the Finder windows, and you just have to trust that it's there.

▼ **Note**

But let's table Love for just a moment so I can express my strictly personal issue with the new Finder windows. The "brushed metal" look of Apple's iLife apps — so very appropriate when you're sorting photos of your bus trip to Branson or buying Tito Puente albums in iTunes — just doesn't work for me as a Finder interface. Exit elegance; enter flash.

They're like putting flame decals on a nice, reliable Volvo. You can pretend all you want but that thing's for hauling kids and groceries and surviving a 70 MPH rollover. It ain't for style. Okay, I'm ready to accept Love back into my heart now.

As we saw in Chapter 3, a toolbar is that strip of buttons at the top of an app's window. Clicking buttons can do many of the things you can do through the Finder's menus. The Finder's standard toolbar is shown in Figure 5-8.

The buttons are as follows:

- **Back/Forward buttons:** The first group of buttons navigate you Back and Forward and they work just like a Web browser's buttons. If you opened your Documents folder and then your Novels folder and then The Importance Of Being Furnished, clicking the "Back" button backtracks you step by step.

- **View buttons:** The second cluster switches you between Icon, List, and Column view (see the section "Finder Window Views" for more information).

- **Action button:** The next item is a user-interface element that's new to Panther: the Action button. It appears in lots of different apps: it's a pop-up menu containing functions that are relevant to whatever mode you happen to be in at the moment. Try popping it from time to time and you'll see that its contents are different when you've selected a file versus a folder, for instance.

▼ **Note**

Incidentally, that doodad on the Action button is a gear. But, of course, there's a swelling movement to call it a flower. Typically, any attempt to put a manly veneer on my milquetoasty geek nature is doomed to failure.

- **The "Gap":** And now you reach The Great Wasteland. It appears to be an empty and useless gap between the Action button and the Search box. It is indeed empty, but it's far from useless: You can drag items into it, such as applications and folders. The item won't be copied anywhere; it will just create a shortcut to it. Boy, is this handy. It keeps useful items right where you can use 'em.

▼ **Tip**

During my frequent and laughable attempts to organize my hard drive, I'll keep a batch of projects and asset folders there in the toolbar, and as I look through a big file list, I'll manually sort them into their proper destinations. And when I'm done, I drag the folders off. Clean and neat, until the next time I save a file, which is when the whole mess starts again.

- **Search fields:** Finally, you've got a Search field. Just tap in part of a filename, and before you've even finished, the Finder creates a list of filenames that contain those letters. Clicking on the magnifying glass lets you limit your search to a specific location.

Like any Mac toolbar, you can customize the Finder. Select View ➔ Customize Toolbar to see what's available. Chiefly, the buttons there duplicate functions you'll find inside the Finder's menu bar.

A LESSER-KNOWN FINDER FEATURE

There's another little feature hiding just above the toolbar. Hold down ⌘ and click on the window's title. Up pops a list revealing the path to the window's contents. For example, if you're looking at Your Documents folder, it will show "Documents>(Your username)/Users/(The name of your hard drive)/(The name of your Macintosh)."

This comes in handy if you place folders inside folders inside folders, and want to make a mental note of where exactly something is. It also lets you navigate back up several steps without going through all the stops in between.

USING THE SIDEBAR

In addition to the three Finder Window views, there is another navigation aid available to you in Finder windows: the sidebar (Figure 5-9).

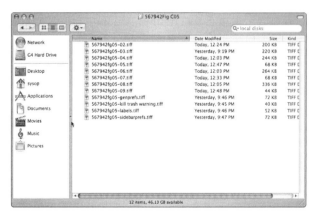

Figure 5-9
A Finder window with a sidebar

You can change the width of the sidebar by dragging the divider to your liking. To make it disappear altogether, drag the divider to the left edge of the window.

The sidebar has two little sections in it. The top section contains a list of all of the volumes currently connected to your Mac. Your built-in hard drive, a CD you've loaded, a memory card in its USB reader, your iDisk, or another volume or folder that you're connected to through a network. The Finder populates this list for you automatically, as volumes appear and disappear. If you want to limit what shows up in this section, click on the Sidebar pane of Finder Preferences.

Underneath that section you find shortcuts to useful folders and locations. Dragging a file into the Documents icon in the sidebar is as good as dragging it into the Documents folder directly.

You can add an item to the sidebar just by dragging it into any blank space underneath or between what's already in there. The list automatically re-sizes itself to make room, if necessary. You can also re-order its contents — move a useful folder to the very top, say — just by dragging it. Clicking on any of the icons in the sidebar opens that item. If the item is a folder or disk, its contents appear in the right side of the window.

To delete an item, just drag it away. It'll disappear in a puff.

▼ Note

Yup. Sidebar. Hate that too. Lots of people swear by it. I think it duplicates functions that are already handled by the Dock and the Finder toolbar. Me, I just close off the sidebar completely to make room for more useful stuff.

FILENAMES: MORE INTERESTING THAN SUPPOSED

You typically name a file when you save it for the first time. However, you can change that name later whenever you want. New folders are given the default name "Untitled Folder." You'll want to change that as well!

To rename an icon on the Desktop or in a Finder window:

1. **Click on an icon or the name of an item to select it.**

2. **Press Enter.** A blue box surrounds the highlighted text of the item's name, as in Figure 5-10.

Name	Date Modified	Size
567942fg05-02.tiff	Today, 12:24 PM	200 KB
567942fg05-03.tiff	Yesterday, 9:19 PM	220 KB
567942fg05-04.tiff	Today, 12:03 PM	244 KB
567942fg05-05.tiff	Today, 12:47 PM	68 KB
567942fg05-06.tiff	Today, 12:03 PM	264 KB
567942fg05-07.tiff	Today, 12:33 PM	68 KB
567942fg05-08.tiff	Today, 12:05 PM	336 KB
567942fg05-09.tiff	Today, 12:48 PM	44 KB
567942fg05-10.tiff	Today, 3:27 PM	236 KB
567942fg05-11.tiff	Yesterday, 9:46 PM	72 KB
567942fg05-kill trash warning.tiff	Yesterday, 9:45 PM	40 KB
567942fg05-labels.tiff	Yesterday, 9:46 PM	52 KB
567942fg05-sidebarprefs.tiff	Yesterday, 9:47 PM	72 KB

Figure 5-10
A filename ready for you to change

3. **Edit the name.**

4. **Press Enter.**

This is as good a place as any to talk about OS X's rules for naming things. The nice thing is that there aren't many rules. You can use just about any character you can type from the keyboard, including spaces. In fact, the only character you can't use is a colon. OS X also won't let you have more than one item in a folder by the same name.

 Note

Oh, and a filename can't be any longer than 255 characters, or 9 average sentences. Maybe when 10.4 is released we can finally live the dream of doing away with files entirely and just putting all of our document contents in the titles.

One of the many things that You Don't Need To Know is the fact that Mac OS X — being a flavor of Unix — puts filename extensions on all its files. That Microsoft Word file's name isn't "Asphalt Pie"; it's actually "Asphalt Pie.doc." The Finder conceals the extension because it's ugly and extensions didn't exist in Mac OS 9. You can have the Finder show all file extensions by clicking on the appropriate button in the Advanced tab of the Finder Preferences window.

CELEBRITY DEATH MATCH? "FIND" VS. SHERLOCK

Oh, so the Finder Finds things! Well, sometimes you *do* run across an Augustus Q. Milkmann who actually delivers yogurt and half-and-half to suburban houses.

Those of you trading up from Mac OS 9 will probably be asking "Finding files in the Finder? But what about Sherlock?" To quote the sober and wise Mob capo Clemenza, who used these words in reference to the whereabouts of a certain member of the Corleone family whose performance was so sorely lacking that an immediate and bloody personnel change was mandated: "Sherlock? Oh, you won't be seein' *him* no more."

Sherlock is still part of X, but it's focused on grabbing info off the Internet. For local file search, Apple has returned to a nice, fast, slim, and *sensible* Find feature. Now, take the cannoli. Leave the gun.

FINDING THINGS

There are literally tens of thousands of files on an OS X startup drive. If you've forgotten where you stored something, finding it by simply browsing through the folder/file hierarchy is little more than an exercise in frustration. But there is a better way: Use the Finder's Find utility.

Find a folder

To find a file or folder:

1. **Select Finder → Find or press ⌘+F.** The Find dialog appears (Figure 5-11).

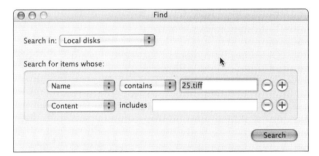

Figure 5-11
The Find dialog

2. **Select where you want to search from the Search in menu.** The options are as follows:

   ▫ **Local disks:** Searches disks in drives physically attached to your computer.

   ▫ **Everywhere:** Searches all local disks plus accessible network disks.

   ▫ **Home:** Searches your account's home directory.

   ▫ **Specific places:** With this option, OS X changes the dialog to display all accessible disks, as in Figure 5-12. Click to place a check in the box next to

all disks you want to search; click to remove the check from those you don't want to search. If you want to search specific folders rather than entire disks, click the Add button. Use the Open File dialog to add a folder to the list of searchable items.

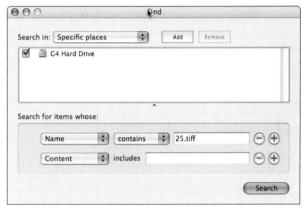

Figure 5-12
Choosing where to search

3. **Select which characteristic of the file or folder your want to search.** The options in the the "Name" pop-up menu are Name, Date Created, Date Modified, Kind, Label, Size, Extension, Visibility, Type, and Creator.

4. **Select the search operator from the "contains" pop-up menu.** The available options for Name are contains, starts with, ends with, and is. Search operators vary depending on the file or folder characteristic you are searching.

5. **Click the Search button.** The result appears in a separate window. As you can see in Figure 5-13, the top portion of the window contains a scrolling list of all items found by the search. The bottom portion shows the path you take through the folder hierarchy to reach the item.

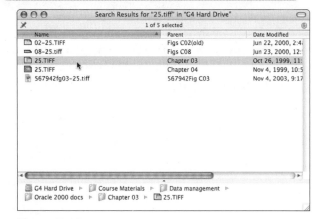

Figure 5-13
The result of a file search

If you want to add more criteria to a search, click the plus (+) button to add another search specification row, as in Figure 5-14. OS X connects each row of search criteria with AND. In other words, a file or folder must meet all specified criteria to be included in the result.

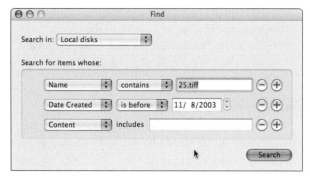

Figure 5-14
Using multiple search criteria

 Note

The path that you take to reach an item is known as its *pathname*. The Mac OS uses colons to separate items in a pathname. Therefore, the pathname shown at the bottom of Figure 5-13 is G4 Hard Drive: Course Materials: Data Management: Oracle 2000 docs: Chapter 03: 25.TIFF. Fortunately, Macintosh users rarely have to use full pathnames.

You can do a number of things with the results of a search that appear in the top portion of the Results window:

- **Open a file or folder.** You do this by double-clicking on its icon.

- **Move an item by dragging it to a new location.** You can find more about moving items in the section "Moving Things Around."

- **Delete an item.** For details, see the section "Trashing Things."

- **Rename an item.**

Searching by a file's contents

The Finder's Find utility can also search file contents. For example, if you can't remember what name you saved a file under, but you do remember that it contained the phrase "Orange frogs playing mixed-doubles with Bea Arthur and Clint Howard," you can search for files containing those words.

There are two problems with doing that kind of search. One: It takes a long time. Two: It takes a long time.

First, it takes a long time because it has to paw through the contents of every file you've got.

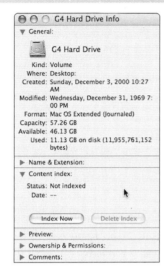

Figure 5-15
Turning on disk indexing

Fortunately, the Finder can use some of its downtime to build a handy index of the contents of all of your files. This takes place in the background, often while you're not even using your Mac. And once this index is complete, a search-by-content takes only marginally longer than any other kind.

Bringing us to Problem Two: building that index takes a long time. At least the first time you do it. But heck, you paid thousands of dollars for that machine. You can either waste your time or its time, and that's a no-brainer. To turn indexing on:

1. **Click the disk or folder whose contents you want to index.**

2. **Select File → Get Info or press ⌘+I.** The Get Info window appears. (You'll find more on this window in the "Getting Information" section at the end of this chapter.)

3. **Click on the triangle to the left of Content Index.** This exposes indexing options, as in Figure 5-15.

4. **Click the Index Now button to begin indexing.** You might want to make this the last thing you do before leaving for the day. It's gonna take a long while.

CREATING FOLDERS

You can create new folders whenever you need them to organize your stuff:

1. **Open the disk or folder in which you want the new folder to appear.**

2. **With the parent disk or folder active, select File → New Folder or press Shift+cmd+N.**

3. **Change the folder's default name ("Untitled Folder") to whatever name you need.**

TRASHING THINGS

Hard disks fill up a lot faster than you think, and it's not hard to end up with a lot of files that you no longer use. When you're ready to clean house, you can delete folders and files:

1. **Drag the items you want to delete to the Trash Can icon in the Dock.** Alternatively, you can select the items and press ⌘+Delete.

2. **Select Finder → Empty Trash.** Alternatively, you can press Shift+⌘+Delete to empty the Trash Can.

▼ Caution

When you move a folder to the Trash Can, you also move everything that the folder contains. Emptying the Trash Can deletes the folder and all its contents.

The Trash Can is a window much like any other Finder window (see Figure 5-16). To open it, click on its icon in the Dock. As long as you haven't emptied the Trash, you can drag any item out of the Trash Can window and return it to its original location.

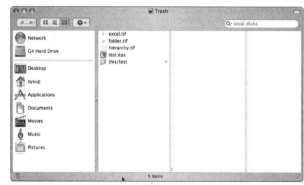

Figure 5-16
The Trash Can window

OS X asks you to confirm emptying the Trash, as in Figure 5-17. If you get annoyed with the warning, and want deletions to proceed without your direct approval, you can turn off the warning.

PANTHER'S VIRTUAL SHREDER

When you empty the Trash normally, the Finder merely notes that it can now overwrite the real estate the data once occupied with new data. The original files are still there and you can retrieve them with a simple utility that looks for stray cattle, so to speak.

If you're trashing sensitive data, use Panther's new Secure Empty Trash option. The Finder will "shred" the data before deleting, making it darn-near impossible for anybody to ever piece it back together.

Figure 5-17
The Trash Can emptying warning

1. **Select Finder → Preferences.**

2. **Click the Advanced button in the toolbar.**

3. **Click the "Show warning before emptying the Trash" option to remove the check, as in Figure 5-18.**

Advanced

General Labels Sidebar **Advanced**

☐ Show all file extensions
☐ Show warning before emptying the Trash

Languages for searching file contents:

(Select...)

Figure 5-18
Turning off the Trash Can emptying warning

MOVING THINGS AROUND

Just drag whatever-it-is from wherever-it-is-now to wherever-you-want-it-to go. Simple, eh?

Yes, for users. For people writing books about simple-to-use operating systems, it's a nightmare. This elegant mechanism does lots of different things, depending on the "where-you-want-it-to-go" bit. Viz:

- **You drag a file from your Documents folder to your Pictures folder.** Both folders are on the same volume (your Mac's built-in hard drive) so the file *moves* from the old location to the new one.

▼ **Tip**

OK, so what if you actually wanted a copy of that file in both places? Apple has thoughtfully given you a shortcut: Hold down the "Option" key before clicking and dragging. The item will copy, and not move, to its destination.

- You drag it from your Documents folder to a folder on an external drive, like your iPod or one of those cool key rings with 128 megs of flash storage. The two locations aren't on the same volume, so the file *copies* to the new location. Two copies now exist.

OK, so what if you actually wanted to *move* that file? Apple has thoughtfully...actually, no, they haven't. You'll have to drag it from one volume to another and then delete the original yourself. What, you don't think the good folks at Apple deserve to take some time off to enjoy themselves every now and then?

THE BEAUTY OF SPRING-LOADED FOLDERS

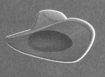

Apple has given us a great time-saver in the form of *spring-loaded folders*. Let's say you don't actually want to move that file into Pictures. You actually want it to go into Paintings Of My Dog, a folder inside a folder named Paintings that's *inside* the Pictures folder. You have to somehow uncover that destination folder so you can drag something into it, yes?

No. Just drag it on top of Pictures, *but don't let go of the mouse button.* After a pause, the folder opens on its own, revealing its contents. Hold it over Paintings Of My Dog and let go. In it goes, and the Finder snaps all those folders closed behind you, neat and clean. You can modify this behavior (or turn it off entirely) via Finder Preferences.

If you don't want to wait, holding down the space bar springs the folder open immediately. I have somehow taught myself how to play an F#m6, the toughest chord possible on the ukulele; so trust me, you can train your fingers to work this shortcut.

CUSTOM LABELS

Custom labels let you color code files and folders. This is particularly useful if you want for example, to identify all files that belong to a single project or that have a similar status (for example, "need to be faxed"). You can spot all the red files at a glance, and when you want to collect all of your project assets together, you can do a Find on that label.

In Icon view, a labeled icon appears with the label color as a background to the icon's name (see Figure 5-19). In List or Column view, the entire row for the icon has the colored background; if you select a row, a dot in the label color appears to the left of the icon name (see Figure 5-20).

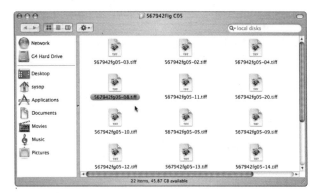

Figure 5-19
A custom label in Icon view

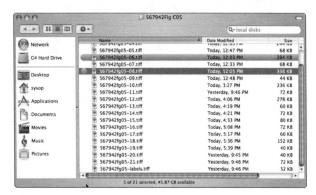

Figure 5-20
Custom labels in List view

To apply a custom label:

1. **Select the item or items to which you want to apply the custom label.**

2. **Drop down the File menu and select the color of the label you want to apply from the last line of the menu, as in Figure 5-21.** You can also hold down the Control key and click on the item, then select the label you want from the resulting contextual menu.

Figure 5-21
Choosing a custom label

To remove a label from an icon, repeat the above procedure, selecting the X at the left of the bottom line in the menu.

Although you can't change the label colors or have more than seven labels, you can customize the text for each label. To do so,

1. **Select Finder → Preferences.** The Labels dialog appears.

2. **Click the Labels button in the toolbar.** This displays the Labels pane (Figure 5-22).

3. **Edit the label text as desired.**

Figure 5-22
Changing custom label text

GETTING INFORMATION

One of the coolest parts of moving to Mac OS X is the way that the Finder presents you with so much useful information, all at a glance. When did I last access that file? Who created it? If it's a document, what does it look like? In Mac OS 9, you needed the Finder's Get Info feature, *plus* a bunch of third-party software to get what you get today by just looking at a standard window.

The role of Get Info has changed somewhat. It still presents much the same information as it did in OS 9 but its function has shifted more towards the utilitarian. Here's where you manipulate various settings that control how this file (folder, app, volume) looks and behaves.

To display an item's Get Info window:

1. **Select the item in a Finder window or on the Desktop.**

2. **Select File → Get Info.** You can also press ⌘+I.

Exactly what you see depends on the type of icon selected, and we'll be covering a lot of the entity-specific stuff in later chapters. Figure 5-23 is the Get Info window for a hard drive.

There are some elements that are common to most Get Info boxes, however. The General section is filled with cool trivia, mostly repeating what you can see in the Finder's Column view. Name & Extension is a quick place to rename items, as well as peek at those hidden filename extensions, and there's a Comments box for free-form notes about a file.

▼ **Tip**

Comments are wretchedly underused. Remember that this resource is available to you and you'll wonder how you did without it. Every time I install new software, for instance, I copy its registration code into its "Get Info" comment. That way, when I upgrade to a new Mac I can just drag my commercial software onto the new hard drive without having to go back and look up all those numbers from the original CDs. You can use Comments in search fields, too.

Figure 5-23
The Get Info window for a hard drive

You can also change an item's Finder icon just by doing a Get Info on the thing, clicking on its icon in the General pane, and then pasting in a new graphic.

Why would you want to do that? First, because it's cool. Second, because it makes a folder or volume visually unique. All of the drives on my Macs have custom icons. When I'm away from my desk and need to connect to my Desktop to grab a file, Mac OS X gives me a list of available servers, and I know in a tenth of a second that the one with the icon of a guy with an Apple logo spray-painted onto his head is the Documents folder of my Desktop G5.

Hmm. I still feel like I've shortchanged you. Tell you what:

Every U.S. paper bill weighs exactly 1 gram. So if you know how much an item costs and how much it weighs (in metric, of course), you can quickly see if it costs more or less than its weight in dollar bills.

So while the Power Macintosh G5 may cost $2,499, at 18 kilograms it costs merely a fraction of its weight in dollar bills. You could buy *seven* G5's for that $18,000, so when you look at it *that* way, by letting you go buy one, your spouse is actually saving the household over $15,000.

I haven't given you a chapter on Ownership & Permissions, but I *have* given you the lever you need to replace the perfectly good Mac you already have with Apple's top of the line. S/he'll either see the logic of your argument or s/he'll conclude that you're so desperate that giving you a new G5 would be a humanitarian gesture.

No need to thank me. Just trying to give you as much bang for the buck as I can. Though as your friend I need to point out that if your husband, wife, boyfriend, or girlfriend actually thinks that this argument makes sense, you should probably spend a good evening evaluating the basis of your relationship and the wisdom of continuing it.

MY ENVIRONMENTALLY CORRECT STRATEGY FOR SHOWING YOU HOW TO USE GET INFO

I'm going to say something disappointing; then I'm going to give you some valuable information that you'll use several times a year for the rest of your life, to make it up to you.

Disappointing: there are some bits under Get Info that, in a longer book, would merit a whole chapter, "Ownership and Permissions," for example. Now *there's* some sweet mojo. The stuff you can do — both "totally not evil at all" and, well, the other thing — is fantastic. But alas, deforestation is a huge problem. I don't know what this "ozone" stuff is, but lots of folks seem to get themselves all lathered up over it and it's just simpler to limit the number of pages of this book than to get into that whole big rhubarb again.

So instead of giving specific detail to everything you'll find in Get Info, I've chosen to pepper the rest of the book with ways to use it effectively. When I talk about folders later on, I'll tell you how to use Get Info to make one of your folders into a "drop box" that other folks using your Mac or the network can see and copy files into...but not open.

The Useful Advice: The theme to *Gilligan's Island* was based on a rather ancient sea song, the same tune that was morphed into *Amazing Grace*, coincidentally. So it is both possible and highly amusing to sing the inspirational lyrics to the greatest hymn ever written to the tune of the worst piece of junk that Sherwood Schwartz ever put on the air.

See? I told you it'd be worth it.

The Dock, and Why It Doesn't Stink Even a Little

In This Chapter

Meet the Dock • Dock Basics • What Dock Icons Do
Adding To and Deleting From the Dock • Bouncing Icons • Contextual Menus
But What If the Dock Still Stinks? • One Final Word...

When Apple introduced the Dock, it was the single worst thing they had done to anger the Mac community since they advertised the iMac with the slogan "Power. Speed. Style. Affordability. Oh, and your mother washes her hair with gravy."

As bad as all that sounds, it's even worse because I just made that second thing up to sort of soften things a little. So in truth, dropping the Dock on everybody was in fact probably the biggest shock Apple ever dealt. Many folks did (and do) have an almost genetic-level revulsion to the Dock the same way we humans are programmed against cannibalism.

But please. *Please.* Use the dock until you learn to love it because you will indeed learn to love it. It's a resource that lurks at the margin of every single screen, and if that weren't enough to make the Dock a powerful tool, Apple was smart enough to keep its functionality simple. The end-result is that the Dock is quite often a big part of making your Mac simpler and more convenient in day-to-day use.

MEET THE DOCK

First off, let's thoroughly explain what the Dock is and what it does:

It's a place to put stuff. Moving on....

DOCK SCRIPTING VIA PYTHON/PERL

Using a C++-like syntax and a moderate knowledge of Unix, it's possible to automate Dock functions from any shell command. With....

NO, SERIOUSLY, MEET THE DOCK

But I don't want to make the basic explanation any more complicated than that. Really. "The Dock is a place where you put stuff so it's handy later." Memorize that, and you're golden.

I'll explain it another way. As I write this, I'm sitting on the sofa in my office and I've got my PowerBook in my lap. Obviously, the Mac is the thing I'm focused on right now. But on the cushion next to me, you'll find my phone, the remote for the TV and stereo, and a reference book. On the table to my right, there's my ukulele, a cold beverage, and (because I've got a bear of a cold right now) a box of tissues.

Note

Keeping a ukulele next to your Mac at all times is just plain good, common sense and shouldn't be mocked.

Technically, each of those things belongs elsewhere in the house, but having them within reach makes me more productive. I don't have to get up and trot to the desk when the phone rings, when I need to sneeze I just need to make a quick reach, and if a quick strum of "Honey Pie," enhances my relentless pursuit of *le mot juste,* then enhanced it shall be.

That's the deal with the Dock. You drag useful applications, files, and folders into it. And they'll always be just a mouse-gesture away, no matter what you're doing at the moment. Viz:

- **It keeps essential apps in reach.** There are apps that you use often, but not often enough that you have them launched automatically when your Mac starts up. By putting these all-stars in the Dock, you can launch them with one click, instead of having to navigate through the Applications folder for them.

Note

Even better, having various apps in the Dock gives you flexibility in opening documents. I'm in the Finder, looking at stuff that's landed on my Desktop. I don't know what DSC829388.JPG is, so I double-click on it and it opens in Preview. I realize it's a cool photo of my nephew and now I want to edit it. Instead of clicking back into the Finder, opening the Applications folder, launching Photoshop, and then locating and opening the file again, I can just drag the document icon straight into the Photoshop icon in the Dock.

- **It keeps files organized.** I *try* to be a good boy and keep my hard drive organized, but at least once a week I have to corral stray files and move them to where they belong. By dragging my Documents, Pictures, Music, and other assorted folders into the Dock, I can move files into them without having to untangle a mess of overlapping windows to keep them exposed. Drag the file onto the folder's icon, let go, and it lands inside.

- **It keeps you current.** To make this book look all purty and stuff, talented designers invested immeasurable time and energy to create a comprehensive Style Guide. But here I am on Chapter 6 and I *still* can't keep all of the styles straight. So a few times a day, I need to read the Guide and remember what needs to be formatted with which style. Dragging the Guide into my Dock means I can look things up quickly. By keeping the project folder in the Dock, one click opens up a Finder window with the entire book-in-progress.

It goes on and on. Yes, at first I was a little thrown by the Dock, too. But I quickly appreciated that it's a flexible feature that's right there when you need it and goes away when you don't. In system-wide utilities as well as high-school relationships, that's the definition of perfection.

DOCK BASICS

Figure 6-1 shows a typical, busy Dock that is anchored to the bottom of the screen. Thing o'beauty, innit? Your own Dock will look different, of course, but the Dock has a consistent visual language.

▼ **Note**

Yes, some freaks have their Docks hanging vertically. Don't be frightened; just make sure to stay rock-still if he or she spots you. They hunt mostly by sense of smell and staying still effectively renders you invisible. Well, okay, maybe these people aren't exactly *freaks*. But as someone who keeps the Dock in its default position at the bottom of the screen, it's still pretty *weird*, man.

Notice that about two-thirds of the way along, there's a faint dividing line. Everything to the left of that line is an Application. Some of the application icons sport little triangles. This means that the app is actually running at the moment. And hey, some of them are sporting little badges or blinkers, too, to offer you a subtle bit of info. Apple's Mail app, for instance, stamps its icon with the number of waiting messages. It's handy. You're about to take a break, but on your way over to the DVD Player's icon, you notice that Mail's counter has changed from 3 to 182, indicating the possibility that something you're responsible for is possibly on fire and that you should really check your email.

THE COOLNESS OF MINIMIZED WINDOWS

Cool beans regarding minimized windows: Minimize a movie window, or the browser window of a news site, or any window that contains "live" content. See? The "iconized" window is *always* up-to-date! What once was *Star Wars: The Empire Strikes Back* playing full-screen is now playing at postage-stamp proportions. This is what's known as an incredibly cool way to flaunt the processing power of the mighty Macintosh CPU.

Icons to the right of that line are everything else: documents, folders, windows that have been minimized, and even entire volumes. The Trash Can always appears at the right.

WHAT DOCK ICONS DO

What happens when you click an icon? Depends on what you're clickin':

○ **If it's an application icon, it switches to that app.** It also brings the app's windows to the foreground. If the app isn't running already, the Dock launches it for you.

○ **Ditto if you click a document icon.** The document window pops to the front. If the document isn't already open, the Dock opens it for you, launching its app, too, if need be.

○ **Ditto for folder and volume icons.** Its window pops to the front. If it isn't already open, the Dock opens it. The Trash icon acts just like a folder.

"But how do I tell the difference between six identical folder icons?" you ask. Not to worry. When the mouse hovers over an icon, its name magically appears. Although there's something to be said for having an element of

Figure 6-1
A typical, busy Dock

mystery and spontaneity on your workday, this feature also tells you which icon you're aiming at with the mouse.

It's also possible to drag items onto icons. Dragging a document onto an application icon opens the document with that app. Of course, the app has to know how to deal with that sort of file. If you drag a JPEG over iCal, nothing happens. If you drag it over Photoshop, the icon turns dark, which is its way of saying, "Gimme, gimme, *gimme*."

 Note

What happens next depends on the app. Usually, dragging a doc onto an icon is the equivalent of using the app's Open command. But Mail, for instance, is smart enough to know that you probably want to email that file to someone, so it creates a new email and adds the file as an attachment. For more on applications such as Mail, see Chapter 7.

ADDING TO AND DELETING FROM THE DOCK

Okay, now that the Dock's various settings are well and truly accounted for — again, anything you hated about the behavior of the Dock should be fixed by now, so let the love begin — let's figure out how to get stuff in and out of the thing.

The OS X installer got you started by placing Apple's Greatest Hits in the Dock for you: Mail, iTunes, Safari, and so on. But naturally your first order of business is to add your own items.

And it's as simple as dragging the item in from the Finder. Remember that apps go to the *left* of that little divider and everything else goes to the *right*, but other than that, go nuts. Existing icons scurry out of the way and the Dock automatically resizes itself to make room for the new arrival as you drag, so place it wherever you want. Let go of the mouse when you're hovering over an empty space, and it's in.

If you don't need an icon any longer, drag it off the Dock onto the Desktop. The icon disappears with a little puff.

 Note

Here you see the sole, sad remaining remnant of the mighty Apple Newton MessagePad PDA: The "puff" effect in the Dock is the same animation that the MessagePad used when you scrubbed out a piece of text. Excuse me, I think I need a drink now...

Application icons are automatically added to the Dock whenever you launch them, but if the icon wasn't there to begin with, it disappears as soon as you quit the app. You can make the icon of a running app "stick" to the Dock without manually dragging it in through the icon's contextual menu. For more on using contextual menus in the Dock, see the section "Contextual Menus" later in this chapter.

BOUNCING ICONS

What's the appropriate way for somebody to get your attention? Clear their throat discreetly? Raise their hand and wait patiently to be called upon?

If you have a six-year-old kid, you know that the appropriate answer is, "Jump up and down like a total spaz until the person has no choice but to stop what they're doing and focus on you." And what do you know: That's what the Dock does, too. Even if the Dock is hidden, the icon springs up, Up, UP and down in and out of view, like it's on a trampoline.

When you launch an app via the Dock, it bounces its icon just to let you know that, yes, it did indeed understand your request and the app should be up in just a couple of seconds.

If you're focusing on the "spaz" aspect of this behavior instead of the "necessary feedback" aspect, you can turn it off:

1. **Select Apple → Dock → Preferences to display the Dock preferences panel.**

2. **Click in the box next to the "Animate opening applications" option to remove the check mark.**

But an application can also cause its icon to bounce of its own free will. This happens when Something Bad Has Just Happened, but the app is in the background and so there's a chance that you might have missed it. For example, if you've set up Mail to receive email in the background, you'd want to know right away that you've lost your connection to the Internet and the app can no longer function. You need to know *now*, not 5 days from now, when you're finally curious about why you haven't heard the New Email Has Arrived sound all week and you bring the app to the foreground.

▼ **Note**

And here I understand — a *little* — about why some people hate the Dock. This behavior is controlled by the app itself, and some apps make the icon bounce for dumb reasons. One of my favorite utilities in the

whole world regularly checks to see if there's a new version available and if so: bouncy, bouncy, bouncy. It doesn't care that it already told me about this update an hour ago and I'm *still* too busy to download and install it; It wants me to drop what I'm doing and learn that Version 1.3.4.2 has been updated to 1.3.4.2.1. In a word: Grrr.

CONTEXTUAL MENUS

You access a contextual menu (see Figure 6-2) by either clicking the icon and holding down the mouse button, by holding down the Control key while clicking, or by using your mouse's right-hand button, if it has one.

So, if this running app hasn't been added to the Dock already, you can just click on Keep In Dock and it's as good as gold.

And boy, are Contextual Dock menus fun. They really add the extra *oomph* of power that sends you over the cliff (but it's a plummet of sheer bliss, because you're being so gosh-darned productive):

- **There's a list of all the app's document windows.** Select one from the list and it pops straight to the front. As a total loser who can never keep his desktop organized, I fondly look upon this feature.

- **You can hide the app without quitting it.** Zap! And your 5-dozen browser windows magically hide themselves. Again, I approve. Hold down the Option key while the menu is active, and Hide becomes Hide Others.

- **Or, you can quit the app.** If something's gone wrong and the program's frozen up, the Dock's contextual menu for it will say "Program Not Responding." You can change the menu's Quit to a Force Quit by holding down the Option key while the menu is active.

▼ Note

A Force Quit is the impolite way of ending an app, but it's the only option when things are locked up. For more on what to do when you computer gets stuck, see Chapter 21.

Figure 6-2
The Dock's contextual menu for a running application

- **Depending on the app, you can access some of its most common features.** Mail lets you create a new message or check for new mail, for example.

- **Whether an app is running or not, you can locate the application in the Finder.** After you place an app in the Dock, you may forget where it's physically located, and thus deleting the app (or replacing it with something newer) can be a real snipe hunt. Not so with the Show In Finder command.

The crazy-go-nuts-great contextual feature comes when you've tossed a folder inside the Dock, as shown in Figure 6-3. Get a load of this:

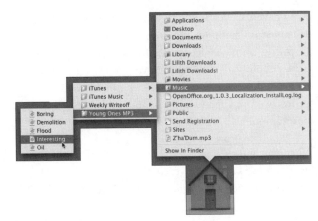

Figure 6-3
The hierarchical menu of a folder or a volume

You can mouse all the way from the top of the folder down to the sub-folderiest sub-folder, entirely through the Dock. Here you see my favorite use of this feature: I've put my Home folder in the Dock. I can access any file or launch any app I have without having to click into the Finder. It's so useful that I also have my Applications folder docked. This way, I can launch even my least-used apps as conveniently as an app that has its own direct Dock icon.

Oh, and I suppose for the sake of completeness I need to say that the Dock has its own contextual menu that you can activate through any part of the Dock that isn't occupied by icons (see Figure 6-4).

Figure 6-4
The Dock's own contextual menu

This capability gives you direct access to the Dock's settings. But that hardly even registers on the excitement scale, after you've seen what happens when you put a folder in there, right? Woo-hoo!

BUT WHAT IF THE DOCK STILL STINKS?

Hey, I appreciate your keeping the faith for this long. Again I say, "The Dock is swell, the Dock is fine. The Dock helps build strong bodies eight different ways." And chances are excellent that no matter what it is that you don't like about the Dock, you can fix it through Dock settings.

Positioning the Dock

Okay, look, I'm sorry about the "freak" crack I made earlier. But no kiddin': Moving the Dock from the bottom of the screen is like when you turn on a talk show and the guest chairs are to the *right* of the host's desk. It's just plain creepy.

But to each their own. Apple lets you customize the appearance and function of the Dock. Including — he said, with a sigh of resignation, knowing that he can't

watch you *everywhere* and that, in the end, you're going to do what you want to do — moving the Dock to the left or right side of the monitor.

▼ **Note**

And I'll admit that it's sometimes a good idea. Mozilla, my Web browser, has a tendency to create new windows that end at the very bottom of the screen, and it's hard to access its scroll arrows without accidentally activating the Dock. Putting the Dock at the side of the screen is great if you have a widescreen monitor. You only tend to mouse all the way to the edge of space through an act of will, and not by accident.

You can change the Dock's location through System Preferences or right in the Apple menu. To use the Dock preferences panel:

1. **Select Apple ➔ Dock ➔ Preferences.**

2. **Click the Left, Bottom, or Right radio button (see Figure 6-5).**

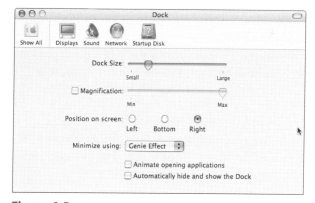

Figure 6-5
Using the Dock preferences panel to chose the Dock's position

To change the Dock's position directly from the Apple menu, Select Apple → Dock and then either Position Left, Position Bottom, Position Right, as in Figure 6-6.

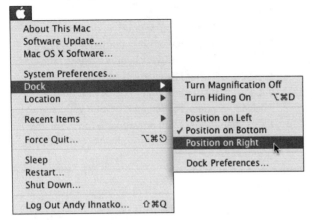

Figure 6-6
Using the Apple menu to choose the Dock's position

Showing and hiding the Dock

The next big deal is whether you want the Dock to remain visible all the time (so you can keep an eye on the wide-screen special-edition of *The Lord of the Rings* as it plays in that inch-wide minimized window) or if it should scurry discreetly out of the way when not in use.

Unless you have a humongous monitor big enough to microwave a potato on your desktop, you'll probably want to turn on the Dock's Hiding feature. There are two ways to turn on automatic hiding and showing:

- **Chose Apple → Dock → Turn Hiding On.** Turn Hiding On changes to Turn Hiding Off so you can turn off this option by repeating the same procedure.

- **Open the Dock preferences panel and place a check in the "Automatically hide and show the Dock" check box.**

With Hiding turned on, the Dock only hovers into view when you mouse into the very bottom of the screen.

Size and magnification

Lucky you: You're just getting started, so you only have a handful of icons in your Dock (see Figure 6-7). Well, I have 50 (see Figure 6-8). As things start to get crowded in there, you need to become intimate with the Dock's Size and Magnification settings.

Size lets you define how small the Dock should ever get. Normally, the Dock automatically shrinks itself to whatever width accommodates all those icons, but you can in effect tell it that the icons are too small to be seen by the human eye, which is, alas, all you happen to be equipped with.

To access Size settings, open up the Dock Preferences panel and play with the Dock Size slider.

▼ **Tip**

You can also change the Dock's size by grabbing that little divider we talked about. Notice that when your mouse hovers over it, the pointer changes to a little grow icon. Just slide it up and down and watch the icons change.

Figure 6-7
The Dock at maximum size

Figure 6-8
The Dock at minimum size

The other balm for your peepers is the Dock's magnification feature. When active, your mouse acts sort of like a magnifying glass as it moves along the dock. Individual icons are magnified to several times their normal proportions, rendering them visible from several hundred yards.

There are two ways to turn on magnification:

○ **Select Apple → Dock → Turn Magnification On.** Turn Magnification On changes to Turn Magnification Off so you can turn off this option by repeating the same procedure.

○ **Open the Dock preferences panel and click to place a check in the Magnification check box.** You can control how big the icons get via the slider control.

▼ **Warning**

Magnification can drive you batty. It's easy to accidentally click on the icon to the left or right of what you are aiming for, particularly if your Mac isn't reacting to your mouse-movements very swiftly. But don't worry. The only time this sort of mistake happens is when you're minutes from a crucial deadline, and the icon you want is right next door to an application that ties up your CPU for a half an hour when launched.

Animating Windows

When you minimize a window, it disappears from the Desktop and reappears in the lower (or right) portion of the Dock. OS X animates the movement from full-sized window to Dock icon. You can choose either a Genie effect, in which the window slurps into the Dock like a grease and hair clog finally disappearing down the drain in a Liquid Plumber commercial, or a Scale effect, in which the window gets smaller as it moves to the Dock but retains its proportions.

▼ **Note**

This is hardly a power-productivity feature. But if you're using an older, less-powerful Mac, you'll find that the Scale effect looks smoother. In fact, this is one of those reasons why I love the Mac. Why do anything the simple way, when a bodaciously cooler method is available and it shows off the machine's processing power? Oh, and watch carefully when you minimize a movie window; yes, the movie is *still playing* even while it's slurping down into the Dock.

To change the minimize animation effect:

1. **Select Apple → Dock → Preferences to display the Dock preferences panel.**

2. **Select Genie effect or Scale effect from the Minimize using pop-up menu.**

Figure 6-9
The Dock with magnification turned on

ONE FINAL WORD...

This is the end of the chapter, so obviously it's the end of my opportunity to honk on about what a great bargain the Dock is and why you should invite it in, give it a hot meal, and ask if it needs anything laundered or pressed.

So I'll end by saying that if I had to give up either the Finder or the Dock, I'd give up the Dock. Actually, I'd just go around *telling* people that I've stopped using the Finder because via the Dock I can quickly hide the Finder when I hear people coming. But I'd be twice as arrogant when insisting that I'd made the right choice.

Just Deal with It: Apps

In This Chapter

Installing Applications • Downloading Applications
Switching Between Applications • Performance Slowdowns • What *Is* That Application Doing?
Taking Care of Comatose Apps • Does the Mac Do Windows?

Here we are, a third of the way through the book, and we're just now attacking the issue of applications. I have become that which I have always despised: the sort of person who writes a book on building a deck and pads the front of it with information regarding tools and fasteners, remaining oblivious to the fact that the reader is eager to rent a nail gun and start causing mayhem with as little preamble as possible.

But, of course, just as a great deal of a pilot's cockpit time is not spent flying, but managing the onboard systems that assist them in flight, a great deal of the user's time is spent acquiring and managing apps. It's hard to bask in the fond embrace of Earth gravity these days and *not* know that you launch a program by double-clicking it, but there's more to know. Particularly when things go wrong, which happens quite a lot. But don't let on if there are any non-Mac people listening.

INSTALLING APPLICATIONS

Fortunately, installing applications isn't like installing a new deck, where you can't barbecue anything until you've measured *this* and built concrete footings for *that*. (Honestly, is the deck industry unaware that I can get a flame-grilled burger just down the street after a mere investment of 99 cents and 14 minutes of my time?) Apps install themselves. With exceedingly rare exceptions, one drag or one double-click is all that's required.

AN "APP" BY ANY OTHER NAME...

And can we please take a moment to mourn the triumph of the word *application* above all other comers? Nobody uses programs or software anymore. Yes, yes, I know that as PCs became more complicated, we needed a special word for the stuff that users run and interact with, as opposed to the stuff that runs behind the scenes and keeps the whole store running.

But I miss referring to my word processor as a program. Whenever I say "application," I wonder if the manager of my bank is going to phone 3 days after I double-click on Microsoft Word to tell me that upon review of my employment and credit history, he is unable to approve a product launch at this time but invites me to apply again at the end of the fiscal year.

Figure 7-1
A disk image mounted on the Desktop

Some downloaded apps cut through all that rigmarole. When you're finished downloading it (more on that later), it's just a double-clickable file. No pretense, no airs — a veritable model for human behavior.

Whether a CD, a disk image, or a humble file, if you're presented with the application itself instead of an Installer (Figure 7-2), you're free to just drag it into the Applications folder without any further ado.

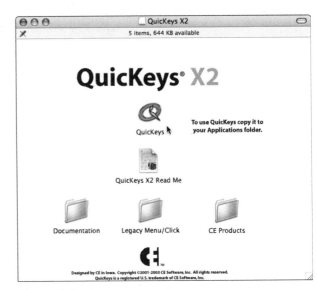

Figure 7-2
An application that you install by dragging it onto the Applications folder

Where do you get apps? They may be supplied on a CD or you can download them from the Internet. If the app came on a CD, just pop it in. If you downloaded it, it might appear as a disk image file. As Chapter 9 explains, when you open a .dmg file it mounts on the Desktop as if it were a removable disk. So if you find that you have a file with that *.dmg* extension, you need to do the following to reach the applications files:

1. **Double-click on the file to mount it.** You'll see an icon like that in Figure 7-1.

2. **At this point, it's just like any other disk. Double-click on the disk icon to open it and reveal its contents.**

3. **When you're done with it, click the Eject button to remove it from the Desktop.**

YOU CAN STORE 'EM ANYTHERE!

But just because Apple has thoughtfully provided an Applications folder for you, should you just drop all your apps there? Of course not. What, are you just trying to cause trouble or something?

You can actually install apps anywhere on your hard drive. But I'm sitting here trying to think of a good reason *not* to use the Applications folder and coming up dry. The only useful reason for skipping the Applications folder is if you have an app that you don't want other people to readily find. On your office Mac you'll probably want to put Tony Hawk in a different folder, unless your boss actively encourages her employees to play skateboard games on company time.

If instead of a draggable application you're presented with an Installer program, thank your lucky stars because you've been saved a great deal of trouble.

Some software exists as more than one application file. Maybe it comes with sets of fonts, too, and it also wants to add a doodad to your menu bar and it has to install an invisible app that gives you some added features even when the "real" app isn't running. The Installer program takes everything you need and puts it everywhere it needs to go.

With the release of OS X, Apple started using a new standard Installer that many (but not all) developers include with their software. You probably saw it the first time you installed OS X yourself. Although installing the operating system requires that you not run other programs, the same is not true of most application Installers. The full installation process goes something like this:

1. **Double-click on the Installer icon to launch it.**

2. **Read the Introduction (see Figure 7-3).**

3. **Click Continue.** This usually opens an Important Information screen.

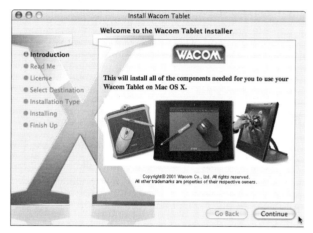

Figure 7-3
The Installer installation window

4. **Read the Read Me information (see Figure 7-4).**

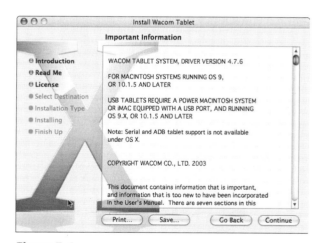

Figure 7-4
The Installer Read Me window

▼ Note

And for the love of all that's good and decent in the world, *read that information*. Oftentimes it's the only place to learn that there's a desperately horrid incompatibility between the software you're about to install and something you previously installed. So read it, unless of course you were sick and tired of having a Mac that's never crashed and taken the entire contents of your hard drive down with it.

5. **Click Continue.** This opens a Software License Agreement screen.

6. **Read the Software License Agreement (see Figure 7-5).**

7. **Click Continue.** In most cases, you will be asked to agree to the license agreement in a separate window.

8. **Click Agree.** You usually see a screen for selecting a destination for the software.

9. **Select the destination disk for the installation by clicking on the icon of the disk you want to use (see Figure 7-6).**

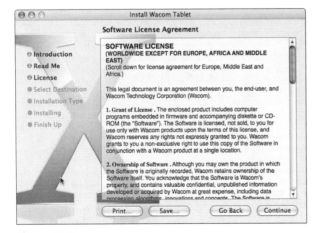

Figure 7-5

The Installer Software License Agreement window

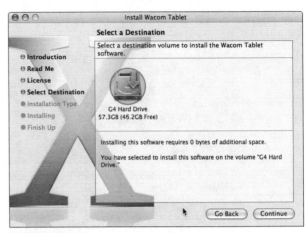

Figure 7-6

Choosing the destination disk for new software

10. **Select either an Easy Install (the Installer makes choices as to which components should be installed) or Custom Install.** By default you get an Easy Install. Click Customize to perform a Custom Install. If you choose to customize the installation, you see a list of components of the application like that in Figure 7-7. You must then remove checks from the check boxes of those components you don't want to install, or, if check boxes are empty, click to add checks to those components you want installed.

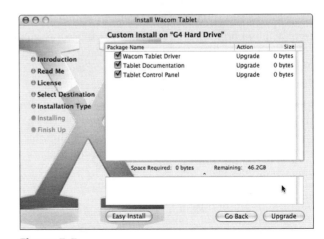

Figure 7-7

An example of a components list for a Custom Install

Note

Nine times out of ten you should just cruise straight to the Easy Install, but it's often worth at least *looking* at what's listed under Custom Install. It gives you a snapshot of what's being written to your hard drive. As a practical matter, I only choose Custom Install when disk space is starting to become slightly precious and I'd rather have an extra 27MB of storage than a big folder of Uzbekistan language infrastructure and fonts.

11. **Click Continue (or whatever the rightmost button at the bottom of the Installer window happens to say).** If the Installer needs to modify system files, it asks you for an administrator password, as in Figure 7-8.

12. **Type an administrator password and click OK.** Why does an Installer ask for an administrator password? Forbidding ordinary users from installing software helps keep a Mac happy and healthy when several users are sharing it. If the whole office has standardized on Word, you don't want somebody installing LambadaWrite. If this Mac is supposed to be used for homework and email, then Junior shouldn't be installing games. Et cetera.

Figure 7-8
Supply the administrator password for a software installation

13. **The Installer installs the software on the destination disk.** You don't need to do anything at this point but sit back and wait, as in Figure 7-9. The Installer finishes up its job and lets you know it's done (see Figure 7-10).

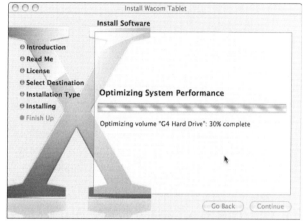

Figure 7-9
The Installer's window as it actually installs files on a hard disk

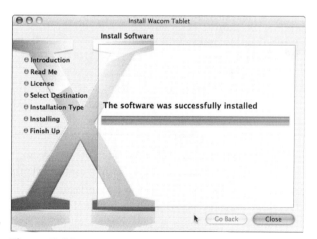

Figure 7-10
Finishing up an installation

▼ Note

And, in some cases, the wait will be ambitious enough that you may want to go get a snack, phone some old friends, perhaps get a start on that cathedral you've been meaning to build in the backyard...that sort of thing. Some installs are intricate enough that the Installer has to check and optimize the entire system before pronouncing the operation complete. The lesson here is that you shouldn't install software unless you're certain that you can (conceivably) do without the use of your Mac for an undeterminable length of time. The other lesson here is that just as you learned when your Dad pointed at your 3/4-acre yard and told you where the push-mower is, sometimes when people tell you they're "just trying to optimize your performance," they're really just out to waste your time and cause you endless frustration.

14. **Click Close to exit the Installer.** The final step to any installation is, of course, giving your added options for getting at the app. Make an alias to the app and put it on the Desktop. Drag the app into the Dock, or into the toolbar area of a Finder window so that you can easily drag files on top of it.

▼ Note

Not all installations use every phase of the process you just saw. Depending on the needs of the particular application, some of the steps in the list at the left of the Installer window may be left out.

Although many Installers were updated to use the framework you've been reading about, some applications still use the classic Mac OS Installer, such as that in Figure 7-11. This may look like an OS 9 application, but if you look at the controls in the top left of the window, you can see OS X window controls, indicating that this is indeed an OS X program. Or it might use another Installer program entirely, such as InstallerVISE. But the basic principles are the same.

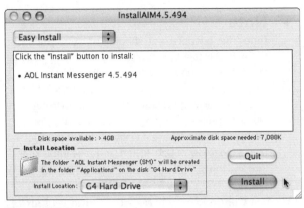

Figure 7-11
The classic Mac OS Installer running in OS X

DOWNLOADING APPLICATIONS

When the Macintosh debuted, you got your applications on a floppy disk. Even when hard disks were standard equipment, you still spent a lot of time disk swapping during an install, and it seemed an eternity until CD-ROM drives became so widespread that it was feasible to ship on CD rather than disk.

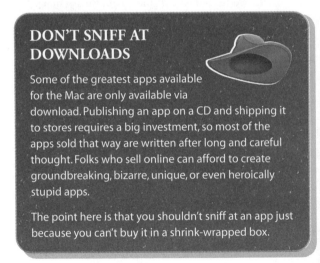

DON'T SNIFF AT DOWNLOADS

Some of the greatest apps available for the Mac are only available via download. Publishing an app on a CD and shipping it to stores requires a big investment, so most of the apps sold that way are written after long and careful thought. Folks who sell online can afford to create groundbreaking, bizarre, unique, or even heroically stupid apps.

The point here is that you shouldn't sniff at an app just because you can't buy it in a shrink-wrapped box.

Today, you can still purchase an application on CD. In fact, most large programs are available only in that format. However, you can download small commercial apps from a vendor's Web site. You can then make a credit card payment and receive an activation code through email. Delivery is immediate and the cost savings (no duplication, packaging, or mailing costs) are often passed on to the purchaser. In addition, you may choose to download freeware or shareware applications from the Internet.

Downloading a commercial application, especially an upgrade to a program you own already, is a relatively safe download. In other words, it's unlikely to be accompanied by an attempt to steal your credit card number or identity. Downloading from the Internet is riskier, although as you discover in Chapter 16, it's a whole lot safer for Macintosh users than anyone else.

Where can you go to find shareware and freeware that is relatively safe? Here are a few of our favorite sites:

- **Version Tracker (www.versiontracker.com):** Version Tracker not only has freeware and shareware, but it also carries beta (not yet ready for prime time) versions of commercial software, updates to commercial software, and demos of commercial software. One of its great strengths is the user ratings and feedback attached to nearly every file; you can quickly tell if a specific download is any good, or has the features you're looking for.

- **Download.com (www.download.com):** This CNET site is differently organized, which makes it a little easy to browse when you have no idea what you're looking for, specifically. It's also Jan's go-to-place for games.

- **Apple (www.apple.com/downloads):** Apple Computer showcases selected bits of shareware and freeware.

A file that you download won't arrive on your hard drive as a double-clickable app or Installer. It had to be packed into a different format for travel. You'll probably see one of these file extensions:

- **.zip:** A ZIP archive. ZIP is the classic Windows file compression and archiving format that is now becoming a standard across all platforms.

- **.gzip:** A GZIP archive. GZIP is the Unix variety of ZIP.

- **.bin:** A Macintosh binary file that hasn't been archived or compressed.

- **.hqx:** A BinHex file. Files in any of the preceding three formats may have been translated to BinHex, so there is nothing wrong with a file whose extension includes two formats, such as *.sit.hqx*.

Before you can install the app, you have to unpack it. If you have Aladdin Systems' StuffIt Expander (a free download from www.aladdinsys.com) you can unpack it automatically just by double-clicking.

Note

Expander has a commercial big brother called StuffIt Deluxe, which lets you create nearly every archive and compressed-format file that exists. So it's a handy thing to have around if you're often swapping archives with your non-Mac pals. The Finder can create ZIP files through its Create Archive command, but naturally StuffIt Deluxe is way more flexible.

So now you've downloaded a running, useful app. Do you have to pay for it? It depends. Some apps are *freeware* — as the name implies, the author has released this app as a bid for good karma and demands nothing in return from the user. Some apps, however, are *shareware;* if you use them and enjoy them, you should send the author the (usually piddlingly small) registration fee he or she requests.

All others are *demoware* or *crippleware*. There's some sort of "gotcha" involved until you send in some greenbacks. You can only launch it ten times, or you can only use it for a month, or you can create files but not save them, et cetera. At least you get to try the software before buying it.

SWITCHING BETWEEN APPLICATIONS

The beauty of multitasking is that you can have multiple applications running at the same time. Although you can only work with one app at a time directly — you are only Human — some apps can continue what they're doing in the background while you do something else. For example, many programs can transfer files over a network or print files in the background. This is very handy because network transfers and printing can take a long time and you have better things to do with your life than wait for a computer.

Once you have started a background process, or if you need to change applications for some reason (perhaps simply because you need or want to do something else), you can bring a new application to the foreground in several different ways:

- **Click on any open window belonging to the application.** If (as is always, always, always the case with my own Mac) the window you want is covered by something else, use Exposé to temporarily "unshuffle" all of the windows on your Desktop.

- **Click on the application's icon in the Dock.**

- Use the *application switcher.*

The application switcher is something new to Panther. To use it, hold down ⌘ and press Tab once. (Be sure to keep holding down ⌘. Otherwise, the application switcher disappears.) Icons for all running applications appear across the center of your startup monitor, as in Figure 7-12.

Figure 7-12
The application switcher

Hold down ⌘ and press Tab to move from one icon to another (from left to right). If you hold down the Shift key, you'll Tab from right to left. When you get to the application you want to use, release ⌘. You can also click directly on the icon of the app you want.

PERFORMANCE SLOWDOWNS

All of a sudden I'm no big fan of delaying the payoff, so I'll cut straight to it and say that if all of a sudden your Mac is running as slowly as a snail wearing a pair of stylish but particularly uncomfortable stilettos, you should quit any running apps that you're not using, and if that doesn't help, you should restart your Mac (see Chapter 21 for more on troubleshooting Mac performance problems).

Now for the reason; in a nutshell, it's *virtual memory*. Your Mac has hardware main memory (its RAM, or *random access memory*) that's measured in megabytes (like 512MB) or low numbers of gigabytes (such as 1GB), and that's where software is loaded into so it can be run.

Problem is, folks like to run lots and lots of apps at the same time, and there's a finite amount of RAM. Solution: Virtual Memory. You only have 512MB of memory (let's say), but you have (ibid) more than 12GB of unused disk space. So the operating system bamboozles everybody into thinking that some of that empty space on your hard drive is actually RAM.

The catch: Information moves through "real" memory at warp speed. Information moves to and from a hard drive about as fast as Katherine Hepburn (circa 1993) could walk on her hands. So the more virtual memory you use, the slower your Mac becomes, as the OS spends more and more time swapping chunks of your running apps to and from the hard drive. Hence, quitting apps allows more of the remaining apps to sit in that cozy, fast, real memory. So why restart?

Again, blame memory. Specifically, blame a pernicious and nearly impossible-to-isolate software bug known as a *memory leak.* Normally, apps and the OS work together to make sure that not a single scrap of memory is wasted. When you open a document, the app tells the OS that it needs a little more memory to work in. The OS finds some memory and allocates it. When you close the document, the app thanks the OS kindly and says that it doesn't need that extra memory space any more.

This system ought to work great, but maybe a few kilobytes get "lost" in every transaction. When the Mac has been running for an afternoon, that's not enough to cause a problem. But when it's been up for ages, it all adds up. Suddenly, huge tracts of fertile land are inaccessible, and the OS's reliance on Virtual Memory swells higher and higher.

You can poke your Mac with a big stick, but that won't dislodge any of that missing memory. The only way to fix the problem is to restart.

Memory is dirt cheap. One of the smartest things you can do is to buy the maximum amount of RAM that your Mac can use. It helps build strong bodies nine different ways, I swear.

 Note

I could have *really* impressed you with the importance of this advice by saying, "Look, if you can't afford it, I'll buy it *for* you," but there's some sort of legal thing about my actually having to deliver on that promise. I tried to tell the guy that the chances of anyone spelling my name right on the subpoena were slim, but he insisted on being a spoilsport. Nonetheless, please buy more RAM.

WHAT *IS* THAT APPLICATION DOING?

That dreaded spinning colored beach ball — it's been making an appearance whenever you move the mouse over any window belonging to one particular application. You can't do anything with the application. What *is* that application doing?

OS X provides two utility programs that can let you — or a technical support person whom you have asked for help — find out what your computer is up to. You can have the most fun with Activity Monitor, but Console can be useful to very technical sorts and you should at least know where to find it in case someone asks.

Activity Monitor and Console are located in the Utilities folder, within the Applications folder. They are standalone programs that you run like any other app.

Launching Activity Monitor displays a window like that in Figure 7-13. The scrolling list of items in the middle of the window is a list of *processes.* A process is a program, or a part of a program, that is vying for time in your computer's CPU. The display in Figure 7-13 has been set to show just processes that the user started. However, if you choose All Processes from the Show pop-up menu, you see process names that don't correspond to programs you've started (see Figure 7-14). These processes, such as *kernel_task* and *init*, are OS X system processes. They are programs that form part of the operating system itself and are running in the background to enable your Mac to function.

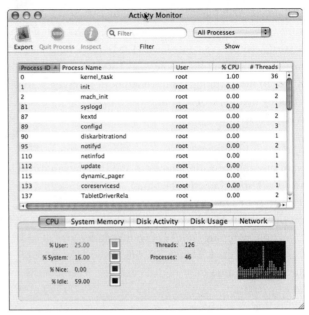

Figure 7-14
Watching all processes and CPU activity

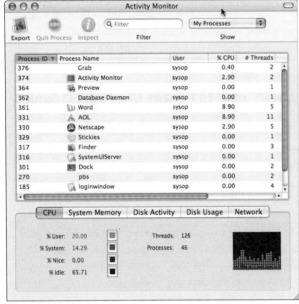

Figure 7-13
Watching user processes and CPU activity

Each process that OS X runs is given a process ID number, which appears in the leftmost column of the Activity Monitor window. Unless you are working at the Unix command line, you almost never need to use this value. The Process Name column is the name of the program corresponding to each particular process. Next to it is the name of the OS X user that currently owns the process. System processes are owned by *root*, the operating system itself. In the example you have been seeing, the human user is *sysop*.

Probably the most important column for everyday use purposes is % CPU, which tells you that percentage of overall CPU time that a process uses. When the screen shot in Figure 7-15 was taken, Microsoft Word and AOL were using the largest percentage of the CPU time, but neither was hogging the CPU. Even when actively working with Word, the CPU usage rarely goes over 25 percent. Therefore, if you see a process that is consuming more than 25 percent of CPU time, and it's not doing something CPU-intensive such as rendering a 3D graphic, then the process is probably in trouble: It's hung.

 Tip

I'm a big fan of keeping Activity Monitor's floating CPU window up. If you turn the window on (through the Monitor menu) a slim little thermometer hugs the side of your screen, letting you know how many RPMs your CPU is pulling at the moment. I keep it up partly because it's cool to look at. But it's useful, too; if it stops twitching, you know your system is hopelessly locked up. When it pulses high for no reason, you know that some app is throttling the CPU and it's time to check things out.

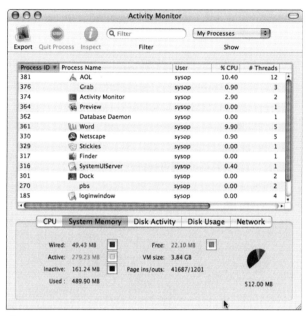

Figure 7-15
Monitoring main memory usage

The information at the bottom of the Activity Monitor window can be fascinating. Figures 7-13 and 7-14 show a live graphic of CPU activity — if your Mac has multiple CPUs, you see multiple graphs — the colors depicting the proportions of user and system processes. Clicking the System Memory button changes the bottom display to show main memory usage, as in Figure 7-15. Although the display doesn't show you how much memory each process is using, it can let you know if you are running out of hardware RAM space. If red and yellow wedges dominate the pie graph, it's time to re-read that bit in the previous section regarding how cheap RAM is and how important it is that you buy some more of it.

The Console application provides access to OS X system error messages and logs. The initial display, which appears

when you launch the application, shows error messages that OS X generated since you booted the computer (see Figure 7-16). Don't worry if you can't understand what the error messages are saying: You really need to be a programmer or a Unix guru to make sense of them.

▼ Note

There are loads of different logs and many of these items aren't even error messages per se. There's a whole formal log that records all of the software updates that have been installed, for example. Even some of the error-ish notations are more like notations of the little aches and pains that the OS likes to complain about but nobody takes seriously. I consider the latter to be Apple's tribute to Marvin, the Paranoid Android from *Hitchhiker's Guide to the Galaxy*.

LIKE A STALLWART COURT REPORTER, YOUR MAC IS TAKING CAREFUL NOTES

But *do* take some time to open the Console app and examine what's there. It saves time when something goes wrong and a tech-support person asks you to read him or her what's in there.

It's also useful to poke around in system.log when you suspect malfeasance. If someone's been snooping in your Mac, the OS logs simple activity. It's not enough to prove that Slugworth was searching for the Everlasting Gobstopper files on your hard drive, but at least you're warned that *somebody* was behind the keyboard at such-and-such date and time, when you were at home watching TV.

If you look in Console's Preferences, you see a check box that brings the console window to the front for a moment whenever anything is logged. Even I — who adore geeky messages that don't really help me very much — consider this feature an annoyance.

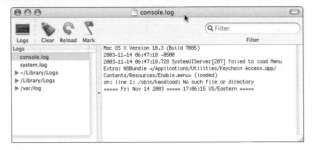

Figure 7-16
The initial Console display

Because OS X is an implementation of Unix, it keeps a number of logs that indicate what it has been doing and where it encounters problems. You may need to share the contents of some of these logs with tech support people, but, otherwise, you generally won't need to worry about them.

Two logs you may be asked to consult are the console log and the crash log. As you can see from Figure 7-17, the logs are accessible through the hierarchical list at the left of the Console window. Expanding the console log hierarchy lets you display any of the previous ten logs.

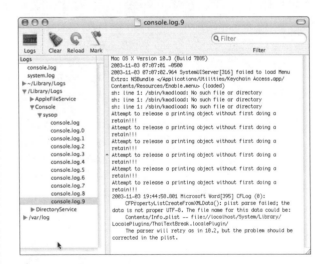

Figure 7-17
Displaying a historical console log

The crash log records information about processes that have terminated abnormally. Sometimes, as in Figure 7-18, the problem is actually a bug in the program. Regardless of the cause of the crash, the information in the log can give a tech support person information about what the program was attempting to do when the fatal error occurred.

There's also the panic log, which records the Gran Mal of all system crashes, the kernel panic. See it and know fear.

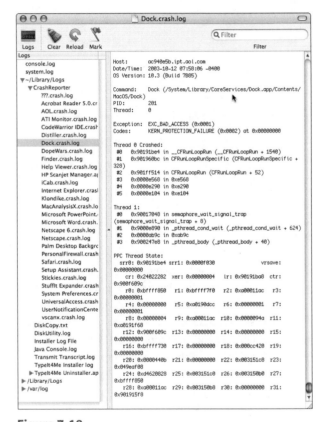

Figure 7-18
The crash log tells you about good apps gone bad

TAKING CARE OF COMATOSE APPLICATIONS

Sometimes the spinning beach ball doesn't go away. Sometimes it sticks around and keeps spinning and spinning and spinning until you begin to see it not as a mouse cursor, but as the whirling portal to a hellish dimension that you don't deserve to have been sent. It is no longer a beach ball cursor: It is The Spinning Beach Ball (or Pizza) Of Death. The SPOD.

You're desperate to move on with your life. In Mac OS 9.*x* days, you'd breathe in and breathe out and acknowledge that just as night follows day and any meal worth eating requires about 90 minutes of kitchen cleanup, the price of using a Mac is having to restart your whole Mac every time one single app digs its heels in.

Welcome to Future World. In OS X, we can just spank the one app that's acting up, leaving all other apps (and all of their unsaved files) safe and sound. It's actually called a *Force Quit*, although the word "spank" is so much more satisfying.

▼ Note

A Force Quit is indeed impolite. When it's 1 a.m. and your party guests still won't leave, etiquette demands that you emerge from the bedroom carrying all of their coats and hats, make a big show of explaining what an early day you've got tomorrow, and then thank everyone for coming and insist that you all do this again sometime. A Force Quit is akin to pouring gasoline around the sofa and then scratching the flint of your lighter in a meaningful way. Both methods will clear the room, but if you use the latter method there might be some serious repercussions.

The app won't follow the formal, "safe" quit procedure that its programmers laid out for it. The OS simply "kills"

(that's a Unix term) all of its processes. So you shouldn't do this as a time-saver. If the app is locked into a SPOD death spiral, take a break. Go downstairs and make yourself some waffles. When you come back, the app might have collected itself enough that you can quit it politely.

Also, be sure of the culprit. Bring up the app's contextual menu in the Dock (hold down the Control key while clicking on its icon). If the app is truly fried, the Dock reports "Application not responding." There'll be a contextual menu to Force-Quit the app.

You can also bring up the Force Quit dialog:

1. **Press Command-Option-Esc to display the Force Quit window (Figure 7-19), or open it through the Apple menu.** You might first have to switch to another app.

Figure 7-19
The Force Quit window

2. **Double-click on the name of the application you want to force quit.** OS X displays the window in Figure 7-20, asking you to confirm your action.

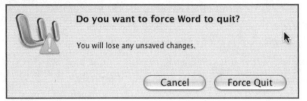

Figure 7-20
Confirming a force quit

3. **Click the Force Quit button.** OS X kills the application for you.

4. **Click the Force Quit window's close box to remove it from the screen.**

▼ **Caution**

Forcing an application to quit will result in the loss of any changes to documents that you haven't saved to a disk. Therefore, don't force quit unless the application won't respond to anything you try to do.

DOES THE MAC DO WINDOWS?

You may not do the windows in your house, but the Mac can do Windows (that "other" operating system). If you find yourself in a situation where you have no choice but to use a program that isn't available in a Macintosh version (and fortunately, this happens with decreasing frequency these days), there is a solution that can keep you from giving up your Mac.

Virtual PC, an application original developed by Connectix but now developed and supported by Microsoft, is software that emulates a PC running Windows XP. Once you install the software, you get a single file that acts like a Windows format disk drive. When you launch the Virtual PC application, it loads Windows from that virtual disk drive and displays the Windows screen in a Mac window. You can do just about anything with Virtual PC that you can with a standalone PC. In addition, you can copy items between the Mac and PC clipboards and drag files to copy them.

▼ **Note**

For more information about Virtual PC, go to www.microsoft.com/mac/products/virtualpc.

A FAMILIAR FACE IN PARTS OF THE MAC WORLD

VirtualPC (VPC) is a venerable Mac app. It's single-handedly responsible for the appearance of many Macs in PC-only offices: Many PC administrators find that it's a lot easier to service the network from a Mac running VirtualPC than a real PC.

It ought to be reiterated that VPC is often convenient but rarely necessary. If there isn't a Macintosh version of whatever PC app you need, chances are excellent that there's a Mac app that's file-compatible.

Coping with Files and Folders

One of the great things about a revolution is that what with the waving of red banners and tarring and feathering of local magistrates and such, you forget that you're in the middle of one until it's all over with. And by *then,* you're so used to the new stamps and the new currency and the huge portraits hanging in every room of a guy who was sorting mail in your hometown 3 years ago that you forget that it's happened.

But we shouldn't. The Mac OS introduced lots of labor- and stress-saving features for handling files and folders, both in the Finder and in every Mac app out there, and Panther has successfully taken things a step forward.

CREATING, OPENING, AND SAVING FILES

In most applications, you create a new document file by selecting File ➜ New or pressing ⌘+N. You can have multiple document windows open at the same time in the same application, although there are a few applications that are an exception. The app just creates a blank document without form or content, and you don't even give it a name until you save it for the first time.

The standard Open/Save dialog

Whenever you open or save a file, the Mac OS throws up a standard, consistent user interface element that lets you point to the file (or if you're Saving, name the file and point to where the file should go). Figure 8-1 shows you what happens when you save a new document in Microsoft Word:

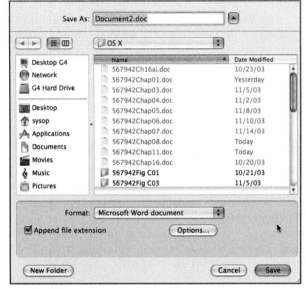

Figure 8-1
The Save File dialog

The interface is nearly identical to that of a Finder window. Everything that makes navigation convenient in the Finder also works in the Mac's standard Save and Open dialogs. All of your sidebar favorites carry through, even down to the order in which they appear; and if you select the Column View, you can walk all the way through your hard drive with just a few clicks.

So if you've ever used the Finder, you're probably 84 percent of the way towards understanding how to open and save files. To open files:

1. **Navigate to the file's folder.**

2. **Select the file.**

3. **Click Open.**

When you're opening files, it's handy to use the Column View by clicking the Column View icon. Because just as in the Finder, when you click on a file, the rightmost column contains a preview of the file's contents. It's a big time-saver, particularly when your Pictures folder contains 13 variations of the filename Jen and Bob's Wedding Photo.

Some files will be disabled (dimmed out; when you click on them, nothing happens). This is because the application can tell Panther what sorts of files it's capable of opening. Adobe Photoshop can't open Microsoft Word documents, so Panther thoughtfully removes them from consideration.

SIZE MATTERS

For reasons beyond mortal man's capacity to comprehend, Apple also presents the Save dialog in a so-called Collapsed View. The key feature of this alternative view is that it's much, much smaller, which would be a big bonus if we were paying for our user interface by the square inch. As it is, you can't help but notice that whereas the expanded view gives you all sorts of useful information and navigational aids, the collapsed view just lets you specify a filename and choose from a slim, prefabbed list of folders to save it in.

If that punified thing is what you're looking at, click on the blue triangle next to the filename to turn the Collapsed View into the Expanded one. My advice about the Mac's standard Save box is the same as my advice about James Cameron's undersea epic, *The Abyss*. Forget that anything other than the Expanded Edition even exists.

WHEN IT COMES TO OPEN AND SAVE, APPLE DOESN'T PLAY FAVORITES

The new Open and Save dialogs are one of the Big Wins of Panther. Apple finally delivers features that folks have been clamoring for practically since Mac OS 7.

One beef, though: There's no way to add a Favorite folder to the permanent list of defaults. In Jaguar, if you're opening or saving a file and you navigate to a project folder that you think you'll be using frequently, you could click a button and bang, that folder would always sit in a list of Favorites.

No more. Panther remembers recent folders, and you can go into the Finder and add a folder to the sidebar, but (a) that's way more steps than just clicking an Add to Favorites button, and (b) it clutters up the sidebar. Oh, well.

Saving files is little different:

1. **Navigate to the folder into which you want the file saved.**

2. **Type a filename.** Remember that a filename can't have any colons in it.

3. **Click Save.**

The Save dialog appears only the first time you save a document. After that, using the Save command simply saves the changes you've made without throwing up a dialog. Most apps give you a Save As command that takes the existing file and lets you save a second copy under a different name. This is handy when you're making revisions to an important document. If you mess things up, you still have the original tucked away in its pristine state.

Naturally, these are just the standard elements that you'd find in nearly all apps. The app can add other features to the dialog when appropriate. Word, for example, also gives you a pop-up menu so you can specify what format the new file should be — modern Word, Word's old file format, Rich Text Format — so other word processors can open it, and so on.

▼ **Note**

And remember once again that man is born unto trouble as surely as the sparks fly upward. Translation: When disaster strikes, it'll strike when you haven't saved your files recently. A famous novelist once compared pausing every few sentences to hit the Save keyboard shortcut (⌘+S) to the way authors would pause every few sentences to dip their quill pens into the ink. It becomes reflexive and invisible.

Opening files from the Finder

Gosh, my hair just flew back from the collective force of 100,000 readers saying, "Duh!" after I said, "You just double-click on its Finder icon, or select it and then select Open from the File menu, right?"

There's some subtlety to be explored, though. When you double-click on a file, the Finder chooses which application to open it *with* by looking at the file's type. But you might have several apps that are capable of opening a JPEG, for example. What if the Finder always opens them in its built-in Preview app, but you'd rather they opened in Photoshop?

You can easily change the default app for opening certain file types. In this case:

1. **Select the file in the Finder.**

2. **Open the file's Get Info window by selecting the menu item under Edit or pressing ⌘+I.**

3. **Click the triangle next to Open with.** A pop-up menu appears containing the name of this file's default app. You can see this in Figure 8-2.

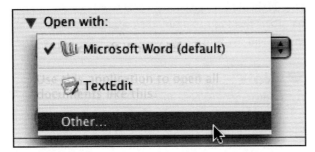

Figure 8-2
The Open with: section of a file's Get Info window

4. **Click the pop-up.** The Finder has assembled a list of all of your Mac's installed apps that are capable of opening the file. Choose the app you want. If it doesn't appear, you can select it manually by clicking Other.

5. **Click the Change All button.** Now your decision applies to *all* files of this type that you open.

HIDING BEHIND AN ALIAS

An *alias* is a file that represents a shortcut to another file, folder, or volume. It doesn't contain a copy of that file or folder. It's like a wormhole in space that zaps you to wherever the original is.

You can make as many aliases to something as you want and keep them anywhere, which is the point. Opening any of these aliases opens the original file, folder, or volume. Opening any of these aliases has the same effect as opening the original, except you didn't have to open an alias, you open the original. What does this buy you? A couple of examples:

- You can put an alias of a folder in a handy, easy-to-access location like on the Desktop, while keeping the

HAVE ALIAS, WILL TRAVEL

You can make an alias of a folder on a remote server, for example, and put it in a Finder sidebar. When you click the folder, it connects you to the server (asking you for a password, if necessary) automatically without having to go through all the steps you'll learn in a later chapter.

Aliases are handy things, and you can move them anywhere. I have an alias to my home Mac's Documents folder on my USB key ring. Wherever I am in the world I can plug this key ring into any Mac, double-click on that folder, and (assuming I have a network connection) I connect to the folder back at my house.

original in a more organized place such as your Documents folder.

- You can make several aliases of a single file and scatter them in several different locations. You get the convenience of having the file in every place you're likely to want to find it, with none of the added cost in storage space.

And cooler still, you can move the original file around, and the aliases still work. When the Finder moves an aliased item from one folder to another, it makes a note of it so that all of its aliases can track it down when they need to. This is because the alias stores not just a reference to the original item, but all the information it needs to *reach* that item.

To create and place an alias where you need it:

1. **Make the Finder the current application.**

2. **Find and select the item for which you want to create an alias.**

3. **Select File ➔ Make Alias, or press ⌘+L.** An alias file appears. As shown in Figure 8-3, the new alias file has the default name of *original_name alias* and has a curved arrow in its lower-left corner.

Figure 8-3
An alias icon

4. **Move the alias wherever you need it.**

FILE PERMISSIONS

One advantage that OS X's Unix base has over the classic Mac OS is more sophisticated file permissions, which become an integral part of OS X security. It's sort of an enhancement of the permissions mechanism we had in Mac OS 9. The OS knows who *owns* a file or folder, and as such it can limit what other users can do to it.

Unix recognizes three types of users:

- **Owner:** A file's owner is typically the user that created the file.

- **Group:** A group is a collection of users that have the same access rights to files. A user can belong to one or more groups, but a file belongs to only one group at a time.

- **World (or Everyone):** Any user anywhere.

When you create a new file, you have all rights to it: You can read, write, and perhaps execute the file. OS X assigns default rights to a group and everyone else.

Fooling around with permissions is powerful stuff. You can do great things with this feature, but you can also mess up your files in a mighty and legendary fashion. Sailors visiting foreign ports will sing songs of the time when you locked yourself out of your own hard drive because you got bored some Tuesday afternoon. Instead of playing that new online Scrabble game you came across the other day you decided to mess around with permissions.

PERMISSIONS EQUAL PRODUCTIVE POWER

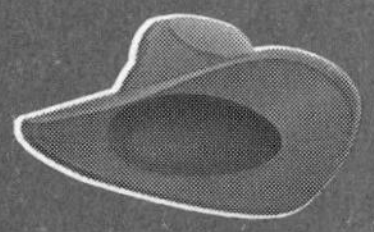

Twiddling with permissions has logical effects. Let's say that I manage an office of 100 people who write reports all day. All reports are based on the same document template, and Step One of any project is to grab a copy of that template off of my Mac. I don't want people to accidentally mess up this master template, but there are four or five people who handle the design work and they need to modify it if necessary.

Without tweaking permissions, all I can rely on is my threat to fire the next freakin' one of youse all who messes up that danged template file again. *With* permissions, all I have to do is create a group containing the users who are designers. I give myself and the designers Read & Write permission to the file, and Others: have Read only access. So the folks with the authority to make changes can make changes, while everyone else can't do squat.

Permissions will also come into play when we get into networking and sharing. See Chapter 11 for more on networking.

You can do some minor tweaking of file permissions from the Get Info dialog. As you can see in Figure 8-4, you can change owner, group, and other permissions — to any of Read & Write, Read only, and No Access — but not the owner or group.

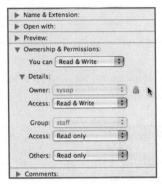

Figure 8-4
Using the Get Info window to change file and folder permissions

MORE FUN WITH GET INFO: LOCKING FILES AND MAKING STATIONERY

You can protect files and maintain template files through a couple of simple features in the Finder's Get Info window (see Figure 8-5).

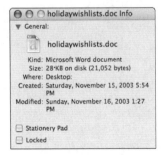

Figure 8-5
Using the Get Info window to lock files and create stationery

Clicking the Stationery Pad option does something very simple but very useful to the file. It becomes a special kind of file called a Stationery Pad that you can open, but not save. Opening this file is like creating a new, untitled document containing all of its contents; when you click Save, the app prompts you for a new filename and location. You use it for letterhead, logos, document templates — anything that you're likely to base lots and lots of new files on.

Clicking Locked is the same as setting a file's permissions to Read only. Nobody — not even you, the document's owner and creator — can save changes to it. The Finder throws a little padlock onto the file's icon for good measure (Figure 8-6).

Avengers Fear Factor.doc

Figure 8-6
A locked file or folder

▼ Note

The Locked feature is also known as the "Please, somebody, protect me from *myself*" feature. I can't tell you how often I've set myself back entire *days* because I merrily took a document that was finished, perfect, ready to go and messed it up because I mistook it for one that I still needed to process or fix.

So now, when a project is completed, I click the Locked option. It's simple to unlock it if need be, and in the meantime it prevents those painful bruises that result when I'm forced to pound my head against the desk over and over and over again.

PLATFORM-INDEPENDENT FILE FORMATS

Although we might wish that everyone used a Macintosh, the world just hasn't ended up that way. We therefore often find ourselves in the position of having to exchange files with people who are using Windows or Unix. The task has become a great deal easier for two reasons: There are some file formats that are platform-agnostic (just about any operating system can read them), and OS X provides significant support for those formats.

What a friend we have in Microsoft Office

Nearly all offices have standardized on Microsoft Word and Excel. Microsoft Office is also available for Mac OS X, but the added bonus is that the Windows and Mac file formats are absolutely identical. You can email a Word file to your Windows buddy and he can open it without any file translation whatsoever. He can save changes and send it back to you, and, ditto, it's welcomed home with open arms and nary a whiff of suspicion.

What a friend we have in TextEdit

But if you don't own Office, try opening that Word file in TextEdit, Panther's built-in simple word processor. The Panther edition can open and save files in Word format. It also supports Rich Text Format, which is an elderly but still rather spry platform-generic, word-processing file format.

The hitch is that TextEdit doesn't have Word's features (in much the same that I can't run quite as fast as a Boeing 777 can fly). But for simple documents without complicated formatting, it'll serve in a pinch.

What a friend we have in PDF

If you need to share documents with complicated formatting (lots of fonts, columns of texts, graphics, and photos... no limitations whatsoever) the cheapest solution is going to be to save it in Adobe's Portable Document Format (PDF).

TAKE THAT, WINDOWS LOVERS!

As the little fish in the pond, it's always been important for the Mac to embrace as many different file types as possible. Many times, an IT manager's claim that, "We can't have Macs in this office because they can't exchange files with the Windows machines," has been dashed when an employee silently stuck a Windows CD into a PowerBook, double-clicked on a file, and then before the manager's unbelieving eyes the Microsoft Word for Windows document opened in Word for Mac OS X without any ado.

At which point he said, "We can't have Macs in this office because they don't match the drapes." But at least we won the intellectual part of the argument.

Adobe promotes PDF files as digital paper; the recipients of a PDF file may or may not be able to edit its contents, but they can certainly read it and print a publication-perfect copy.

▼ Note

And, in fact, that's one of PDF's handiest features. When you're sending your sister's wedding program to a print shop to be professionally typeset, you can't send the file you created unless you're *sure* the shop owns the exact same software and the exact same fonts, and that all of your images and stuff stay together. With PDF, the whole thing's already been rendered, text, graphics and all, and it'll look the same coming out of a $20,000 typesetter controlled by a Linux box as it did coming out of a $100 inkjet connected to your Mac. The federal government enjoys and trusts PDF for distribution of tax forms and informational documents...why won't you?

Until recent versions of the Mac OS, you needed to purchase Adobe Acrobat to create PDFs, although Acrobat Reader was and is available free for most operating systems. The Macintosh, however, can now print to a PDF file.

To create a PDF:

1. **Prepare your document as desired.**

2. **Select File → Print or press ⌘+P.** This displays the Print dialog.

3. **Select Output Options from the pop-up menu without a label (the third one).**

4. **Click the PDF option to place a check mark in it, as in Figure 8-7.**

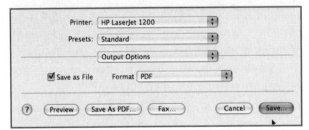

Figure 8-7
Creating a PDF file

5. **Click Save.** A Save File dialog appears.

6. **Name the file — give it a .pdf extension — and select a storage location for it.**

7. **Click or press Enter.** OS X creates the PDF file and stores it on your hard drive.

To view the PDF, use Acrobat Reader; you won't be able to modify it. If you want to modify the file, you need to purchase the full Adobe Acrobat package.

Graphics file formats

In terms of graphics files, there are four file formats that are relatively platform independent:

- **GIF:** GIF is one of two formats used primarily on the Web. Its specialty is compressing images into relatively small files that you can quickly download and view.

- **JPEG or JPG:** JPEG is the second graphics format designed for Web use. JPEG files are generally larger and of somewhat higher quality than GIF. You can save them in a wider range of sizes.

- **TIFF:** TIFF is used primarily for print publishing. It generates significantly larger files than GIF or JPEG and therefore was never suitable for Web use.

- **EPS:** EPS is a PostScript format that is used extensively in publishing. When the image can be described in terms of lines, curves, and shapes, it provides excellent scalable output at a small size.

▼ Note

TIFF is a great format for when you don't want to compromise image quality. When an app saves a JPEG file, it compresses it to make it smaller so that you can transmit faster. But there's always a drop in image quality. You can usually save TIFF files in an uncompressed format, so the file is as crisp and clean as the original. Obviously this is only a big concern when you're doing high-end work, but it's good to know, nonetheless.

Graphics programs such as Photoshop can handle GIF, JPEG, and TIFF files. You need a program such as Macromedia Freehand or Adobe Illustrator to work with EPS files.

FILE FORMAT TRANSLATION

If you receive files from someone who is using software that you don't have (especially Windows software), you may need to translate the file format into something that an application that you do have can handle. By the same token, you may need to take one of your files and translate it into something you can send to someone using different software.

There are several ways to go about this. The trick is to use an application that can read or write the file format in question. If you want to translate graphics formats, for example, OS X's Preview application can do quite a bit for you:

1. **Open the document that you want to convert using Preview.**

2. **Select File → Export.** A Save As dialog appears.

3. **Select the format in which you want to save the file from the Format pop-up menu that appears, as in Figure 8-8.**

4. **Click Save.**

Many other application programs have built-in translation facilities. For example, as you can see in Figure 8-9, Microsoft Word can handle some generic formats (RTF and plain text) as well as a variety of Microsoft formats, such as Word and Excel for Windows.

Unfortunately, Word doesn't translate files created with other word processors. So, what can you do if someone sends you a Word Perfect file, for example? Are you stuck with simply recovering the text? Not necessarily. What you need is a file format translation program such as MacLinkPlus from DataViz (www.dataviz.com/products/maclinkplus/index.html).

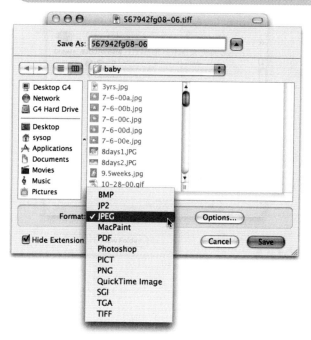

Figure 8-8
Using Preview to convert graphics file formats

MacLinkPlus can handle nearly 75 MS-DOS, Windows, and Macintosh file formats, some of which are from older software that isn't used any more. This is a major boon if you find that you need to get to older files whose programs won't run at all, even under OS 9!

MacLinkPlus not only translates formats, but also allows you to view the contents of a document even if you don't have the application with which it was created. MacLinkPlus also can extract files from Stuffit, ZIP, and tar archives, as well as decompress MIME and BinHex files.

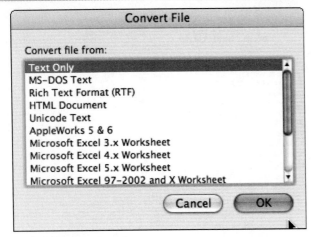

Figure 8-9
Microsoft Word's built-in translators

 Tip

Chances are excellent that you'll never need MacLinkPlus. The Word format has become so ubiquitous throughout the industry that it's become the *lingua franca*. Bookmark DataViz's Web site all the same. I think most of its sales come from people who unexpectedly get a VisiCalc For Solaris Workstations file from someone who promised them a spreadsheet they could just drop into their report and print!

I have some blank space here so I'll just share one of those Big Pronouncements About The Future Of Technology that everybody was making a long time ago, but which hasn't come to pass and never, ever will. The whole concept of *files* is hopelessly quaint, and that by the 1990s we'd consign them to the scrapheap of history, like the buttonhook, and people who major in communications with the actual hope that this will help them get a job some day.

It's certainly a good idea. Remember that keeping data organized into files with names and organized into folders is a burden that's fallen on the shoulders of the users. Is this unavoidable? Well, no. Ask someone who loved Apple's discontinued Newton PDA. It didn't save anything as files. Everything you created was tossed into a soup of data, and it was the Newton OS's responsibility to figure out that you now wanted to get your hands on that note you wrote last Tuesday about this hot new music group you've just come across: "Wham!"

But we're stuck with them. Not because we lack the technology and the firepower. We can't change the basic interface of a car to anything other than a steering wheel, foot pedals, and a shifter. It's just too deeply ingrained into society at this point.

That doesn't prevent us from hoping there's a better way around the corner, though. I don't give up hope. I still keep praying that *Star Wars Episode III* will turn out to be better.

Using Hard Drives, CDs, DVDs, and Other Silos of Data

In This Chapter

And Volumes Are...? • The Boot Volume • Mounting and Unmounting Volumes
External Drives: USB and FireWire • Burning CDs and DVDs • Memory-Based Storage
Networked Volumes • Using Target Disk Mode • Disk Images • Keeping Volumes Healthy

Slide a floppy disk into a drive, you hear a mechanical *ch-CHNGK* and a whirring of motors, and a second or 3 later an icon appears on the Desktop. Double-click the icon and a window opens revealing all the files on that disk.

Ah, the good old days of 1985. The mid-1980s had its downsides (as I recall, I was forced to play a lot more dodgeball than I would have liked, plus, it was the sort of artistic environment in which groups like Culture Club and the Thompson Twins were able to thrive), but the unsophisticated storage devices of that era's computers made it a pretty sweet time to learn about computers.

Today, things are different. When we talk about Something-We-Store-Files-On, we're talking about an abstract construct. You don't call it a disk because you only use actual disks in Cuba these days, and even a *drive* is imprecise because a hard drive can contain several independently mountable areas. And how should we describe that Something when it's not part of our own hardware setup, but a device that we connect to via a network?

Hence, we start talking about *volumes*. There's a lot to know about accessing, caring for, and feeding the little darlings, and a topic that broad needs a phony-baloney and only marginally clear technical term.

AND VOLUMES ARE...?

So what *are* we talking about when we speak of volumes? You can stick with the description I gave you in the intro: It's a discrete place to store files. And so long as you don't think too hard about that, it'll probably do you just fine.

In real truth, volume is a well-selected term because it does a really accurate job of explaining the technical side of file storage without forcing us to haul out the *H. Poindexter Nerdly Guide To Obfuscational Linguistics*.

Think about all the volumes you have on your bookshelf right now. I'm glancing to my right and reading four titles at random: Andrew Chaikin's *A Man on the Moon,* Larry Kaniut's *More Alaska Bear Tales, The Calvin and Hobbes Tenth Anniversary Book* by Bill Watterson, and Roger Ebert's *Book Of Film.*

▼ Note

The *Bear Tales* book is the second in the series and contains hundreds of pages of first-person accounts of what it's like to be attacked by a bear. I try to keep it handy while I work. Writing is a challenging, lonely business, and at times reading a tale of a camper being dragged by his left ankle through a stream by a grizzly bear helps to keep one's hardships in proper perspective.

These are all separate books. Each has its own title page, its own unique Library of Congress number, its own table of contents, and its own index. Moreover, you can format each of these books in its own special way. The Calvin and Hobbes book is horizontal and consists almost entirely of comic strips, for example.

Got that? Well, congratulations. You now understand what volumes mean to a computer. Whether a volume is a hard drive, a networked volume, a CD, or a bit of flash memory on a USB key ring, it has its own independent file directory and data structures and its own method of laying out

information — so you can make one volume a Mac-for-matted drive, another a DVD-ROM prepared for Windows machines, and a third an audio CD. And you can access them all at the same time.

Finally, they're separate entities. You can close one book and put it away without disturbing any of the others that are still open on your desk (or your bed, which in my case is far more likely).

THE BOOT VOLUME

Your Mac can have many volumes attached to it, but one of these volumes is special. A *boot volume* contains a properly installed copy of the operating system on it that your Mac can load in and execute on startup. You can recognize a Mac OS X boot volume by the presence of an enormous folder named System. Macs that can boot into Mac OS 9 have a totally separate folder called System Folder. Try not to let it confuse you; though I won't think any less of you if it did.

BOOT VOLUME TRIVIA

Many commercial disaster-relief utilities (such as Alsoft's *DiskWarrior,* mentioned later in this chapter) ship on bootable CDs, and thank heaven for that. You probably won't use a magical piece of software that fixes a petulant and recalcitrant volume until that volume stops working. If it's the boot volume, your Mac can't start up and run the utility!

This is also why I have a minimal Panther installation on my iPod. I know that if push came to shove, I can connect it to my PowerBook and boot it back to life. It's like the CPR paddles you see on *ER.* Plus, this functionality was just the practical excuse I needed to allow me to buy the 40GB model instead of the 20.

So you're only going to have one boot volume, right? Well, most likely. Out of the box, your Mac's hard drive is formatted as one big volume, and there's just one copy of the OS on there. But there are instances in which you can have more than one boot volume available, namely:

- **You have more than one drive attached to your Mac.**

- **You have a disc in the drive that's bootable.** Whether you have Panther on a DVD packaged with your new Mac or bought it as a four-disc boxed set, one of those discs is bootable.

- **You've partitioned your hard drive into multiple, independent volumes.** In that case, you can place a different bootable OS on each volume.

- **You have another volume elsewhere on your local network off of which you can boot.**

When multiple boot volumes are available, you can select which one the Macintosh should use the next time it restarts or starts up when you turn on the power:

1. **Launch System Preferences by clicking on its icon in the Dock.** Unless you've moved things around in the Dock, the System Preference icon is the second or third icon from the left.

2. **Click the Startup Disk icon.** The startup disk panel appears, as in Figure 9-1.

3. **Select the disk volume from which you want to boot.**

4. **Exit System Preferences.** If desired, restart the Macintosh immediately to boot from the newly selected volume.

Figure 9-1
Choosing a startup disk

MOUNTING AND UNMOUNTING VOLUMES

Most Macintosh volumes will mount themselves. For example, hard disks mount when you start or restart the computer; CDs or DVDs mount as soon as they spin up to speed in a drive and can be read.

▼ Note

The term *mount* is a charming holdover from the early days of computing when huge mainframes relied on disk packs the size of spare tires. Over in the Math Building you'd be at a terminal making a request to load up some software, and some computer-science grad student wearing earth shoes and an I'm With Stupid shirt had to physically mount the pack inside a piece of equipment. I missed out on this part of the computing era, but I imagine that part of the fun of playing Solitaire back then was the knowledge that your idle whim to waste some time was going to require an anonymous stranger to manhandle a 15-pound piece of equipment into position. It must have been the same feeling that King Louis had when he ordered his human chess pieces around. Ah, the good old days...

Mounting volumes

Occasionally, you may find a volume that won't mount even when inserted into a disk drive. In that case, you can try to mount the volume manually using Disk Utility:

1. **Open the Finder, the Applications folder, then the Utilities subfolder.**

2. **Launch the Disk Utility program by double-clicking its icon.**

3. **Select the name of the volume from the list of recognized volumes.** You find this on the left of the window (Figure 9-2).

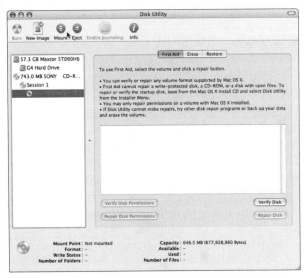

Figure 9-2
Mounting a volume manually

4. **Click the Mount button in the toolbar at the top of the window.** OS X mounts the volume and adds an icon for the volume to the Desktop if it can.

▼ Note
Whereas the Finder doesn't give you useless, confusing information about the devices you're using, Disk Utility strips it all buck-naked. Not satisfied to merely list G4 Hard Drive (the name of the boot volume in Figure 9-2), Disk Utility tells you that it's physically located on a mechanical hard drive of a specific make, model, and capacity. Disk Utility is one of my most-often-used utilities. If they came out with a tee shirt for it, I'd buy it and wear it while I exercise. And when that cute girl with the long black hair comments on it, I'd say, "Oh, yeah, I've been using it for *years*, way before it started getting national airplay and stuff." She would giggle and wonder why she's never really noticed me before.

Unmounting volumes

Unmounting a volume removes its icon from the Desktop. The physical drive might still be connected and spinning, but as far as the Finder is concerned the unmounted volume doesn't exist anymore, at least until you mount it again.

To unmount a volume, drag its Finder icon into the Trash. If it's a network volume or a volume on a hard drive, it disappears from the Desktop. If it's a removable volume like a CD, it is ejected. You can do the same thing by just clicking the little Eject button next to the disc's name in the Finder.

▼ Note
"Wait...when I drag a volume *into the Trash,* it just unmounts it? It's not going to, um, well, *delete 2 years of my life's work in an instant* or anything?" No. I don't know whose idea it was to encourage people to drag volumes into the Trash, but it was a bad one, and a serious stretching of the Trash metaphor. It confuses (and concerns) a lot of people, which is why in Mac OS X, Apple set up the Trash to turn into an Eject symbol when a volume is dragged onto it.

You can also use Disk Utility to unmount a volume without removing the disk from its drive. This is useful mojo. If a multisession CD is in your drive, each session appears in the Finder as a separate volume. That's a lot of clutter;

just unmount the ones you don't need. It's also handy to unmount any external drives you're not going to use. It's a hassle to unplug my little pocket drive when I go off to lunch but by unmounting it, it's unlikely that anyone's going to paw through its contents while I'm away.

To unmount a volume via Disk Utility:

1. **Open the Finder, the Applications folder, then the Utilities subfolder.**

2. **Launch the Disk Utility program by double-clicking its icon.**

3. **Select the name of the volume from the list of volumes.**

4. **Click the Unmount button, visible in Figure 9-3.**

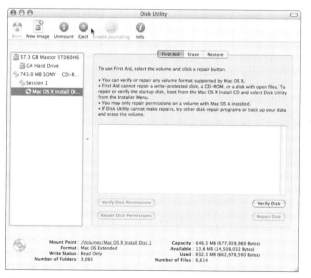

Figure 9-3
Moving the cursor to the Unmount button and clicking unmounts a volume manually

▼ Caution

Disk Utility does not stop you from unmounting a hard disk, including your boot volume. If you accidentally unmount your boot volume and don't remount it before you quit Disk Utility, you need to reboot the computer to get the drive to mount again.

▼ Tip

If you look again at Figure 9-3, you see an Eject button in the window's toolbar. This allows you to eject removable media (in particular, CDs and DVDs) without leaving Disk Utility.

EXTERNAL DRIVES: USB AND FIREWIRE

The back of your Macintosh has USB and FireWire ports, places where you can plug in external devices. Both are *plug and play* (plug the device in, perhaps install some software, and go) and *hot-swappable* (plug and unplug devices while your computer is turned on).

USB hard drives are pretty tough to find these days. USB is slower than FireWire by a whole order of magnitude and was never really intended for the sort of throttling that a hard-drive interface gets. It's more introspective, taking life as it comes, and was designed for low-speed devices like keyboards, mouses, and printers.

Both FireWire and USB devices are set up so that multiple devices can hook up to a single Mac FireWire or USB port. You do it either through *daisy chaining* (the device has its own USB port in the back, where you can plug in a second device) as in Figure 9-4 or through a *hub*. A hub (they're made in FireWire or USB flavors) is a harmonica-looking device that sports several connectors and can serve to connect four or more devices into the same Mac port. Figure 9-5 shows you what I mean.

ONE DOWNSIDE OF USB AND FIREWIRE

Both USB and FireWire are big improvements on the interfaces they replace: Apple Desktop Bus and SCSI. SCSI in particular deserves to be given a stern talking to and sent out to the yard to pick weeds until suppertime. Whereas today you simply plug a FireWire drive in and expect it to work, attaching a SCSI device to a Mac means that you are in for a real way-hey-hey of an afternoon (and evening and early dawn).

One of these new interfaces' best features spawns one confusing element, however: Both interfaces can serve as an electrical connection as well as a data connection. So, my pocket FireWire drive connects with just one cable; no AC adapter is necessary. When you start attaching several devices to the same port, some of those devices may sputter and stop working. There just isn't enough power on that USB port to run all those input devices *plus* that new Waring blender. A good hub comes with its own power supply capable of pumping out more than enough electrons to keep all of your devices happy.

Oh, yes, and about that hot-swappability I mentioned. It's a big boon to disconnect a drive and put it away without having to shut down your Mac first, but don't just yank out the cable. You absolutely, positively *must* unmount the drive's volumes first. Just go to the Finder and drag its volumes to the Trash.

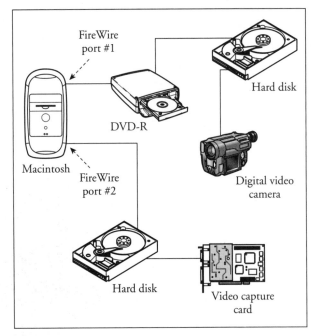

Figure 9-5
Using hubs to connect multiple USB devices

Why? Because you never know when some app on your Mac is working with the thing. If it's saving that previous Word file to it when you yank the cord out, kiss the file goodbye. If the Finder is writing critical directory information, well, you can kiss something *else* of yours goodbye.

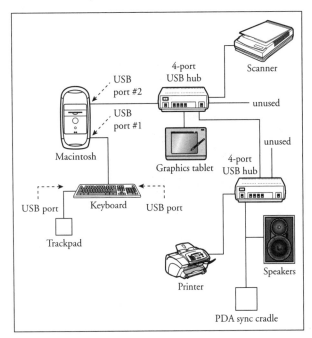

Figure 9-4
Daisy chaining FireWire devices

I assure you it's a far more personal item and not as readily replaced as a two-page memo.

BURNING CDS AND DVDS

There's a reason why Apple stopped putting floppy drives inside Macs years ago: They're obsolete. They went out with spats and buttonhooks, steam-powered cars, and even Sylvester Stallone's bankability as the star of Hollywood blockbusters.

Why put 1.4MB on a diskette when you can put 650MB there instead? Or how about more than 4 whole gigabytes? Diskettes still had a place in this modern pushbutton world when recordable CD and DVD media were expensive. Once, a blank DVD would have set you back 10 or 20 bucks. Today, you can buy them in spindles for about a buck a throw, and CDs are down to mere pennies.

Recordable discs give you vastly increased amounts of removable storage, but they're a bit less convenient than floppies. A computer can write a file to a floppy immediately. With optical discs, it's a big production; it has to blast all of its contents onto the disc at once. You can fill it up in several blasts spaced days, months, or weeks apart — this is known as *multisession* recording — but the fact remains that you have to maintain a slightly different mindset when working with discs than you do with floppies.

The burning process

Writing to a CD or DVD is known as *burning* the disc, and OS X makes the process extremely easy:

1. **Insert a blank CD-R, CD-RW, or writeable DVD into the appropriate drive.** OS X mounts the disc on the Desktop as Blank CD (or DVD). If the disc is blank, Panther opens a dialog that asks for a name for the disc. Type any name you prefer.

BURNING A DISC: BEHIND THE SCENES

When you're burning a CD or DVD, the Finder mounts that disc on the Desktop as a new volume, after which you can start dropping folders and files. What *actually* happens is that a section of your hard drive, the size of that disc, is set aside, and all the files you drag onto the CD icon get copied there. Only when you burn the disc is the data actually written.

For this reason, Panther won't let you work with a recordable disc unless you have an amount of free space on your boot drive equal to its capacity. It can be a minor hassle, but keep in mind that in the olden days (that is, back during Clinton's second term in office) the Finder couldn't deal with blank optical media at all. You had to do everything through a third-party app.

2. **Select the type of disc you want to create (music or documents) and the application you want to use on the Action pop-up menu** (Figure 9-6). This menu varies depending on the type of disc you have inserted. For example, if you insert a CD-R, you can open the Finder or iTunes. However, if the disc is a writeable DVD, you'll also be invited to use iMovie. In all cases, you can select an alternative application.

3. **Click OK.**

4. **Drag the files you want to burn onto the disc icon or window.** You can open the disc's window in the Finder at any time and rearrange and rename files. You can also create new folders as needed. Organize the files as you want them to appear on the disc.

5. **When all files are in place, make the Finder the current application.**

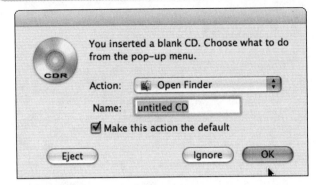

Figure 9-6
Naming a blank writeable disc

6. **Select File ➔ Burn disc (Figure 9-7) or drag the disc icon to the Trash.** Alternatively, you can click the yellow and black Burn button next to the disc icon. In any case, OS X asks you what you want to do with the disc.

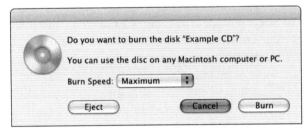

Figure 9-7
Lighting the match before burning a disc

7. **Select your burn speed (see the related sidebar on this page), then click the Burn button.** This begins the burning process (see Figure 9-8).

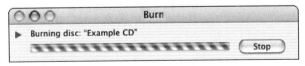

Figure 9-8
Watching the progress of a disc-burning session

BURN SPEED: FASTER AIN'T NECESSARILY BETTER

So, why *wouldn't* you just select the maximum speed from that pop-up menu? For the same reason the Connecticut State Police nailed me for doing 90 in a 55. Not everything is rated for the top possible speed. Look at that bundle of discs before purchasing. It's possible that the reason it was such a bargain is that they can't be burned at your SuperDrive's full 16x speed.

Let the Finder try the maximum speed by default. But if it spits out the disc and says, "No bleepin' way, mate," be prepared to click on a slower speed, like 4x.

(What does 16x, 8x, and so on mean? 1x is the speed of the playback of a normal audio CD; it takes about 70 minutes to read it from start to finish. So, a drive that can write at 16x speed can [technically] burn a CD-R full to the brim in roughly 5 minutes.)

Burning an optical disc

Burning an optical disc takes more time than writing to a hard drive. OS X shows you a progress bar as it works. Nonetheless, be prepared to wait a bit while the disc burning proceeds.

Alternatively, you can use Disk Utility to control writing to optical discs using a previously prepared disk image. The advantage to this is that you can create a multisession disc, which is a disc that you can continue to write to until it is full.

Each time you write to the disc, you create a volume for the burn session. This means that you must place the files that you want to write to the disc during any given session into a single, top-level folder. You create a disk image from that folder, which is then burned onto the disc. (You'll learn more about disk images later in this chapter.)

To create a disc that can accept multiple write sessions:

1. **Copy or move all the folders and files you want to write to the disc into a single, top-level folder.**

2. **Open the Finder, the Applications folder, then the Utilities subfolder, and launch the Disk Utility program by double-clicking its icon.**

3. **Select Images → New → Image From Folder.** An Open File dialog box appears.

4. **Locate the top-level folder you prepared in Step 1, and click the Open button.** The Convert Image dialog appears.

5. **Name the disk image and select a location for it** (Figure 9-9). OS X creates a disk image file (a *.dmg* extension). It then appears in the Disk Utility window as a disk (Figure 9-10).

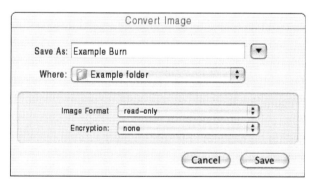

Figure 9-9
Creating a disk image using Disk Utility

6. **Insert a blank, writeable optical disc into the drive.**

7. **Click the disk image.** This has been done in Figure 9-10.

8. **Click the Burn icon at the far left of the toolbar.** The dialog box in Figure 9-11 appears.

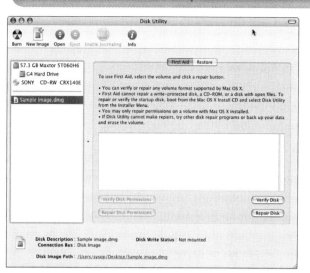

Figure 9-10
A disk image in the Disk Utility window

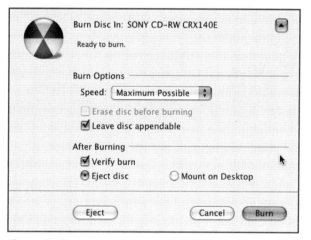

Figure 9-11
Disk Utility: She burns, she burns!

▼ Note

If you don't see the large dialog in Figure 9-11, click the arrow at the top right of the dialog to show the entire window.

9. **Click the Leave disc appendable option.** This makes the disc multisession.

10. **Click Burn to burn the disc.**

Throughout this section I've mentioned CD-R and CD-RW. There are actually two kinds of optical media: CD-Recordable and CD-ReWritable. They both burn the same way, but with a CD-R once the thing is full, it's full. That's all she wrote. With CD-RW, you have the option of erasing and reusing the disc.

This used to be a bigger deal than it is today. Once, discs were expensive and you hated to waste 'em. But, do you want to know how cheap CD-Rs are these days? About 10 to 20 cents. Earlier today, I needed to copy about 80K worth of files from one Mac to another. I could have used Panther's way-cool and way-powerful networking features to move those files through my home network, but at the time it seemed simpler just to burn them onto a disc and carry it to the other Mac.

 Note

> Incidentally, putting a file on a disc and hand carrying it to another computer is a recognized and time-honored standard networking protocol known as SneakerNet. It's low tech and it ain't as fast as Ethernet... *but it always works.*

And yes, when I'm done, I just drop the CD into the trash. Fifteen cents and I have 500 of 'em here.

There's one advantage to CD-RW: You can indeed erase them. So when you throw them out, you don't have to worry about someone fishing them out of your wastebasket and poking through their files.

There's one *big* advantage of CD-R, though: If you burn audio onto a CD-RW and stick it into a standard CD player, it probably won't play. Some players are finicky about

all recordable media, but CD-R was designed specifically to hew as close to the standard as possible, so it works with the greatest number of players.

The same differences and caveats apply to DVD-R and DVD-RW, though at this writing, recordable DVD is where recordable CDs were several years ago. That is, when you show off your new DVD-RW drive, people say, "You lucky bum," instead of, "Yeah, so what?"

MEMORY-BASED STORAGE

If you have a digital camera, you have some type of memory card in that camera to store images. Most of these cards use flash memory — that special RAM that can retain its contents with no power applied — known as either Compact Flash, Memory Stick, or Secure Digital. These cards mount on your Desktop like any standard volume.

But how? If it's inside your camera, it mounts as soon as you connect the device to your Mac's USB port, using the cable that came with the camera. You might find it more convenient to take it out of the camera and stick it inside a card reader instead. This is a little device the size of a cassette tape. It plugs into your USB port and typically has slots for all three or four different kinds of memory.

Either way, everything should be plug and play. Panther comes with all the know-how to mount your memory card built in. So just plug it in, wait a second, and then copy the card's files to your hard drive.

▼ **Note**

> Of course, Panther has a marvelous plan for your life. So if it recognizes that you have connected a camera, it automatically activates iPhoto and asks if you'd like to slurp all those image files straight into the iPhoto library. It can do the same thing with card readers, too.

DON'T BE CAUGHT WITHOUT YOUR KEYCHAIN

Yes, my young apprentice, you do want a keychain drive. You can't have your Mac with you at all times. You might own a PowerBook, but carrying a 7-pound object with you at all times marks you as the enemy of good posture and the best friend of the chiropractic industry.

But you *do* always have your keys in your pocket. So it's possible to always have your Safari bookmarks, all of your passwords (read the Keychain section of Chapter 16), and the collection of documents your life is revolving around at the moment. All that and plenty of room left over for the full-screen trailer to the first *X-Men* movie. Stick it into the USB port of any Mac — even one at a nearby Apple store — and you're good to go.

There's another kind of flash storage: keychain drives. These are memory chips ranging in capacity from 64MB all the way up to a gigabyte that are mounted on what looks like the end of a popsicle stick. A keychain drive has its own USB connector at one end and a little hole at the other end so you can keep it with your keys. Just plug it into any USB port, and it mounts automatically and operates just like an ordinary drive.

NETWORKED VOLUMES

To this point, I've assumed that all the volumes you use are physically part of your computer, but that may not be the case. You can reach any number of volumes on a remote server over a network and have Panther treat it like it was a hard drive plugged into your Mac.

The server can run nearly any operating system: OS X, an earlier version of the Mac operating system, a flavor of Windows, Unix, Linux, Novell. Panther also supports connections to SMB/CIFS, NFS, and WebDAV servers without any extra encouragement from third-party utilities. In addition, you can access the contents of a Public/Shared folder on an OS X or Windows computer, assuming that the owner of the machine has turned on file sharing.

▼ Note

I'm just typing stuff to impress you because, in truth, you don't need to know any of this. It's enough that Panther knows this stuff. It'll figure out the networking hoodoo for you.

Connecting to a server

Connecting to a server is handled almost automagically:

1. **Click the Finder.**

2. **In the Go menu, select Connect To Server.** The Connect To Server dialog appears (Figure 9-12).

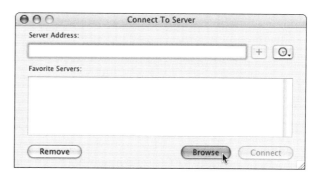

Figure 9-12
Preparing to browse for available servers

3. **Click Browse.** You can consolidate steps 2 and 3 by simply clicking the Network item in the sidebar of any Finder window. Panther sniffs through your local network looking for machines with which it can share files. This might be a big noisy rack of XServe file servers in the basement of your office. It could be the Macintosh in your home office that's been set up for file sharing, or a Windows machine with one or more shared folders on it.

▼ Note

I'm rather clumsily avoiding the use of the word server. Technically, a server is indeed that big, noisy machine that does nothing *but* serve files to other machines across a network. But in this modern push-button age, almost any computer on the network can share files. If my little G4 Cube wants to call itself a server, let it, I say. So from now on, where you see the word server, you can substitute "any machine capable of sharing files."

The window ultimately fills up with available servers (Figure 9-13). Expect them to straggle in like children assembling in the kitchen on the first school morning after Christmas vacation. It takes a while to discover every available server.

Figure 9-13
A list of what you can connect to at the moment

4. **Double-click on a server to access its contents.** You are presented with a login box (Figure 9-14). So, do you have permission to use this server? If so, its owner should have set you up with a user name and a password.

5. **Enter your user name and password in the fields provided, and click Connect.** If you don't have an account, click Guest instead. The person in charge of the server might have set up folders that folks are free to access without a user account.

Figure 9-14
Who goes there? Identify yourself to the server

And you're in. Where you can go and what you can do on this server is limited to the permissions that the server's owner has set for you (Figure 9-15). You might have *carte blanche* to open any folder, copy files onto the server, and modify what you find there. Or you may encounter a single folder that you can't open, but into which you can copy files. This is what's known as a Drop Box, and it's a simple way to let people send you files without having to manage a whole lot of accounts or worry that the boss will see what you've *really* been doing with the company pension fund.

Figure 9-15
Voilà! A network server mounted on your Mac

▼ Tip

You know what else is cool? Remember when I mentioned that Panther's standard Open and Save dialogs are functional duplicates of the standard Finder windows? Yes indeed, that means that when you're in Microsoft Word and you're about to save the file you just created, you can connect straight to your supervisor's Mac (or even his or her Windows machine) and save it right into the public folder. Send Apple a dollar right now. Whatever you paid for Panther, it just wasn't enough.

Finding the address of a piece of hardware

It's possible, however, that Panther can't locate some servers automatically. That's why the Connect To Server dialog contains a field in which you can type the network address of a known piece of hardware.

It's easy to find this address:

1. **Go (actually walk) to the Mac to which you want to connect, and under System Preferences click Sharing** (Figure 9-16). There it is, in English.

▼ Note

If the owner of this Mac is (a) right there in the room and (b) one of those suspicious types, you might want to start a small fire in a disused corner of the office as a distraction. Or just dramatically point at the window and shout, "Look! A big distracting thing!" Use your imagination.

---

2. **Jot down the gobbledygook that begins with afp://, and then go back to your own Mac.** Type it in the Server Address: field of the Connect To Server dialog.

3. **Click Connect.** The login dialog from Figure 9-14 appears.

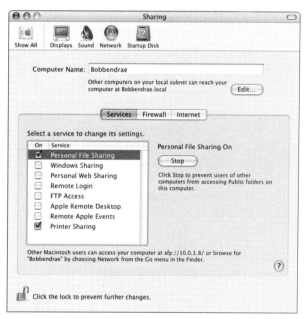

Figure 9-16
Finding the network address of a target Mac

Note

You know, that afp:// thing looks a *lot* like a URL, doesn't it? I wonder what would happen if you were to type it into the Address field of your Mac's Web browser? (sigh). I was hoping that this would inspire you to go off and try it. But alas, my skill as a writer has left you on tenterhooks. So the answer is that yup, it switches to the Finder and tries to mount that server. It's called synergy, kids.

Other networked volumes: FTP and iDisks

FTP is the most popular (but by no means the most sophisticated) way to shuttle files from one computer to another using a network. Panther's version of the Finder can access FTP servers on its own:

1. **Use Connect To Server, and use the server's FTP address as, well, the server address.** You'll be presented with a login window (Figure 9-17):

Figure 9-17
Panther's FTP login window

2. **Give it your user name and password, and you're in.** It mounts in the Finder just like any other server.

Note

There's just one problem: The Finder can only read files from FTP servers. You can copy files to your local Mac, but you can't upload to the server. To upload, you must open the Terminal and use a built-in command-line FTP program, or you can get a slick, graphical third-party utility like Fetch or Interarchy. You can access many servers through Safari or any other Web browser, as well.

And then there's the iDisk. Apple has this big, nifty online service called .Mac. It costs about a hundred bucks a year, and you get an email account and Web server space. It's pretty slick because most of your iApps are set up to interact with your private .Mac space. You can publish a photo album so that Aunt Estelle and all the other relatives can view it online by accessing a Web page on Mac.com.

iDisk is part of this ginchiness. An iDisk is, in effect, a private file server that you own, hosted on Apple's .Mac servers. If you keep your important documents and your iCal and Address Book data on your iDisk, nearly any Macintosh with a high-speed connection to the Internet becomes like your own personal Mac.

And your iDisk is the simplest sort of network server there is:

1. **Go to iDisk under the Finder's Go menu, and click My iDisk.** One time and one time only you'll have to provide your .Mac member name and password.

2. **Type in your .Mac member name and password.** Every time thereafter, the thing just magically appears, kind of like Pottery Barn catalogues.

Even if you don't lay out a hundred clams for a year of .Mac membership, you can mount any existing .Mac member's iDisk by clicking Other User's iDisk. Completing the trifecta of iDisk ginchiness, each .Mac member's iDisk has a special Public folder that anybody can access without a password. It's a handy and reliable way to distribute a file to loads of strangers, like a piece of software you wrote and want to give away, or your band's demo tunes. Just select Other User's Public Folder, and enter the dude's .Mac account name. No password necessary.

 Note

> Steve Jobs has a .Mac account. His account name is Steve.

No matter how you mount a network volume, when you're done using it, you can terminate the connection by dragging its Finder icon to the Trash or by clicking the Eject button next to its name.

USING TARGET DISK MODE

Ah...a new Mac has just been unpacked and is sitting on your desk. Your only dilemma is how to transfer files from your old machine to your new one. Using the company's network would be pretty slow. (If you're a home user, you may not have a network!) So, what to do? You can boot one machine in *target disk mode*, where its hard drive mounts on the Desktop of the second machine. Then all that remains is to drag the files you want to copy from one hard disk to the other.

All you need for target disk mode is a FireWire cable. If one or both of the computers has a low-speed FireWire port, use a six-pin FireWire cable. However, if both computers support the faster FireWire 800 version, you can use a nine-pin cable to transfer data faster.

Here's how you do it. In these instructions, the target Mac is the machine whose hard drive you want to mount on

another Mac. For additional clarity, let's say that you want to mount my PowerBook's hard drive on the Desktop of my Desktop Mac. Just keep in mind that this works with any modern Mac.

1. **Shut down the PowerBook.** Sleep won't do; you have to power it off completely.

2. **Connect the PowerBook to the Desktop Mac using their FireWire ports.**

3. **While pressing the T key on the PowerBook, press the Power button.**

4. **Release the T key when the Desktop appears.** Instead of the standard startup process you see a big, colorful FireWire logo on the PowerBook's screen.

The PowerBook now behaves exactly like an external FireWire drive without restrictions. When you're done with it, put it away as you would any other FireWire drive: Drag its icon to the Trash and then disconnect. Turn off the PowerBook by holding down the Power button. It can now reboot normally.

DISK IMAGES

Disk images are special files that contain all or part of a volume. As you read earlier in this chapter, they are useful for creating multisession optical discs. However, they have other uses as well:

- **You can use a disk image to duplicate a CD or DVD when you have only one drive.** Create an image of the disc, which then resides on a hard drive. Then, copy the image to a new, blank disc.

- **You can use a disk image to distribute a collection of files.** In fact, a lot of the software that you download over the Internet (whether freeware, shareware, or commercial) is supplied as a disk image.

▼ Tip

I also use disk images to maintain a set of Good Samaritan files on my PowerBook. For example, at a trade show, a pal was all frantic because his Mac wouldn't boot up. My own drive contains disk images of the complete Panther install set and a couple of different emergency bootable CDs. A quick stop at the drugstore for a couple of blank CDs and I can produce a disc that'll bring his Mac back to life.

A disk image behaves like a removable disk. When you double-click on a disk image (which has the .dmg filename extension), Disk Utility opens the image file and mounts it on the Desktop as a standard volume (see Figure 9-18). You can copy to it and from it. You can add folders and move files and folders as necessary.

Figure 9-18
A disk image file and disk image mounted on the Desktop

Creating a disk image for use as a removable disk is very similar to what you do when you create a multisession CD:

1. **Launch Disk Utility.** To do this, open the Finder, the Applications folder, then the Utilities subfolder. Launch the Disk Utility program by double-clicking its icon.

2. **Click the New Image button.** This is located at the top in the toolbar (Figure 9-19). The New Image dialog appears (Figure 9-20).

3. **Provide a name and storage location for the image file.**

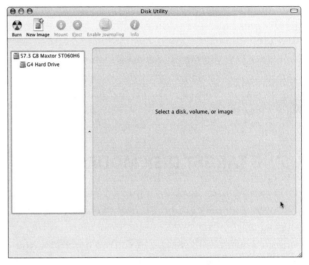

Figure 9-19
Beginning to create a disk image using Disk Utility

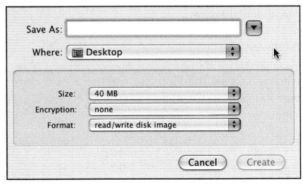

Figure 9-20
Naming and locating storage for a new disk image

▼ Tip

To expand the New Image dialog so that you can browse through your disk hierarchy to find a storage location, click the down arrow at the right of the Save As text box.

4. **Select the size of the disk image from the Size pop-up menu** (Figure 9-21).

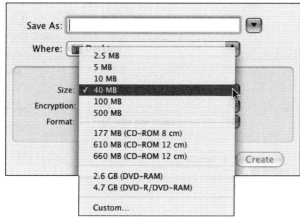

Figure 9-21
Selecting the size of a new disk image

5. **Click Create.** Disk Utility creates the image file and mounts the empty disk image on the Desktop. The image also appears in Disk Utility as a mounted disk (Figure 9-22).

6. **Drag files and folders to the mounted disk image as necessary.** As you can see in Figure 9-23, a mounted disk image window looks and acts just like any other Finder window.

When you are finished working with the disk image, you can unmount it by dragging the mounted disk image to the Trash or clicking on the Eject button to the left of the disk's name in its Finder window's sidebar. All of the volume's files are packed into the .dmg file, and there they'll slumber until the next time you double-click the file.

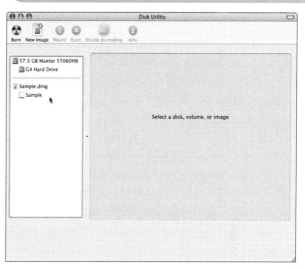

Figure 9-22
A disk image file appearing in the Disk Utility disk list

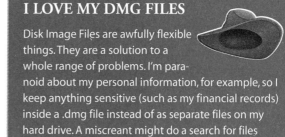

I LOVE MY DMG FILES

Disk Image Files are awfully flexible things. They are a solution to a whole range of problems. I'm paranoid about my personal information, for example, so I keep anything sensitive (such as my financial records) inside a .dmg file instead of as separate files on my hard drive. A miscreant might do a search for files named Tax deductions/2004, but because I unmount that disk image when I'm not using it, that data defies all conventional search utilities.

I intend to continue to pursue these aggressive security ideas all the way to the point where I begin to stroke my Macintosh and mutter *my preciousssss...they wants you...but I won't lets them HAVE youuuu!* I think that's quite reasonable.

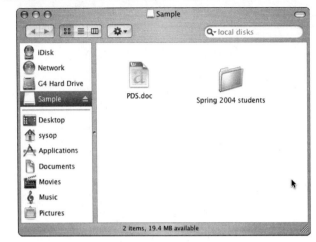

Figure 9-23
A disk image window

KEEPING VOLUMES HEALTHY

Because a hard disk relies on mechanical parts to access locations on the disk, it is one of the slowest components of your Mac. A hard disk running at optimal speed, nonetheless, doesn't slow most of us down. However, over time the software that manages the files and folders stored on a hard drive can become corrupt. The result is significantly slower disk access and/or the inability to launch applications.

One of the major culprits in slow access and preventing files from opening is file and folder permissions. OS X's Unix underpinnings use file and folder permissions to determine whether a user has the right to use each file and folder (and there are tens of thousands of them!). When the permissions become damaged, you are likely to encounter problems. The solution is to use Disk Utility to repair the permissions:

1. **Open the Finder, the Applications folder, then the Utilities subfolder.**

2. **Launch the Disk Utility program by double-clicking its icon.**

3. **In the disk list at the left of the window, select the disk whose permissions you want to repair.** (Figure 9-24.)

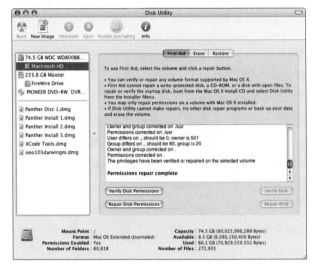

Figure 9-24
Repairing file and folder permissions

4. **Click either Verify Disk Permissions or Repair Disk Permissions, both located at the bottom of the window.** Click Verify Disk Permissions to determine whether the permissions are a problem for your disk. Click Repair Disk Permissions to both verify and repair in the same step.

▼ Note

Disk Utility can repair permissions only on a startup volume (in other words, a volume with OS X system files on it). Repairing permissions is one of those "things you try when something's wrong and you don't know what to try." That is, it certainly won't make any situation *worse*, and file permissions is such an arcane and potent concept to Panther that there's a decent chance it'll fix things up.

If repairing permissions doesn't solve your disk problems, you may want to try a more generic verification or repair. This process checks and/or repairs disk partitions, the data that describe how the disk is formatted, and the structure of the file/folder hierarchy. You can verify any disk (even a write-only disk such as a CD) but only repair a disk with no open files. If you want to repair the startup disk, you need to boot from a CD or another hard disk.

To verify or repair a disk:

1. **Make sure that all files on the target disk are closed.**

2. **Open the Finder, the Applications folder, then the Utilities subfolder.**

3. **Launch the Disk Utility program by double-clicking its icon.**

4. **In the list of disks at the left of the window, select the disk** (Figure 9-25).

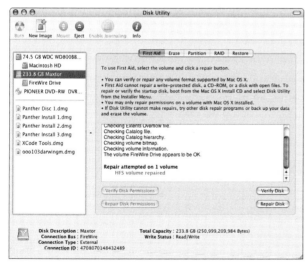

Figure 9-25
Verifying or repairing a disk

5. **Click either Verify Disk or Repair Disk**. Click Verify Disk to verify the integrity of the disk. Click Repair Disk to both verify and repair in the same step.

 Note

Prior to OS X, Mac users were told to *defragment* hard disks frequently. Defragmentation places each file in contiguous storage and then writes all files next to each other on the disk. The theory is that this speeds up file access. The theory works fine for OS 9 and earlier, but Unix keeps files spaced out on the disk to avoid having to break files up into small fragments, providing a significant amount of protection from file corruption. (If a part of the disk goes bad, only the single file on that portion of the disk corrupts rather than parts of many files.) The bottom line is that defragmenting a Unix-based file system can make things worse instead of better.

Tip

No disk lasts forever, no matter how often you repair it. Your best hedge against disk corruption is to make good backup copies. (Make a mantra out of it: "Backup, backup, backup.")

Finally, realize that there are limits to what Apple's built-in utilities can do for you. Sometimes you have to call in a hired gun, and by far the most important soldier of fortune in this product category is Alsoft's *DiskWarrior*. DiskWarrior analyzes your hard drive down to the sub-muon level. As a guy who's used this utility since Version 1.0, I can calmly say that the only problem that DiskWarrior *can't* solve is when you accidentally cut a drive in two with a band saw. Even so, if you run DW on the affected volume, a dialog appears reading "A repair cannot be attempted. This drive has been cut in half with either a band saw or an angle grinder." Now *that's* service.

Archiving to Analog Pulpware Substrate (Printing)

In This Chapter

Printing Concepts • Setting Up OS X for Printing
Changing the Page Size and Orientation • Printing from Within an Application
Can I *Please* Click the "Print" Button Now?!? • Managing Printing • Faxing

It's a world gone mad, but only a paltry 3 percent of Americans have presented themselves at their local participating True Value hardware store to have a Bluetooth chip permanently fused to their anterior brainstems. If more of you were to get on board, chapters like these would be wholly unnecessary. We technology pundits have spent some of the best years of our lives carefully explaining to you people that print is dead, but have you listened? No. There's a reason why we're still at least 6 years away from being able to enjoy Thomas Hardy's *The Return of the Native* in convenient, cherry-coated pill form, and I for one know *exactly* whom to blame.

Okay, so fine. *Print* your documents. *Fill* your homes, condos, and apartments with flammable papers. In 6 months, not *one,* one of those Bluetooth implants has ever caused a house fire (yes, except for that guy in Nebraska, but he was using beta drivers), but I suppose that as a technology pundit, it's my job to educate, not to cast judgment, except again for that pill thing.

PRINTING CONCEPTS

One of the advantages of building a whole new OS from scratch as Apple did with Mac OS X is that it presented a big opportunity to clean house and consolidate features. Printing in Mac OS X is both familiar and very different compared to OS 9. It's familiar because there are so few totally new features available to you in Panther. But it's different because features that were once presented to you as A Big Deal are now integrated into the entire printing system. You can take full advantage of every modern ultraconvenience without being terribly aware that you're doing it.

As I go along, I'll talk about specific steps for setting up and using printers. But at a bare-bones level, using Panther's Print command causes two things to happen:

- The application and Panther talk to each other, and together they transmogrify your document into data that your chosen printer can understand.

- Panther waits until the printer is available and then sends this data on over.

Simple. Barely worth breaking out the bulleted-list thingy to explain it. But it's a good way to bring up two points, namely:

- **When you tell your Mac to print something, nothing happens.** This is normal. You're just used to the idea of the printing process holding your computer hostage until the last page gets spit out onto the floor. In Panther, issuing a Print command only holds you up for as long as it takes to tell your Mac what it needs to know. I bid you faith, patience, and calmness, young Jedi. The printed page will come when your spirit is ready to receive it. And, um, when that crummy $79 inkjet printer you got free with your system is done grinding through the job.

- **You don't even *care* about what happens during the second bullet above.** In other books in other eras, you'd need to master the concept of print queues and networked printers and submitting jobs to a server. All those concepts come into play, and you can manipulate things directly if you wish, but just as Bill Gates and Steve Jobs haven't the foggiest idea how the coffeemaker in the executive-level lounge works, you can

simply relax. Other entities know how the system works, and all you need to do is to tell this minion what you want.

Note

And incidentally, this is another area in which you — the user — get a lot of added functionality for free, so to speak. Mac OS X is built upon the Unix operating system, and Unix offers incredibly muscular printing architecture to all of its apps. You don't need to understand how or why this mojo is happening. All you have to do is sit back and enjoy that pine-fresh scent.

SETTING UP OS X FOR PRINTING

This section is either going to be a short one or a long one for you. One thing that confused me when I started using Mac OS X was that printers were so *bloody* difficult to install and configure. Where was the Chooser? After I've unearthed the disc containing the driver for my printer, how do I install it? Wait! Holy cow. I've just checked the printer manufacturer's Web site, and it doesn't even have Mac OS X drivers available for download!!!

Then I discovered that the moment I plugged my printer into a USB port, OS X had automatically found it, configured it, and made it available to all of my apps.

Well, *okay* then.

Mac OS X ships with printer drivers for nearly every printer you're ever likely to come across. When you do a basic installation, you're ready to rock and roll. In Chapter 2, which covers installing, one of the specific options the Panther installer makes available is a batch of extra printer drivers. This is why you're always encouraged to install everything that's available to you. You have scads of hard-drive storage available, and installing every driver just saves a lot of hassle.

▼ Note

This is particularly good advice if you're installing the OS on a PowerBook or iBook. If you take your Mac with you over the river and through the woods, you want to have as many printer drivers installed as possible. At a friend's house, at a Holiday Inn Express in Dearborn, Michigan, or at the satellite office way across the Iberian peninsula, the difference between printing a crucial document in three mouse clicks and enduring a process not unlike that faced by some of those poor trogs in the Old Testament is having a Mac that's prepared to work with anything.

Still, this world being naught but a vale of tears and all that, it's possible that your printer *won't* appear automagically within your apps' Print dialog box, and you'll have to add it manually through the Print Setup Utility.

Adding printers

To make a printer available for use:

1. **Turn on the printer.**

2. **Launch Printer Setup Utility.** The Printer Setup Utility is in the Utilities folder inside the Applications folder. The Printer List window appears.

3. **Click the Add icon** (Figure 10-1). The window for adding a printer appears (Figure 10-2).

Figure 10-1
Getting ready to add a printer

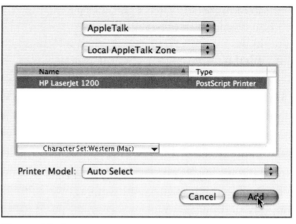

Figure 10-2
Adding a printer

4. **Select the manner in which the computer will communicate with the computer.** You do this from the top pop-up menu, as in Figure 10-3. OS X looks for available printers.

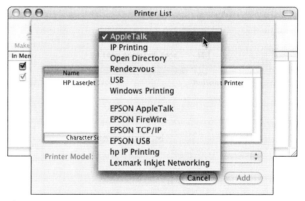

Figure 10-3
Choosing a printer communication language

If your printer is networked, you typically use AppleTalk to communicate with it. However, some networked printers require IP printing. You need to consult the printer's documentation to determine which is available. If you are sharing a printer connected to another Macintosh on your network, select Rendezvous. (You can find more information about Rendezvous and using IP to print in Chapter 11.)

▼ Note

And don't get thrown by all of these steps. We're talking worst-case scenarios, here; much if not most of this configuration will be handled by Panther on its own. You'll just confirm that the printer that Panther found is indeed the one you mean to install.

5. **Select the name of the printer from the list of printers in the middle of the window.**

6. **If OS X can't identify your printer by model, click the generic printer name in the list of printers and then select the manufacturer of the printer from the Printer Model pop-up at the bottom of the window** (see Figure 10-4).

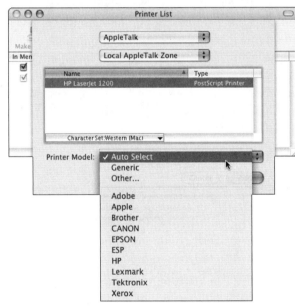

Figure 10-4
Choosing a printer

7. **Select the printer model from the list of models and click Add** (see Figure 10-5). If you are setting up a PostScript printer, OS X will search for a PPD (Post-Script Printer Description) file, as in Figure 10-6.

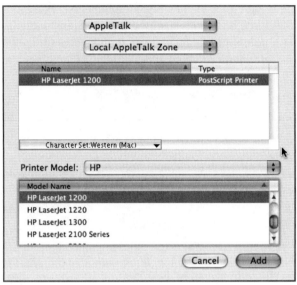

Figure 10-5
Choosing a printer model manually

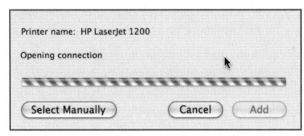

Figure 10-6
Finding a PPD for a PostScript printer

8. **If there is no PPD for a PostScript file, click the Select Manually button, and click the printer model that is closest to yours.** If you can't find anything close, select Generic. In most cases, it will work just fine.

▼ Note

And what's a PPD file? It just tells the printing system about the features that set this printer apart from the run-of-the-mill variety. It's got two different paper sources, it has a special mode for double-sided printing, it has a little taser-like coil that can be triggered whenever the cat curls up in the output bin for a nap. That sort of thing.

9. **Repeat the above procedure for each printer you want to add.**

Printers that you have configured using the preceding steps appear in a list of printers in the Print dialog so that you can select them when you print a document. One printer is the *default printer*. Unless you specify differently, the default printer is the first printer that you added.

To change the default printer:

1. **Launch Printer Setup Utility.**

2. **Click the printer that you want as the default printer.**

   Select Printer ➜ Make Default. Alternatively, you can press ⌘+D, or click the Default button at the left edge of the toolbar.

Creating desktop printer icons

One of the biggest problems with having Printer Setup Utility buried in Applications ➜ Utilities is that it isn't particularly handy when you are in the middle of printing. It also doesn't make it easy to drag a document item to a printer to print it. You can simplify your life by creating Desktop printer icons, such as those in Figure 10-7, for each of your printers. Yes, indeed, photorealistic icons

SUPPORTING UNSUP-PORTABLE PRINTERS

What if — horrors compluviated! — you're using an old, possibly Soviet-made printer that Panther doesn't actually support? And you've already checked the Web site of Metaliya Printsvertsk and found no downloadable drivers?

Well, head on over to gimp-print.sourceforge.net/ and download the (free, free, free) Gimp-Print driver package. It adds support for dozens of printers that Panther has never heard of.

And Gimp-Print is worth knowing about even if Panther supports your printer directly. It's an open-source, community effort to create the highest-quality print drivers possible, and oftentimes using one of Gimp's drivers instead of one provided by the manufacturer yields noticeable improvements in print quality.

representing your printers. Automatically installed. It's a prime example of a feature that doesn't really make things work any better, but will certainly make things work *cooler*. Features like these make me want to send Apple an extra dollar or something.

To create a Desktop printer icon:

1. **Launch Printer Setup Utility.**

2. **Click the name of the printer for which you want to create the Desktop icon.**

3. **Select Printers ➜ Create Desktop Printer.** OS X asks you to select a location for the icon.

4. **Select a location.** A Desktop printer icon appears immediately on your Desktop. You can print any document just by dragging its icon to that printer.

Figure 10-7
Desktop printer icons

 Tip

I don't use Desktop print icons much — like, when was the last time I could actually *see* my Desktop? — but they're handy. They act like any other file on your Desktop, so if you want, you can copy them onto another drive, like that USB flash drive you keep on your keychain. If you move around from Mac to Mac in your building, you can always route printouts to the printer in your office, just by inserting your USB keychain and dragging the file onto your home printer. *Another* reason to send Apple a dollar.

CHANGING THE PAGE SIZE AND ORIENTATION

Before you can print a document, you have to tell the print what size paper you're using. You must do this before you can print your document, which is discussed in the next section "Printing from Within an Application."

Not all paper is created equal: It comes in different sizes. In addition, you may want to print sideways on the page. The Page Setup dialog, such as the one in Figure 10-8, handles these types of settings.

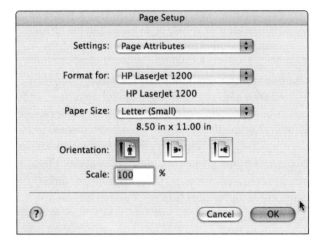

Figure 10-8
The Page Setup dialog box

To set up your paper:

1. **Select File ➡ Page Setup.** Notice that the first panel sets Page Attributes.

 Tip

Many applications support Shift+⌘+P as a keyboard shortcut for File ➡ Page Setup.

2. **Select the printer you want to use.** You do this in the Format For pop-up menu.

3. **Select the paper size from the Paper Size pop-up menu** (Figure 10-9). If you can't find the paper size you need in the pop-up menu, skip to Step 4; otherwise, continue with Step 7.

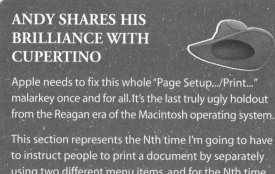

ANDY SHARES HIS BRILLIANCE WITH CUPERTINO

Apple needs to fix this whole "Page Setup.../Print..." malarkey once and for all. It's the last truly ugly holdout from the Reagan era of the Macintosh operating system.

This section represents the Nth time I'm going to have to instruct people to print a document by separately using two different menu items, and for the Nth time I'm going to have to say, "No, I don't know *why* they decided to do it that way." I'm picturing a Monday deadline and a long-planned weekend trip to Six Flags, but I can prove nothing, so I must remain mum.

It's clumsy. It's not elegant. It's *non-Maclike*, for heaven's sake.

▼ Note

Do notice that when you change the paper size, your document automatically reformats to reflect the new page dimensions. Or at least it should, if the app you're using conforms to Apple's guidelines. Some programmers are like wild stallions, unbroken, untamed. Many of them have customized vans with art airbrushed on the sides, amplifying that theme.

4. **If you don't find the paper you need in the Paper Size pop-up menu — say you're printing on some sort of oddball label paper — select Custom Paper Size from the Settings pop-up menu at the top of the Page Setup dialog.** The Custom Paper Size panel appears (see Figure 10-10).

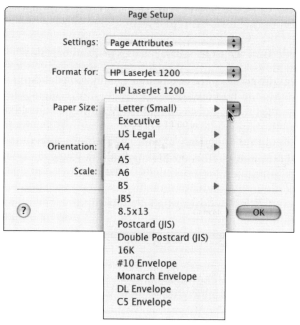

Figure 10-9
Choosing the paper size for printing

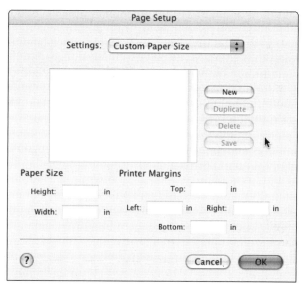

Figure 10-10
Defining a custom paper size

5. **Click the New button.** This creates a new custom paper.

6. **Give the paper a name, and type its dimensions.**

7. **Select the page orientation** You do this by clicking on the icon (straight up or sideways) that represents how you want contents to flow on the page.

8. **To see a summary of your page settings, select Summary from the Settings pop-up menu** (Figure 10-11).

9. **Click OK.** Your changes are applied.

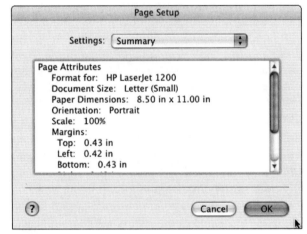

Figure 10-11
Viewing the Page Setup summary

In addition to the panels you have just seen, many applications have their own Page Setup panels. For example, in Figure 10-12, you can see the Microsoft Word panel.

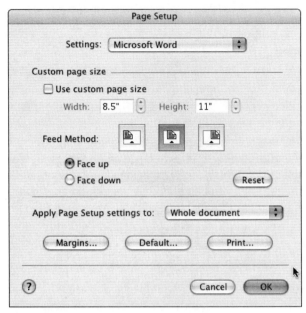

Figure 10-12
Application-specific page setup options

PRINTING FROM WITHIN AN APPLICATION

If you just want a paper copy of a document, there's little more to printing than turning on your printer, selecting File ➜ Print, and pressing Enter. But this is OS X. There are a million printing options (well, maybe a few hundred) that you can select before you print. Remember that the options presented in the Print dialog do not cover options to change the size of the page on which you want to print. To do that, rewind a bit to the previous section "Changing the Page Size and Orientation."

The most common way to print a document is to use the File ➜ Print command or to press ⌘+P. The Print dialog box appears showing the Copies & Pages panel, as in

Figure 10-13. Obviously, a graphics program like Photoshop has different printing features than a word processor like Microsoft Word, which has features unique from Microsoft Excel. We're using Word as an example here, but on your own Mac prepare yourself to see a celebration of variety.

There are so many different kinds of settings that Panther organizes the Print dialog into several pages that you navigate between via the pop-up menu under the Presets menu. It starts you off in Copies & Pages because in most operations that's all you mess with before clicking Print. However, OS X presents more options in the Layout, Scheduler, Paper Handling, Paper Feed, and Summary pages. To give you an overview of all the options available to you, the following sections discuss all the Print pages' options in excruciating detail.

▼ Note

Remember, that none of the options presented in the rest of this section are required. If you don't want to deal with all the options, all you have to do is click File ➜ Print, or press ⌘+P.

The Copies & Pages page

So, here it goes! After accessing the Print dialog, the Print dialog appears already on the Copies & Pages page (Figure 10-13). This page lets you set options for the number of copies you want to make as well as the range of material you want to print. Mac OS X has one option that appears at the top of the Print dialog no matter what page you're on: the Printer option. I'm covering it here because it's the first thing you see on the default page.

To use a different printer, select the printer's name from the Printer pop-up menu (Figure 10-14). Printers that are not available to you at the moment are marked with an

exclamation point. And notice that there's a whole submenu for printers that are attached to other Macs but available to you over the network through Panther's Printer Sharing feature.

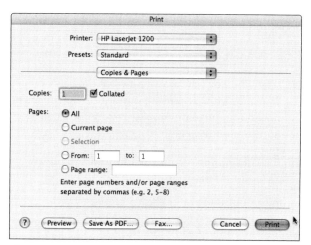

Figure 10-13
The Print dialog

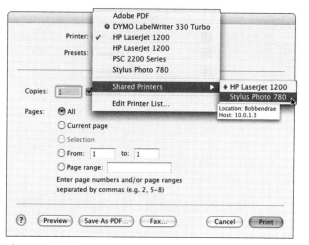

Figure 10-14
Selecting a printer

▼ Tip

If you hold your mouse over a shared printer, it'll helpfully tell you what Mac it's physically connected to and what that Mac's network address is. Just to help you keep things straight.

The options on the Copies & Pages page include the following:

- **Copies:** If you want just one copy of the entire document on your default printer, press Enter. (You're done.) To print more than one copy, type the number of copies you want in the Copies text box.

- **Collated option:** If you want the copies to print collated, click the Collated option.

- **Pages options:** You have options to print all pages, just the current page, or whatever text you've selected. To print just a limited range of pages instead of an entire document, click the From option and specify a page range. Alternatively, you can click the Page range option and type the range of pages you want to print.

The Layout page

This page allows you to print more than one page on a sheet of paper, and includes options for the page's layout and borders. The point of all that: If you're just printing something to proofread it, printing two or four pages per sheet speeds the printing process and saves paper. And by being a little creative with the four-page layout and the paper direction, it's possible to make quick-and-dirty two-sided booklets. Print, fold twice, and you can walk into the next comic-book convention with a slick list of all the issues of *Cerebus the Aardvark* you need to complete your collection.

To access this page, select Layout from the third pop-up menu in the dialog (see Figure 10-15).

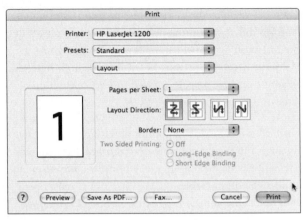

Figure 10-15
Printing multiple document pages per piece of paper

The options on this page include the following:

- **Pages per Sheet:** Choose the number of document pages to print on a piece of paper from the Pages per Sheet pop-up menu.

- **Layout Direction:** Select the layout direction that matches the order in which you want the pages to be placed on paper.

- **Borders:** In the Border pop-up menu, select the type of border you want to appear between the pages.

The Scheduler page

If you want to print 400 copies of a six-page concert program for your daughter's middle school, I urge you to use this feature and schedule the job to take place at night, when nobody else is in the office, particularly if you're sharing this printer with everyone else on the floor and someone might need to print just *one* page before leaving for the day.

There is a man in my office who's the *only* one in the company parking garage whose tires *always* have the air let out of them and whose door panels *always* get dinged and whose backseat upholstery *always* seems to get set on fire. He's also the *only one* who has no idea why these things keep happening to him. Don't be That Guy. Be considerate and schedule big printing jobs for later times.

If you want your document to print at a later time and day instead of right away, select Scheduler from the third pop-up menu in the dialog box (see Figure 10-16). Then:

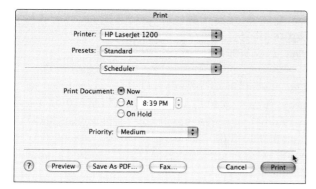

Figure 10-16
Scheduling printing

1. **Click the At option and type a specific time at which you want the document to print.** Alternatively, you can click the On Hold option to place the print job in the print queue without printing.

2. **Clicking a priority level in the Priority pop-up menu.** Higher-priority print jobs will bubble to the top of the print queue faster than lower-priority ones.

The Paper Handling page

To control the order of page printing, select Paper Handling from the third pop-up menu in the dialog (see Figure 10-17). The options on this page include:

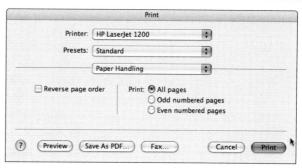

Figure 10-17
Choosing page handling options

- **Reverse page order:** This option lets you print from the highest page number to the lowest.

- **Odd numbered pages or Even numbered pages option:** Obviously, these allow you to print only odd or even pages.

The Paper Feed page

To change the source of the paper for printing, select Paper Feed from the third pop-up menu in the dialog (see Figure 10-18).

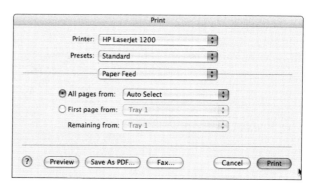

Figure 10-18
Choosing paper feed options

The options on the Paper Feed page include

- **All pages from:** If all pages are to come from the same source (a paper tray or manual feed), click the All pages from option and select the source from the associated pop-up menu. The Auto Select option is available for those printers that can detect the presence of paper in the manual feed slot and select that paper automatically. Otherwise, select the paper tray or manual feed. (Exactly what options appear in the pop-up menu depend on the specific printer.)

- **First page from and Remaining from:** To take the first piece of paper from a source different from where the paper for the rest of the document will come (for example, to print a first page on letterhead), click the First page from option and select sources for the first page and remaining pages from the associated pop-up menus.

 ## Note

Remember, if you own a bare-bones printer that's so cheap you got it for free when you ordered an AOL signup CD, you're not going to see a lot of these features.

The Summary page

To see a summary of all your settings, select Summary from the third pop-up menu in the dialog box (Figure 10-19).

The Preset option

Good heavens, that was a lot of effort. Well, again, usually all you'll do is press ⌘+P, and click OK to print one copy of whatever it is that's in front of you.

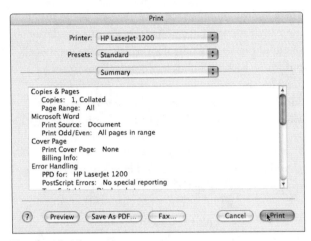

Figure 10-19
Viewing a summary of printing options

And you don't need to go through that *every bloody time*, either. If there's a group of settings you keep reusing (like, every time you need to proofread a document you always print double-sided, four to a page, borders around all pages), you can just set it up once and then save it inside the dialog's Presets (see Figure 10-20).

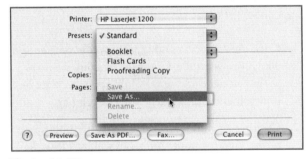

Figure 10-20
Saving your customized Print settings

Just click the pop-up next to Presets and select Save As to save these settings as a permanent option. You can store as many customized settings as you want.

CAN I *PLEASE* CLICK THE "PRINT" BUTTON NOW?!?

Well, sure, I mean, if that's what you really want. Really? All you want to do is Print?

Okay, it's a free country. But there are a couple of other neat alternatives. First, there's Print to PDF (discussed in Chapter 8). One click and boom, the whole document is "printed" as a Portable Document Format file with all graphics and formatting intact. It's like digital paper; you no longer need the original app to view or even print the doc, and if you give it to a friend who uses Windows or Linux, he or she can read and print it using the free PDF reader that you can download from Adobe.com.

The Preview button performs a similar mojo. Have you ever tried to print something, you know, tricky? For example, you've just bought plane tickets and now the travel site displays an electronic ticket that you need to print and bring with you to the airport. Printing Web pages from a browser is always a hit-and-miss proposition. Namely, you miss old-fashioned paper tickets and you want to hit the person responsible for the system we're stuck with now. Thank you! *Goodnight!*

To get an idea of what the printed page will look like *before* that piece-of-junk printer wastes 3 hours printing it, click File ➔ Print Preview instead of File ➔ Print. Panther images the document just as it would if it were sending it to a printer, except it ultimately sends it to Panther's built-in Preview app instead (Figure 10-21):

That's exactly what will be sent to the printer. Click Print to actually commit the baby to the mashed-up bits of tree bark.

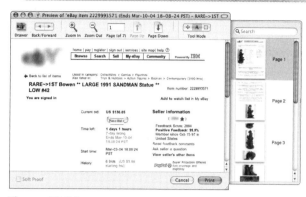

Figure 10-21
Previewing a printed document before you waste time and paper on it

MANAGING PRINTING

I meant what I said at the top of this chapter (see the section "Printing Concepts"). After you click Print, this document is someone else's problem, and you never need to get involved in the nuts-and-bolts of what happens next.

But let's return to one of our previous examples. It's 5 p.m. You can't leave the office until you print a two-page memo. But when you walk to the printer you share with the rest of the floor, you see nothing but C. Estes Kefauver Middle School Presents: *Death Of A Salesman!* A New Musical Revue By Mr. Earls and Mrs. Troiani. Page after page after *page* of it, with no end in sight.

Sometimes it's *you* who messed up your life by giving your printer a ton of documents to print all at once. But a consistent theme of this book is that I'm on *your* side, so I'd much rather build a mythical outside evil influence that's out to get you.

Time to open the Printer Setup Utility and learn about what happens after you click Print. What actually happens is that your document is placed in something called a *print queue*, which is a list of all the printing jobs lined up for the printer to service. Fortunately, it's possible to see how many jobs are ahead of you, temporarily suspend a job that's in progress, or kill it altogether.

▼ Note

But you can only manipulate the queue if you're actually at the keyboard of the actual Mac that the actual printer is actually plugged into. This is a good thing. If anyone anywhere could instantly pop his or her print job to the top of the list, well, you'd have a *Lord of the Flies* situation on your hands in no time flat.

Accessing the print queue

Each printer that you have configured for OS X has its own print queue. There are several ways to reach it:

- **The Printer Setup Utility:** Launch Printer Setup Utility from the Utilities folder. When the application window appears, double-click the name of the printer whose queue you want to manage.

- **The printer's icon:** If printing is in progress, click the printer's icon in the Dock.

- **The Desktop printer icon:** If you have a Desktop printer icon, double-click the icon.

Regardless of how you reach the print queue, you see something like Figure 10-22.

Canceling a print job

You can cancel a print job that is currently printing or one that is waiting in the queue:

1. **Click the job in the print queue window.** See the previous section to access the window.

2. **Click Delete in the window's toolbar.**

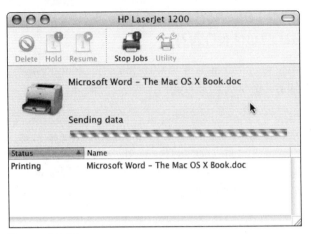

Figure 10-22
A print queue window with one job

Canceling a job that is being printed doesn't always work the way you would expect. It stops the printing of those pages that haven't been sent to the printer only. If part of a document has been transmitted and is in the printer's memory, the only way to stop those pages from printing is to turn off or reset the printer.

Suspending and resuming a print job

If you want to postpone a print job, temporarily preventing it from printing:

1. **Click the job in the print queue window.**

2. **Click Hold.** OS X places the job at the bottom of the print queue and does not send it to the printer.

To make a postponed print job active again:

1. **Click the job in the print queue window.**

2. **Click Resume.** OS X makes the job active again and places it at the end of the other active jobs in the print queue.

Starting and stopping the print queue

You can stop (and restart) all the jobs in a print queue at once. To do so:

1. **Open the print queue window for the printer whose print queue you want to stop.**

2. **Click the Stop Jobs button in the toolbar.** When you have stopped the print queue, the Stop Jobs button changes to read Start Jobs. You can restart the queue by clicking the Start Jobs button (which, as you would expect, then changes back to read Stop Jobs).

▼ Note

Printers continue to appear in the Print dialog even when their print queues have been stopped. They appear even if the actual printer isn't actually available, either. You can, for example, write a brilliant term paper inside a coffee shop on your PowerBook and Print it to your home printer, which obviously isn't there. Panther sticks the document into the printer's print queue, and as soon as you go home and plug your printer back in, bang, it prints right up.

Changing assigned printers

If you have more than one printer (a laser printer and a color inkjet, say) and you did something stupid like print an e-ticket to your color inkjet right while it's tied up printing a huge poster, you're not stuck waiting 3 hours for the poster to finish up. You can just drag the e-ticket's print job out of the inkjet's print queue and into the laser printer's queue provided the job hasn't been started yet.

Pooling printers

Which leads us to a rather ginchy feature called Pooling. If you have several printers, why should you have to wait at *all* for a document to print? It'd sure be keen if you could

have a special printer definition that says, "Look, I don't care *which* device prints this document; find a printer that's not doing anything and print it *immediately*."

Aren't you glad you own a Mac? Just create a Printer Pool.

1. **Open the Printer Setup Utility.** This opens a list of all available printers. If you don't see the list of available printers, press ⌘+L.

2. **Select all of the printers that you want to group together in the pool.** Use ⌘+click to make noncontiguous selections.

3. **Select Pool Printers under the Printers menu.** When you do so, you see Figure 10-23.

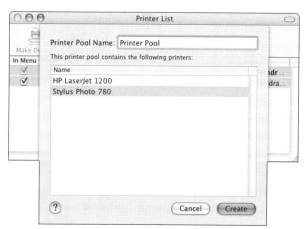

Figure 10-23
Making several printers act as one via a Printer Pool

4. **Determine the order of the Printer Pool:** At this point, you can choose the order in which these printers will receive jobs by dragging their names in the list. The printer at the top gets first crack. If it's busy, the job goes to the next on the list, and so on.

5. **Give the new pool a name, and click Create.**

BETTER KARMA THROUGH PRINT POOLING

Pooling printers is just good for morale. Remember: flattened tires, keyed and dinged door panels, the occasional load of Sak-Krete hardening in someone's front seat. Ensuring that people can print what they want when they want goes miles toward improving everyone's love for their fellow man, until someone goes into the break-room fridge and discovers that his or her yogurt is missing, even though it was *labeled* and everything. Then, boy, find a doorframe to stand under because the earth's gonna start moving. But at least it wasn't the printer's fault this time.

And that's it. The new pool appears in Print dialogs as if it were another printer. You can still use these pooled printers individually.

Pooling printers is a great idea for busy offices with heavy printing demands. You can spend megabucks on a high-speed, high-volume printer — or you can just buy four or five cheaper ones and pool them together. This means that when *one* printer breaks, jams, or runs out of toner, it won't cripple the office's whole ability to print stuff. Another dollar goes into Apple's tip jar for this one.

FAXING

This may seem like a strange place to discuss sending faxes, but sending a fax is really just another form of printing. You print to a fax modem, which acts just like a printer with its own job queue. (And we're covering receiving faxes here because it makes sense to keep sending and receiving together in the book!)

▼ Note

No, actually, it *doesn't* make sense to discuss faxing here. Here, meaning in a book about computers written in the Miraculous Pushbutton World Of Tomorrow. Bad *enough* that I'm still encouraging you folks to actually (brrrr) *print* stuff.

By now, faxing just seems so...well, *quaint*. Faxing a document — as opposed to emailing it — seems like churning your own butter or meeting your future bride without the help of a Web site directory of lonely, single Russian women. Like I said: *quaint*.

Sending a fax

To send a fax:

1. **Make sure that your computer's modem is connected to a telephone line.**

▼ Note

You don't need to set up the modem to send or receive a fax, nor do you need an ISP. All you need is the phone number of the fax machine you want to call.

2. **Prepare the document you are going to fax.** Make sure the naughty cartoon you've included on Page 4 won't lead to any unfortunate actions, that sort of thing.

3. **Select File ➜ Print or press ⌘+P.** This opens the Print dialog.

4. **Click Fax at the bottom of the Print dialog.** The Fax dialog appears (Figure 10-24).

5. **Type the number of the fax machine you are calling in the To text field.**

6. **Type a subject for the fax in the Subject text field.**

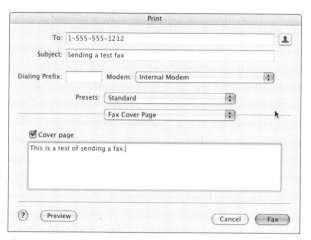

Figure 10-24
Entering information for sending a fax

7. **Type a prefix.** If your phone system requires a dialing prefix (for example, a 9 to reach an outside line), type that prefix in the Dialing Prefix text field.

8. **Select a modem.** If you are using a modem other than your computer's internal modem, choose the modem from the Modem pop-up menu.

9. **Click the Cover page option.** If you want a cover page, click the Cover page option and type the text for the cover page in the text field below the check box.

10. **Click Fax.** This sends the fax. The modem then appears in the Dock just as if it were a printer. You can open the modem's window to view the fax queue, view the status of faxes, and manage the fax queue, just as you would manage a print queue.

▼ Note

All of the printing features we've already covered can also help you out in the Fax department. Layouts, page ranges, the whole whack. Here, though, the Schedule option is of particular interest. If you're sending 30 pages to Beijing, you probably want to make that international phone call at 1:38 a.m., when it'll cost you a mere fortune, instead of a caliph's ransom.

Receiving a fax

Receiving a fax is only a bit more involved than sending. You don't need to do any special configuration of your hardware, but you do need to tell the computer to answer incoming telephone calls:

1. **Launch System Preferences.**

2. **Click the Print & Fax icon.** This displays the Print & Fax preferences panel (see Figure 10-25).

3. **If necessary, click the Fax button.** This displays the Fax pane.

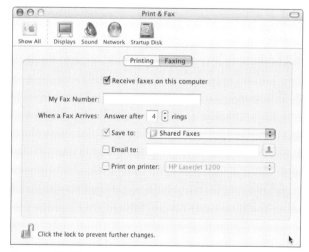

Figure 10-25
Setting up OS X to receive faxes

4. **Click the Receive faxes on this computer option.**

5. **Type the telephone number at which you receive faxes in the My Fax Number text field.**

6. **Type the number of rings after which the modem should answer in the Answer after text field.**

7. **Decide what to do with the incoming fax by selecting an option:**

   ▫ **Save to:** This saves the fax as a file. Use the pop-up menu to identify the folder in which you want fax files saved.

   ▫ **Email to:** Click this option and type an email address to email the fax file automatically.

   ▫ **Print on printer:** Click the Print on printer option and select a printer from the associated pop-up menu to print the fax automatically.

Okay, so we've done printing now. The principles I'm willing to bend for the sake of you kids...

The (surprising, shocking, temporary suspension of ennui-inducing...pick one) fact is that I'm not totally kidding when I say that print is dead. I have three printers here in my home office, including a really spiffy high-volume 1200 dpi laser printer and a professional-grade photo printer. And I've just leaned back and sipped thoughtfully at my Dr. Pepper and blinked a lot of times and then leaned forward again and misjudged where the edge of my mousepad was and accidentally set the can back down on an edge. It spilled onto the keyboard, and I shouted a whole bunch of words that my goldfish didn't approve of and frantically started dabbing at the keyboard with the tail of my MacHack 23 tee shirt but forget it, that keyboard was toast. So I looked through my closet and found another one and replaced the ruined one and now I've quite forgotten where I was going with this.

Oh, yeah. printing. Well, I can't remember the last time I actually printed something on *paper*. Perhaps I should try it sometime. It'll give me a good nostalgic sense of how Dickens used to write novels on *his* Macintosh way back in 1986, before the days of the Internet.

Networking on Copper, Air, and a Prayer

In This Chapter

The Wired Part: Cables, Hubs, and Switches • The Wireless Part: AirPort and Base Stations
Cable Modems and DSL Modems • Modems: The Adorably Quaint Way to Connect
Dialing and Connecting • Antisocial Networking: Direct Mac-to-Mac Networks
FireWire Networking • Juggling Lots of Different Network Connections
Locational Guidance Counselor • Sharing Your Internet Connection • Bluetooth

When we talk about networking, we're talking about two things: connecting computers to each other and connecting computers to the Internet. And when we say "connecting," some parts of your network connect to each other through physical cables that tether machines together like some Fritz Lang version of an assault on Mount Everest. Some parts accomplish the same exact things with radio waves, through wireless cards built into your Macs that talk to each other and to a base station that plugs into your wired network.

Simple. But if Truth-In-Marketing laws in this country had real teeth, every time you bought a new computer and tried to make it work with a network, you'd launch a setup program and see this (Figure 11-1):

Because that's the way networking tends to work. Either you click a few buttons and it works flawlessly, or you do everything the right way and you *still* can't connect to the Internet. Either way, you're dealing with some complex mojo and for all you know, the whole system works because Tinkerbell owed Murray, the Missing Car Keys Gnome, a favor.

WHAT ABOUT RENDEZVOUS?

I pitched a book about Rendezvous, Panther's built-in networking scheme that automatically finds and exploits the resources of other Macs and bits of hardware on a network and makes them available to you. It'd be the easiest $300 I ever made; one page containing the sentence I just wrote, then three or four hundred pages of musings about the reasons why NASA beat the Russians to the moon.

So this is a chapter on networking. Why is there no section on Rendezvous? Because it works on its own and there's nothing to discuss. Look around through Panther: Rendezvous doesn't have its own helper app or its own System Preferences pane or its own *anything*. It's the epitome of how technology is *supposed* to function. All users know is that in iTunes they can click on other music libraries across the network and play albums remotely. When they open up iChat inside a lecture hall, any Mac user within AirPort suddenly is available for communication.

Teach Rendezvous? To explain it is to not understand it, littlegrasshopper, for to understand Rendezvous is to merely trust and accept it. Rendezvous is like Batman. It's a force of good that lurks everywhere unseen, emerging only to kick some serious butt and then withdraw once again to the shadows of legend.

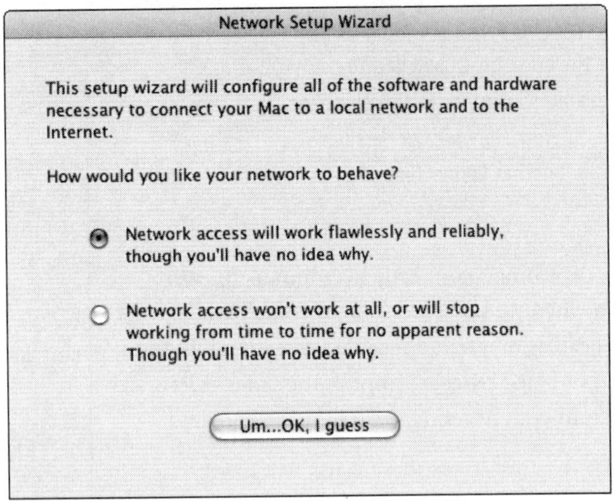

Network Setup Wizard

This setup wizard will configure all of the software and hardware necessary to connect your Mac to a local network and to the Internet.

How would you like your network to behave?

- ⦿ Network access will work flawlessly and reliably, though you'll have no idea why.

- ○ Network access won't work at all, or will stop working from time to time for no apparent reason. Though you'll have no idea why.

(Um...OK, I guess)

Figure 11-1
Telling it like it is

So networking can be intimidating. Even to me — and I'm the guy who once tried to access file servers through the infrared features of his Casio digital watch. (And it would have worked, too, except I was really quite exceptionally drunk at the time. Rum is that most subtle and seductive of liars, kids; never forget that.)

Fortunately, networking under Panther is actually as simple as things can get. It's one of those rare operating systems where you really *can* just run the installation wizard program, close your eyes, commend your soul to God, and have faith that everything will work out pretty well in the end. Even the advanced features that make networking — do I dare say it? — actively and passionately *cool* are easy to take advantage of.

THE WIRED PART: CABLES, HUBS, AND SWITCHES

Step One of networking your Mac is to physically connect it to your network. Yes, I know, how disgustingly analog. Newsreels from the '30s promised that by 1982 we'd have robots that would string network cables across our offices for us, but keep in mind that the culture that made that promise also told us that it was possible to feed and clothe a family of four on a salary of $1,300 a year. So we're talking about some pretty big idiots here.

FAST, FASTER, AND FASTEST ETHERNET

Speed is the other thing to consider when you're standing there in the office superstore and wondering just how much you really want to spend. Every few years, the industry kept coming up with new ways to shoot data across Ethernet cables at faster speeds. Originally, Ethernet moved at 10 million bits per second. That sounded grandma-ish to some people, so new network hardware was developed that worked at a hundred megabits. Modern Macs ship with gigabit Ethernet, which is another order of magnitude zippier. At this writing, 10GB Ethernet is on the horizon.

All you need to know is that Ethernet is Ethernet. When a machine with an older Ethernet interface swaps data with a new machine, the faster machine downshifts to match the slower speed. No sweat. But if you bought a cheap 10MB switch to network all those gigabit Macs together — congratulations: you saved yourself $20 — but your network is a hundred times slower than it needs to be. Word to the wise.

Incidentally, while 100MB Ethernet is technically referred to as fast Ethernet, this is much like making a reference to color television. It instantly dates you. The younger, cooler people will bounce you right out of the dance club, fake tattoos and all, while hails of "Narc!" rain all around you. Avoid.

Every Macintosh that isn't either inflatable or made out of marzipan comes with a built-in Ethernet port. Ethernet is the international standard for getting hardware to talk to each other over copper wire, and at this level it refers both to the standards for the hardware and the cables and the standards for slurping digital information across it.

On the hardware side, an Ethernet port looks like a phone jack with a pituitary disorder. Plugging in cables is as easy as unpacking your new answering machine, without all the fuss and bother of finding a way to sing an outgoing message to the theme song from *Silver Spoons*. So, if you have three Macs plus a cable modem that give you a high-speed connection to the Internet and you want to network them together with Ethernet cable, you just connect their ports together and bang...instant network, right?

Alas, no. You old-timers who got to see *Pulp Fiction* in an actual movie theater probably remember AppleTalk, the Mac's early networking standard. Ethernet kicks AppleTalk's butt so no big loss there, but one of the keen things about the old way was that its networking boxes had two jacks. You could just daisy-chain Macs together — networking cable goes in one jack, a second cable runs from the second jack onward to the next machine. No such luck with Ethernet.

Instead, you use external devices called *hubs*. An Ethernet hub acts just like your USB or FireWire hub. It splits a single connection into several. A typical hub (and by typical I mean "$100 buys you this hub, a DVD of the latest Pixar movie, plus dinner and a movie if you're a cheap date") allows you to connect four computers together, though the more expensive ones have more jacks.

A simple hub is adequate for the needs of nearly anyone who wants to get his or her networking advice from a book instead of a consultant who went to school for this sort of garbage. But if you want to spend a little more dough, you can do a little better by buying a *switch* instead. A hub is a dumb device that (more or less) just takes all the cables that are plugged into it and mashes them all together. All of the traffic on this part of the network becomes a single, thick stew, so when one Mac is generating a huge amount of chatter, it slows down everyone who's using the network.

But a switch is slicker and more sophisticated. If your Macs are networked together through a switch, data can move directly from Mac A to Mac B without becoming part of the stew. The upshot is that when you connect to another Mac's hard drive over the network and copy 20 megabytes of photos, it doesn't matter that your son D'Artagnian is using the same network to watch an *incredibly* educational bit of streaming video via the Internet at the same time. That scenario would choke a hub, but a switch silently creates separate connections. Mac A talks directly to Mac B; Mac C talks directly to your cable modem; and if any of these users are experiencing unhappiness in life, network-related speed hits aren't a large contributor.

To actually set up a wired network, just plug everything together through the hub or the switch. You don't need to shut down all your hardware first, though your Macs and any other gear probably won't be able to see each other until you do.

THE WIRELESS PART: AIRPORT AND BASE STATIONS

There are times when I must acknowledge that not all people share my unique viewpoints regarding interior design and see dozens of thick, multicolored Ethernet cables snaking in and out of every room as something less than a sign that this home is owned by a true forward-thinker.

Well, it takes all kinds to make a world, I suppose. Enter wireless Ethernet, in which a doohickey projects a bubble of network access around itself.

▼ **Note**

I say doohickey because it's a sturdy, satisfying word, and because although wireless Ethernet has become as popular as Diet Coke, the industry has yet to fall behind one single word for the aforementioned bubble-projecting device. Some folks call it a base station; some call it an access point. They mean the same thing, but I'll stick with base station from here on out.

Any computer — a Mac, a Windows machine, even a PDA — inside this bubble can potentially find and communicate with this base station, provided that the computer's equipped with a wireless networking card. If so, it's golden. This wireless connection is as good as being connected to the network through copper. If you set up this base station as a connection to the Internet, it means you can be out in your backyard lifeguarding your houseguests Uma Thurman and Halle Berry as they frolic in the pool while you watch the live restart of the Iditarod dogsled race via streaming video. (It could *so* happen. *Shut up!*)

Apple was nice enough to be perhaps the very first major computer maker to fully embrace wireless Ethernet. The specification for wireless is an industry standard but it's saddled with a terrible name: 802.11b, later to be upgraded to 802.11g, a flavor that's completely compatible with the old standard but an order of magnitude faster. Seven syllables, including punctuation: That's not very Mac-like. So Apple adopted those standards but started calling them AirPort and AirPort Extreme.

Plugging a base station into your network is no more difficult than plugging in your Mac. If you're using your AirPort base to provide wireless access to broadband Internet, connect its Ethernet port to an Ethernet connector on your cable or DSL modem. If you're using it to provide access to your local wired network, plug it into an available connector on your hub or switch. AirPort Extreme base stations can easily accommodate both, with separate Ethernet jacks for both broadband and local-network connections. Plug it into AC power and the hardware end is over and done with.

But while hubs and switches are simple devices with no free will, under the hood a base station is actually a fairly sophisticated computer that needs to know what sort of world it's been born into. You'll need to run the AirPort Setup Assistant to spank the base station on its polycarbonate bottom and get it breathing oxygen instead of amniotic fluid (Figure 11-2).

BUT WIRELESS IS WIRELESS

Still, AirPort is based on those generic standards, so it isn't an Apple-only club. The AirPort card inside your Power-Book is as happy to talk to a third-party, no-name 802.11g base station as it is to talk to something slick and UFO-shaped with an Apple logo stamped on it. And when you prove how open-minded you are by actually allowing your Windows-user friends over to your house, the 802.11g cards in their notebooks can find and use your Airport base station just fine.

In light of all this, it bears mentioning that AirPort base stations can cost two or three times as much as a third-party model. Are they worth it? Well, they're a lot easier to install and set up, and they work more intimately with Mac OS X. You'll probably be happier with an AirPort. But if the price is out of reach, you can lead a rich, fulfilling life with a Linksys or D-Link 802.11g router, too.

Figure 11-2
Configuring an AirPort base station

The Setup Assistant not only sets up base stations, but also configures individual Macs to connect to networks wirelessly. The Assistant makes the process fairly automagic. In Figure 11-2, you start by describing how it should connect to the 'net.

- If it's going to use its built-in modem to establish a dial-up connection, you need to have an account with an ISP. The Assistant needs your account name, password, and the dial-up's phone number. You can get these from your ISP.

- If it's connected to a broadband modem (a cable or DSL modem), it needs to know if your service uses a system known as Point-to-Point Protocol Over Ethernet. With PPPoE, your Mac must activate connections to the Internet manually; this is why few broadband providers use it. It's likely that your broadband connection to the Internet is always active and uses a flavor of DHCP.

DHCP? Whuzzat?

Oh, it's a flippin' godsend, is what it is. I want you to put this book down, go out into the yard, turn east to face the rising sun, and say, "Thank you, o loving universe, for creating the Dynamic Host Configuration Protocol." I would specifically direct you to turn and face the home of the Dynamic Host Configuration Working Group of the Internet Engineering Task Force, but — like love and hope and all good things — they're everywhere.

DHCP is the reason why the Orwellian nightmare of getting networking hardware to actually do something useful is now a thing of the past. A hundred years ago, we had to make our own soap by killing animals for the fat and rendering it down. Now, we head to the drugstore and pick up a bar of Life Buoy. Similarly, adding a computer to a network or (for those who have already largely given up the last shreds of their faith in a kind and loving God) getting it to reliably connect to the Internet was a hugely complicated process of looking up and punching in endless series of network addresses, routing codes, name servers...I seem to remember at one point having to correctly guess the number of piña colada–flavored jellybeans in a 50-gallon aquarium, but I might just be misremembering.

DHCP changes all that. Your hardware and the network simply have a little chat and work out for themselves how they need to configure everything. And holy, dancing Zagnuts on a rotisserie...it actually works.

▼ Note

DHCP is, frankly, the reason why it's possible to discuss networking in a single chapter of a book instead of taking up an entire volume on the subject. Nearly all Internet service providers support DHCP. Nearly all hardware manufacturers support DHCP. Nearly all software publishers support it. Why? Because it's Human and it's Humane, and it's the difference between a product that people can actually install and use and a product that costs the manufacturer tens of thousands of dollars a month in tech support.

WHERE TO STICK IT

Many folks complain that they're not getting anywhere near the football field-sized range they've been promised. I hear ya. Every wall, floor, and ceiling between your Mac and the base station degrades the signal, so in a worst-case scenario (a clay brick wall separating the two) you'll be lucky to get 12 feet.

You can improve the base's broadcast penetration by plugging in an external antenna, but be prepared to move the base around to find a magical place and orientation that cures most ills. Remember that higher is better than lower, and mounting the base station vertically can often work wonders.

You'll notice that I'm not going to spend 50 pages lovingly explaining every possible way to configure a Mac for use on a network. It's because DHCP has collapsed all sensible advice down to two, and only two, states: (1) Check DHCP and let the devices configure themselves, and if DHCP isn't supported, then (2) contact your network administrator or broadband provider and ask them for the specific settings required to get your hardware running on his or her network.

But back to AirPort

Once you click Continue in the Setup Assistant in Figure 11-2, you're asked to give some information (Figure 11-3):

- **Network Name:** You'll need to give this base station a name. This name will apply to this specific piece of hardware.

- **Wireless Security:** You'll also need to name your new wireless network.

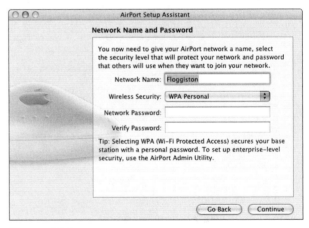

Figure 11-3
Naming your new wireless network and securing it from no-goodniks

SECURITY COUNTS

And yes, it's very, very easy for some weasel to pluck your email and password out of the air when a base station is not secure. There's actually software you can run on a wireless-enabled computer that simply waits patiently and builds a list of passwords and account names it spots in the wireless data stream. This isn't James Bond stuff; it's a free download from just about anywhere.

In some situations, you want your base to be wide-open. If you're running a coffee shop and are using free broadband access as a way of pulling in customers, you don't want your put-upon serving staff to have to spend 10 minutes coaching a Mocchalito and Scone through the sign-on process. But otherwise, you want to protect your base behind an encryption scheme and a password.

▼ Note

It's possible to have many base stations and many separate networks. I happen to have two; one base station is set up to have little or no security and is a snap for visitors to access. The second is tightly protected and also allows access to my private home network. So choose network names carefully.

○ **Network Password:** Speaking of protection, you also need to choose a method of securing the signal, both to prevent some schmo in a Hyundai from parking outside your house and exploiting your connection to the Internet, and also to ensure that this same schmo can't pluck your email and passwords out of the air.

Fortunately, your Mac can remember AirPort passwords automatically; so for *you,* the honest, authorized user of your network, you'll never notice the added

security. Turn to Chapter 16 for other AirPort security tips.

You'll also be asked to create a separate password for maintaining the AirPort base station. Without it, any weasel could run their own copy of the AirPort Admin Utility and turn off your base's security features. That's no good. When you've completed the setup process, AirPort Setup Assistant uploads all of your settings to the base station and causes the base to restart itself.

Using the Setup Assistant to configure your Mac to join AirPort networks is actually pretty anticlimactic. All of the necessary software is already built in, and the only thing the Assistant really does is tell your Mac that you're really quite fond of this particular base station and would like to use it to access the network. It's nothing that can't be done through the AirPort menulet.

Connecting to an AirPort network

When you connect all those Macs together using Ethernet, the network exists without having to explicitly tell any of this gear that they are now part of a network. There are really no settings to manage, so there's nothing to set and adjust.

AirPort's different. Panther puts an AirPort icon in the menu bar (Figure 11-4).

This menu is workin' for me even when I haven't pulled it down. The icon in the menu bar tells me that I'm currently connected to some sort of AirPort network and that the strength of the radio signal is pretty good; three of the icon's four bars are darkened in, which is about as strong a signal as you can expect without actually holding the base station between your knees as you type. When no base stations are in range, the entire indicator is gray.

Figure 11-4
The AirPort menu

The menu gives you access to a bunch of handy options:

- **Turn AirPort Off.** Turning off your Mac's internal AirPort interface is like physically disconnecting an Ethernet cable. It gives you a little extra assurance that no one can see (and possibly exploit) your Mac.

▼ Note

If you're using a PowerBook, turning off AirPort when you're not using it also extends the charge in your battery. Keeping a radio transmitter/receiver running burns energy, after all.

- **Choose available AirPort networks.** Panther lists all of the different AirPort networks it can see inside that second section. Here, we can only see my home wireless network, Floggiston. If you visited my house, you could use Floggiston just by selecting it from the menu and then (if it's a secure network) entering a password. But in truth, there's a second network in my office named Iron Monkey. But I don't make that one public. To access that AirPort network, you need to use the next menu item,

- **Other.** The fact that wireless base stations broadcast their names to the world is actually a feature; otherwise, how would people know that they existed and are available? But sometimes you don't want folks to even try to connect to your base station. If you've set up a closed network, the base is invisible unless you

know its name. If you select Other from the menu you're presented with the dialog shown in Figure 11-5. As you can see, I have to provide the network's name and password before I'm given access:

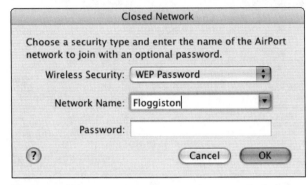

Figure 11-5
Joining a closed network

- **Create Network.** The next option is really pretty special. All along, we've assumed that only an AirPort base station can anchor and establish a wireless network. Well, your Macintosh is a pretty decent piece of hardware on its own, and by clicking Create Network, you can establish a brand-new wireless network using your Mac as a virtual base station (Figure 11-6):

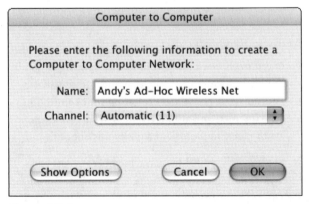

Figure 11-6
Creating an ad hoc AirPort network using your Mac as a base station

1. **Just give it a name.** Clicking the Show Options button allows you to encrypt the signal and password-protect your new network in precisely the same way you'd protect a real base station.

2. **Click OK.** Your Mac now appears in the AirPort menus of any nearby wireless-studly Macs. It's really that simple.

▼ Note

This feature alone is probably responsible for 11 percent of all corporate sales of AirPort-equipped Macs. Why, just 5 years ago if your boss called an all-staff meeting and crowded 30 of you into a conference room to watch a weapons-grade 3-hour PowerPoint presentation on Synergy and Commitment and Excellence, the only dignified way to endure it would be to fake some sort of seizure and hope that someone seizes upon the opportunity and carries you out. Today, though, you silently create an ad hoc network, let your friends in the room find it, open up iChat, and spend the rest of the session making fun of the speaker's tie.

○ **Interference Robustness**. The last item in the menu, this is a (hopeful) solution to living in a cramped environment in which lots of radio devices (like cordless phones and microwave ovens) shriek like harpies all through the day or night, making it difficult to maintain a solid connection between your Mac and the base station. It'll cost you a little in terms of performance, but it gives you a boost in reliability.

CABLE MODEMS AND DSL MODEMS

Fortunately, you're paying people to install this hardware for you. They come right in, drill holes through your hardwood floors, help themselves to whatever looks good in the fridge, and leave behind a box the size of a paperback book with lots of blinking lights on it.

Whether you go with a cable modem or a DSL connection, the actual hookup is simple:

1. **The modem sports an Ethernet connector. Connect this to your Ethernet hub, your Ethernet switch, or your AirPort base station.**

2. **Install the appropriate software.** Your service provider might have also given you a CD-ROM with its own installation wizard. This disc will install whatever special software your Mac requires to access the Internet via this modem, or at the very least it automates the creation of special profiles that make it easier to switch from this new broadband connection to your existing connection and back again.

3. **Restart your Macs or your base station.** DHCP kicks in and each device directly connected to the modem negotiates with it, agreeing on the proper settings for peace, brotherhood, harmony, and access to ESPN.com's live coverage of major-league baseball.

4. **Verify the connect.** After the restart, verify that the connection is working by opening Safari and pulling up Google.com's search page. If it doesn't come up, the problem can probably be traced to one of two causes:

   ▫ **The new cable/DSL modem hasn't found the service provider yet.** It will. Keep it powered up for a half an hour or so. If there's still no joy, call the company up and holler blue murder.

   ▫ **Somewhere in the daisy chain between your Mac and your service provider, a device hasn't negotiated its connection to the device that represents the next step closer to the Internet.** Start downstream with your Mac. Restart it. No joy? Restart your AirPort base station if you have one (I just pull out its power plug for a few seconds). No? Restart the broadband modem. If you're still getting nothing, then it's time for more blue murder.

▼ Tip

This is just good general advice. Not the yelling; the idea that you should restart devices in a downstream-to-upstream order when an Internet connection goes bye-bye. Though a good holler at someone who doesn't know you, never did anything to you personally, and isn't responsible for your current predicament, can occasionally be quite cleansing.

MODEMS: THE ADORABLY QUAINT WAY TO CONNECT

Well, we've spent enough time on fancy, useful, high-speed networks. Now we should move onto that most venerable and (unfortunately) useful method of connecting to the Internet: dialing in through a modem.

And before you sniff at this, reflect upon the fact that there are times when you're visiting your parents or staying at a beach house or have checked into a hotel where broadband access bills at $20 per day. I sure don't have the guts to spend 18 hours without checking my email. Maybe you're simply a better person than I am. I've seen what I look like when I dance so I suppose it's actually pretty likely.

Yes, after all these months of wireless high-speed broadband access to the Internet, I'm sure that getting your email at 56 Kbps after hearing a dial tone and a *whrshhrsh-hhskktktkt* of static seems like walking around your office in bare feet and no shirt...but doing it does serve to keep one humble.

You create a modem connection through the Network panel of System Preferences (Figure 11-7).

Figure 11-7
The Network panel of System Preferences

The Network panel is your dashboard for Panther's network connections, and we'll be coming back to it later. For now, click the pop-up menu next to Show: and select Internal Modem.

Unfortunately, there isn't anything nearly as slick as DHCP for dial-up connections, and you need to type in the connection settings manually. Hey, look; this is a *modem* connection. You're lucky you don't have to scoop data off of your hard drive with your bare hands and physically *carry* it over to the Internet.

Tip

And if you click Assist me, Panther walks you through the entire process step by step, via the Network Setup Assistant. But this is the *one* case where it's actually faster to plug in these settings yourself. The meat is all there in front of you, and you'll be off and running (or walking — again, this is a dial-up connection) toot sweet. But don't be a hero. Nobody's watching, so go ahead and use the assistant if you get confused.

Most dial-ups will use Panther's default settings for PPP, the industry-standard way to establish a dial-up Internet connection, and all you need to do is define the following specifics:

- **Account Name:** Your account name. If your email address on this dial-up is artcarney@queenssewers.com, your account name is *artcarney.*

- **Your password.** You can save this password with your configuration. Otherwise, you'll have to enter it every time you connect to the Internet, and isn't your life a big enough mess as it is?

- **A phone number and a backup phone number.** If you're doing some fancy stuff like dialing 9 to reach an outside line or a calling-card number, you might need to type in a fairly goat-chokingly-large number, but don't let it throw you. Just throw in a comma at every point where you'd like the modem to pause for a second. "9,,,7815551212" ensures that the modem will wait three seconds to give your phone system a chance to find an outside line before proceeding.

Tip

Incidentally, if you like to actually, you know, *connect* to the Internet when you travel, it's a good idea to make sure you don't leave home without downloading a list of all of your dial-up ISP's local access numbers. When I head off to a city for the first time, I visit Earthlink's Web site, ask for a complete list of access numbers, and then use Panther's Print To PDF feature to turn that list into a file I can read offline whenever I want. It is at times humbling to discover that you flew 3,000 miles and only after checking into the hotel realized that Earthlink's online database of access numbers isn't technically going to be available to you until you actually manage to get onto the Internet, you know?

Some dial-ups require some special massaging with customized settings, accessible through the PPP Options... button and the TCP/IP tab. Get in touch with your ISP and get a list of the proper settings, and as with anything you do while setting up a Network connection, don't even think of messing around with these settings unless specifically directed to.

Click Apply Now and your new modem configuration is good to go.

DIALING AND CONNECTING

You use the Internet Connect application to actually dial out and establish a connection to the Internet. You'll find it in the Applications folder (Figure 11-8).

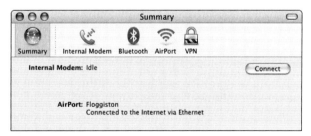

Figure 11-8

Click, bzzz, dial, shriek, connect; dialing with Internet Connect

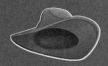

MORE ON INTERNET CONNECT

In the high-schoolish social structure of Panther, Internet Connect is one of the Goths who always eat together and alone in the cafeteria. That is, it's useful and interesting, but people just don't feel a need to interact with it.

The purpose of this app is to show you your connection to the Internet and, in the case of connections that aren't always on, to let you connect and disconnect at will. You'll see that every different method of connecting to the 'net is represented by a different icon in the toolbar. But access to the Internet and access to your local network have been mainstreamed together, so there's no psychological need to keep checking in on your connection to the outside world. And while naturally you're going to want to dial the modem if you're stuck with a dial-up connection, and see how well your AirPort connection is doing, Apple's smart enough to know that you'll prefer to access that hardware through dedicated icons on the menu bar, not by launching a separate app.

So in truth, Internet Connect is actually irrelevant for most people. Goth chicks are cute, and if you compliment them on their Morpheus tattoo they'll read you some of their poetry, plus they're human beings who contribute their own unique spice to human society. But if you never actually interact with Internet Connect, you're not missing much.

Click Connect to start things going. The window updates with status messages to annoy you about the connection-in-progress, and once you're online, it'll be replaced with a clock showing you the amount of time you've been connected. The Connect button changes to Disconnect, and clicking it does more or less what y'all think it does.

Clicking the Internal Modem button in the toolbar opens a more detailed status panel (Figure 11-9).

If you've defined several different modem configurations (for example, you have more than one dial-up ISP) you can switch between them through the Configuration pop-up. It's also a handy spot to temporarily add stuff to the phone number, such as when you find yourself in one of those fascist offices where the ruling class forces the proletariat to dial 9 to get an outside line.

Figure 11-9
More details about your modem connection

The handy bit about the Internal Modem status panel is that it offers you a check box for adding a Modem menu to the menu bar. You're gonna want this. It's as handy as the AirPort menulet, allowing you to check on your modem status at a glance and to connect and disconnect at will (Figure 11-10).

Figure 11-10
The Modem menu

ANTISOCIAL NETWORKING: DIRECT MAC-TO-MAC NETWORKS

It seems like it'd be hopelessly missing the point to create a network of two Macs. Networks are all about openness and shared resources and community; essentially you're saying it's you and this guy, and the rest of the world can go hang itself. It's totally a Whitney Houston/Bobby Brown sort of thing.

Still, networking two and only two Macs together is terribly handy. I usually refer to this as Airplane Networking as opposed to AirPort Networking; networking two Macs together directly is great for when you and a friend are on a 6-hour flight and want to play network games right there in Row 19.

It's called a direct network because it's done by simply connecting the Macs' two ports together with a cable. No hub, no base stations, no larger infrastructure. Just a guy and a

THE OYMANDIAS OF THE CABLING INDUSTRY

Not so fast, Skeezix. Patching two Ethernet ports together with a plain cable works if you have a new-ish Mac, say, one that was manufactured during the George Dubbya Bush administration or later. A direct two-computer Ethernet network *used* to require a special flavor of cable called a crossover cable. A couple of the connectors were switched around and it allowed the manufacturer to charge an extra seven bucks for what to the naked eye was a plain, $5 cable. But this method of networking proved so handy that Apple just went ahead and made its Ethernet ports smart enough to detect when they were directly connected to another machine and make the necessary adjustments automagically. This crippled the crossover cable industry, but in this modern, global economy you have to look at the big picture. Compassion, a sign of weakness in our nation's youth, just slows down the March of Progress and is to be discouraged.

girl fragging each other on a Boeing 727 somewhere over Iowa. It's a natural and a beautiful thing, and it couldn't be simpler to create; just take an Ethernet cable and connect the two network ports together. Depending on what your Macs have been up to lately, you might need to restart, but there's nothing to configure or install.

FIREWIRE NETWORKING

"Blasphemer!" you cry. "And what's the deal with that *hair?*" you add, which, frankly, is unnecessarily hurtful.

Your FireWire port is chiefly there to connect high-speed peripherals like video cameras and external hard drives, but heck, son...it's a high-speed port! No reason why we can't use it for networkin'!

FireWire networking is fairly obscure and it's sufficiently "out there" that when I tell people that such a thing is possible, the scene is fairly evocative of the time when Copernicus made his dramatic and revolutionary announcement that man had evolved from apes and to prove it, he intended to sail three ships to the so-called edge of the world.

"But why bother?" you might ask. The Top Three Reasons:

- **A FireWire cable is a lot smaller than an Ethernet cable and it has no little plastic bits that might snap off in my carry-on bag.** So as an emergency, "I desperately need to create a two-machine network" solution; it's way better than Ethernet. I'm almost certain to have the right cable with me, and it's certain to be in working order.

- **Yes, if you want to mount another Mac's internal drive on your Desktop you can simply connect the FireWire ports and use Target Disk Mode.** This saves you from having to set up FireWire networking on both Macs and doing all the steps necessary to mount it as a remote network volume. But remember that Target Disk Mode requires that you shut down and restart the target Mac, which can often mean wasting 10 or 15 minutes shutting down apps and saving documents. FireWire networking gives you all the speed of Target Disk Mode without the shutdown, and the second Mac continues to act like a Mac with a keyboard and a mouse and windows and junk and everything, not like an external hard drive. So your sweetie can still mess around on the Internet while you're copying that 10-gigabyte iPhoto library.

- **It's just cooler.**

The only hitch here is that — unlike direct Ethernet networking — Panther doesn't automatically look at FireWire and think, "Here we have a connection to a network." So you have to configure it:

1. **Open the Network pane of System Preferences.**

2. **From the Show pop-up menu, select Network Port Configurations.** You'll be shown all of the network connections that Panther is currently aware of (Figure 11-11).

Figure 11-11
Port Configurations: All of Panther's connections to other machines

3. **Click the New button to create a new port configuration.** A sheet drops down (Figure 11-12).

4. **Select Built-in FireWire from the Port pop-up and give your new configuration a likely name.** Click OK.

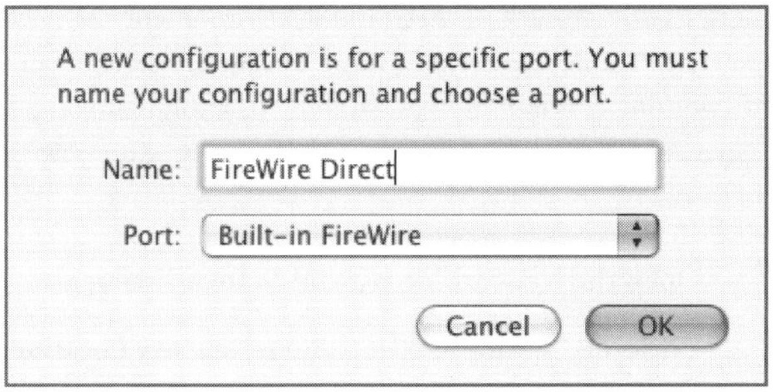

A new configuration is for a specific port. You must name your configuration and choose a port.

Name: FireWire Direct

Port: Built-in FireWire

Cancel   OK

Figure 11-12
Adding a network configuration for your FireWire port

The new configuration now appears in that list of active and useful network ports and is ready to use. No restart is necessary. Just connect the two Macs' FireWire ports together with any FireWire cable and you're good to go...after you make sure that Panther looks to FireWire *first* every time it needs to get a network connection. Which seems like a cue for a transition to a new topic. Hang on, I think I need to put new batteries in the New Section-O-Matic...

JUGGLING LOTS OF DIFFERENT NETWORK CONNECTIONS

Networking is a prime area in which Panther does a stellar job of taking an incredibly tortuous and highly technical subject and eliminating as much of the mental clutter as possible. By skillfully using such distracting verbiage as comparing a form of networking to one of the most troubled celebrity marriages since James Brown married...well, about anybody, really. You've learned about how your Mac can have several different connections to the Internet (AirPort, cable modem, dial-up modem) and even several different methods of establishing a physical network connection in the first place (Ethernet port, Airport, FireWire).

So why aren't you worried about having to juggle all of these different methods and ports? Two reasons: That Whitney and Bobby line was really pretty good; honestly, I'm pretty happy with it. Plus, Panther manages all that stuff for you.

It's called *autohoming* and it's like this: Panther knows all the different ways it can connect to a network, and if one fails, it'll just try another. So there's never any need to specifically say, "Dude, alas the AirPort connection we all enjoyed back at the house is no more; a phone jack is all that lies between this Macintosh and insanity."

If you want to manage these connections manually, open the Network panel of System Preferences and select Network Port Configurations from the Show pop-up (figure 11-13).

Figure 11-13
Changing the pecking order of network configurations

That's a list of networking schemes and the order in which Panther tries to use them. If you're there in Seat 11-A and you've just linked to the FireWire port of your companion in Seat 11-B for a little network game play, you can tell Panther that FireWire is now your number one method of networking by just clicking and dragging FireWire Direct (or whatever you named it when you configured the port) to the top of the list.

It's also a handy way to temporarily disable a port entirely. Deselecting Built-in Ethernet effectively renders your Mac deaf and mute on that port.

LOCATIONAL GUIDANCE COUNSELOR

Of course, you have no idea of what a fool's paradise you're now living in. Your Mac is new, you're configuring it for the first time, everything is pretty much out of the box and minty fresh, assuming that you were gargling mouthwash at the keyboard, read something particularly amusing on a Web site, and sputtered Scope all over your screen, in which case you have much bigger problems on your hands right now.

When you're at home, you have a dial-up connection. When you're at the office, you connect to a server through direct Ethernet. When you're at a branch office, you connect to the main office through a Virtual Private Network. You make plenty of business trips to San Francisco, New York, Boston, and Wahoo, Nebraska, and in each of those places you connect to your dial-up ISP through a different local number. And let's not forget all the time you spend on airplanes blowing up the person seated next to you in your guise as a black-ops Navy SEAL.

Result: colossal hassle every time you move from one location to another. Panther's autohoming helps you out a little, but on the whole, you have to change oodles of

settings every time your networking environment changes. Not so: Panther allows you to save the current state of your networking configuration as a unique location that you can activate with one click. Here's how you create a new location:

1. **Open the Networking pane of System Preferences.**

2. **Click the Location pop-up and select New Location.**

3. **Type a name for your new location and click OK.**

And that's it. Your existing configuration is saved under this new name and you can activate it just by selecting it from the Location pop-up (Figure 11-14).

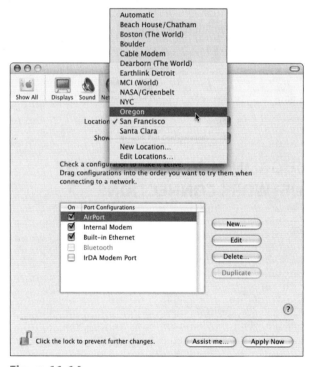

Figure 11-14
Switching settings snappily through lots of locations

Some people have an album of postcards or a shelf full of souvenir snow globes or a string of children all across the country to attest to their world travels. Me, I have a fat Location menu.

Locations are handy enough that you can also switch between them right from the Apple menu.

SHARING YOUR INTERNET CONNECTION

Workers! People! Throw down your tools! Then pick them up again and rise against the hated oppressors of the proletariat! Let us...let us...

Well, I'm not really up on my Commie revolutionary rhetoric. What I'm driving at is that when one individual has so much and the rest have so little, it's a sign of greatness that the former should spread the wealth with the latter. We've already covered ways that your Mac can share its files and printers with others, but how ginchy is it that you can share your Mac's Internet connection, too?

This is easier to demonstrate than to explain. Try these on for size:

- You and your three friends are sharing a beach house for the week. You're all technology-savvy forward thinkers, true warriors of the New Economy (read: geeks who would wet their Spiderman Underoos if they should — God forbid — go an afternoon without checking email). But there's only one phone line, which means that only one of you can dial into an ISP and grab your mail at a time. With Internet Sharing, you can establish a dial-up connection on your Power-Book and then it becomes available to anybody who can reach your PowerBook via AirPort.

- You and your sweetie are at a coffee shop with free wireless access. You have a top-of-the-line PowerBook with AirPort, but she has actual social skills and a good sense of proportion, so she just has a cheap iBook with no wireless at all. You can create a two-Mac network by connecting the two Mac's Ethernet or FireWire ports and then sharing your AirPort Internet connection with her.

IF YOU THINK TWENTY DOLLARS IS A REASONABLE CHARGE FOR A FEW HOURS OF INTERNET ACCESS, YOU NEED TO SWITCH TO A BETTER BRAND OF GIN

I like hotels that provide broadband but hate hotels that seem to think I'm a trust-fund idiot with my own reality-TV show and no perception of the value of a dollar. So if my friends and I are staying in a block of rooms in the same hotel, one of us will connect to the in-room Ethernet and share it with the rooms next door via AirPort.

Shady, yes. Possibly a violation of the hotel's policies. But when I start to feel guilty about it, I realize that for the same amount of money I'd be spending on Internet I access, I can go down to the megastore in Times Square and buy one new DVD for every night I spent here in New York City. Isn't it great to be able to talk your way out of almost any ethical problem?

And then there's the Shady Way To Use This, which I'm a little embarrassed about, and so I'll toss it into a sidebar.

As is typical for Panther networking, sharing your Internet connection is so simple as to be anticlimactic:

1. **Open the Sharing pane of System Preferences.**

2. **Click the Internet tab (Figure 11-15).** All of your available Internet connections are shown in the pop-up menu.

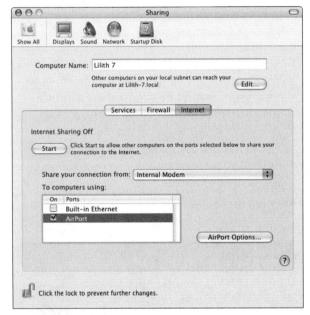

Figure 11-15
Sharing your Internet connection with other folks on your network

3. **Select your source this list.** You can share the Internet across all of your available network ports, or just some. Click the check boxes of all the ports across which you'd like to share the Internet. Any local computer that can reach your Mac through one of the selected ports can access the Internet.

4. **Click Start.**

In Figure 11-15, I've set up my Mac so that I'm connecting to the Internet through my internal modem and sharing the connection with all AirPort-equipped Macs nearby. Just as when you created an ad hoc AirPort network by clicking AirPort Options, you can encrypt the wireless signal and control access to the Internet via a password of your choosing.

▼ Note

But do understand that sometimes, sharing an Internet connection can violate the terms of your agreement with your Internet service provider. Furthermore, when your Mac shares its Internet connection, it works some minor mojo that might temporarily confuse your broadband connection. Nothing permanent, mind you, but it might be enough that you can't use your cable modem until you restart it, and you'll get a testy email from your broadband provider ordering you to knock it off and warning you not to do it again.

And that's really it. All of the examples I've cited happen to have been based on PowerBooks, but this feature will work on any Mac. Believe me, you haven't lived until you've seen a network of four top-of-the-line G5 Macs connected to the Internet through a PowerBook that has a measly cellular-phone dial-up connection. But when a hurricane has knocked out the phones and the broadband and *this* is the only way for an office to get a mission-critical report filed to the main office on time, well, you make do.

I often help out friends who are in a jam, but this was the first time that one was so moved by gratitude that he actually sent me a 14-pound honey-baked ham. Now, I help because I'm a kind, old-world soul, but still, me likes ham.

BLUETOOTH

Bluetooth is a weird name for a wireless networking technology, but if you ask me, it ought to have been called "Godot." When the standard was first proposed and published a few years ago, I — like any good American — couldn't *wait* for the technology to arrive.

Originally, Bluetooth was conceived as a way to eliminate cable clutter in the office. Instead of running a cable between your desktop Mac and your printer, both devices would have Bluetooth chipsets inside them. The Mac could "find" the printer there in the room on its own and start the waterfall of pages. If AirPort is a way of eliminating Ethernet cables, Bluetooth is a way of eliminating USB cables, whether you're connecting to printers, PDAs, or whatever. It's often called a "personal" networking standard because its range is only about 15 yards.

▼ Note

Any time you buy a wireless device (even a cordless phone or a walkie-talkie), please keep in mind that the folks who write the packaging are either (a) incorrigible liars and people of negligible moral fiber, or (b) immigrants from that one country where there are no mountains or valleys and no trees or buildings higher than 2 feet. Here in America, you'll find that most claims of broadcast range are off by a factor of two or three. I find that Bluetooth's maximum reliable range is about 10 feet.

The Bluetooth standard has some wonderful underlying architecture, which makes it far, far cooler than a simple cable replacement. Bluetooth-compatible devices are "discoverable," you see. Any device can "ask around" to see if a certain piece of hardware is within range. I mean, wow!!!

...You're not excited.

No, that's very kind of you, but there's no need to pretend. Okay, imagine this scenario: I'm at a yard sale and spot a big coffee mug shaped like the head of Chewbacca. The guy wants 50 bucks for it, which seems sort of steep. I unpocket my Bluetooth-equipped PDA so I can go on the Internet and look for more info about this item. As soon as I tap www.google.com into Pocket Internet Explorer, my PDA looks around and asks *Hey, are there any devices nearby that can connect me to the Internet?* And my Bluetooth cell phone says *Sure, I'm a phone with modem capabilities...what can I do for you?* The PDA gives it the phone number of my ISP and seconds later, I realize that I'm holding one of the first two *Star Wars* products George Lucas ever conceived, and that while 50 bucks wasn't out of line, I could probably haggle the price down a little.

It's cool because I didn't even have to take my phone out of my pocket. It was within my PDA's "bubble" of Bluetooth connectivity and that's all that mattered. There's no limit to the range of devices that Bluetooth can connect, either. My hands-free headset connects to my phone via Bluetooth, and the same device connects to my PowerBook just as easily. I have a Bluetooth Global Positioning System device. When it's on my car's dashboard, it communicates with a map program on my notebook and gives me directions to the state park. When I get there I dangle it off my backpack and it sends the same sort of positioning information to my PDA.

IT'S A PUSHBUTTON WORLD

I use the term "the Miraculous Pushbutton World Of Tomorrow" a lot and almost always in a snarky way. I just don't think that in this day and age I should be spending *this* much time flipping the bird at inanimate objects. But Bluetooth solutions like these are exactly the way I hoped and expected the Future to be. It's not a Jetsons-style folding hover car, but I bet the insurance on that sort of thing would be a bear.

So there are many, many categories of Bluetooth devices, and the procedures for getting each one to work with your Mac vary from product to product. Step One is almost always "pairing" the device. You don't want strangers to make your cell phone dial an ISP in Kyzyl just by sidling up next to you and tapping into their Bluetooth PDA, so as a security feature, two Bluetooth devices typically have to be formally introduced to each other at least once before they work together

There's a handy wizard for this: the Bluetooth Setup Assistant. You'll find it in your Applications folder, inside Utilities.

After blowing past the usual hello, welcome, isn't it lovely to be assisted, etc. startup screen, you need to tell the Assistant what sort of device you're setting up (Figure 11-16):

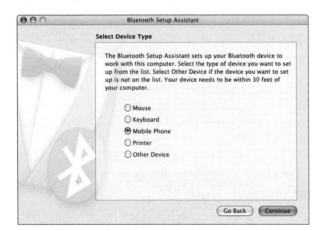

Figure 11-16
Pairing a device using the Bluetooth Setup Assistant

In this example, I'm setting up my Mac to work with my Bluetooth cell phone, but the basic pairing procedure is the same no matter what sort of gear you have. When I click Continue, the Mac starts sniffing the air for any Bluetooth device within the immediate vicinity that identifies itself as a cell phone. Before I do that, I have to make

sure that my phone's Bluetooth features have been turned on and that it's "discoverable." Bluetooth devices are often set up so that they don't respond to any hardware they haven't been formally paired with. It's another security feature. Check your device's manual to see how to activate Bluetooth and turn on discoverability.

Once I proceed, the Assistant looks around and assembles a list of all Bluetooth cell phones it can see. The device's product names appear in a list (Figure 11-17). Highlight the name of the device and click Continue.

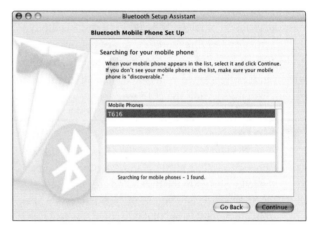

Figure 11-17
Selecting a phone

The device will (probably) chirp to catch your attention and tell you that this weirdo computer has asked to establish a partnership, but that it won't let that happen until you enter a passkey. The passkey is just a one-time deal to make sure that no one pairs themselves to your device without your approval. The necessary digits are generated at random by the Assistant and display in big, fat text (Figure 11-18):

Next, the Assistant asks the device what it's willing to bring to this relationship. Steady income? Good car? A relative with Red Sox season tickets, not farther away from home plate than Section LL? Or in the case of a cell phone: Does it have an address book? A calendar app? Can it serve as an Internet connection? The Assistant reports back with what it's found and offers you a list of options (Figure 11-19). Un-check any items you want to disable.

Figure 11-18
The Magic passkey that pairs your Mac to a device

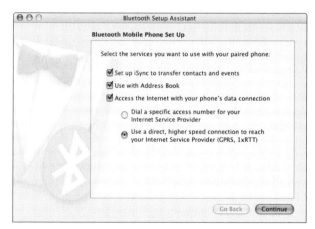

Figure 11-19
Enabling a Bluetooth phone's features

Because this example sets up a cell phone, you also have the option of setting up this phone so that the Internet Connect app can use it to connect to the Internet. You have two options:

- **Dial a specific access number**. If you use this option, the phone will act as a fairly ordinary modem. When you click "Continue," you'll be asked for much the same information you provided if you set up a modem connection through a conventional phone line: number, account name, password. Most cellphones can only support somewhat wretchedly low speeds as a modem, though...typically 9600 bps.

- **Use a direct, higher speed connection**. But if you have a modern cell phone with GPRS features — very likely, if it has Bluetooth — it's actually in contact with your wireless provider's data network to deliver all those email and live sports scores and streaming-media features. You get much higher speeds (typically two or three times faster than using your cell phone as a modem) and depending on your provider, you might still be able to take and receive calls while connected. You'll need a user name and password to access your provider's net, and an ID string to identify your hardware. Get these from your provider.

When you click Continue, you're done. The Assistant shows you a summary page that tells you what features have been enabled (Figure 20).

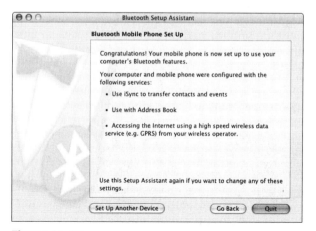

Figure 11-20
The Assistant's summary page

TRAPPED IN A SYNC-HOLE

In the past 2 years, I've gone from not having any sort of electronic address book — I kept one on my Newton MessagePad, but when Apple stopped supporting it, I couldn't find a PDA I liked nearly as much — to having my numbers and appointments on at least five devices: my phone, my PDA, my wristwatch, and my two iPods. It's a fine testament to the strength and power of iSync, but think hard before enabling *all* of a devices sync features. I can edit appointments on my phone *and* on my PDA, which short-circuits the whole point of iSync: It's possible for me to have three conflicting sets of appointments.

I could solve this problem by being a lot more disciplined and organized...or I can simply un-click my phone's iSync features. Which also means that the phone's built-in phone list only contains the 20 or 30 people I actually call on a regular basis, not all 832 people I've apparently swapped business cards and email addresses with in the past 7 months.

Your Mac and your device have been successfully paired. Would that it were that easy for us Humans.

My very first book was about networking. That was more than 10 years ago, and there was no mumbo, no jumbo, no hoodoo, no mojo, no incantation, spell, totem, spirit guide, supplication to Karma, jinx, or other bit of technical or superstitious arcana that went undocumented or uncommented.

Why? Well, there was nothing you *didn't* need to know back then. Networking was like industrial heating and cooling. Nothing about this area of technology was even remotely designed for easy installation or even casual use, and the desire to get a network up and running implied a concurrent desire to learn so much about the standards, protocols, and hardware that the only way to get the same final effect would be to fill your head with angry bees.

Boy, do I feel old today. Every time I went in to describe some sort of deep-mojo tweak or setting, I wound up deleting the paragraph as soon as I typed it. You really don't need to know about TCP header compression. It's all taken care of. Nearly anything you try to connect to anything else will automatically be configured via DHCP with very little intervention on your part.

What's more, when DHCP won't cut it or Panther's default settings can't handle it, you can do far more harm than good by trying to work out the problem on your own. When you're trying to connect to an ISP or a protected file server, for instance, there is no troubleshooting technique that is simpler or more effective than phoning or emailing the thing's administrator and saying, "I'm trying to connect from a Macintosh running Mac OS 10.3. What settings do I need to use?"

You're doing yourself a favor and you're doing the administrator a favor. Even if you managed to get it running on your own, chances are excellent that *something* is subtly messed up. Not so bad as to cause the connection to fail, but definitely bad enough that the connection is slow and unreliable. Meanwhile, at the other end of the connection, the administrator is cursing you out. Your slightly dinked connection is generating no end of minor inconveniences for him or her, as the servers keep spitting out warnings and errors that must be cleared.

And to cheese off a system administrator is to yank the tail of a sleeping dragon. You might be barred from the network. Or you never know, he might be a judge at the next Dragon•Con costume contest, and his might be the deciding vote that keeps your Bride of Boba Fett outfit out of the winner's circle.

WHY "BLUETOOTH?" HEAD FOR BLOCKBUSTER.

I'm going to make an executive decision here. Instead of telling you Where The Name Comes From, I'm going to tell you that *The Stunt Man* and *Smile* are probably the two best movies out of the Seventies that you haven't seen. Or, in the case of *Smile*, haven't even heard of.

Those of you who've been married or in committed long-term relationships will understand why. Your spouse once dumped a whole tureen of guacamole on the lap of the guy who played the dad on *Family Ties*. It's a great story and he or she tells it with such gusto and self-effacing good spirit that the first time you heard it, you knew that you two were fated to bond for life. But you've heard it *93* times since then — you actually worked it out — and you're quite sure that the next time you hear the phrase "...and then I notice that his waiter hasn't given him any dip for his tortillas, so..." it's going to lead to a court date. Divorce, misdemeanor battery, you hope you won't have to find out.

The Story Of The Bluetooth Name is that sort of thing. It won't help you understand this any better, and you'll probably hear it forty times in the next year. So rather than compound one of society's problems, I'd rather clue you in to two really wonderful flicks. Don't even read the synopsis on the DVD. Particularly with *The Stunt Man*, it's good to go in knowing absolutely nothing.

That first book of mine also underscores another point about networking: It's terribly fluid, and new (and wonderful) things are happening all the time. The difference between Mac OS 9 and Mac OS X networking is the difference between crossing the Mediterranean chained to a bench in the ship's bilges, working an oar with the 60 or 70 other guys in your village who thought that these Spartans weren't as tough as everyone says they are, and crossing it while sipping an umbrella drink by the pool of a luxury liner.

See, I insisted to the publisher that this "inter-net" thing was gonna be big, and that connecting to bulletin-board services via modems was going to go the way of the steam-powered gyrocinematoscope projector. No, PPP connections to an Internet Service Provider, connecting to a variety of online services: There's the future for you. But

they wouldn't listen and insisted that I just talk about modems and stuff (I was helping out a pal who'd already come up with the premise), and the rest is history; in a year's time, everything was different.

I suppose I'm making two points here: One, that as cool as Panther's networking features are, this book is being written several months in the past, so always leave your expectations high for future greatness; and two, man alive, that book was 10 years ago and I *still* can't get over it. I was hoping that this would underscore the fact that except where matters of grooming, haberdashery, and racquet sports are concerned, I'm nearly always right, but it's possible that I've simply made an excellent case that I'm a bitter crank. I really ought to think these things through before I write. I really should.

12

The Apps Wot You Get for Nothin'

In This Chapter

Mail • Address Book • .Mac and the *Point* of .Mac
iCal • iChat • Sherlock • Safari • iSync

When you install Panther, you get a whole bunch of apps that aren't *technically* part of the Macintosh operating system, but which are so basic to the experience of using a Mac that they might as well be.

It's just like with the Beatles. You've got your John, your Paul, your George, and your Ringo. But what about George Martin, the producer who taught the boys the difference between being a band that pops pills and plays the Kaiserkellar, and being one that goes into an EMI studio and makes a record? Or Pete Best, who laid the groundwork for the final, successful incarnation of the group by playing the drums not nearly as well as Ringo? Or Yoko Ono, whose obsessive clinginess to John indirectly gave us a supergroup known as Wings, a triple-album known as *All Things Must Pass*, and the 1985 made-for-TV-movie *John and Yoko: A Love Story*, in which a young Mike Myers has an uncredited role as a delivery boy?

Each of these apps makes significant contributions to The Panther Experience. Even if you don't deliberately set out to try these apps, rest assured that your paths shall inevitably cross. One thing that qualifies each of these apps as The Fifth Beatle is the fact that they all work together so transparently, one borrowing features from and communicating with the other.

So, here are some overviews and tips on getting started with these Fifth Beatles. All of these apps are waiting for you in your Applications folder.

MAIL.APP, BACHELOR NUMBER 2, AND BACHELOR NUMBER 3

For practical purposes there are only two commercial alternatives to Mail.app. Microsoft Entourage's big draw is that it integrates tightly with Microsoft Office; in 2004 editions of Office, it practically becomes the dashboard for all of your ongoing projects. Bare Bones Software (www.barebones.com) has Mailsmith, a high-octane app that's hugely attractive to people who have very complicated needs and like to beat their Inboxes into submission with lots of automated routing, redirecting, and message handling.

I've used Mailsmith for a good long while, but it's overkill for most users. Use Mail.app until you feel you've outgrown it...and in truth, you might *never* outgrow it.

MAIL

No longer an exotic function, but as fundamental to the computing experience as running water, you can ably handle the sending, receiving, and processing of email with a built-in app by the name of Mail. Mail (sometimes referred to as Mail.app in order to distinguish it from third-party email apps) has really come along in Mac OS X. In 10.0 it was a laughingstock, a placeholder with a Post-It stuck on it reading "Insert a *real* email app here." But now it's competitive with any email client anywhere.

Before you begin working with Mail, you need to tell it about your email accounts. So, you should start off by getting a little bit of information from your ISP, including

- **Your email address** (for example, icompute@ mac.com).

- **The name of the incoming mail server** (for example, mail.mac.com). You should also ask what kind of mail server it is. It probably uses either IMAP or POP.

- **The name of the outgoing mail server** (for example, smtp.mac.com). The outgoing mail server must use SMTP (simple mail transport protocol).

Once you have the necessary information lined up, you're ready to roll with Mail.

Setting up an account

You can use Mail to manage more than one email account, but for each account, you must give Mail the information it requires to access that account:

1. **Launch Mail.**

2. **Select Mail ➜ Preferences to display the preferences window.** Unless you have accessed this window previously, you see the General pane (Figure 12-1).

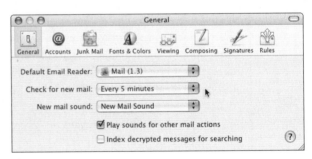

Figure 12-1
The Mail General preferences pane

3. **Click the Accounts icon in the toolbar.** This displays the Accounts preferences pane.

4. **Click the Plus icon in the lower-left corner of the window to add a new account** (Figure 12-2).

Figure 12-2
Adding a new account

5. **Select the type of account from the Account Type pop-up menu.** Your choices are .Mac, POP, IMAP, and Exchange. If you aren't sure which you have, ask your ISP.

6. **Fill in the text boxes.** The text boxes include the following:

   ○ **Description:** A text description of the account. That's just for your own reference.

   ○ **Email Address:** The email address used to send mail to the account. This is the address that's displayed in the From: heading of all the mail you transmit.

   ○ **Full Name:** Your full name. Mail stamps this on all of the mail you send.

   ○ **Incoming Mail Server:** The name of the incoming mail server. You got this from your ISP.

   ○ **User Name:** Your user name, typically the part of your email address that precedes the @. If your email address is gern@blanstev.net, your user name is "gern".

   ○ **Password:** Your account password.

▼ Tip

If you leave the Password text box blank, Mail simply asks for your password every time it tries to access your account. You may want Mail to do this if you're worried that someone in the office is going to wait until you're off at lunch and then use *your* Mac and *your* email account to tell the boss that he can call that thing on his head a Hair Replacement System as long as he wants, but it won't change the fact that it's still a damned *toupee*.

7. **Select Add Server from the Outgoing Mail Server pop-up menu.** The SMTP Server Options window appears.

8. **Type the name of the account's outgoing mail server in the Outgoing Mail Server text box**, as in Figure 12-3. Leave the other information in this window alone unless your ISP has specifically instructed you to change something.

▼ Note

But let's take a moment to look at that "Use Secure Sockets Layer (SSL)" option. You ought to know that on an insecure network — a wired network run by a bad administrator, or a public wireless access point — it's possible for ne'er-do-wells to "sniff" the packets of data whizzing by and grab your mail password. Then, the weasels can download and read your mail just as easily as you can.

Many mail servers support Secure Sockets, which is a way of encrypting and protecting this info before it leaves your Mac. Ask your ISP if it supports SSL, and if it does, ask how to use it. It'll have Mac OS X configuration info handy.

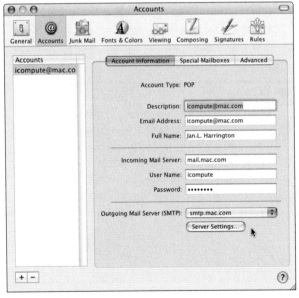

Figure 12-3
Adding a new outgoing mail server

The completed account information looks something like Figure 12-4.

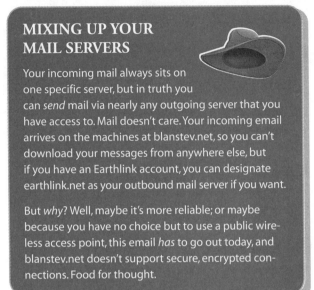

Figure 12-4
Completed account information

MIXING UP YOUR MAIL SERVERS

Your incoming mail always sits on one specific server, but in truth you can *send* mail via nearly any outgoing server that you have access to. Mail doesn't care. Your incoming email arrives on the machines at blanstev.net, so you can't download your messages from anywhere else, but if you have an Earthlink account, you can designate earthlink.net as your outbound mail server if you want.

But *why*? Well, maybe it's more reliable; or maybe because you have no choice but to use a public wireless access point, this email *has* to go out today, and blanstev.net doesn't support secure, encrypted connections. Food for thought.

If you've signed up for a .Mac account, Mail.app configures for you automagically — just one of the benefits of using an Apple Mail.app on an Apple operating system with an Apple ISP.

You can repeat this process for each of your email accounts. Maybe you have an account on the mail system at work, a personal account for home, and a third Hotmail account that you use on Web sites and such, to avoid attracting spam to your "real" email addresses. Mail.app collects mail from all three accounts every time you tell it to check for new messages. Speaking of which...

Receiving email

Reading your email is really a two-step process. First, Mail needs to retrieve the email from your ISP's server and then you can look at it:

1. **Launch Mail.** If necessary, connect to your ISP. Mail checks each of your accounts for new mail. By default, it continues to check again automatically every 5

minutes. (You can change that interval in the General preferences pane, which is shown in Figure 12-1.) If you've got new mail, Mail places it in the In box, one of the built-in mailboxes that Mail.app creates for you. To see all of those mailboxes, go to the View menu and select Show Mailboxes. A drawer opens on one side of the Mail window (see Figure 12-5).

Figure 12-5
The mailbox sidebar

Notice that the In box's name is in boldface, and there's a number next to it. That's the app's way of tipping you off that unread mail lurks within.

2. **Click the name of the mailbox.** A list appears at the top of the Mail window (see Figure 12-6). A preview of the currently highlighted message appears below.

You can double-click a message in the list to view its complete contents in a separate window.

Figure 12-6
New mail listing

Incidentally, Mail also sticks a little badge on top of its Dock icon that contains an up-to-date total of the number of your unread messages (see the Figure 12-7).

Figure 12-7
11739 new messages? You're loved!

Yes, indeedy. If you ever become an internationally beloved industry pundit who's never hidden his email address from the public, you, *too,* may end up having nearly 12,000 unread messages waiting for you at the end of the day. And that's only *after* all of my personal and business mail has been read. I don't ask for your pity. I already have your money, and that's enough.

Mail automatically indexes all of your mail as soon as it's received so you can perform lightning-fast searches. Mail's Search box works exactly the same way it does in all other Mac apps. If you're looking for that email your Aunt Midge sent you last week, just type Midge in the search field, and by the time you get to "g" Mail hides all emails but hers.

If you use the magnifying glass pull-down menu, you can limit the search to just one element of the messages, such as the emails' subject lines, just the From address, or the entire contents of the messages.

Figure 12-5 showed you a rather basic set of mailboxes. It's pretty much the minimum set you get out of the box. Here's a simplified peek at my own mailbox setup (see Figure 12-8).

This shows off two features of Mail that simplify your Mail-readin' experience: having Mail detect and remove junk mail for you automatically, and organizing your mail into separate mailboxes.

Screening out junk

Having Mail handle your junk is as easy as going into Preferences, clicking the Junk Mail tab, and clicking the option labeled Enable Junk Mail Filtering. Mail then uses a fairly sophisticated set of rules to determine whether or not a piece of incoming mail is spam. If the message fairly

reeks of Nigerian herbal mortgage enhancements, Mail automatically diverts it to a new Junk mailbox. You can see the Junk mailbox in Figure 12-8.

Figure 12-8
A more fanci-fied set of mailboxes

The filter is uncannily good from Day One, but it's not flawless. If a piece of spam winds up in your In box, just select it in the main Mail window, and then click the Junk button. If you click the Junk mailbox and see that a group holiday letters from your Aunt Midge got mistakenly tagged as Junk, select the group of letters and click the Not Junk button that appears. Mail.app learns from its mistakes and slowly but surely will do better in the future.

Organizing your mail

As you can see in Figure 12-8, I've defined several mailboxes. That way, personal emails don't get mixed up with reader mails, and important messages from my editors are always just a click away.

You can create new mailboxes by clicking the plus sign at the bottom of the mailbox list and giving the new mailbox a name. Then, just drag messages straight into the new mailbox from the In box.

▼ Tip

But that's not what *I* do. I use a Mail feature known as Rules. By creating a Rule for each different easily identifiable kind of mail, Mail automatically sorts my mail into the proper mailboxes. Everything that my editor, Gern Blanstev, sends me is of A1 importance, so I want it to go straight into my From Editors box instead of in the enormous pile of stuff in my main Inbox. So, a Rule tells Mail what to do whenever I receive a message from Gern.

Specific tutorials on creating Rules is beyond the scope of this chapter, but it's worthwhile to open Mail Help and type "Automatically processing email" in its search box.

Sending email

You can send email either by composing a new message from scratch, replying to an existing message, or by forwarding an existing message.

To compose a new message:

1. **Click the New icon in the Mail window's toolbar.**
   An empty e-mail message window appears (Figure 12-9).

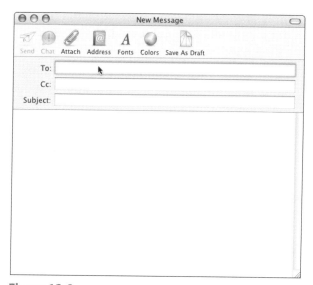

Figure 12-9
The new message window

2. **Type the necessary information in the text boxes:**

   ▫ **To:** Type the email address of the recipient. Separate multiple recipients with commas.

▼ Note

Why Mail.app Is Cool: If the name you type matches a name or an address in Panther's Address Book, or the name or address of someone you've corresponded with recently, Mail automatically completes the data for you.

   ▫ **Cc:** Type the email addresses of those you want to receive copies of this email. Separate multiple recipients with commas.

- **Subject:** Type the subject of the message. Given the amount of junk mail floating about the Internet and the Herculean efforts of people to filter the junk, it makes sense to enter as descriptive and specific a subject as possible.

3. **Type the body of the message.**

4. **Attach the files you want to send.** If you want to attach a file to the message — photos of your big trip to see Yakov Smirnoff in his Branson dinner theater, an important spreadsheet, anything — click the paperclippy Attach button and select a file. An icon representing the file (or the actual image, if the file is a picture) appears at the insertion point. You can even skip this step entirely and just drag the file straight from the Finder into the Mail window. Mail handles all the magic for you. The file automatically transmogrifies into a form that any Mac or Windows machine can receive. Just let Mail do the work.

5. **Click the Send button.** Mail places the message in the Out box and attempts to send it immediately.

Replying to a message or forwarding a message isn't much different from composing a new message. To reply to a message:

1. **Display the message to which you want to reply.** You can do this either in the message's own window or at the bottom of the main Mail window.

2. **Click the appropriate Reply button.** Click the Reply button to reply to the sender only; click the Reply All button to reply to other recipients and the sender. By default, Mail includes the message to which you're responding so that the recipient has some bloody idea of what you're talking about. Unless you think ahead and just select a single relevant passage before clicking Reply, Mail includes the entire message.

"OUT" DOESN'T MEAN "SENT"

If the email you're sending is intensely important, keep a wary eye on that Out box to make sure the mail was actually sent. If Mail encounters an error (say, you're not currently connected to the Internet), that critical financial report will just *sit* there while your boss fumes in a faraway office and decides who's going to get your swivel chair and your red Swingline stapler.

Mail does heroic things to get that message sent. It tries to send the message again automatically, and if you have more than one mail server set up, failure to transmit via one server prompts Mail to ask if it's okay to try a different server instead.

3. Compose and send the message as you would if it were a new message.

When you forward a message, Mail automatically includes the entire message from the original email in the new email. To forward a message:

1. **Display the message you want to forward in its own window.** Alternatively, you can **select the message in the list of messages in the main Mail window.**

2. **Click the Forward button in the toolbar.**

3. **Compose and send the message as you would if it were a new message.**

That's the basics of Mail.app, and as much as could be squeezed (squozen?), well, crammed into the space available. But we've only hinted at the features and power of this application, so I'm begging you to go to Mail's Help menu and read as much as you can stomach. I'll even go so far as give you a dollar if you do it right now, so long as we both agree that there's no way in Helena-Bonham-Carter that I'll ever actually cough up the dough.

ADDRESS BOOK

"But I've never really needed to use a Desktop address book!" some of you are complaining. And I think under those shouts I heard others among you grumble that you're perfectly happy with the contact manager you have already, thank you very much. Well, before Mac OS X's Address Book app, I was one of you.

But my chief reasons for not using a Desktop address book were that I'm obnoxious and disliked, and had erected this wall of technology around me mostly to keep myself isolated from humanity. So any app that caused my Mac to actually encourage interaction instead of providing me with a substitute for it seemed to be counterproductive to the whole master plan.

Trust me. In OS X, it's not just about walking over to your Mac every time you need to look up a phone number. Address Book is a fundamental service of the Macintosh operating system, placing contact and personal information about your friends and co-workers right where you need it, when you need it. Whether emailing a co-worker, addressing a Christmas card, or calling the local Domino's through a USB phone interface, the implications of having one database serving all apps is too good to pass up.

The Address Book display

The Address Book uses a card metaphor to store contact information. As you can see in Figure 12-10, the default view includes three areas:

- **Group:** This column lists groups of cards. When you launch Address Book for the first time, you see a group named All (all cards belong to this group) and an icon named Directories for any network directories to which you may have access.

- **Name:** This column lists the names of all cards in the currently selected group.

- **Card:** The right of the window contains the card for the name selected in the Name column.

Figure 12-10
The three-column Address Book display

To view just the card (for example, Figure 12-11), select View → Card only, or press ⌘+2. You can display the columns again by selecting View → Card and Columns or pressing ⌘+1.

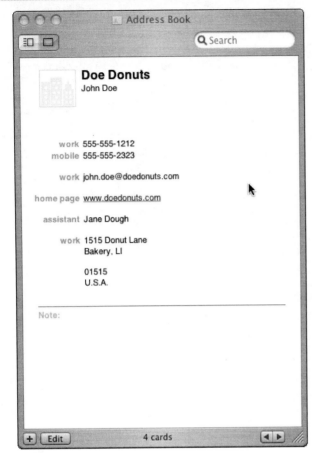

Figure 12-11
Viewing only the Address Book card

Adding a new card

The Address Book comes with two cards for Apple computer. Adding more is up to you. To add a new card:

1. **Click the plus (+) button at the bottom of the Name column.** Alternatively, you can select File ➜ New Card or press ⌘+N. A blank card appears (see

Figure 12-12). Notice that each data field is labeled in boldface. The placeholders for data appear in gray type.

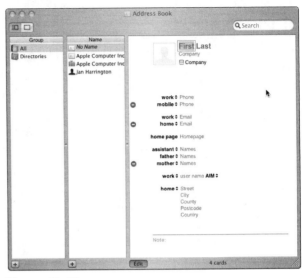

Figure 12-12
A new card

2. **Enter contact information.** Click each field for which you want to enter data, and type the field's contents:

   ▫ To remove a field that you don't want, click the red minus (-) button to its left.

   ▫ To add another instance of an existing field (for example, to include more than one work phone number), click the green plus (+) button to the filled field's left.

3. **Add a picture.** You do this by doubling-clicking on the image square next to the contact name fields. The window that appears provides three ways to add the image (see Figure 12-13):

   ▫ Drag an image into the square in the middle of the window.

- Click the Choose button to display an Open File dialog box for locating the image file.

- Use a video camera to capture an image.

Figure 12-13
Adding an image to a card

If the card represents a company and, in particular, doesn't include a person's name, click the Company check box underneath the company name field. This tells Address Book to alphabetize the card using the company name rather than the fields for a person's name.

The little arrows next to some of the field labels display menus that affect both the field labels and field formatting. For example, in Figure 12-14 you can see a pop-up menu that lets you select a field label. If you don't like any of the existing choices, you can click Custom to type your own label. You can select the subfields of an address field by choosing a country from the field's pop-up menu (see Figure 12-15).

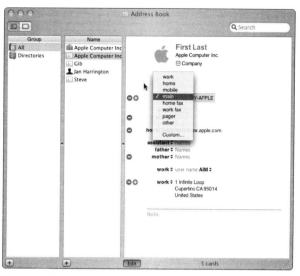

Figure 12-14
Choosing a field name

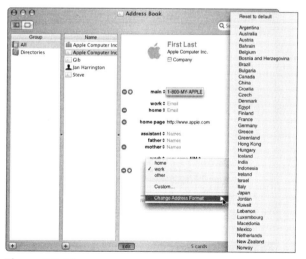

Figure 12-15
Choosing address field format

If a field you want to include isn't present on the card, you can add it:

1. **Go to the Card menu and highlight the Add Field submenu.** A list of additional fields appears (Figure 12-16).

2. **Select the desired field.** It appears in the current address card.

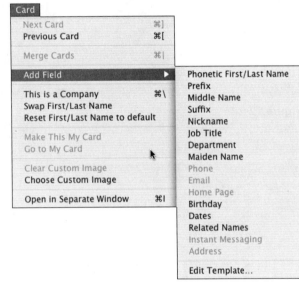

Figure 12-16
Using the View menu to add a field to a card

 Tip

Remember what I said about all these Fifth Beatle apps being tightly (and almost subliminally) integrated? Well, you can also add new people to Address Book just by clicking on their names when you read their email in Mail.app. Some users may actually attach their personal, Address Book–friendly business card to the email, and Address Book automatically fills in all of the data — including a photo.

Editing a card

To change the contents of a card:

1. **In the Name column, click the card you want to change.**

2. **Click the Edit button below the card.** The fields and their controls become visible, as in Figure 12-17.

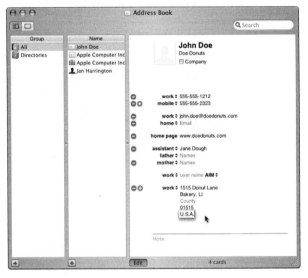

Figure 12-17
A card ready for editing

3. **Click in a field whose contents you want to change.**

4. **Edit the text in the field as necessary.**

You can also add and/or delete fields, change field labels, and change field formats.

Deleting a card

It pays to clean out your Address Book every so often. If you can't remember who someone is or why you have a card for a company, then it's time for that card to go! To delete a card:

1. **In the Name column, click the card you want to delete.**

2. **Select Edit → Delete Person.**

▼ Note

Of course, Address Book doesn't give you the added rush of tearing an unfaithful boyfriend's or girlfriend's page out of a book, spitting on it, crumpling it up, throwing it to the floor, and then jumping on it. That is, you can *do* it, but it'll probably cost you another iBook.

Finding cards

As long as the number of cards in your Address Book remains small, finding a card isn't much of a problem. You can simply browse the Name column. But what should you do when your list of contacts grows to several hundred? Do you want to spend time browsing? If not, you can use Address Book's search feature to locate cards:

1. **Begin typing in the search box.** Note that the search box has a magnifying glass at its left edge. Address Book has a search box that — God bless Apple — works the same way as it does in the Finder, Mail, and nearly every other Mac app. When you type in the search box in the upper-right corner of the Address Book window, Address Book narrows the names in the Name column to include those that start with the typed characters. For example, in Figure 12-18, Address Book selected the two Apple Computer cards by the time the user had managed to type "App." (Because they are the only cards that begin with "A," they are actually selected when the user types the first character!)

2. Continue typing characters until you have located the card you want.

To clear the search, restoring all cards to the Name column, click the X at the right edge of the search text box.

Figure 12-18
Searching for cards

Choosing default card contents

When you create a new card, Address Book provides you with an empty card containing a selection of fields. You can control which fields appear through the Address Book preferences:

1. **Select Address Book → Preferences.**

2. **If necessary, click the template button.** A template similar to that in Figure 12-19 appears.

3. **Add fields to your template:**

   ▫ Click the Add Field pop-up menu to add extra fields.

   ▫ Click the red minus (-) buttons to remove fields.

   ▫ Click the green plus (+) buttons to add more fields of the same type.

Figure 12-19
Editing the Address Book card template

Your changes to the template are saved automatically when you close the Preferences window.

Working with groups of cards

Bulk emails drive most of us crazy, but there are, nonetheless, some legitimate reasons for sending the same message to a group of people. Perhaps you want to announce a meeting or let everyone know that the class reunion has been postponed. Whatever the reason, you can use Address Book to group cards so that you can work with the contacts in that group as a single unit.

The first step is to create a new group:

1. **Select File ➔ New Group.** Alternatively, you can click the plus (+) button at the bottom of the Group column (Figure 12-20).

Figure 12-20
Adding a new group

2. **Type a name for the group and press Enter.** Now you can add names to the group.

3. **Select a group in which the card you want to add to the new group appears.** In many cases, this will be the default All group.

4. **Drag the card you want to add from the Name column to the new group.** This action *copies* the card to the new group; it remains unchanged in its original location.

.MAC AND THE *POINT* OF .MAC

We're about to hit a couple of Fifth Beatle apps that work even spiffier if you subscribe to Apple's .Mac service, so now's probably a good time to answer that musical question, um...dot-*what*, now?

.Mac is Apple's foray into creating an online service for Mac users. "Ah! An online service!" you say. "So if I subscribe, I bet I get

- **An email account with my own gernblanster@ mac.com address.**

- **My own Web page,** albeit a personal one intended for showing off photos and home movies, not something I can run my own nationwide online carpet-cleaning business from.

"Plus, lots of little apps, games, and utilities that Apple licenses from third-party commercial publishers, free exclusively for .Mac subscribers! Great gobs of hydrogenated canola oil! That's a lot of service for just 99 clams a year!"

And you would be right. (Though I'd go easy on the caffeine; it's a nice deal, but places like Hotmail and Yahoo! will give you *free* email accounts, and it's also possible to find free places to post your photos online, too. So all I'm saying is steady on, so far.)

.Mac goes way beyond a simple, run-of-the-mill online service. It's tightly integrated into Panther, so it's more accurate to describe your .Mac account as "a bubble on the Internet onto which you can project bits of your Macintosh experience."

▼ **Note**

For the record, I have never in my life felt more like a peace-love-granola-spouting hippie as I have after writing that last phrase. I have made a note to myself to go out and get a big, greasy drive-through burger as soon as I'm done with this chapter and then toss the wrapper into a protected wetland afterward. Just to restore the balance, you see.

Viz:

- **You also get an Online iDisk, with 100MB of storage.** You can mount this on the Desktop of any Mac anywhere in the world, so long as it has an Internet connection. Store all of your important docs on your iDisk and any Mac can, in effect, be *your* Mac. An iDisk is the source of unspeakable ginchiness, and we spoke highly of it back in Chapter 9, when we talked about Volumes.

- **.Mac makes it easy to swap and synchronize information between multiple Macs.** Because all Macs are familiar with the concept of an iDisk, all of your different Macs can access files there to swap and synchronize information among each other. If up-to-date copies of your appointment calendar and address book sit on your iDisk, your office Mac, your home Mac, and your PowerBook can easily synchronize themselves to your iDisk so that they always contain the same contacts and calendars. Ditto for your browser bookmarks file and other esoterica.

- **Apps can interact with your .Mac account directly, without any configuration.** Many of the iLife apps (iPhoto, iMovie, and so on) are hip to the concept of wanting to let your friends and relatives see all the photos and video you shot during your big road trip to Lowell, Massachusetts, to see the World's Largest Shoehorn. Because they're Apple apps and (again) are hip to the iDisk concept, publishing all this media to your iDisk in the form of Web pages that anyone can read and enjoy is a matter of one or two mouse clicks.

So, .Mac is actually much bigger than the familiar email and personal Web page service you get from other services. But is it worth it? It is unwise to tip the vessel of knowledge, young padwan. By which I mean...um, I dunno.

The good news is that you get to try .Mac for free for 2 months, and that's time well spent. Click the .Mac button within System Preferences to get going.

iCAL

It's almost wrong to call iCal an appointment calendar. It does a jim-dandy job of recording birthdays, meetings, trips, auditions for reality-TV shows, and the like, but it goes way beyond that.

iCal has two big, yippee-inducing features:

- **You can create "layers" of calendars.** Each of your major projects at work can have its own uniquely colored calendar, as well as each of your kids' sports teams, your training regimen for the Boston Marathon, and all of your spouse's piddling little commitments that he or she seems to think are *soooo* danged important. When you want to focus on one aspect of your life, you can hide everything. When you want to try to figure out how you can bring in your company's quarterly actuals on deadline, get your teeth cleaned, *and* make sure that your son D'artagnian gets picked up from stage fighting class all within the same 3 hours of the same day, you can see where your commitments overlap each other. Rescheduling a commitment is as simple as dragging it from one day and time to another.

- **iCal also helps you out by making it easy to share calendars with others.** With just a few clicks, iCal can transmogrify your calendars into Web pages that anyone with a browser and an Internet connection can view. So when it looks like you're going to get stuck working late at the office, you can easily go to the Web, look at your spouse's iCal schedule, and see that there's nothing preventing him or her from picking up D'artagnian from stage fighting class and driving him to his Blockfløte recital.

In Figure 12-21, you can see a sample iCal display. The center of the window shows a single calendar week.

SO WHY DON'T *I* SUBSCRIBE TO .MAC?

I suppose I shouldn't be so glib about my advice about .Mac. I tried it for 60 days, then spent the dough for a year's subscription ($99, at this writing). But then I didn't renew it.

iDisk is a tremendously elegant solution to a lot of problems, particularly the problem of sharing data between multiple Macs many miles apart. But, as a guy with his thumb in a great many online pies, I found that most of .Mac's services are duplicated elsewhere, often inside other services for which I was already paying. I have my own Web site, I have commercial software for publishing movies and photos, and I already have more email accounts than I can manage. Also, as a one-man-company, all of my work is kept here on Lilith, my PowerBook, and when I need to tote files from place to place, I do it on this 128MB flash drive on my keychain. But your experience may be different and a .Mac account might swat at several problems with a single club.

I shall close by saying that to my knowledge, there is no giant shoehorn to be found in Lowell, Massachusetts. But if there were, I'd road-trip to see it. I'm a big fan of having my picture taken next to oversized novelty community monuments, and so you should be, too.

The right side of the window contains the current to-do list. Current calendars appear at the top left, and a small overview of the current month appears at the bottom left. Calendars to which this copy of iCal subscribes have an arrow at the right edge of their names; the calendars without arrows are local calendars — those that this copy of iCal uses.

Clicking the Day button at the bottom of the window switches to a view of the currently selected day (Figure 12-22). Clicking the Month button provides an overview on an entire month (Figure 12-23).

Figure 12-21
The iCal week display

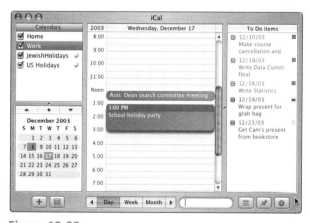

Figure 12-22
The iCal day display

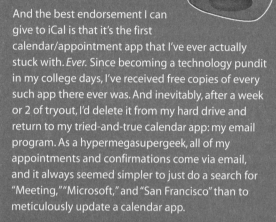

ASK THE MAN WHO OWNS ONE

And the best endorsement I can give to iCal is that it's the first calendar/appointment app that I've ever actually stuck with. *Ever.* Since becoming a technology pundit in my college days, I've received free copies of every such app there ever was. And inevitably, after a week or 2 of tryout, I'd delete it from my hard drive and return to my tried-and-true calendar app: my email program. As a hypermegasupergeek, all of my appointments and confirmations come via email, and it always seemed simpler to just do a search for "Meeting,""Microsoft," and "San Francisco" than to meticulously update a calendar app.

Like Address Book, though, it's iCal's tight integration into the rest of my swingy Macintosh lifestyle that sold me. That, and, er, the increasing number of times I wound up triple-booking myself for meetings and briefings during trade shows.

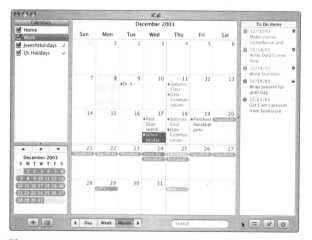

Figure 12-23
The iCal month display

Some items are events rather than appointments: a birthday, a weeklong conference, or the Iditarod dogsled race, for example. iCal displays these as a stripe at the top of the day rather than attaching them to a specific time.

You can see the starting time of a timed event and as much of the name of an event that the window can display. The details of an event appears in the Info window, which pops out as a drawer attached to the side of the calendar display (see Figure 12-24). You can use this window to enter or edit event information. The Info window also handles to-do list items.

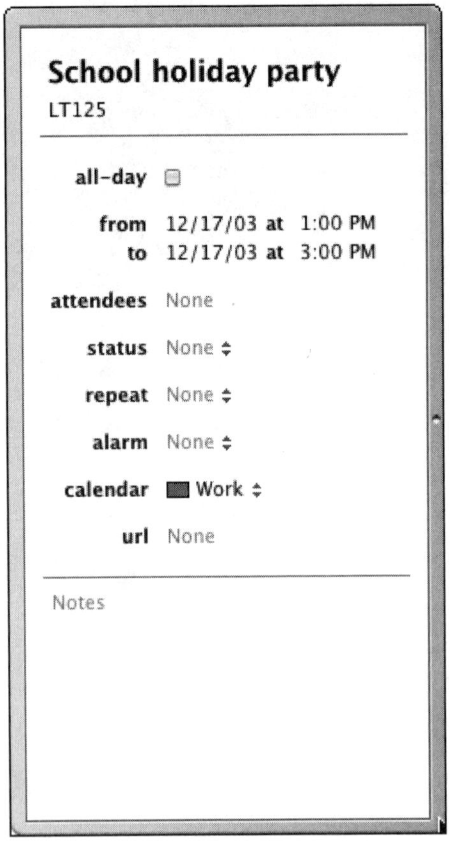

School holiday party
LT125

all-day	☐
from	12/17/03 at 1:00 PM
to	12/17/03 at 3:00 PM
attendees	None
status	None ↕
repeat	None ↕
alarm	None ↕
calendar	▉ Work ↕
url	None

Notes

Figure 12-24
The iCal Info window

Adding and editing events

The first thing you are likely to do when setting up your electronic calendar is to add some events:

1. **Click the day on which you want to add the event.** If you want to click and drag to create the event rather than typing the date and time, day or week view works best.

2. **On the Calendar, click in the Calendars column to which the event belongs.**

3. **Select File → New Event or press ⌘+N if you want to type all the information about the new event.** Otherwise, click and drag from the starting to ending time of the event. iCal changes the ending time in 15-minute increments as you drag. If you accidentally place an event in the wrong place, you can drag it to a new location. You can also use this technique if the day or time of an event changes.

4. **Complete the details of the event by typing in the Info window** (see Figure 12-25). Click a gray field placeholder to highlight it, and then type what you want in the field. The Info window includes the following items:

   ▫ **Event name field.** Replace New Event with a descriptive name of the event. You can also edit the event description directly on the calendar display.

   ▫ **The all-day option:** Click the all-day option to create an untimed event such as a birthday or anniversary.

   ▫ **from and to fields:** Click on any portion of the starting or ending dates and times, and type any necessary corrections. For example, if you have an event that starts or ends at a time other than an even quarter hour (for example, 9:05 rather than 9:15), you can type the time in this way.

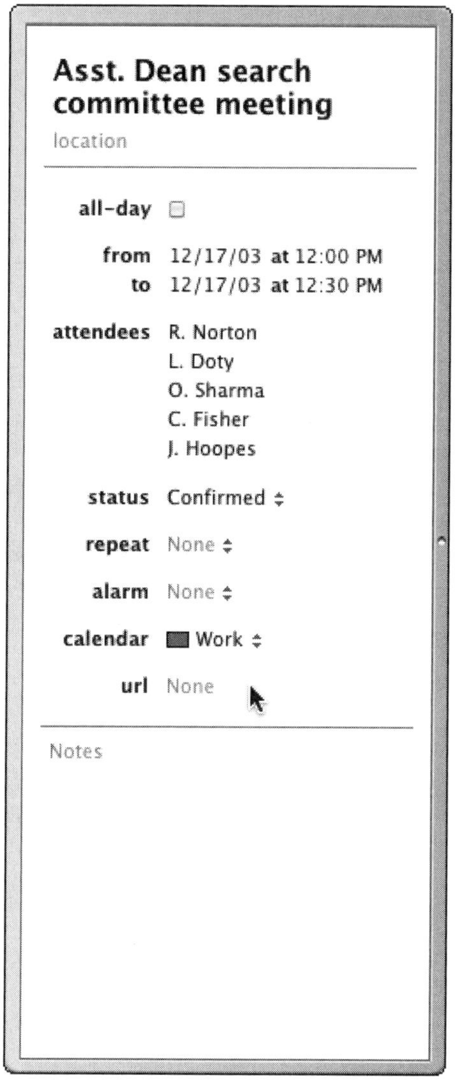

Asst. Dean search committee meeting

location

all-day	☐
from	12/17/03 **at** 12:00 PM
to	12/17/03 **at** 12:30 PM
attendees	R. Norton
	L. Doty
	O. Sharma
	C. Fisher
	J. Hoopes
status	Confirmed ⬍
repeat	None ⬍
alarm	None ⬍
calendar	▪ Work ⬍
url	None

Notes

Figure 12-25
Completing event information

That's a basic appointment. Most of the extra-credit options are available, too, namely:

▫ **attendees:** Click None next to attendees to enter a list of people invited to an event. The people in the list must be in your Address Book. (If they aren't, you can type them into the list, but when you click on another field, they'll disappear!)

▫ **status:** Click the arrows next to the None following status to set the status of the event (None, Tentative, Confirmed, Cancelled).

▫ **repeat:** Click the arrows next to the None following repeat to set up a repeating event. As you can see in Figure 12-26, events can repeat every day, week, month, or year, or you can create custom repeat intervals.

MY LOVE FOR iCAL KNOWS MO' BOUNDS

Actually, I think that the steps on this page are a cumbersome way to enter appointments. I prefer to type new appointments manually by pressing ⌘+N and then filling in the blanks in the sidebar. And I'm not a big fan of *that* method, either. iCal's a great app; hey, I'm all about love and light and stuff, but all too often it tries to *help* me by auto-filling appointment data. Good impulse, iCal, but you keep guessing wrong and forcing me to correct you.

I think nearly all calendar apps are fundamentally annoying, come to think of it. iCal is just the *least* obnoxious of the lot. It still needs work, though. What's so difficult about an event that starts at 11 p.m. and continues past midnight? But at this writing, iCal will still cuss me out and insist that I'm a heretic who's trying to create an appointment that *starts* at 11 p.m. and *ends* at 1 a.m. that same day, 22 hours earlier.

Of course, it could just be me. Mom always said that a few years in the Army would have done me a world of good, given me some structure and stuff. Well, who's to say?

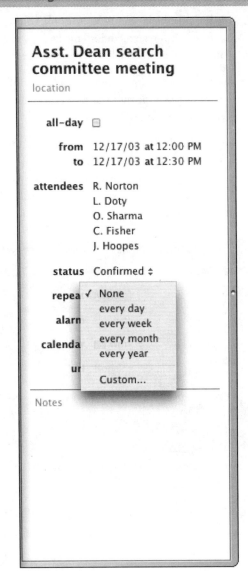

Figure 12-26
Choices for repeating events

When you select day, week, month, or year repeats, you must then indicate when you want the repetition to stop (Never, after a set number of repeats, or on a specific date, as in Figure 12-27). If you click after, type the number of times the event should repeat. If you click on date, type the date of the final repeat.

If you want to create a custom repeat, you can use the shaded box at the bottom of iCal's window drawer (Figure 12-28) to specify when the repeats should occur. You can select daily, weekly, monthly, or yearly repeats. Daily repeats occur for a specified number of days. Weekly repeats can occur for any number of weeks and on a specific day during the week. Monthly repeats allow you to specify a date within the month (for example, the 15th of every month) or a day of the week (for example, every Wednesday).

alarm: Click on the arrows next to the None following alarm to select the type of alarm you want to occur when a time event is imminent (Figure 12-29). Message means iCal will throw an alert box up on your screen where you can't miss it, with or without a sound to further distract you from whatever Web site you are surfing instead of actually working. Or you can have iCal email you (a boon if you're like me and use your email app as the interface to your whole world) or open a file. You may also specify when you want to be alerted. If you just want to remember to phone your broker at 4:00, a minute's notice will do, but if you have an appointment at a doctor's office a half-hour's drive away, being reminded 5 minutes beforehand is sort of counterproductive.

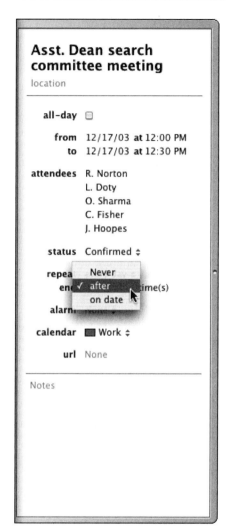

Figure 12-27
Stopping a repeating event

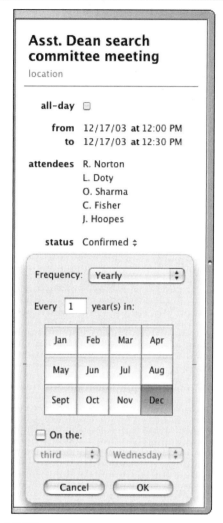

Figure 12-28
Creating a custom repeat

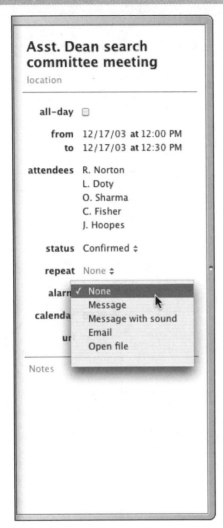

Figure 12-29
Choosing an event alarm

 Tip

And I'm a big fan of the Open File alarm. This is *supposed* to help you out by automatically opening your client's spreadsheet file 10 minutes before your conference call, so you can refamiliarize yourself with the full depth and darkness of the financial hole your bourbon-fueled investment plan has left him in. But any file will do. Have it open one of your MP3 files; have it open an AppleScript file. It'll perform the instructions scripted therein. This one feature can do the work of a brace of expensive third-party utilities.

- **calendar:** Click the pop-up menu next to calendar to assign this event to one of your calendars.

- **url:** Click None next to url to enter the URL of a Web site that is applicable to this event.

- **Notes:** Use the Notes area at the bottom of the window to type any text you want about the event.

To edit an event, highlight the event in the calendar display (any view) to display the event's details in the Info window. Then use any of the techniques just described to change any information about the event. You can also reschedule an event by clicking and dragging it to a new spot on the calendar.

To delete an event, click the event in the calendar display and press Delete. Alternatively, click the event in the calendar display and select Edit ➔ Delete.

Adding and editing To-Do List items

To-do items flit around in their own separate little world, unconstrained by dates and times, free to just *be*, the lucky little buggers. Sigh. But still, individual to-do items are associated with specific calendars that help you keep all the goals of a project or process together with the events, meetings, and deadlines. To create a new to-do list item:

1. **Select File ➔ New To Do.** Alternatively, you can press ⌘+K. A new item appears at the bottom of the To Do items column and the item's details appear in the Info window (see Figure 12-30).

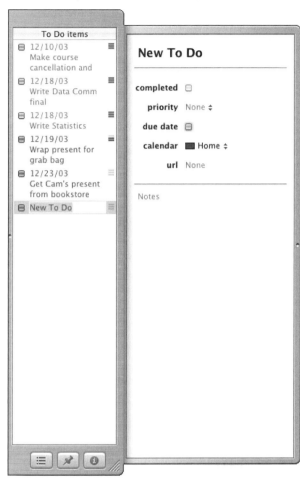

Figure 12-30
Creating a New To-Do list item

2. **Complete the details of the list item by typing in the Info window.** The Info window includes the following items:

   ▫ **Name field:** Replace the text "New To Do" with a description of what is to be done.

   ▫ **completed option:** Do not click the completed option.

▫ **priority:** Select a priority for the item by clicking the double arrow next to None on the priority line. An item can have no priority, be Very Important, Important, or Not Important. If you look carefully at the To Do items in Figure 12-30, you see a square to the right of each item. A completely filled square represents Very Important priority; a two-thirds-filled square stands for Important priority; one-third filled represents Not Important; and an empty square is no priority.

▫ **due date:** If there is a specific date by which the item must be completed, type the date following due date. iCal fills in a time left field for you. To be reminded when the due date is approaching, set an alarm by clicking the double arrows next to None following alarm. As with events, you can choose to receive a text message, a message with an audio alert, an email, or to open a file.

▫ **calendar:** If necessary, select a different calendar for the list item.

▫ **url:** If a Web site is associated with the list item, replace None following url with the appropriate URL.

▫ **Notes:** Type information about the item in the Notes section at the bottom of the window.

When an item is completed, click the check box to the left of its entry in the To Do items list.

To edit an item, click on it in the To Do items list to display its details. Use any of the techniques just discussed to modify information as needed.

To delete an item, click on it in the To Do items list and select Edit ➜ Delete or just press Delete.

ROOM FOR FUTURE IMPROVEMENTS

Unfortunately — and I've pointed out this omission to Apple personally — there's no option for Do You Want It Done Fast, or Do You Want It Done *Right?* There used to be an option labeled Knuckle under to The Man and all his plastic, petty rules, but it was removed after the ruling class boasted that this concept was so relentlessly ingrained into the psyches of the industrial proletariat that repetition was no longer necessary.

Which reminds me: Mark July 17, 2006, on your iCal. That's the day we finally raise the red banner of revolution and fill the skies with the glorious sound of a million chains breaking. Clambake to follow; not a word to the aforementioned ruling class, right?

Creating and editing your own calendars

Most users quickly populate iCal with separate calendars for organizing each area of their lives. If everything is in one hodgepodge, it's hard to make sense of individual schedules and prioritize events.

▼ Note

But don't get hung up on the fact that we're referring to these entities as separate calendars. It's not like you close your calendar of FluffyPuff Marshmallow Ad Campaign deadlines and meetings when you switch to a calendar of upcoming *Babylon 5* reruns. In concept, iCal calendars are more like iCal categories. iCal deals with all of your events and appointments as one big collection; calendars just control how much visual clutter you're dealing with at once.

To add a calendar:

1. **Select File ➜ New Calendar.** Alternatively, you can also press Option+⌘+N. A new, unnamed calendar appears in the Calendars list, and the Info window shows the new calendar's details.

2. **Replace New Calendar with a name for the calendar.**

3. **Select a color for the calendar's events and to-do list items from the pop-up menu to the right of the calendar's name.** See Figure 12-31. This helps you easily distinguish one set of events from the other when they're all hunkered down in the same window together. If you don't want to use one of the preset colors (or if you've used all the preset colors already), select Custom. A color wheel appears from which you can choose any color your Macintosh can display.

4. **Replace the word Description by typing a description of the calendar.**

To modify information about a local calendar, click the calendar in the Calendars list to display its details in the Info window. Make any necessary changes in that information.

To delete a calendar, click the calendar in the Calendars list and choose Edit ➜ Delete or press Delete.

Publishing and subscribing to calendars

There are a lot of calendar applications available, but iCal is special. Why? Because you can share your calendars using the Internet. When you want to make a calendar available to others, you *publish* it; when you want to use a calendar prepared by someone else, you *subscribe* to it.

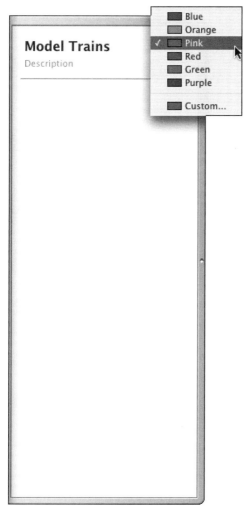

Figure 12-31
Choosing a color for a new calendar

iCal can check for updates to calendars to which you have subscribed. If it finds that the calendar has changed, it updates your copy of iCal to reflect that change.

To subscribe to a calendar:

1. **Get the URL of the calendar to which you want to subscribe.** Many people publish calendars on their personal Web sites, but there are a couple of big, central depositories containing great heaping piles of different calendars, including sports schedules, astronomical events, DVD and feature film releases, and dates when celebrities are due to be paroled. Try www.apple.com/ical/library on Apple's site, or www.icalshare.com for an even larger collection.

2. **Launch iCal.** Make sure that you have a live Internet connection.

3. **Select Calendar → Subscribe or press Option+⌘+S.** A sheet drops down (Figure 12-32).

4. **Type the URL of the calendar to which you want to subscribe.**

5. **Select the options you want:** The calendar options are as follows:

   - **Refresh:** If you want iCal to check for updates to the calendar automatically, click this option. Select the refresh interval (15 minutes, once an hour, once a day, once a week) from the pop-up menu.

   - **Remove alarms:** Click this option if you want to remove or retain any alarms set in the calendar.

   - **Remove To Do items:** Click this option if you want to remove or retain any to-do list items included in the calendar.

6. **Click Subscribe.** iCal downloads the calendar and merges it into your copy of iCal.

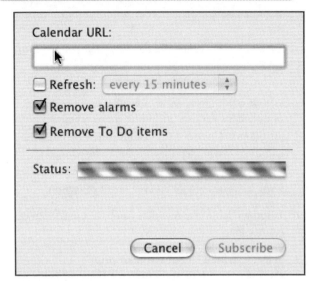

Figure 12-32
Subscribing to a calendar

The information you supply when you subscribe to a calendar is summarized in its Info window. (For an example, see Figure 12-33, a calendar of U.S. holidays.)

To manually refresh a subscribed calendar, select Calendar → Refresh or press ⌘+R.

You can remove a subscribed calendar in the same way you would delete a local calendar. In the Calendars column, click the calendar and select Edit → Delete or press Delete.

To publish a calendar, you must upload it to a server that runs WebDAV. You can use .Mac or a free calendar-hosting site such as iCal Exchange at www.icalx.com. When your calendar is ready for sharing:

1. **Make sure that you have a live Internet connection.**

2. **In the Calendars column, click the calendar.**

3. **Select Calendar → Publish.**

Figure 12-33
The Info window for a subscribed calendar

4. **If you are publishing to .Mac, you must provide the following information or select the following options** (Figure 12-34):

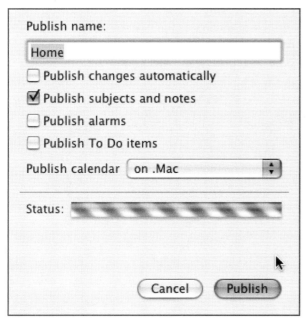

Figure 12-34
Publishing a calendar to .Mac

- ⬚ **Publish name:** Type a descriptive name for the calendar in the Publish name text box.

- ⬚ **Publish changes automatically:** Click this option if you want iCal to send changes to the calendar to .Mac automatically.

- ⬚ **Publish subjects and notes:** Click this option to remove the check mark if you don't want to include that data in the published calendar.

- ⬚ **Publish alarms:** Click this option if you want to include alarms.

- ⬚ **Publish To Do items:** Click this option if you want to include to-do list items.

5. **To publish to a WebDAV server.** To publish to a WebDAV server, you must select a WebDAV server from the Publish calendar pop-up menu (see Figure 12-35). You must then fill in or select the options discussed in step 4. Then you must fill in the following information:

Publish name:

Home

☐ Publish changes automatically

☑ Publish subjects and notes

☐ Publish alarms

☐ Publish To Do items

Publish calendar [on a WebDAV server]

Base URL:

Login: **Password:**

Status:

[Cancel] [Publish]

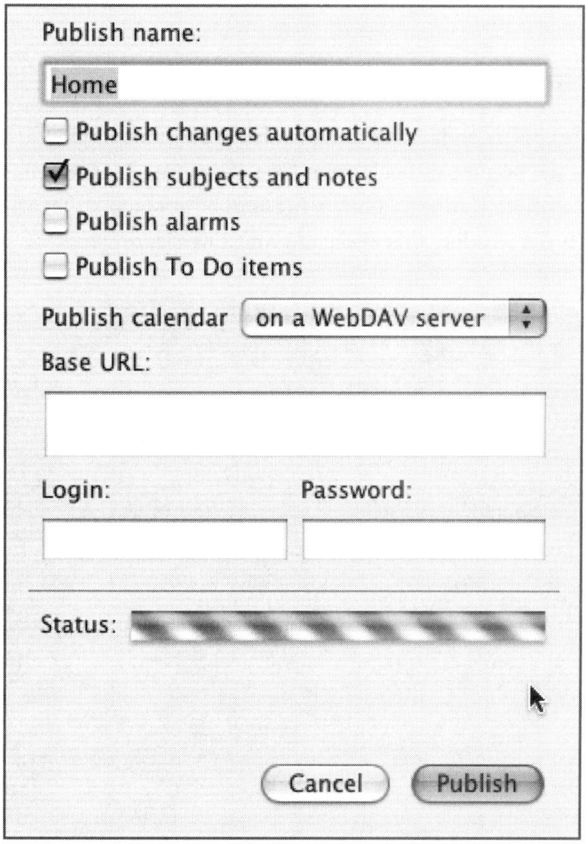

Figure 12-35
Publishing a calendar to a WebDAV server

- **Base URL:** In the Base URL text box, type the URL of the Web site to which the calendar is to be published.

- **Login:** Type your user name on the WebDAV site in the Login text box.

- **Password:** Type your password on the WebDAV site in the Password text box.

6. **Click Publish.** iCal uploads the calendar for you.

Finding events and to-do list items

As your calendars and to-do list items continue to grow, it can become difficult to find specific events. "Just when *was* that meeting?" "Johnny needs to be at practice when?" "Is the wedding this weekend or next weekend?"

YOU GET POWER BECAUSE APPLE GETS IT

Incidentally, Apple didn't exactly invent these basic technologies. iCal can achieve this level of ginchiness because the app supports the network-savvy ICS format for calendar data, and because Panther supports WebDAV access servers. This means, in turn, that (a) iCal can swap event data with any modern calendar app on any OS or hosted on any Web site, and (b) it can interact with that remote host pretty intimately without any direction, intervention, or incantations from the user.

Some day I should write up a list of Important Concepts That Apple "Gets." When I do, the topmost item will be that when you support and enhance a useful nondenominational standard, Great Things Happen.

The easiest way to locate events and to-do list items is to search for them. iCal's search feature is fairly straightforward: Type search text in the search text box (the one containing the word Search at the bottom of the calendar display). iCal performs a *contains* search on all entries — winnowing the results as you type more letters — and displays the results, as in Figure 12-36. To go to a specific item in the search result, double-click it.

Figure 12-36
The results of searching for iCal items

Handling outdated events and items

One of the most frustrating things about many calendar applications is that there is no automatic way to remove past calendar items and completed to-do list items. You end up either going back to delete them manually or having a calendar file that continually grows in size. This is something that you can avoid using iCal. To set the disposition of past events and completed to-do list items:

1. **Select iCal → Preferences.**

2. **Click the Delete events and To Do items after option.** Type the number of days in the text box to the right of the word after. (See Figure 12-37.)

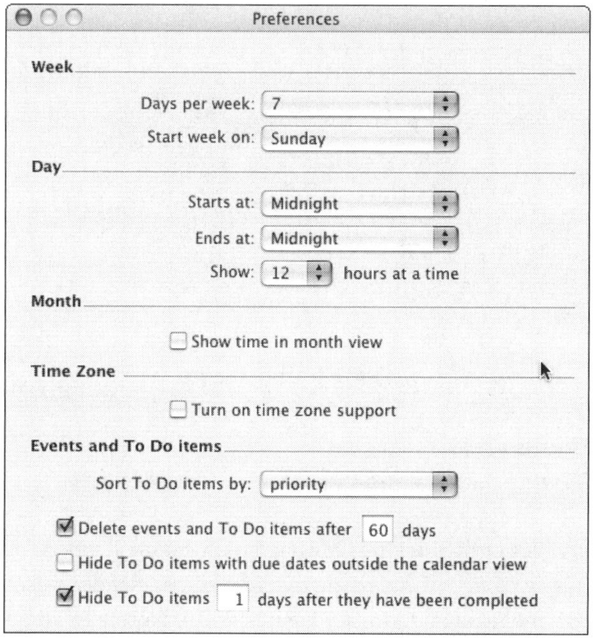

Figure 12-37
Setting the deletion interval for outdated events and items

▼ Note

I never delete old appointments. You never know when you're going to need an alibi for something. Plus, come on, you're tying up18GB of hard drive space with video of your 10-month-old showing off his special "Stare off at an indeterminate point in midspace" trick, and you're worried about wasting a few kilobytes keeping records of past meetings?

iCHAT

iChat just goes to show you that the worst curse possible is to have one of your wishes granted. I've always disdained telephones as being *way* too analog for my tastes, hoping that it would one day disappear and be replaced with something far more Jestons-ey. Enter the basic concept of online chat as a vector for human conversation, and (a couple of years later) iChat in particular.

It's digital. I'll *give* you that. But in my darker moments it seems to me like iChat is a Frankenstein of the least-palatable elements of all the various forms of communication that replaced it. It gives you all the hassle of having to type email and all of the hassle of having to drop what you're doing at the moment and take part in live communication.

▼ Note

And I'm being serious, here. Do you fear burglars? Compact nuclear weapons being stolen from former Soviet republics and winding up in the hands of people who don't intend to use them for deer hunting? Biting into a candy bar and instantly tasting something that you know isn't chocolate, caramel, or peanuts? I'll take any of those over hearing iChat trill at me and seeing a window pop open, representing a vague acquaintance who's so *consumed* by the dynamics of the question "What's Up?" that he simply couldn't feed or bathe himself until I weighed in on the subject.

Still, props and overall shout-outs to iChat all the same, in addition to text messaging back and forth, it supports audio and live video, and can take the place of long-distance phone calls and even actual visits in which there's a danger of experiencing person-to-person contact with another Human.

To use iChat, you need either an iChat account or an America Online Instant Messenger (AIM) account. You do not need to subscribe to AOL to have a free AIM account, however. If you want to set up an AIM account, go to www.aol.com and click on the AOL Instant Messenger button. Download the software and use it to set up your AIM account. Once the account is set up, you won't need the AIM software; you can use iChat instead.

You don't need to subscribe to .Mac to get an iChat account, either. To set up an account, go to www.mac.com/ichat/. You can sign up for a free iChat account and get a free 60-day trial of .Mac. Even if 60 days go by and you choose not to subscribe to .Mac, the iChat account keeps functioning forever.

Setting up iChat

The first time you run iChat, you must provide information about your AIM and/or .Mac accounts. Your account represents your presence to other users, and it's the name people will use to locate and connect to you.

1. **Launch iChat.** The software runs its setup utility automatically.

2. **Type information about your .Mac account, as in Figure 12-38.** If you prefer to use your AIM account, select AIM from the Account Type pop-up menu, then type the account name and password.

Figure 12-38
Configuring iChat to use a .Mac account

3. **Click Continue.** If you have a camera and/or microphone attached and turned on, you can see them in the window in Figure 12-39. This window is really just to test your connections; there is nothing for you to change or enter unless you don't see an image in the square (if you have an operational camera) or a live audio meter underneath the square (if you have an operational microphone).

4. **Click Continue.**

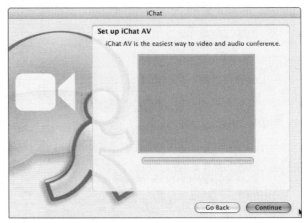

Figure 12-39
Testing camera and microphone connections

5. **Set up Rendezvous Messaging.** If you use Rendezvous to contact iChat partners, click the Use Rendezvous messaging option (see Figure 12-40). Normally, you can only chat with people once you've plugged their chat names and accounts into iChat's Buddy List; Rendezvous lets you automatically discover people on your local network. During a crowded keynote address, the Rendezvous Messaging window lights up like a Christmas tree.

Figure 12-40
Deciding whether to enable Rendezvous messaging

6. **Click Continue.** At this point, you are done with iChat setup (Figure 12-41).

7. **Click Done.** You can now begin chatting.

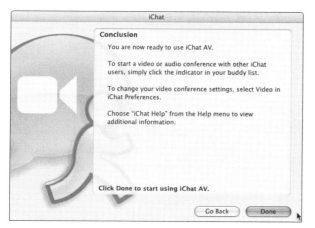

Figure 12-41
Finishing the iChat setup

Using the iChat Buddy List

The center of your iChat universe is iChat's Buddy List. As you can see in Figure 12-42, it displays a list of the people

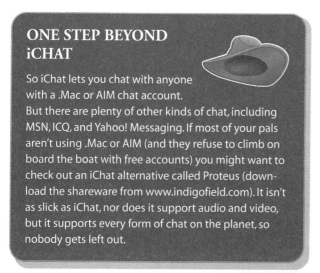

ONE STEP BEYOND iCHAT

So iChat lets you chat with anyone with a .Mac or AIM chat account.
But there are plenty of other kinds of chat, including MSN, ICQ, and Yahoo! Messaging. If most of your pals aren't using .Mac or AIM (and they refuse to climb on board the boat with free accounts) you might want to check out an iChat alternative called Proteus (download the shareware from www.indigofield.com). It isn't as slick as iChat, nor does it support audio and video, but it supports every form of chat on the planet, so nobody gets left out.

with whom you might want to initiate a chat. If the button next to a name is green, the person's account is online and available; if it is red, the person is online but not available. In the latter case you often see an *away* message.

Figure 12-42
iChat's Buddy List window

At the far right side of each chat partner's name you can see the person's current chat icon. It might be something generic (for example, the AIM running person) or an image that the person has selected for his or her chat sessions. You might find an icon indicating that the person has audio or video capabilities just to the left of the chat icon. In Figure 12-42, for example, I have a video camera plugged in and ready, and thus can do video and audio. My pal Sam has a microphone.

To get iChat to recognize a chat partner, you must add that partner to iChat's Buddy List:

1. **Click the plus sign (+) in the lower-left corner of the Buddy List window.**

2. **Select Buddies ➔ Add a Buddy, or press Shift+⌘+A.** The window in Figure 12-43 appears. You can select someone who has a card in your OS X address book (continue with step 3) or add a new person (skip to step 6).

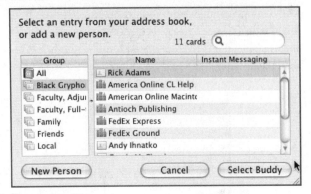

Figure 12-43
Adding a new buddy from the Address Book

3. **To add a person from your Address Book, click the group in which the person appears in the Group column.**

4. **Click the person in the Name column.**

5. **Click Select Buddy.** iChat adds the person to its Buddy List and searches the Internet to determine the person's status. If the person is online and available, you are ready to initiate a chat.

6. **To add a new person, click the New Person button.** The window in Figure 12-44 appears.

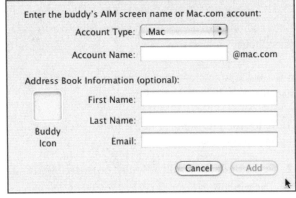

Figure 12-44
Adding a new buddy who isn't in the Address Book

7. **Select the Account type from the Account Type pop-up menu.** This could be AIM or .Mac, for example.

8. **Type the account name in the Account Name text box.**

9. **Type information to complete this entry in the Address Book.** iChat automatically adds new people to the Address Book. Although you can delete iChat buddies from your Address Book without affecting the iChat Buddy List, you may want to at least include a name so you can identify the Address Book entry.

10. **Click Add.** iChat adds the new person to its Buddy List and searches the Internet to determine the person's status. If the person is online and available, you are ready to initiate a chat.

Status messages

Notice that little menu underneath your name in the title of your Buddy List (see Figure 12-42). You can use this to set your chat status.

Remember when I told you how annoyed I get when I'm busy and people try to iChat me for no real purpose? Well, it really shouldn't be a problem at all because I can just tell people to buzz off through this little status line. If I set my status to Away, a red dot appears next to my name in my pal's buddy lists, and the software won't allow anyone to interrupt my pursuit of *le mot juste*.

As you can guess from the word Away, this specific choice is intended to tell people you're not at your desk. This message is "broadcast" to all of your buddies. It might be more accurate to change it to "I'm Busy," which tells people (like your boss) that you're chained to your desk with your nose at the grindstone and not over at Six Flags hitting on the woman who makes change at the Skee-Ball pavilion. Viz:

1. **Click the Status pop-up (it's actually the status text), and click on the Custom item.** You can find this at the top of the Buddy List (see Figure 12-42). The Status pop-up changes into an editable text field.

2. **Type a brief message that you want your Buddies to see.** For example, you can type "Buzz off, I'm trying to WORK!"

3. **Press Return to apply the change.** iChat adds your custom message to its list of prefabbed status messages. This allows you to select this message at any time. You can create new Available (green dot) messages as well.

▼ Note

People use that status message in ways that Apple never intended. It's a good way to quickly communicate a message to a lot of people because it's right there in their Buddy Lists. There are also AppleScripts that automatically change your status message to reflect what's going on in your office. One connects to a weather service and turns your status line into a constantly updated weather forecast. A popular one always lists whatever track is currently playing in iTunes. Apparently, while the hippies of the preceding generation feared Big Brother, the generations that followed are only worried that strangers aren't interested *enough* in the minutiae of their daily existence. (Refer to *The Real World*, and any holiday family letter written and distributed after 1996.)

If you want *complete* privacy, there's an item in the Status menu labeled Offline. This logs you off of iChat's chat-server completely, rendering you invisible until you log back in again.

Being chatted

So you've told people about your new iChat account and alerted them to your desire to be bothered at all hours of the day by people who want to know what you thought of last night's episode of *Law and Order*. What happens when people try to start a chat with you?

You see a window that looks a little like Figure 12-45. You then have several options:

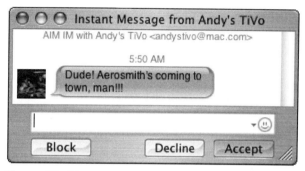

Figure 12-45
An invitation to chat with someone

- **Accept:** Click Accept to open an iChat chat window and start jabbering away.

- **Decline:** Clicking Decline says thanks, but no thanks.

- **Block:** Block is a necessary side effect of allowing Humans — of all people — to use chat software. It's possible that some thumb-sucking jerk may gain access to your chat ID and continue to pester you with instant messages. If so, click Block and iChat ignores this balloonhead forevermore.

Chatting

So you see someone with whom you want to chat is online and available. Now what? Initiating a chat is easy:

1. **Click the person's name in your Buddy List.** See Figure 12-42 for an example of the Buddy List.

2. **Click one of the three icons at the bottom of the Buddy List window:**

   - **A icon:** This invites the person to a text chat.

   - **Telephone receiver icon:** This invites the person to an audio chat.

   - **Camera icon:** This invites someone to a video chat.

   The type of chat to which you can invite someone depends on the equipment that each person has available. If iChat detects a camera, all three types of chat are available. If iChat detects a microphone but no camera, then you can select a text or video chat only. If no AV equipment is present, then you can conduct a text chat.

   But *receiving* audio and video is handled entirely by software. So if you have a camera but your chat partner doesn't, you can select One-Way chat mode from the Buddy menu. Your buddy can see you, but naturally you can't see him.

   ## ONE-WAY BAD CRAZINESS

   iChat AV's One-Way chat mode led to one of my happiest little hacks. I wrote an AppleScript that allows me to do a one-way video iChat between my TiVO video recorder at home and me. I set my iChat status to Watching TiVO wherever I am in the world. Back home, my Mac sees the status and invites me to chat. My TiVO is plugged into a box that converts its analog signals into iChat-compatible digital video, and bango —I can see and hear the show that my TiVO is currently tuned into.

   This is what is known as an Act of Heroic Stupidity.

3. **Wait for the person to accept the chat invitation.**
   In Figure 12-46, you can see the window that appears when waiting for a response to an invitation to a video chat. The Buddy List icon of the invited person appears at the top of the window. The current image coming from the sender's camera appears in the body of the window. Figure 12-47 contains the window that appears when you wait for a response to an invitation to an audio chat.

Figure 12-46
Waiting for a response to a video chat invitation

Figure 12-47
Waiting for a reply to an audio chat invitation

If your chat partner accepts the invitation, the Waiting for reply window becomes your chat window. Exactly what you see depends on the type of chat you are conducting, of course. Figure 12-48 shows a typical video chat. The person with whom you are chatting appears in the body of the window; the small inset contains the image coming from your camera.

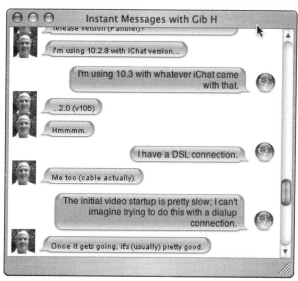

Figure 12-50
Conducting a text chat

To end a chat, close the chat window.

Figure 12-48
Conducting a video chat

An audio chat (Figure 12-49) shows an audio meter. A text chat (Figure 12-50) contains what you and your chat partner type.

Figure 12-49
Conducting an audio chat

Swapping files

Okay, I've been joking around about how I hate having to chat with people. In truth, I'm a salt-of-the-earth, Falstaffian character whom dogs trust implicitly and without reservation. But if you had been nodding your heads while I railed on about not wanting to interact with my fellow man, I've got a bonus for you.

iChat is one of the simplest ways to transmit a file from person-to-person, whether across the office or across the world. All you have to do is drag the file onto his or her icon in your Buddy List. At the other end, your buddy sees a pop-up window that looks something like Figure 12-51.

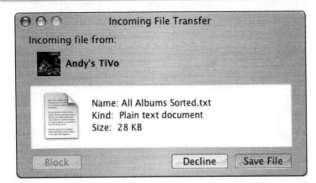

Figure 12-51
Receiving a file via iChat

Click Save File to download and save the file to the computer's hard drive.

 Tip

> Man, is that cool. Finally, a method of shuttling files from one Mac to another that's actually an *improvement* over simply copying it onto a disk and walking it over there yourself!
>
> And it gets slicker. If you're in the middle of a chat with someone, and you drag in a JPEG or GIF, the image file displays right inside the chat window. Them boys & girls at Apple, they's a thinkin' bunch, all right.

SHERLOCK

Sherlock is a tool for searching for information on the Internet. Which might seem pretty funny to you. In this day and age if you utter the phrase "searching for information on the Internet" in front of one of the smarter breeds of dog, the animal reflexively starts pawing the ground as though attempting to type www.google.com into a Web browser. A dedicated app for 'net searches might seem redundant.

The idea behind Sherlock isn't to help you research the social and economic leverages that acted as the flashpoints to the Sino-Russian War; it's to give you a faster and easier way to find a Chinese restaurant in Dedham, Massachusetts, or to find out if the airline delayed your sweetie's flight, or to learn why your spell-checker failed to flag "corf" as a typo.

Note

> A Corf is "A wooden frame, sled, or low-wheeled wagon, used to convey coal or ore in a mine." As a bonus, I'm happy to point out that in *The Meaning Of Liff*, Douglas Adams' dictionary of words that don't exist but should, a "Corfe" is a newspaper being read by a fellow passenger on a subway, identical to yours in every way except that for some inexplicable reason it contains far more interesting articles.

Each type of information that Sherlock can search for gets its own "channel," i.e. its own button in Sherlock's toolbar. Clicking on a channel's button brings up a user-interface tailor-made for searching for exactly that sort of info. To get you started, here's how you search for a public golf course near Norwood, Massachusetts:

1. **Launch Sherlock.**

2. **Click on the Phone Book tool.** Sherlock opens an interface that's handy for doing Yellow Pages–type searches for businesses and public resources. (Figure 12-52):

3. **Click on the Business Name or Category field and type what you're looking for.** In this example, it's "Golf." Sherlock has dozens and dozens of categories built-in, and it auto-completes the category information as you type. You can also click the pop-up tab for partial category matches to what you've typed, or for a list of the most popular categories.

4. **Click on the Find Near field and type a location.**
This example uses "Norwood, MA." As with the Category field, Sherlock tries to auto-complete the name as you type, matching your keystrokes against its database of placenames and zip codes.

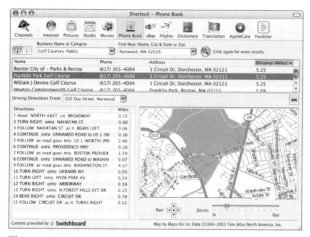

Figure 12-52
Searching for addresses using Sherlock

5. **Click the green Search button.** Sherlock percolates for a moment and then returns a list of the ten public golf courses closest to Norwood, Massachusetts. In the interests of getting you answers quickly, Sherlock only displays the first ten items it finds. If you don't see something you like, click on the green Search button again and the app spits out the *next* ten. Just keep in mind that the results that are farthest down the list are the farthest away from the search city.

Sherlock also appreciates that you might want to actually *go* to one of these joints...so clicking on any item in the list brings up a street map of the area with the location marked with a star. You can zoom in and out on the map with the slider control.

The Phone Book tool can give you driving directions as well, if you tell it what street address you're starting from. Click on the Driving Directions From: box and type it in. As soon as you hit Return, turn-by-turn directions appear below.

SAFARI

In the abstract, you really need to spend a great many nights sleeping in a freshly painted and poorly ventilated room to look at Microsoft Internet Explorer — hands-down the most dominant Web browser on all the planets *I've* been to — and think, no, our company should do away with it and replace it with something better.

Conceptually, the walls at Apple's company headquarters are always bright, clean, and colorful.

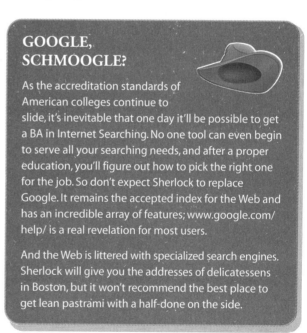

GOOGLE, SCHMOOGLE?

As the accreditation standards of American colleges continue to slide, it's inevitable that one day it'll be possible to get a BA in Internet Searching. No one tool can even begin to serve all your searching needs, and after a proper education, you'll figure out how to pick the right one for the job. So don't expect Sherlock to replace Google. It remains the accepted index for the Web and has an incredible array of features; www.google.com/help/ is a real revelation for most users.

And the Web is littered with specialized search engines. Sherlock will give you the addresses of delicatessens in Boston, but it won't recommend the best place to get lean pastrami with a half-done on the side.

And indeed, the browser Apple came up with proves the point: You *can* do way better than Explorer. A little history: Apple started off with great material. It looked at an open-source (i.e., built by the Internet community at large and owned by everyone) Web-browser engine called KHTML and took it under its wing. It made vast improvements to the existing software library and gave those improvements back to the open-source community. Then Apple added its own dose of elfin' magic (the same basic principles that make Fudge Shop Cookies so danged tasty), rolled in some Mac-specific features, and out popped Safari.

Safari offers a great many improvements over Explorer. The first improvement you'll notice is its sheer *speed.* No browser can render HTML pages faster than Safari. It's like having a whole new Mac.

It also has three major features that are unfamiliar to Explorer users: simplified Bookmark creation and management, the Google box, and SnapBack. You're probably already familiar with Explorer so I'll just focus on the differences.

Bookmarks

It's easier to create and organize bookmarks in Safari than it is in nearly any other browser on any platform. Safari places a Bookmarks button — the dingy that looks like an open book — in the toolbar of every window. When you click it, the current Web page is replaced with a display similar to Figure 12-53.

Like most of Apple's iApps, Safari uses collections to organize bookmarks. The main portion of the window shows you the bookmarks in the currently highlighted collection.

Some of the collections have special purposes:

- **Bookmarks Bar:** Any bookmarks in this collection appear in the Bookmarks Bar above the window's main display area.

- **Bookmarks Menu:** Any bookmarks in this collection appear in Safari's Bookmarks menu.

- **Address Book:** The Address Book collection contains any URLs that are in your OS X Address Book.

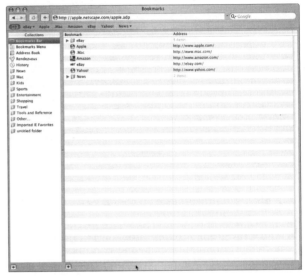

Figure 12-53
Safari's bookmarks display

- **Rendezvous:** The Rendezvous collection automatically searches through your local network for available Web servers, such as your company's private internal Web site, routers that use internal Web servers for creating and manipulating hardware settings, and personal Web sites hosted on individual Macs.

- **History:** The History collection really isn't a bookmark collection at all. It provides access to the Web sites you've visited, as in Figure 12-54.

Figure 12-54
Safari's History list

The remaining collections are for the usual type of Web site bookmarks.

To create a new bookmark collection:

1. **Click the plus sign (+) in the lower-left corner of the bookmark display.** Safari adds an "untitled folder" at the bottom of the Collections column.

2. **Type a name for the new collection.** The real heat happens when you add a bookmark.

3. **Press ⌘+D when you are viewing a Web page.** A dialog scrolls down (Figure 12-55), prompts you to type a name for the bookmark, and offers you the chance to specify a location to keep the bookmark.

▼ **Note**

The location feature alone justifies Safari's existence. Before, nearly all browsers simply dumped new bookmarks at the end of the Bookmarks menu, leaving it to you to wade through it later on and organize them by subject and topic. Safari lets you do this while the bookmark is fresh in your mind. Result: no impossibly cluttered and nigh-useless Bookmark lists.

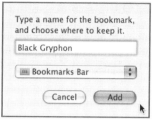

Figure 12-55
Adding a bookmark for a Web site you are viewing

4. **Type a name for the bookmark.**

5. **Select a collection for it.**

6. **Click Add.** Safari adds the bookmark to the appropriate collection.

▼ **Tip**

You can also create bookmarks just by grabbing the URL — the little icon to the left of the address serves as a grabable handle — and dragging it wherever you want it to go, such as into the Bookmarks menu or straight onto the toolbar.

Note that through the Collections pane, it's possible to actually store collections of bookmarks within the toolbar; clicking the name in the toolbar displays a whole menu of bookmarks, and you can drag new bookmarks straight into one specific toolbar collection.

Copying and deleting a bookmark is easy: To copy a bookmark from one collection to another, Option-drag the bookmark in the bookmarks display. To delete a bookmark, click the bookmark in the display and select Edit ➜ Delete or press Delete.

The Google box

The Google search site has become so intractably the rice in the great beef burrito known as the Internet that Apple decided to make Google searching part of Safari's top-level interface.

See that search box in the upper corner of the window (Figure 12-56)? That's a direct line to Google.

Figure 12-56
Googling straight from Safari's search box

To access Google, follow these steps:

1. **Click inside the search box.**

2. **Enter your search terms just as you would if you were on Google's Web site.**

3. **Press Return.** Safari submits the search for you and displays the results in the browser window.

 Note

And all of Google's advanced features work, too. If you type "seventeen ounces in liters" Google responds with "Seventeen US fluid ounces = 0.502750005 liters". If you type a FedEx tracking number, it responds with tracking information for that package. See, now *this* is why I don't use Sherlock. I can Google for nearly anything I'd Sherlock for, without any additional overhead. I reiterate that Sherlock's developers, promoters, and users are kind-hearted, salt-of-the-earth types who'd probably like me a lot if they ever met me socially. I'm all about the love.

SnapBack

Here's the situation: You've hit the Jean-Luc Picard Trivia Page to find out what flute-like musical instrument the

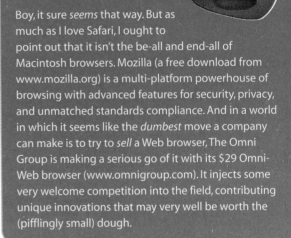

IS SAFARI THE ONLY MAC BROWSER?

Boy, it sure *seems* that way. But as much as I love Safari, I ought to point out that it isn't the be-all and end-all of Macintosh browsers. Mozilla (a free download from www.mozilla.org) is a multi-platform powerhouse of browsing with advanced features for security, privacy, and unmatched standards compliance. And in a world in which it seems like the *dumbest* move a company can make is to try to *sell* a Web browser, The Omni Group is making a serious go of it with its $29 OmniWeb browser (www.omnigroup.com). It injects some very welcome competition into the field, contributing unique innovations that may very well be worth the (pifflingly small) dough.

Enterprise captain played and where he first learned to play it. But when you get there, there's a link to a Sci-Fi convention that you wind up clicking, and it takes you to a costume contest, and then to the personal Web site of this guy who made this *awesome* set of Imperial Stormtrooper armor, and...

Whoops, the flute thing. To get back to the page you started on, you have to carefully pick your way through the browser's History menu and rewind.

Not so with Safari. When you create a new window and navigate away from your first URL, Safari leaves an orange arrow in the address bar (Figure 12-57).

Clicking the arrow rewinds you back to the original Web page. Safari remembers the original page automatically, but if you want to mark a different page as the SnapBack page, just go to the History menu and while the page is visible, click Mark Page for SnapBack.

Figure 12-57
Safari's SnapBack button

iSYNC

If you have an iPod, a PDA, a modern cell phone, or several Macs and a .Mac account, you'll think iSync is the greatest single invention since the Hide-A-Key. If you don't fall into any of these categories, well, go ahead and take the rest of the chapter off. I won't take it personally.

As the name implies, iSync's *raison d'être* is to synchronize a collection of information (chiefly your iCal and Address Book data) among multiple devices so that changes made to the info on one device ultimately propagate through the entire collection. Your appointment calendar is only moderately useful to you if it's all trapped on your desktop Mac; iSync slurps a copy of all that data from iCal straight onto your Palm. And when your blind date goes swimmingly well and you agree to go on another date the next weekend, the moment you set your Palm back into its HotSync cradle it transmits the date and time and the meeting place at the *Battlestar Galactica* convention back up to your iCal database.

And ultimately, that same data goes into your iPod *and* your cell phone. Welcome to the twenty-first century, Buck Rogers.

▼ Note

> Wait, *Buck Rogers*? Terrible show. Even worse than *Battlestar Galactica*, which I remember perceiving as *Love Boat In Space*. Once one has seen *Star Wars* in 70mm THX, one develops high standards.

Figure 12-58 shows you all of the different gizmos that hold my Address Book and calendar, thanks to iSync.

Figure 12-58
Handhelds of a feather sync together.

Here you see my .Mac account, all *three* of my iPods, my cell phone, my Palm PDA, and my PocketPC. How does iSync know how to handle all of these devices? Actually, it doesn't. iSync chiefly acts as a go-between for all the apps and drivers that your devices came with when you bought 'em. That's a *good* thing. Every device has its own unique advantages and features, and a custom add-on conduit that comes with each of the devices you buy (or which is offered as an added option) is better than iSync having one lame, limited solution that works with everything. The third-party iSync conduit that makes my PocketPC work goes beyond iCal and Address Book. For example, it syncs selected photo albums from iPhoto and specific iTunes playlists onto my PDA.

It also means that Apple has created an infrastructure that makes manufacturer support largely irrelevant. Microsoft makes the PocketPC operating system and has never

ONE THING iSYNC CAN'T DO, BUT SHOULD

Obviously I'm a big fan of iSync, but it does have one big shortcoming: It'd be a whole order of magnitude more useful if it could sync two folders of files on two different Macs on a network. You come home after a long business trip, you open your PowerBook, and iSync leaps to life, discovering that while you were traveling you changed three of the files you'd copied over from your desktop Mac and created two new ones. A little wireless networking action and before you've even kicked your shoes off, your desktop Mac is updated with all the changes you made during the road trip.

Alas, no such luck...at least not for now.

shown any interest in supporting Macs. Well, who cares? The day PocketMac shipped, every PocketPC ever invented was as well supported by Panther as any iPod.

And it's all so simple. Figure 12-58 is the sum total of the iSync interface, and you don't even need to look at it; it all works automatically. But follow your manufacturer's directions for configuring each of your devices for iSync.

Synchronizing to an iDisk via .Mac

Things are a bit more complicated if you're syncing to your iDisk, though.

Syncing to an iDisk is a desirable function. If you have a .Mac account, iSync can also sync your calendar to your iDisk, and from there you can sync to every Mac you own. Ditto for your Safari bookmarks.

You need to register each Macintosh that you want to use with the iSync server.

1. **Make sure that you have a live Internet connection.**

2. **Launch iSync.**

3. **Click the Sync Now button.** The iSync window expands to let you know that you need to register the computer (Figure 12-59).

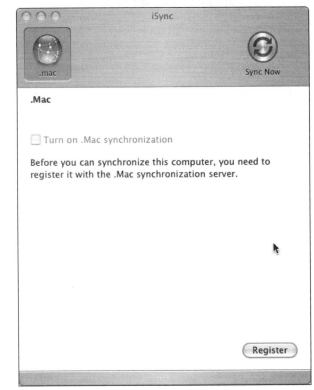

Figure 12-59
Beginning the iSync registration process

4. **Click Register.**

5. **If necessary, type a name for the computer, as in Figure 12-60.** iSync suggests the computer's network name, but you can change it.

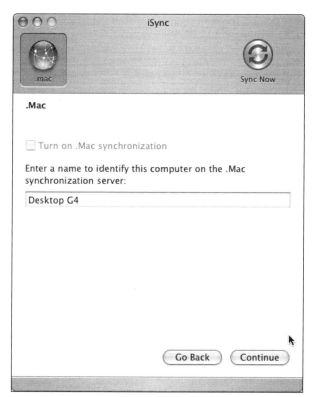

Figure 12-60
Naming a computer for use with iSync

6. **Click Continue.** iSync registers the computer (Figure 12-61).

At this point, you can synchronize this computer by uploading from your applications and/or downloading what is stored on your iDisk.

Figure 12-61
iSync registration in progress

Syncing with iDisk

Once your computer is registered, you can sync with your iDisk.

1. **Click the .Mac button to select the device with which you want to sync.** The window expands to show you the sync options (Figure 12-62).

2. **If necessary, make changes to the options.** For example, if you don't want to sync your Safari bookmarks, deselect the Safari Bookmarks option. Otherwise, leave all the settings alone.

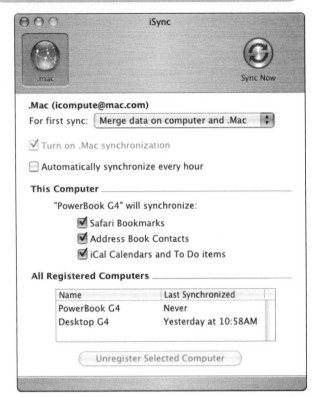

Figure 12-62
Synchronization options

3. **Click the Sync Now button to start the synchronization.** iSync uploads and downloads data as necessary, showing you the progress in the iSync window (Figure 12-63).

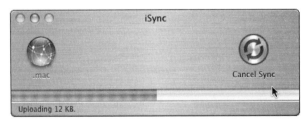

Figure 12-63
 A synchronization in progress

If iSync changes more than a set percentage of the data on your computer, it warns you (see Figure 12-64). You can either accept the changes or cancel the sync. The percentage of changes that triggers the alert is set in iSync's Preferences (Figure 12-65). Select any, more than 1%, more than 5%, or more than 10% from the pop-up menu.

Figure 12-64
A data change alert

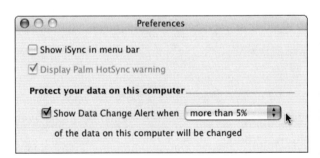

Figure 12-65
Determining the percentage of changes that trigger an alert

If iSync finds any conflicts between settings on your computer and what you have stored on the iDisk, it alerts you and lets you select which settings you want to use. For example, in Figure 12-66, there is a conflict between the colors assigned to a calendar. To resolve the conflict, click the setting you want to use and click Continue. (When you reach the last conflict, the Continue button reads Finish.)

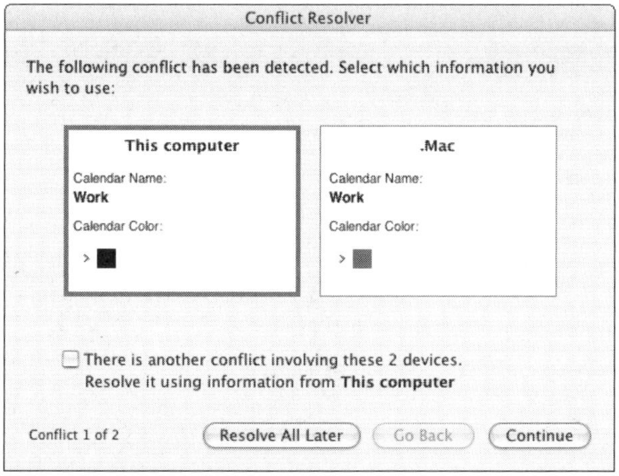

Figure 12-66
Resolving settings conflicts

Wowzers. I feel like Willy Wonka. I've taken you all on a whirlwind tour of some of the most fantastic creations produced in one of the most amazing 12 acres of light-industrial real estate in town. (i.e., While many of you came through the experience with horrible physical and mental scars, I'm sure it's left you with a proper sense of the biggest and brassiest creatures lurking inside your

Applications folders, and with a firm handle on what can be done with them.)

Actually, the chief reason why I feel this way is because I wrote this entire chapter while wearing a purple crushed-velvet frock coat and a thickly upholstered top hat. Yes, it's a foolish and uncomfortable getup, but it was a Christmas gift from my Mom; and if she doesn't see me wearing it at least once, I'm in for a long winter and spring of quiet fuming.

If this were an ABC Afterschool Special, this is where I'd be suggesting additional reading if you want to pursue your Safari and Mail and Everlasting Gobstopper education further. Do hit the individual apps' Help content. Each one is arranged as a pretty healthy tutorial to the apps in general and is a wonderful starting point.

Whoops! I see by the plaid light on the big Georgian-era brass status board that a little Austrian boy has gotten his ears stuck in the high-velocity, nine-stroke extrusion machine! Gotta run; I can already hear the song cueing up, and if I'm not there for the baritone part, the warehouse staff will be terribly disappointed.

13

More Built-in Apps: The Junior Varsity

In This Chapter

TextEdit • Grab • The Calculator • Stickies
DVD Player • Chess

In the last chapter, we talked about big, incredibly powerful and useful apps that allegorically are only a whisker lower in importance than any of the Beatles. But now here we are, soon to be talking about a program that takes something as simple and straightforward as a Post-It note and tries to Digital it to death.

What I'm saying is that there are some useful, and dare I even say Keen, free apps there in your Applications folder. And if they could never be called an iApp or even a Fifth Beatle, they're still worth reading about.

▼ Note

Now that I think of it, it's possible that putting this chapter after the preceding one might have been a tactical error. However, it'd be reasonable to point out that if I put the preceding chapter *after* this one, then it would cease to be the preceding chapter and we'd wind up with a whole *new* mess on our hands. The lesson here is that blinkered ignorance and carelessness for details is the only thing that keeps things moving forward, and explains a lot about why certain people get promoted to middle management while you're stuck in a cubicle ordering toner.

TEXTEDIT

What a long, strange trip this app has taken. Apple has always included a word processor of *some* sort with their operating system. Apple bundled MacWrite with the very first Macs, under the thinking that for $2,500, a computer should do more than show a smiley face during startup. Then they *un*-bundled it and replaced it with TeachText, a hugely low-level little text editor intended just to give you a way to read the little "Read Me First!" docs that (then as now) came with nearly every app you install.

TeachText gave way to SimpleText, which ultimately became TextEdit under Mac OS X.

 Note

This leads to lots of situations in which I wind up speaking like a parent who had eight kids within a short span of time and made the mistake of giving them names that were too close to each other. I cannot say the word "TextEdit" without saying "Teach-Text" and then correcting myself twice.

But whatever the name, one thing was consistent: This was never intended for use as a "real" word processor. It was like the spare tire in the well of your trunk. Puny and undersized, it'll get you off the highway and back home and then to your service station, but that's it.

Imagine my reaction when I launched the Panther version of TextEdit for the first time. "By the sainted banjo of Emmylou Harris!" I exclaimed. "All of a sudden, TextEdit is a *real* word processor!"

Here are the features that make it a credible vehicle for writing simple papers and reports.

It's file-compatible with Microsoft Word

Previous editions could save, open, and edit generic text files and files in the multiplatform Rich Text Format (RTF). But *this* TextEdit can handle files from Microsoft Word as though they were its very own.

Its default file format is still RTF, but saving a document as a Word file is as easy as accessing a pop-up menu in TextEdit's Save dialog (see Figure 13-1).

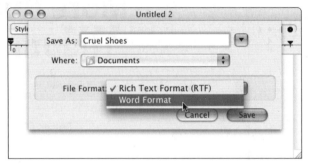

Figure 13-1
Saving a TextEdit document as a Microsoft Word file

And you can just keep right on writing and editing. Any Mac OS X–compatible version of Microsoft Word will treat that file as though it were one of its own.

 Note

That includes the edition of Word found in Microsoft Office XP, so this is a dirt-cheap way to exchange data with your Windows-slinging friends and co-workers.

Opening Word files is even more direct: You just double-click on the file. Unless you already have Word installed, TextEdit launches and opens the file. If you *do* already have Word, you can open the file in TextEdit by dragging the document onto TextEdit's icon.

Note

But for Heaven's sake, *why?* Well, because TextEdit launches in precisely seven one-hundredths of an instant. If all you want to do is check the contents of a file before emailing it to someone, TextEdit gets you in and out faster than Word.

OS X introduced TextEdit, a much more richly featured piece of software that you can use as a very simple word processor. You can't use it to prepare the company newsletter or write a book — you'll need a real word processor for tasks like those — but for a short memo or note, it will do quite nicely.

By default, TextEdit saves files in Rich Text Format (a file extension of .rtf), a generic file format that most word processors can read. It includes a wide variety of formatting options, although you can't set page margins, create multiple column layouts, or any other types of sophisticated page layout arrangements. Panther's version of TextEdit can also save plain text files.

Finer control over text and paragraph formatting

Previous versions of TextEdit could format text in all of the basic ways. There's a ruler at the top of the document window, and all of the basic, familiar word-processing controls are there: tabs (Left, Center, Right, and Decimal), left and right margin controls, and a T-shaped control for setting the indentation of the first line of a paragraph. Figure 13-2 shows you some of the fancy formatting possible with TextEdit.

The Panther edition has gassed things up a little by also allowing you to fine-tune line spacing. To change the line spacing of text:

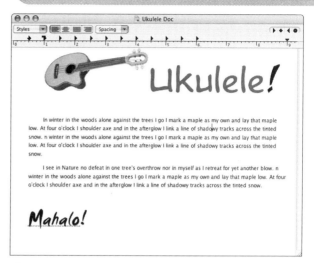

Figure 13-2
A nicely formatted TextEdit document

1. **Select the text you want to change.** If you don't select a range of text, TextEdit only applies your changes to whatever paragraph the blinking cursor happens to be in at the moment.

2. **For simple changes, go to the Spacing pop-up menu in the document's toolbar and select single or double spacing.** The changes will be applied immediately.

3. **For tighter control, go to the menu and select Other.** A dialog drops down and presents some new options (Figure 13-3). Line height multiple, Line height, and Inter-line spacing are three different ways of dictating the height of individual lines within a paragraph. Using all three of them from top to bottom, you can tell TextEdit, "Make each line of this paragraph three times higher than the line of text it contains, but make sure it's at least 24 points high, and make sure there's at least 12 points of space between it and the line above and below it."

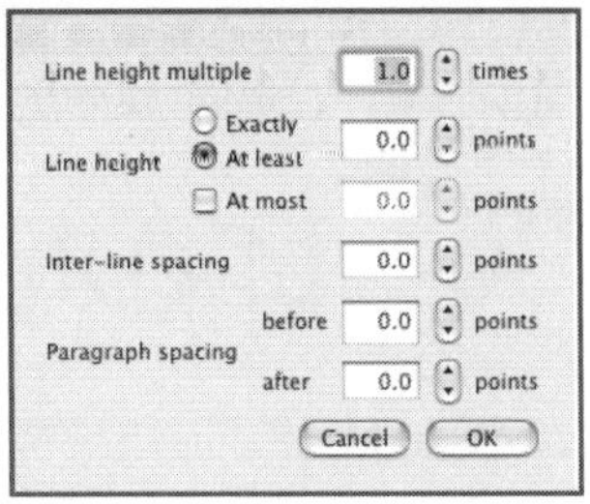

Figure 13-3
Paragraph-formatting options

4. **To control how much padding will be inserted above and below each separate paragraph, enter numbers in the "before" and "after" slots.**

Combined with the previous edition's ability to fine-tune the spacing between individual characters in a word (to make sure that the letters of a word like *AVATAR* snug nicely into each other's nooks and crannies), TechEdit has nearly all the low-level formatting features you'd find in a big-time professional word processor.

It's got styles!

This is the feature that knocked me on my heels. Not because it's an unprecedented, Jetson's-era feature, but simply because it's so common in "real" word processors.

So remember how in the previous section we spent so much time tweaking the appearance of a paragraph? It'd be a bummer to have to make each of those tweaks all over again every time we want to format another paragraph the same way. Thus, TextEdit lets you save these formatting definitions as *Styles* and apply them through a new pop-up menu thereby named. Typically, the difference between a text editor and a real word processor is the inclusion of a timesaving feature known as *Style Sheets*.

OKAY, I'M A GEEK

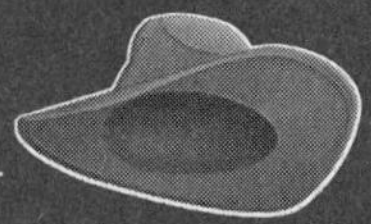

Yes. *Yes.* I was actually excited that Panther's free, basic word-processor now supported style sheets. I will also tell you that as I write this, I've got both a 1977 vintage Chewbacca ceramic mug *and* a rather detailed bust of Boba Fett on my desk next to the keyboard. If you're up to Chapter 13 and haven't figured out that I'm a freakin' geek yet, either you've been skipping around a lot or you just haven't been paying attention.

Or you're in the bookstore and just flipped to this page at random. In which case I say: You can make no finer purchase than the book you are now holding. You will look back on this moment years from now and recognize that this was the day when you're life really turned around for you. Hey, look, the cash register right next to the espresso bar has just opened up. No lines! You'll thank me later.

The Panther edition has all of the same text-formatting features as its predecessors. You have all of the familiar ruler controls for adding tabs, indents, and changing margins. You can change the appearance of text as much as you want, choosing different fonts, sizes, and type colors.

To create a new style based on existing formatting:

1. **Prepare the text with all the characteristics you want in your new style.** Font, size, line spacing, tabs, color...everything counts.
2. **Select the text that represents the new style.** You can set styles based on individual text or a whole paragraph, which includes line and paragraph spacing. TextEdit shows you a sample of the selected text's formatting.

3. **Click Document Styles and then click Add To Favorites.** A new sheet of settings appears.

4. **Give the style a name and specify whether you want both the type styles and the ruler formatting to be included in the definition.** You might, for example, want to create a font-only style for putting headlines in big purple type, without affecting whether the text is centered on the page.

And you're done. To apply the new style's formatting somewhere, just select the desired text and then choose the style from the pop-up Styles menu.

▼ Tip

If you've created a bunch of styles and forgotten what they might actually look like, select the Other menu item. You'll see the same sheet as Figure 13-4, but those playback-looking buttons let you scroll through all of the defined styles and see what the selected text will look like with the formatting of each. Click Apply to apply the style.

Figure 13-4
Creating a new style

But what are its limitations?

Well, at this point I confess that TextEdit isn't a *perfect* word processor. It's missing so many basic features, like

- **Flowing text through multiple columns.**

- **Sophisticated graphics handling:** You can drag pictures (and even movies) into a TextEdit document, but (a) they'll only print at the resolution of your Mac's screen, so they won't look very nice, and (b) you can't plop them down just *anywhere*.

- **Basic Elements:** Headers and footers, Footnotes. Tables. Management tools for large projects. Groupware features. Advanced search and replace...

...Rather a lot, really. But in its defense, unlike Microsoft Word, if you ever — *ever* — see an annoying animated paperclip or dancing Macintosh while you use TextEdit, you can blame the expired tub of cottage cheese you ate for lunch, not the app's programmers. And TextEdit is sophisticated enough that it was able to open, edit, and save this very chapter without a single burp.

GRAB

There are times when you need to explain the operation of your Mac to an interested third party and need to convert images from your Mac's screen to graphics files that you can toss onto a printed page or into a presentation. Grab's the baby for you. Its whole operational motif is based around a camera. You get the screen looking the way you want it and then you snap a picture.

Grab is a really easy utility to use. Here's how:

1. **Launch Grab.**

2. **Tell Grab whether you'd like to capture an image of the whole screen, or just a portion.** You have four

different ways to capture what you want. You can capture the whole screen, a portion of the screen, a window, or you can capture on a time delay. After you capture what you want, Grab displays the image in a window as an untitled document.

- **Grabbing the whole screen:** To capture, the entire screen, select Capture ➜ Screen or press ⌘+Z. The dialog in Figure 13-5 appears. Click anywhere outside the dialog to trigger the screen capture.

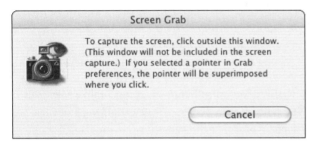

Figure 13-5
Capturing the entire screen

- **Grabbing a portion:** Select Capture ➜ Selection or press Shift+⌘+A. The dialog in Figure 13-6 appears. Drag to select the rectangular area of the screen you want to capture.

▼ Note

Don't worry about Grab's own little dialog. It won't appear in the final screen image you make.

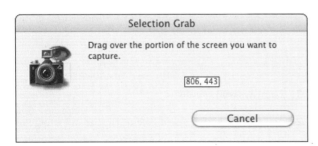

Figure 13-6
Capturing a selected portion of the screen

GRAB: ONE HECKUVA HANDY UTILITY

Even if you're *not* writing about Panther for a major name-brand publisher of instructional books, Grab is a handy utility. If you're going into the Genius Bar at an Apple Store to get advice about a technical problem, it's helpful to come in armed with screen shots. Tech-support people give off a strawberry-scented aura that puts technology in a happy mood, and reproducing an error for the benefit of these people can be notoriously difficult.

I'm also in the habit of Grabbing images of my network settings. When I need to configure a new Mac to work on this hellaciously complicated network setup, all I have to do is make its Network Settings look like the picture.

And yes, technical-support people do indeed smell like strawberries. All of them do. You're probably just remembering wrong, that's all.

- **Grabbing a window:** To capture a window, select Capture ➜ Window or press Shift+⌘+W. The dialog in Figure 13-7 appears. Click on the window you want to capture to make it active. Then click on the Grab dialog's Choose Window button.

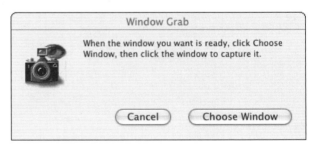

Figure 13-7
Capturing a single window

- **Grabbing with a delay:** To capture the entire screen following a 10 second delay, select Capture → Timed Screen or press Shift+⌘+Z. The window in Figure 13-8 appears. Click the Start Timer button to begin the 10-second countdown. Set up the screen the way you want it to appear in the screen shot, including dropping down a menu. Wait until the timer goes off and the image appears in a Grab window before releasing any menu you have shown.

- **Grabbing with a delay:** To capture the entire screen following a 10 second delay, select Capture → Timed Screen or press Shift+⌘+Z. The window in Figure 13-8 appears. Click the Start Timer button to begin the 10-second countdown. Set up the screen the way you want it to appear in the screen shot, including dropping down a menu. Wait until the timer goes off and the image appears in a Grab window before releasing any menu you have shown.

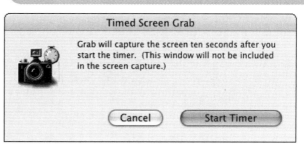

- **Grabbing with a delay:** To capture the entire screen following a 10 second delay, select Capture → Timed Screen or press Shift+⌘+Z. The window in Figure 13-8 appears. Click the Start Timer button to begin the 10-second countdown. Set up the screen the way you want it to appear in the screen shot, including dropping down a menu. Wait until the timer goes off and the image appears in a Grab window before releasing any menu you have shown.

Figure 13-8
Performing a delayed screen capture

▼ **Note**

You'll want to use timed Grab to capture an image of an action-in-progress, such as pulling down a pull-down menu. Start the timer, run over to the app, pull the menu down, and wait.

3. **Select File → Save As or press Shift+⌘+S.** A Save File dialog appears.

4. **Save the image file.** Grab saves files in TIFF format, but if you need a file in another form (like JPEG for use on the Web), you can easily open the file in the Preview app and convert it.

▼ **Tip**

There are more direct ways of activating Grab, too. It appears under the Services menu of every running application, so you can access its features immediately without leaving home. It's also assigned to a couple of different keyboard function keys. ⌘+Shift+3 will Grab the entire screen. ⌘+Shift+4 will bring up a set of crosshairs that allow you to Grab a selection. The command keys often work when Grab doesn't, such as in the middle of a game.

Unless you specify otherwise, Grab includes the mouse pointer in a screen capture (assuming the mouse pointer is on the portion of the captured screen). You can specify the shape of the mouse pointer or exclude it altogether using Grab's Preferences panel:

SNAPZ: A VERITABLE MISSILE OF A SCREEN CAPTURE UTILITY

If training and teaching people is a big part of your daily life, you might want to download Snapz Pro from Ambrosia Software (www.ambrosiasw.com). Where Grab is a bow and arrow, Snapz is like the missile that Slim Pickens rode to his fate at the end of *Doctor Strangelove*. It's much more flexible in isolating parts of the screen for capture, can scale the image up or down to any size, can save in multiple formats, and it can even capture *movies* of the screen.

Yes: Instead of a static picture of the mouse activating a menu, you see the mouse move to the menu bar, you see the menu drop down, you see the pointer scroll to the last item, you see the menu roll back up again and you see a new window opening.

Incidentally, it's also the only way to make a screen capture from Apple's DVD Player. In an uncharacteristic move, Apple apparently chose to tread lightly with the Motion Picture Association Of America and block users from the nightmare scenario where they might actually use a favorite image from *Hope Floats* as their desktop picture.

And (cough) Snapz can also capture the actual video itself and save it as a QuickTime movie. Gosh, given how honorable the MPAA has acted in the past, you don't know how *angry* that feature makes me...

1. **Select Grab ➔ Preferences.** The window in Figure 13-9 displays.

2. **Click the square that corresponds to the mouse pointer shape that you would like included in screen captures.** The top-left square is empty, which means that you want no mouse pointer.

3. **Close the Preferences panel.**

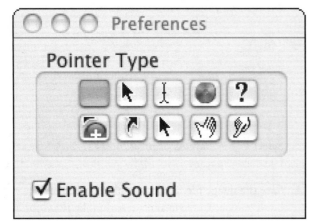

Figure 13-9
Grab Preferences

THE CALCULATOR

I've already made the comment about having a Chewbacca and a Boba Fett on my desk here, so you can probably guess that I don't own a Rolls-Royce. But I've read about Rolls-Royces, and looked on plaintively at them as wealthy dowagers and newly minted rap stars, who apparently have never seen the M.C. Hammer episode of *E! True Hollywood Story*, cruise on past me and my Schwinn. So I'm confident in comparing the dashboard clock on a Rolls-Royce to the Mac's Calculator app.

That is, the Mac's Calculator app remained unchanged since the very first day the Mac appeared, even as the years

kept screaming by and it became less and less elegant and more and more crummy in comparison to what everyone else was using. Fortunately, with recent editions of OS X, the Calculator is once again a handy little thing to keep within mouse-reach.

At first glance, it looks like a simple, four-function calculator (Figure 13-10). You can operate it by clicking on the buttons in the Calculator window, using the keys on the main keyboard, or using the keys on the numeric keypad.

 Tip

If you're using a PowerBook, you can turn the center of your keyboard into a numeric keypad by pushing the Num Lock key at the top of the keyboard. If you use the keypad a lot, though, you might want to spend 20 (measly, stinking, piddly) dollars on a little standalone USB numeric keypad instead.

ME? PARANOID?

If you open Calculator's Help topics, you'll find the phrase, "The results of my calculations aren't correct," smack-dab in the middle. Don't let this throw you because (a) the math is just fine and it's just warning you of some common mistakes that humans make, and (b) it's always good to have a scapegoat when the company comptroller points to a shortfall in the August actuals and seems to be making sinister implications about the gold tooth you've been sporting since September.

And when you read Help's explanation referred to in (a) and make inevitable comparisons to what the HAL-9000 computer said before killing all the astronauts in hibernation, murdering another during a spacewalk, and nearly killing Dave Bowman, well, don't let that throw you, either. I honestly think you ought to calm down, take a stress pill, and think things over.

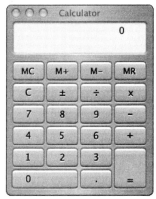

Figure 13-10
The default calculator window

Figure 13-12
Viewing the paper tape window

You can expand the calculator to perform more sophisticated mathematical operations. Choose View → Advanced to expose the keys that you see in Figure 13-11. Clicking the 2nd button gives you the reciprocals of the trigonometric functions.

By default, the calculator does not keep track of calculations as you perform. However, if you open a paper tape, you can see the electronic equivalent of a paper trail. To see the tape window, choose View → Show Paper Tape. You'll see a display something like Figure 13-12.

If you need to keep the contents of the paper tape, choose File → Save Tape As or press Shift+⌘+S. You'll see a Save File dialog for locating and naming a text file for the tape.

A COOL LITTLE PAPER TAPE FEATURE

The Paper Tape window is also handy because it allows you to perform a little Soviet-style revisionist history on the numbers. Let's say you scroll back and discover that an hour ago you typed in 1827782.872881 instead of a 1827782.872887. All the calculations that followed were based on that number, and now there's a good chance that the remorseless killer cyborg that you're designing – the one that's supposed to travel back in time and make sure that the parents of the person who conceived and produced the show *Dr. Quinn, Medicine Woman* never meet – won't do much at all.

No problem. Just highlight the bad number, type in the good one, and click the Recalculate Totals button. All shall be put right. The fact that you're scratching your head right now and muttering, "Doctor...Quinn, did he say?" attests to the efficacy of this fine feature.

Figure 13-11
Advanced calculator functions

You can control both the precision of computation results (the number of places to the right of the decimal point) and the type of display:

- To set the precision, select View ➜ Precision ➜ *number_of_decimal_places*, as in Figure 13-13.

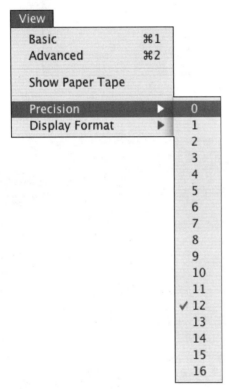

Figure 13-13
Setting the precision of display results

- To set the display format, select View ➜ Display Format ➜ *desired_format*, as in Figure 13-14.

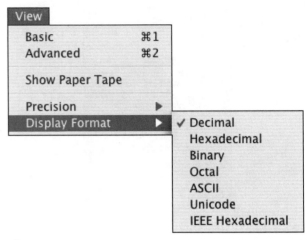

Figure 13-14
Setting the display format

Calculator can convert many types of units of measure, and also features a currency converter (Figure 13-15):

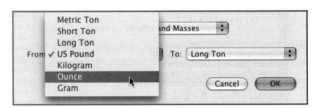

Figure 13-15
Converting Ounces to Long Tons

1. **Type in a number to convert.**

2. **Select the kind of conversion you need from the Convert menu.**

3. **Use the From pop-up to define what sort of units the number represents. Use the To pop-up to define the units you'd like to convert to.**

4. **Click OK.** The converted number appears in the Calculator's display.

Figure 13-16
The Stickies font panel

STICKIES

There's very little on this good, green Earth that we can't claim is obsolete and turn into something digital that doesn't work without a $2,000 computer behind it. From that philosophy, the Stickies app – an analogue to those familiar Post-It notes – represents an inspirational symbol of Mankind's desire to be ever voyaging.

To get started, launch Applications: Stickies. If you have no existing messages, Stickies opens a single yellow sticky note for you. To create a new note at any time, choose File ➜ New Note or press ⌘+N.

Stickies has limited editing capabilities—it's not meant to be a text editor—but you can set font characteristics. To do so, choose Font ➜ Show Fonts or press ⌘+T to open the Font panel, as in Figure 13-16. Notice that this is the same font panel as TextEdit uses, the details of which are discussed in the TextEdit section earlier in this chapter.

By default, sticky note windows are movable, but other windows can hide them. If you want a note to remain on top of all other windows, select the note by clicking on it and choose Note ➜ Floating Window or press Option+⌘+F. In contrast, if you want other windows to show through a sticky note, select the note and choose Note ➜ Translucent Window or press Option+⌘+T (see Figure 13-17).

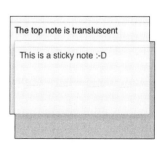

Figure 13-17
A translucent sticky note

Although the default sticky note is yellow, you aren't stuck with yellow notes. To change the color or a note, select the note and choose a color from the Color menu.

The Stickies application automatically saves the contents of all notes when you quit the application, either manually (with File ➜ Quit) or when you shut down or restart your computer. However, you can also save the notes by choosing File ➜ Save All or pressing ⌘+S.

When you close a sticky note, it will be deleted unless you save its contents to a file. Stickies therefore asks you to confirm whether you want to close it. If you click the Save button, you see a special Save As dialog. Choose the format for the file (text or RTF) from the pop-up menu. Then name and locate the file before saving it.

▼ **Tip**

If you use Stickies regularly, let OS X launch it for you each time you boot the computer. For information about startup applications, see Chapter 2.

If you have just migrated from OS 9, you may have sticky notes from OS 9 that you want to include in the OS X Stickies application. You can do that easily by choosing File ➜ Import Classic Stickies. You then see an Open File dialog to use for locating the OS 9 Stickies file from which the notes should be taken.

DVD PLAYER

How quickly doth – can I say the word "doth" in a family publication? – the exotic become the mundane. A computer with a built-in DVD player once seemed like the acme of wretched excess...but now, they're found in all but the budget-oriented machines.

If you have a Mac with a built-in DVD drive (be it a combo drive that reads and burns CD-ROMs but are read-only for DVDs, or a Superdrive that can burn DVD-R discs, too) Panther makes a judgment call whenever you insert a DVD. The DVD is mounted by the system just like any disc, but if it's a video DVD (as opposed to a DVD-ROM you burned with 4 gigabytes of files and stuff), it'll automatically launch DVD Player, an app that turns your Mac into a video player with onscreen controls that will be instantly familiar to anyone under the age of 70, as shown in Figures 13-18 and 13-19:

Figure 13-18
A DVD in progress

DVD Player works exactly like a conventional player works. We can stop talking about it right now, really; most of the menu items (Scan Forward/Backwards, Closed Captioning) are what you'd find on any DVD remote control. If you go to the Video menu you can change the size of the video window so that it's either tiny enough to share space with your running apps or make it so big that it fills the entire screen, banishing the menu bar, the Dock, and any other Mac-ish element that might distract from the full cinema experience.

Figure 13-19
The DVD controller

What happens when DVD Player launches? It depends on how you've set DVD Player's preferences. Open Preferences and click the Player tab (see Figure 13-20).

So if your druther is for your Mac to assume that when you insert a DVD, you want Player to launch, enter full-screen mode, and start the movie from the beginning, just click the appropriate boxes.

Are we done here?

Hey, cool...if you look at the bottom of the Preferences, you'll see that the Player's smart enough to mute the audio whenever you're audio-iChatting with somebody, so your aunt won't hear all that blue language in the *South Park* movie.

Oh, of *course* there's more. Previous editions of the Player were downright lame. They lacked ambition; Apple was satisfied to duplicate the functions of a home DVD player and no more. But the Panther version is actually aware that it's running on a sophisticated computer with a full user interface!

Player's coolest new feature is Bookmarks. The restored director's cut of Sergio Leone's *Once Upon A Time in America* runs *3 hours and 47 minutes*. No problem for *me*, of course. I'm self-employed. But what about those of you watching movies on company time? Four hours is an *awfully* long time to stare at a computer screen without touching the keyboard. Looks very, very suspicious.

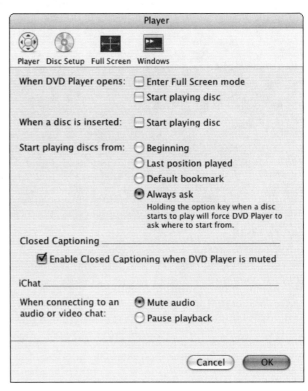

Figure 13-20
Telling Player what to do when a DVD is inserted

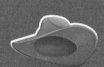

MAC DVD: JUST LIKE BEING AT THE MOVIES?

Um...*do* you get The Full Cinema Experience with DVD on your Mac? Sure. Yes, I'll say yes. The Dolby Surround information is encoded in the standard stereo signal, so if you've plugged Dolby-compatible 5.1 speakers, you will indeed get fill surround sound.

Plus the video quality is probably way better than what you've got in your rec room, believe it or not. When you watch movies on a computer, the movie stays digital from disc all the way to the display, resulting in truer color and crisper images. Find a friend with a 20-inch iMac and play a Pixar movie on it. Except for the size of the screen, the image kicks the butt of most home theaters.

Now, if only La-Z-Boy made a recliner that can scootch up to my desk...

So this version of Player automatically creates little book-mark files for each disc you use. Every disc has its own unique identifier, so when you eject it in mid-scene, it's a simple matter for Player to make a note of the chapter and cue point it was at when the Mac spit it out. The *next* time you insert that disc, it retrieves that bookmark file and (depending on how you've configured Player in Figure 13-20) can automatically resume playback right where you left off...whether it's an hour or a year later.

You can also create your own custom bookmarks. If the film you're watching has reached your favorite bit and you want to be able to zip *straight* to the moment when Fredo panics and fumbles with his gun as Don Corleone is being gunned down, all you have to do is

1. **Pause playback at the point where you want to set the bookmark.**

2. **Under the Controls menu, select Add Bookmark.** You'll see a dialog like Figure 13-21.

3. **Give the bookmark a name.** If you want this to be the default bookmark for this disc, click the check box. Whenever you insert this disc, playback commences from your new bookmark.

4. **Click OK.**

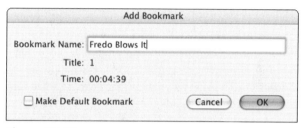

Figure 13-21
Creating a bookmark so you can zip straight to the good stuff

Navigating to an existing bookmark is as easy as selecting it from the Bookmarks submenu under the Go menu (see Figure 13-22).

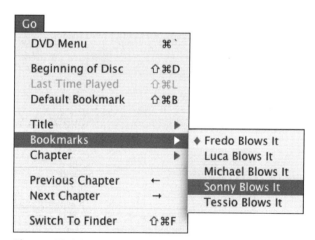

Figure 13-22
Navigating to specific bookmarks on a disc

CHESS

And because all work and no play makes Jack a dull boy — actually, if Jack is in a snowbound and deserted resort hotel with Shelly Duvall and an axe, Jack really comes alive, as Stanley Kubrick has pointed out — Panther includes a game. Unfortunately, it's Chess.

As you can see in Figure 13-23, the Chess game uses a traditional set of chess pieces.

If you want to get a different perspective on the action (or "action"), hold down your mouse button anywhere inside the window and drag. A four-arrow controller appears allowing you to pitch, yaw, and roll the board to whatever orientation you like (Figure 13-24):

GEEK VS. GEEK

Chess has become known as "the dividing line between the bottom-most strata of the high-school caste system," putting the chess geeks below the Dungeons & Dragons geeks.

Why were the chess geeks lower than the D&D geeks? Only because if you were a jock and your choice of target was between a kid who, last Halloween, was seen pacing the halls in a hooded leather robe and a 4-foot claymore, and another kid who doesn't carry anything more lethal than an asthma inhaler, well, who would you single out for swirlies?

Figure 13-23
OS X's chessboard

Figure 13-24
Thrills! Spills! 3D Hauptmann-Rauss Gambit Action!

▼ Note

This is, incidentally, the most fun you're likely to have with this app. There isn't a hidden cheat mode where you can knife the knight, steal his ride, and then gallop all over the board in first-person perspective collecting weapons and powerups and shooting zombies in the face. Believe me, I've tried every key combination possible. Oh, don't even listen to me. I'm just one of those people who've bought dozens of chess books but never got much beyond the "OK...so my horsie can jump *this* way, right?" skill level.

When you are ready to play, choose File ➜ New Game or press ⌘+N. You can then choose to play against the computer, play with two Humans, or have the computer play itself (Figure 13-25). You can also choose the type of game (Regular, Crazyhouse, Suicide, Losers) from the Variant pop-up menu.

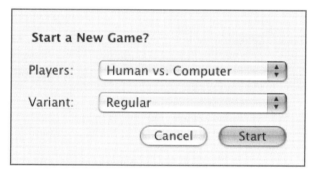

Figure 13-25
Starting a new Chess game

To move a piece, drag it from its current location to the square where you want it to land.

If you aren't sure of the move you should make, you can ask the computer for a hint: Choose Moves ➜ Show Hint.

You'll see a red arrow pointing toward the suggested move (Figure 13-26).

Figure 13-26
Getting a hint for a move

You can configure the game's behavior from the program's preferences panel: Choose Chess ➜ Preferences to display the panel (see Figure 13-27) and then

- Use the Style pop-up menus to change the look of the board and chess pieces.

- Use the Speech check boxes to determine whether the computer should speak to the player.

- Use the Computer Plays slider to determine the expertise of the computer's play. As you can see in Figure 13-27, the computer can play quickly or it can play more expertly.

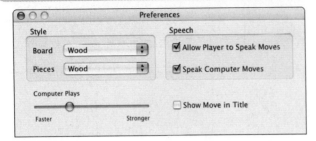

Figure 13-27
Setting Chess preferences

Two final thoughts before we move on. First, although I'm just as disappointed as you are that the one game Apple gives you for free is a cerebral exercise in tactics and lateral thinking, it just occurred to me that this might be the reason why so many studies suggest that Mac users are far more productive than their Windows-saddled brethren. Every time I drive over to visit my folks and I catch my dad at his Dell, he's busy playing either Solitaire or FreeCell. Whereas we Mac users really have nothing distracting us from just cracking our knuckles and getting a jump on next year's tax forms.

Second, it might seem weird that we've spent two whole chapters talking about nothing but Apple applications, and we haven't even mentioned any of the iLife apps. Not even iTunes, which is a *free* download, for crying out loud.

There's a simple reason: We're trying to get some more money out of you. There, I said it. All of the iLife apps will be lovingly and thoroughly detailed in another book in this series, co-written with Tony Bove. You wouldn't want us to talk about iLife in here, anyway. We'd have room for like three pages on each app, tops.

But chiefly I just need the money. It's not for me, you understand: It pains me to see my dad living out his golden years in such squalor, and I think the man deserves an iMac.

Coal-Fired Submarines, Mac OS 9, and Other Relics

In This Chapter

The Classic Environment • Starting Classic

Closing the Classic Environment • Final Classic Malarkey

Good afternoon. My name is Jennifer Walters, associate counsel in the firm of Goodman, Lieber, Kurtzberg and Holliway. I am Andy Ihnatko's intellectual-property attorney.

After prolonged arbitration with the publishers of this book, it has been agreed that Mr. Ihnatko's original draft of this chapter may be allowed to stand as-is, provided that it is preceded by the following points:

1. MANY PEOPLE rely on old software for their day-to-day business. This software has not now and likely never will be upgraded to take full advantage of the features of Mac OS X.

2. MANY PEOPLE own useful add-on accessories, peripherals, and handheld electronics that can only be configured by software running on a Macintosh, said software that has not now and likely never will be upgraded to take full advantage of the features of Mac OS X.

3. MANY PEOPLE consider it cost-prohibitive to upgrade some of their major existing Mac OS 9 software to Mac OS X editions, though such editions are commercially available.

4. UNDER THESE CIRCUMSTANCES, the so-called "Classic Environment" of Mac OS X Panther is a functional and useful feature.

These points are attested to and agreed with by the Author on this date. Andy Ihnatko. [Signature]

This document has been properly notarized and filed with the Clerk of the Suffolk Superior Court, Commonwealth of Massachusetts, and is made available by the clerk magistrate for public viewing during normal office hours.

THE CLASSIC ENVIRONMENT

I mean, *honestly.* Like the TV show *Family Ties*, there was once a time when the thing was relevant, even important. The Mac community would never have abandoned *all* of its existing Mac OS 9 software and Mac OS 9 hardware and jumped to Mac OS X when it was first released. Yes, Mac OS X 10.0 was crashproof, but that wasn't much of an accomplishment — for an application to cause an OS to crash, it needs to exist in the first place. And when 10.0 first came out, it could run Microsoft Internet Explorer and a really minor-league version of Mail and that was it.

 Note

Incidentally, note the difference between those two names: "Mac OS 9" and "Mac OS X." Yes, there must, there must, there *must* be a space between the Mac and the OS, Apple told us technology pundits. David Lee Roth refused to knuckle under, and look what they did to *him.* So, I for one just shrugged my shoulders and agreed to play ball.

But today, there's absolutely no reason to run it. There was a moment when companies continued to develop new Mac OS 9 software, but there was also a moment when *The Macarena* was a hit record. The moment has passed. If you've still got Mac OS 9 apps, new versions are available. If there aren't, I guarantee you that something even better has been written to replace them.

 Note

"Guarantee" does not represent a guaranty or warranty of any kind, expressed or implied, and will not be honored. – *JW*

I see you nodding your head. I've effectively shot and killed Mac OS 9 before your eyes, but allow me to shoot his hat into the grave with him, a la the final scene in *The Good, The Bad, and The Ugly*:

- The Classic Environment is actually a Mac OS X application that bamboozles old software into thinking it's running under Mac OS 9. Not all old software runs properly using it.

- Because of the bamboozlery, Mac OS 9 software runs noticeably more slowly in Mac OS X under Classic than it would on a Mac that's capable of running 9 on its own.

- Mac OS 9 apps will *run,* but they won't receive any of the benefits of Mac OS X. All of the old OS's ghosts are still haunting the joint: If one OS 9 app freezes, *every* OS 9 app running under Classic freezes. If one OS 9 app crashes, *every* OS 9 app crashes.

- Don't count on your Mac OS 9 apps being able to see your printer, scanner, or even bits of your network. Remember, you're not running two operating systems. You're still running Panther. It's just that you also have this Classic Environment that bamboozles old apps into thinking they're in familiar surroundings. Panther is handling all of the drivers that let apps locate and communicate with hardware and networks, so it's out of Mac OS 9 apps' reach entirely.

- When you launch a Mac OS 9 application, be prepared to wait and wait and wait. Your Mac isn't just launching that app, it's also launching the entire Mac OS 9 infrastructure necessary to run it.

- In some counties, using Classic on a regular basis is grounds for Child Protective Services to put your children in temporary foster care.

STARTING CLASSIC

You're still reading this? I guess I should shrug and say, "It's your funeral," and just get on with the explanations.

Classic starts automatically whenever you open a Classic application (aka an app written for Mac OS 9.*x* or earlier). Panther throws up a status dialog like the one in Figure 14-1.

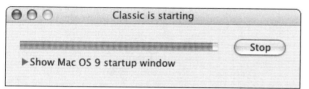

Figure 14-1
The Classic startup dialog

Sit back and enjoy it because you're going to be watching that progress bar for a minute or so while Panther sets up the Classic environment and it boots Mac OS 9 into Classic's space.

If you want a little more visual pizzazz on the screen, click the triangle in the dialog (marked "Show Mac OS 9 startup window") to witness the "fake" Mac OS 9 loading (see Figure 14-2).

Ah, sweet nostalgia; it's been years since I've seen the March of the Icons.

IT'S NOT REALLY OS 9

Booting Mac OS 9 into Classic's space is not like the Panther boot process, nor even like when you reboot your Mac with your Mac OS 9 System Folder set as the startup disk. This threw me the first time I launched Classic. I *imagined* that there'd sort of be a Mac OS X "mode" and a Mac OS 9 "mode," and I'd be switching between the two. Not a bit of that. So it's best to just think that Panther's simply loading in the software libraries it needs in order to run old software.

Figure 14-2
The Mac OS 9 startup window

You should be dramatically unimpressed by the results. The windows of the Classic app you've just launched mixes and mingles with the Panther windows you already have. No need to switch between separate modes at all (see Figure 14-3).

Figure 14-3
Classic apps cohabitate with Panther apps just fine

THE TATTOO RECORD OF MY LIFE

Incidentally, I finally came up with a tattoo concept that I could *really* get behind. The Classic Mac OS starts off by loading in system extensions and components one by one, each marked by a different icon, making stately progress from one side of the screen to another. How about a set of system icons representing the progress I make loading in the Human operating system, complete with social extensions?

The first icon represents birth. Then, breathing air. Next come distinguishing light from dark, pattern recognition, digesting solid foods, crawling, walking, speech, abstract thought, all the way through the landmarks of teendom, education, adulthood, First Tattoo, marriage, parenthood, home ownership, the whole ball of wax; just a line of little square icons marching from my left wrist to my right one. Every blank spot of skin in between would remind me that I've still got more skills and learnin' to do before I've got the complete OS and am ready to move on.

The only trouble is that while I can make up most of these icons as I go, it's important that I pick a good death icon straight away. And I'll have to carry it in my wallet and have some sort of organ-donor-type boilerplate forcing my estate to have it applied at the end of my startup screen before planting me.

I mean, that's just the sort of unfinished business that (if Stephen King's word can be trusted) dooms one's spirit to wander the Earth as a wraith for all time.

...Hmm. I've suddenly lost my nerve on this whole project. The great thing about a Yosemite Sam "Keep On Truckin'!" tattoo is that it will do little to bar your progress from this world to the next. I think I know why they're so popular, all of a sudden.

Your only tip-off is that the Classic app's window has the Classic user interface (naturally), and when it's the front-most app, the Panther menu bar switches to a Mac OS 9–style one.

Incidentally, the tip-off that you're about to launch a Classic app is in the icon, as shown in Figure 14-4. A Classic app icon on a Mac OS X application Dock looks slightly like a mule lurking in a herd of gazelle.

Figure 14-4
Can you spot the Classic app slinking among the Panthers?

CLOSING THE CLASSIC ENVIRONMENT

Not necessary. When you're done with that old app, just quit it. The Classic Environment will still be floating around somewhere in memory, ready to leap into action in an instant; but if there aren't any Classic apps running, the environment uses practically no system resources.

If you *do* want to close or restart Classic — let's say you've just used a Classic application Installer, and it's told you that you need to restart your Mac, unaware that the Mac it's running on is a fake one set up within Panther — you can do so within the Classic pane of System Preferences (see Figure 14-5).

Click Start or Restart, whichever you require. And there's also a Force Quit button for use in the incredibly, amazingly, holy *cow* is it ever unlikely event that one of your Classic apps crashes and locks up the whole Classic environment. (Note: sarcasm.)

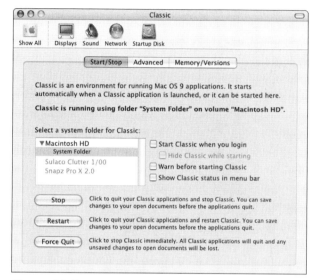

Figure 14-5
The Classic settings window

FINAL CLASSIC MALARKEY

There are still more caveats to know about. Locally mounted hard drives and CDs are available to Classic apps, but network volumes might be hit or miss. And remember that zero Panther resources are available to Classic apps. So when you print, you use the Mac OS 9 Chooser to select printers. Unless you've installed Mac OS 9 drivers for your local printers, you're out of luck. And you're limited to just the fonts that are installed in the Mac OS 9 System Folder (the folder marked, oddly enough, *System Folder* in your directory).

If you're a Mac OS 9 user, you know that keeping the thing running requires that you have a bunch of little system tricks at your disposal. They're easy to pull off if you're running Mac OS 9 for real, but you can only do 'em under Classic through its System Preferences Advanced tab (see Figure 14-6).

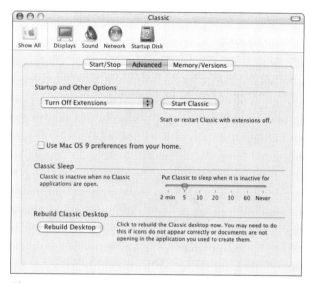

Figure 14-6
The Classic Advanced settings window

Here you see such golden oldies as

- Turning off System Extensions because the whole thing keeps crashing at startup. Select this through the Startup and Other Options pop-up, and click Restart Classic.

- Pressing a certain key combination during startup because, for example, one of your third-party system extensions defaults to Italian mode unless you press E for "English." Select Use Key Combination from the Startup pop-up, and then press the keys you need.

- You have no idea why Mac OS 9 is screwing up, but it's screwing up, so just as legions of Mac users did before Mac OS X, you want to rebuild the Desktop file to see if *that* magically fixes it. Click Rebuild Desktop.

- There's also an option called Classic Sleep. The Classic Environment goes to sleep — that is, switching to a mode where it uses the barest minimum of Panther's system resources — when there are no Classic apps running. If you keep Classic apps open but use them rarely, you can get back most of the performance they suck away from Panther by adjusting this slider.

And it's stuff like that which makes me wonder why *anybody* would want to go back to Mac OS 9, even to run a quick app. I had finally put all that junk about System Extensions and rebuilding the Desktop out of mind. Classic Mode just brings back the nightmares. I mean, when a burglar finishes serving his three-year sentence, he doesn't go *back* to the joint voluntarily, does he?

If you want nostalgia, rent *American Graffiti*. For gosh sake, don't launch Classic apps.

15

I Love People! I Want to Share My Mac!

In This Chapter

Multiple Users on the Same Mac • Sharing Volumes and Folders
Sharing Services • Sharing with Windows Users

It's hard to look at any of the basic philosophies that the original Macintosh development team came up with that were completely and utterly wrong. But they *were* rather insistent upon redefining computing as a "one computer, one person" concept, which, of course, trended dramatically toward baloney-dom as the years sped on. It was a reactionary concept to begin with, a fist being waved at the hegemony of university and corporate mainframes shared by dozens or hundreds of terminals. One big centralized computer amounted to Big Brother. Hundreds of personal computers meant independent free thought.

Well, the Big Brother computing concept was a Big Win for the folks in the *1984* commercial, wasn't it? That blonde with the hammer certainly wasn't going to show up at the branch office and go from cubicle to cubicle smashing individual *desktops*, was she?

I have to believe that a lithe, athletic woman running into the auditorium in shorts and a tank top and doing a few spins did wonders for the morale of every last one of those gray drones in attendance. "Best Friday all-staff meeting *ever!*" THX-1138 said to DDY-8172 as they rode the elevator back to their floor. Big Brother was pretty steamed about the broken big-screen TV, but when he saw what that little stunt did for both group and individual sales the next week, he arranged for attractive male and female decathletes to barge in and disrupt a *lot* of meetings from then on.

In this pushbutton world of the twenty-first century, we've found the happy medium. Mom, Dad, and little D'Artagnian don't each need to have their own computers. A Mac securely supports several users on the same machine, so what's Mom's is Mom's and what's Dad's is Dad's. There's no longer the implication that a computer is a closed box of data and resources. If a document, folder, or volume might be useful to a co-worker, then he or she can access your Mac and use it, with your permission. And everyone in the building can share a single printer.

Let's see, what else did the Mac's original designers get wrong? Hm. Well, I remember that they put this ultra-gnarly, high-voltage capacitor right next to where you grab the circuit board to remove it. I installed 512K of memory in my Mac in 1988, and I think the hair on the back of my right hand only started growing back a month or two ago.

So here's where we start to talk about sharing your Mac's data and resources. This is the flip side of Chapter 11, which is where we hoarded resources and files from the Macs of other people.

▼ Tip

Remember, it is always better to give than receive, unless, of course, you're a contestant on *$100,000 Pyramid*, and your celebrity partner in the final round is a former reality-TV show participant.

MULTIPLE USERS ON THE SAME MAC

Of the many Big Deals of Mac OS X, the ability to support multiple users is certainly one of its Big Deal-iest. Yes, even under the single-user Mac OS 9 it's *possible* for Dad, Mom, and their two children, D'Artagnian and Felicity, to share a Mac. But look at what happens:

- Felicity wants to download a couple of big movie trailers, but there's no room left on the hard drive. So she deletes a 3.1GB folder of stuff she doesn't recognize.

This folder contains — or should I say *contained* — all of the photos and videos D'Artagnian shot when he toured Skywalker Ranch and the full Lucasfilm Archives, led around by George Lucas himself.

- Dad installs an MP3 player. At the last step in the installation process, the installer asks, "Would you like to make LambadaJukebox your default player for all of your Mac's media files, even though it's a total load of dingo's kidneys and iTunes is vastly superior in every conceivable way?" Dad, who's been drinking, clicks OK. Now everybody in the house is stuck using LambadaJukebox until someone puts things back the way things were.

- Mom feels as though she's stuck in a loveless marriage that was formed largely due to her parents' expectations of her as a teenager, and has determined that as soon as the kids are grown, she's filing for divorce and moving out of the house. But that's 5 or 6 years away, so she's just laying the groundwork. Dad notices a set of AmeriTrade bookmarks in the family Mac's browser, clicks it, and discovers that the household has $57,000 in investments he never knew they had. Two days later, Mom is surprised to see a brand-new purple Humvee with leather interior and four built-in video screens parked in the driveway.

Bottom line: A single-user OS causes a great deal of strife and is the third-leading cause of divorce in the state of California, behind bad vibes and an affair with the pool guy. With a true, multi-user OS, these things wouldn't happen because

- **Each of the Mac's authorized users has his or her own protected area in which to store files, and one user can't delete or even view another user's files without permission.**

- **Some users have greater power than others.** Some users are empowered to install new software, while other users can only use whatever software is already there.

- **While users do happen to share applications, they don't share application settings.** So when D'Artagnian clicks Safari, he sees his own bookmarks, not Felicity's. When he runs iTunes, he uses his own music library and not anybody else's. And so, the multigenerational male teenage tradition of being able to thrill to the illicit delights of bubblegum pop in the privacy of his home while still being able to say to his friends, "Aw, *hell* no! That's my sister's music. I wouldn't listen to that weak, old junk if you *paid* me," comes to a sad end.

Just what exactly is a *user*?

A *user* is an account on a computer running OS X. Each user has his or her own preferences and home folder, which is stored in the Users folder.

There are actually two different types of user accounts:

- **Standard:** The type who acknowledges that the Manager of Information Technology was hired for his expertise in this field and that if he or she says, "Don't download stuff from the Internet and install it on one of the company's computers; it might contain a virus or a Trojan horse that'll cripple the whole network," well, maybe he knows what he's doing.

- **Administrator:** The kind who thinks, "I'm not just some 24-year-old nerd in jeans and sneakers...*I'm* a vice president with a law degree! And *I'm* installing this cool dancing chicken screen saver that came unsolicited in my home email from a person with an invalid address!"

▼ **Note**

Sorry. It's been a decade since I was in charge of running a company network, and I still don't think I'm fully recovered yet.

PICK YOUR PASSWORD, PARDNER

Fortified with the power to astride the contents of this Macintosh like a Colossus, the password protecting access to the Administrator's account should be the safest and hardest-to-guess password there is. Choose wisely, and reflect well upon the lessons of Chapter 16.

And don't worry about choosing a password that's so tough to guess that you might forget it. To encourage you to choose tough passwords, you can reset admin passwords by inserting Disc 1 of your Panther install package, rebooting off the CD (restart and press the C key), and then selecting Reset Password from the Panther Installer program.

Only the Panther install CD that actually installed this System can reset your password via this method. So make sure you keep that disc somewhere safe, where you can't lose it and ne'er-do-wells can't find it.

A *Standard* account is your plain, average, everyday user. Nothin' special here. But an *Administrator* account gives someone nearly free reign over the entire Macintosh. That person can install new software, update the operating system, change system settings, even poke around in other people's user directories.

You can have more than one Administrator account — so both Mom and Dad can install software and muck around with the kid's files, for example — but ideally you'd only have one such account on each machine. If everyone has administrator powers and can muck around everywhere and do anything, why bother having multiple accounts? When every man is Superman, Superman is a mere Everyman. That sounds like a lyric to a Bob Dylan song but I swear, I just made it up a moment ago and it's quite apt.

Why the wretched misanthrope should add users

"Andy, I admit freely that I am obnoxious and disliked. I am both riff and raff. I *want* to reach out to people, but fear getting hurt, so I build these walls around me that people often misinterpret as hostility and ego. I am solitary and brooding by nature, enigmatic, yes, but the keeper of secrets both cryptic and unknowable. Bottom line: I have no intention whatsoever of sharing my Mac with *anyone*, so why would I ever bother creating additional user accounts?"

Well, Senator, it's actually advisable to have a few extra accounts, and here's why:

- **A second account is a real lifesaver if your Mac suddenly decides it wants to stop working.** It's possible that the problem is with your usual account and not Panther or your Mac in general. If you restart and log in as a different user, you'll be back up and running. If your virgin, never-been-messed-with user account experiences the same problems, you'll know that you have a problem that might require reinstalling Panther from scratch.

- **Second accounts are great for presentations.** I know that you don't intend to go out on the Internet looking for pornographic drawings of Captain Kirk of *Star Trek* gettin' it on with Captain Janeway of *Star Trek: Voyager*. It just sort of magically appears in your Pictures folder all of a sudden. Well, because God loves a good laugh, particularly at your expense, he'll make sure that something causes that cartoon to pop up on the screen while you're in the middle of a presentation to 800 members of the United Council of Churches. Having a user account that's specifically set up for presentation use ensures that nothing untoward — not even a Desktop cluttered with icons — hinders your presentation.

- **Guest accounts are a good security measure.** There are times when lending your PowerBook to someone or allowing him or her to come over and use your Mac is just a friendly gesture. But you sure don't want that person pawing through your files, even accidentally, so a special Guest account is a good thing to have ready.

That's just a partial list, of course, but it presents ample reason to set up one or two extra accounts...even if you *do* consider yourself a pariah of society.

Creating new users

Your Mac already has at least one user: the Administrator account that was created for you automatically when you first installed Panther.

▼ **Cross-reference**

Way back in Chapter 2. Remember Chapter 2? Those were good times, weren't they? Can you believe the clothes and the music back then? I was listening to Disc 2 of the *Best of Peter Sellars* boxed set instead of Disc 6, and I used to wear a ripped pair of jeans and this really ratty old Newton Messagepad tee shirt that...oh, wait; that's what I'm wearing right now. I should probably take a break now and do some laundry. This might be the reason why the FedEx guy tossed his clipboard to me yesterday morning when he needed a signature, instead of just handing it over.

You can create accounts for additional users through the Accounts panel of System Preferences.

1. **Launch System Preferences.**

2. **Click the Accounts icon to display the Accounts panel (see Figure 15-1).**

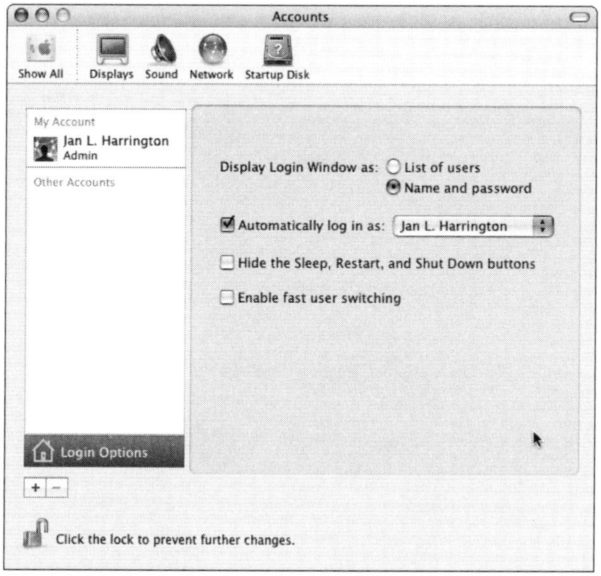

Figure 15-1
The Accounts preferences panel

Figure 15-2
Typing information about a new user

3. **Click the plus sign (+) in the lower-left corner of the window.** The right side of the window will then contain spaces for typing information about the new user, as shown in Figure 15-2. Each new user needs a name that the Humans will recognize, a shorter one that the OS will use internally to name its user directories and stuff, and a password (which you'll have to type twice, for safety).

▼ Note

Actually, you don't *need* to define a password. If you *want* to create an account that allows absolutely *anybody* to access your Mac even if that user is a bass player for a particularly disreputable Midwestern cover band for the love of Mike...well, that's your funeral. But your Mac agrees with me that this is a terrible idea. It'll warn you 12 times to Sunday before meekly complying with your request.

You can configure OS X to display an optional password hint after a user types the wrong password three times. If password hints are not turned on, OS X asks you to confirm the use of the hints, as shown in Figure 15-3. Use this carefully. I mean, come on...who *doesn't* know the answer to a question like, "The first man to space walk without the assistance of umbilical tethers to a spacecraft"?

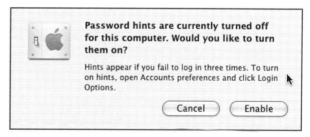

Password hints are currently turned off for this computer. Would you like to turn them on?

Hints appear if you fail to log in three times. To turn on hints, open Accounts preferences and click Login Options.

Cancel   Enable

Figure 15-3
Confirming the use of password hints

4. Click the Picture button to choose a picture for the user (Figure 15-4). The picture appears next to the user's name in list of users. If by some strange quirk of fate you *don't* happen to look like a dog, cat, or some species of insect, you can insert a custom user picture. You can Edit, and a window like the one shown in Figure 15-5 appears. You can insert your own picture in three different ways:

- Drag it into the window from the Finder.

- Click Choose to pick it from a standard Open dialog bog. If you use iChat, all of your most recent personal chat icons will be arrayed in the Recent Pictures pop-up menu.

- If you have an iSight or another video camera attached, click the Take Video Snapshot button to snap a quick self-portrait.

Figure 15-5
Inserting a custom user picture

No matter what method you use, you'll have the opportunity to scale and crop the image inside the window's unshaded box before clicking Set and accepting your changes.

Figure 15-4
Choosing a picture to represent a user

5. Click the Limitations button to determine the files to which the user will have access (see Figure 15-6).

Figure 15-6
Setting user access

The Limitations section is there because some people are fiends draped in human flesh or kids who don't know better or grown-ups who don't know better or corporate executives who know better but have never quite gotten the knack of connecting actions to consequences. Thus, you can give a user access to your Mac, but clamp down on what that user can do at the keyboard, viz:

- **Open All System Preferences:** Deselect this if you think this user is the sort of person who'll fool around, change the Displays setting to the smallest possible screen size, not know how to change it back, and then blame you for an afternoon's lost productivity.

- **Change Password:** Deselect this if you think this user is apt to forget his or her password and then blame you (et cetera), or if you want to retain the ability to log in as this user from time to time.

- **Modify The Dock:** Deselect this if you think this user is apt to remove important apps from the Dock and then not know how to launch Safari and then blame you (et cetera).

▼ NOTE

You begin to understand: Users are trouble. This is why so many professional system administrators prefer not to learn their names. If you start to get emotionally attached to them, you start to think of them as human beings, and that sort of compassion only gets in the way of your job.

- **Burn CDs and DVDs:** Deselect this if you think this user is apt to walk off with information that ought to stay on this Mac, or if he or she is not likely to appreciate that those blank DVD-Rs cost you two freakin' bucks *apiece* and you don't keep them there in the drawer so your stupid roommate can burn a copy of a 40K JPEG of Ensign Sulu and Lieutenant Ohura showering together that he downloaded from alt.lonely.nerd.pathetic.

- **This user can only use these applications:** Panther gives you the hugely useful ability to restrict a user's access to certain applications. If you select this option, Panther builds an outline listing every application available to this account. If little D'Artagnian has been breaking the house rule of "no surfing the Web or using online chat unless Mom and Dad are home," you can easily turn off Safari and iChat entirely. Or, if he was mouthy when you confronted him, turn off all apps except for TextEdit and Chess. *That'll* teach him.

Finally, Panther has a special Simple Finder mode, which is attractive for users who (a) are intimidated by a computer even as simple as a Mac, (b) have a tendency to click every button and pull every menu and thus get into a lot of trouble, or (c) you don't really like very much and who you feel need to be taught a lesson. Figure 15-7 gives you the gist of the Simple Finder experience. To enable the Simple Finder, click the Simple Finder button in the Accounts preferences.

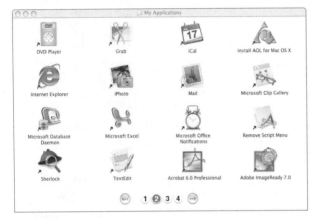

Figure 15-7
A user account with Simple Finder enabled by the administrator

That's pretty Spartan. After 14 chapters of working with Panther in all its glory, this is like walking into your house after a week's vacation and discovering that you've been burgled, isn't it?

A grand tour of the nothingness: You've got one Applications window, and it only shows those apps that the administrator has allowed this user to access. The Dock is nearly empty. The user can access his Documents folder and the Shared folder, but that's it. The menu bar has been abbreviated like a Fox Network production of *Nicholas Nickleby*. The user can put the Mac to sleep, log out, Force Quit an app, and that's it. He can only switch to the "real" Finder if an administrator comes along and types a password.

 Note

Man alive. If the Bergman-esque bleakness of this image doesn't immediately make you think of your Mom or Dad yelling, "And you'll *stay* here and *think* about what you did until *I* say you can come out again!," then clearly you didn't get into as much trouble as a kid as I did.

Changing login options

Okay, you have successfully set up accounts for additional users. *Now* what? Well, now it becomes important to think about making changes to your login screen, that little box that comes up when you fire up your Mac, the one that asks you who exactly you think you are and *why* in God's name should this Mac allow you in to use its apps and resources? It's possible that you've never even looked at the login screen before; there was only one user, so your Mac logged you in automatically.

But with several sets of mitts clawing at your keyboard, it now becomes rather important to make some changes to your Mac's welcome mat. Back in the Accounts pane of System Preferences, there's a big button that exposes your Mac's login options (Figure 15-8).

Most of these options have subtle but important effects on your Mac's security and stability.

- **You can have the login window display a list of registered users.** The user clicks on the name and types a password. That's convenient, but it automatically gives a ne'er-do-well an opening. Said NDW can click on Gern Blanstev's name and maybe Gern has set a password hint and maybe the NDW can guess it. If you leave this first option set to Name and Password, the egg-sucking weasel will have to correctly guess a password *and* a valid user name.

Figure 15-8
Twiddling your login preferences

- **You can have one user logged in automatically at startup.** You turn on your Mac and blammo, it boots up under this user's account without any passwords or typing. That's perfectly fine if you live alone, but if you're sharing a Mac with other folks, you'll want to deselect this option.

▼ **Note**

But this feature isn't without its uses. When I have to set up a Mac for more or less public use — in the lobby of an office, for example, where folks are welcome to look things up on the Web or something while they wait for an appointment — I set up a guest account that's limited to Web browsing only and have the Mac automatically log in to that account. Other folks in the office can still log in and access all of their services, but when they log out it's the browser-only account that remains active.

- **You can hide the login window's Sleep, Restart, and Shut Down buttons.** It's safer to keep these buttons hidden. Even someone who doesn't have an account on this Mac would have the ability to turn it off, and if this is a Mac that the whole building relies on to handle network printing, that ain't so good.

Switching between users

Good heavens, this is like model rocketry, isn't it? Scads and scads of preparation until we get to the actual "it" of it, which only takes about a second.

So, now you've done everything you need to do to turn your one-man Mac into a hippie commune of activity. When one user finishes searching the Internet for the best deal on *Mork and Mindy* original costumes and memorabilia and is ready to move on with his or her life, that user selects Log Out from the Apple menu (Figure 15-9).

Logging out politely quits all of your running apps (asking you to save any unsaved changes in open documents first) and leaves your Mac idling at the login screen, awaiting the arrival of another registered user.

▼ **Note**

It's important that you officially tell your Mac that you're walking away, and you're not coming back for a while. Typing a user name and password is a minor hassle, and there's no guarantee that one of the people who shares your Mac won't prefer to just sit down and surf the Web under *your* account instead. So, logging out when you leave is a security thing. It also ensures that if someone tries to buy a $200 DVD boxed set containing every episode of *Monty Python's Flying Circus* ever aired, it'll be charged to *his or her* Amazon.com account, not yours.

The downside of all this is that you *do* have to log out — as in, quit all your apps, close all your docs, start again from the beginning when you come back. Not all Mac users are sufficiently hippie-crunchy in philosophy to see this as a ritual of cleansing and renewal. Most, in fact, look upon this as a profound pain in the posterior.

Figure 15-9
Logging off of your Mac

Well, Panther brought with it a new feature that benefits multi-user Macs: Enable fast user switching. You have to enable it through Login Options (back at Figure 15-8).

With Enable fast user switching turned on, a new menu appears at the extreme right end of the menu bar (see Figure 15-10).

The title of the menu is the current user. Just select another user, pausing to provide that user's password, and instantly, your Mac switches from *your* account and *your* settings and *your* protected directories to that user's.

You don't have to wait for all your apps to close. Your apps are still running and your documents are still open; you just can't see them or access them until you switch back to your account. So, this feature doesn't just offer convenience, it also brings added flexibility. If iMovie is going to be spending an hour compressing and outputting your latest video masterpiece, it doesn't have to tie up the whole Mac for the rest of the house. It can continue its work in the background while Junior switches over to his own account and does a little work on his next novel.

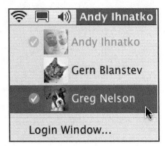

Figure 15-10
Doing a quick change from one user to another with fast user switching

---

▼ **Note**

If Enable fast user switching is so universally ginchy, why does Apple warn you that you shouldn't turn it on unless you trust the other users of this Mac? Well, I *suppose* it's *possible* that in an *uncontrolled* environment, an individual bent on malfeasance could exploit Enable fast user switching to pull a fast one. It's more a conceptual thing than anything else: Are you okay with the idea that while you're happily writing a letter to the *Oprah Winfrey Show*, unbeknownst to you a Mail app running under someone else's account is sending out 120,000 bulk emails on behalf of the Drunk Drivers Against Literacy Foundation? I wouldn't worry about it, but it's something to be aware of.

Deleting users

When you no longer want to give a user access to your computer (he or she has been humming the "Plescheyevo Lake" theme from Prokofiev's *Alexander Nevsky* score all

FAST USER SWITCHING, GAME SHOW STYLE

I really need to talk about the way that Panther accomplishes the visual transition when changing user accounts under fast user switching because it's sort of at the heart of the whole Mac experience. There seems to be no way for me to make a shot of the screen as it happens, but Panther pulls off a 3D effect wherein your desktop and the next user's desktop are on adjoining facets of a screen-filling cube, and it simply rotates from the first desktop to the second, with full shadow, perspective, and lighting effects.

(Basically, if you've ever seen a 1970s game show on The Game Show Network, close your eyes and imagine what happens when there's a shot of a pile of yellow vinyl luggage on a rotating stage and Johnny Olsen says, "And you're going to *need* that new luggage because you're going on a deluxe vacation...tooooo...*Mexico!*" That's the baby.)

Yes, it would have been just as effective to simply replace one screen for another. But even in such casual, offhand matters, it's important for the Macintosh to flex its arrogance: "I have *so* much computing power and *such* a robust set of code libraries that a visual trick like this is more or less as simple to pull off as calculating the cube root of 1928738 to 30 decimal places, and incidentally, an advanced OS and CPU like mine considers the cube root of 1928738 to be such a trivially boring exercise that we make the keyboard controller chip do it."

God, I love the Mac!

freaking day and you've finally had it), you can delete the user.

1. **Launch System Preferences.**

2. **Click on the Accounts icon to display the Accounts panel.**

3. **In the list of users at the left of the window, click the name of the user you want to delete.**

4. **Click the minus (-) button at the bottom of the list.** OS X asks you to confirm the delete (Figure 15-11). If you want to save the user's home folder in a folder named Delete Users, click OK. This is the equivalent of firing an employee, but dumping the contents of his or her desk in a cardboard box so the stuff can be returned later. Awfully sporting of you. If your hatred of this person is so intense that you can't even bring yourself to extend the *simplest* basic human courtesy, click Delete Immediately.

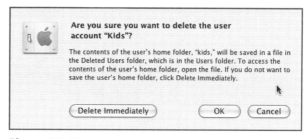

Figure 15-11
Confirming the deletion of a user

SHARING VOLUMES AND FOLDERS

If you've read Chapter 9, you know about using volumes that are available for you to share over a network. Now you'll begin to take a look at making resources on your own computer available to other users, thus putting the shoe on the other hand.

Turning on File Sharing

To allow other users to share volumes and/or folders on your computer, you need to turn on Personal File Sharing:

1. **Launch System Preferences.**

2. **Click the Sharing icon to display the Sharing preferences panel (see Figure 15-12).**

3. **Click the Personal File Sharing option in the list of services at the left of the window or click Start to the right.** Panther will percolate for a moment while it pumps the accelerator pedal and squirts hairspray into the carburetor and does all the little things that have to be done to make your files available to other folks on the network. Once it's done, the Start button becomes a Stop button; clicking it will turn Sharing off.

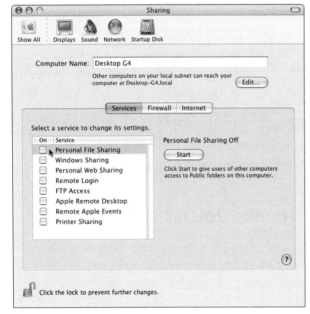

Figure 15-12
Turning on Personal File Sharing

The Public folder

Personal file sharing works without any further setup on your part because every account has a couple of prefab shared folders already on it, ready to go (see Figure 15-13).

Figure 15-13
Your Public folder, or, mine, actually

Every user directory contains a folder entitled Public. You can find yours at the very top level of your home directory (the one with your user name on it).

The Public folder is designed as an official visitor's lounge to your Mac's hard drive. Anyone with access to your network — whether that user has an account on your Mac or not — can "see" this folder on your Mac and open it. Other users can take any files they find in there and copy them to their own local hard drives. They just can't change the Public folder's contents. They can't delete or rename files and they can't add any files themselves.

There's also a special folder entitled Drop Box. Visitors can copy files from their local Macs into your Drop Box but they can't open the folder, which means that they can't see what's inside and they *certainly* can't copy anything within.

So you can understand the usefulness of a Public folder, if you manage it properly. You use your Public folder for items that you want to share with friends and strangers, like a document template file for the standard letterhead you want everybody to use when writing company correspondence. When someone else on the network wants to send you an item that isn't for everybody's eyes — his half of an internal report on which you're collaborating, for example — he sticks it in your Drop Box. That way, the file becomes for your eyes only.

 Note

Incidentally, your Public folder is also public to every other user of this Mac. So, if you tell your daughter Felicity to give you a copy of her American history homework so you can check it, she can put a copy in your Drop Box even though she doesn't have access to your directory. Incidentally, if your chief interaction with your genetic offspring is that she can send you documents via multi-user write-only access to a folder, it's probably time to call Dr. Phil or something.

If you subscribe to .Mac, your iDisk has a Public folder, too. Files you place in your iDisk Public folder become available to any Mac user on the planet who goes to the Finder and selects Go ➜ iDisk ➜ Other User's Public Folder from the menu bar.

Turning on Personal File Sharing allows users with accounts on your machine to log in and access the volumes to which you've given them access. Users without accounts — those who log in as guests — have access to the contents of a folder named Public.

The Shared folder

You can use your Public folder to share personal files with other users of your Macintosh, but your Mac also sports a special folder entitled Shared. The Shared folder is at the top level of your Mac's Users folder, which you can find by clicking the icon of your hard drive.

The Shared folder acts as sort of the common atrium that connects all of this Mac's user directories. There's just one Shared folder among all users. Any user can access any file you drop in there.

DON'T GET TOO PERSONAL IN PUBLIC PLACES

Personal File Sharing becomes an issue when you use this feature on a notebook. Inside the confines of your home, it's a wonderful convenience and a real slam-dunk. Your whole home network is on Airport, so you can easily sit down at your desktop Mac and grab a few files off your PowerBook's hard drive.

Then you head off for work, and you stop off at a coffee shop for a cup of double-blahbah with a half-shot of whatever (I'm sorry. Truth be told, I've never bought a cup of coffee in my *life*). You sit down at a table, open your PowerBook, and read over some documents you'll discuss in a meeting later on.

But...oh, *shazbot*...you *forgot* that Personal File Sharing was still *on*, didn't you? So anyone else in the coffee shop with a wireless notebook can grab and read any file that you put into a publicly accessible folder.

So *please* be aware of when this service is on and when it's off. Chapter 11 discusses how to create different network Locations. Create one called Away in which file sharing is turned off; this makes it really easy to button down your PowerBook when you're away from home.

Making other folders public, or sort of public

The Public and Shared folders are just the folders that Panther prefabs for you. They're designed for simplicity and security. You can modify the behavior of the Public folder — or give people network access to some of your other folders — by manipulating the folder's Permissions.

For example, what if you want to make your Public folder more ambitious. Let's say you have a dozen people in your office working together on a big presentation. You want to use your Public folder as the central depository for presentation resources — text, pictures, music, the whole schmeer. Folks need to copy things to the folder, but they also need to copy things *from* it to their local drives.

Piece o'cake:

1. **Select your Public folder in the Finder.**

2. **Do a Get Info.** A window appears showing the information for the Public folder. Get Info lets you give or take away access and lets you apply it to three different categories of users: Owner, Group, or Others.

3. **Click the triangle next to Ownership & Permissions.** This exposes that batch of info. You're interested in the bit labeled Others at the bottom of the window.

4. **Click the closed padlock so you can make changes** (Figure 15-14).

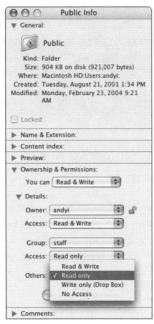

Figure 15-14
Changing Permissions on your Public folder

BE CAREFUL WHEN MESSING WITH PERMISSIONS

Okay. We're a little drunk with power — okay, *and* that case of generic lite beer I got at the Dollar Store this afternoon — so let's calm down for a moment. Messing with Permissions is an easy way to make wonderful things happen on your Mac, but it can also lead to boatloads of trouble. Remember that as a general rule, giving *greater* access to your files and folders is dangerous and should be avoided. In this sense, your folders are a lot like your emotions. Turn your back on hope and love. That's what I say.

There are no labels on this beer. Now that I read that last sentence back I wonder if this is actually the full-strength stuff.

▼ Note

Get Info lets you give or take away access and lets you apply it to three different categories of user. This was covered in Chapter 8, but for those of you who are skipping around: Owner is you, usually. Group means a collection of defined, known users — defined through a hoary process that involves the Net Info Manager utility, a half-gallon of bourbon, and a friend or relative who you suspect enjoys a better than nodding relationship with either advanced Unix system administration, Satan, or (ideally) both.

Others is, well, everybody else. If Apple enjoyed 90 percent market share, it might have had the jocularity to label this Schmoes instead because that's what we're referring to: strangers; just your basic, average guy; anyone not already defined in one of the previous two categories.

5. **Click on the Access field just above Others.** This field lets you designate four different kinds of access:

- **Read & Write means full access:** It's as though users created the folder themselves.

- **Read only:** This is how you normally access a Public folder set. Users can look, but not touch.

- **Write only:** Apple helpfully explains that this is Drop Box behavior; users can toss stuff inside but they can't *look* inside.

- **No Access:** You, sir, are *dead* to me. I drop a funereal shroud over your worthless head. I cup my ears and turn toward the South to hear the keening lamentations of your loved ones. I breathe air tinged with sweet morning dew and the melodies of songbirds, and I am content, for I do not acknowledge that you even exist and I live in a world in which I never knew you in the first place. No, seriously, dude; do *not* get on my bad side.

6. **Click Read & Write, close the Get Info box, and you're done.** Your Public folder is now a two-way street.

You can use this same technique to make *any* folder of yours act like a Public folder or a Drop Box folder. Just do a Get Info and change the access level for Others to whatever's appropriate. The only hitch is that other people can't see it in the first place unless it's inside a folder that's publicly accessible. So, if you have a folder of Batman artwork inside your Pictures folder, assigning Read only access to Others isn't enough. You also have to make your Pictures folder Read only.

SHARING SERVICES

Up till now, we've just discussed the clean, sweet-smelling, warm and fuzzy ways of opening your Mac to other people. What follows are methods that aren't quite so bright and shiny. They're useful, but (a) they're not quite so easy to use, and (b) many of them leave your Mac a bit more vulnerable to attack.

Which is why Panther leaves most of these features turned off until you specifically turn them on. Each one of these services is like a big, double-wide doorway through the castle walls. The wheels of a siege machine could nicely squeeze through the jamb, so it's best to keep the door shut, barred, and put a lower-level minion with a crossbow on duty nearby, preferably with a horn loud enough that he can raise an alarm before the advancing French stick a pike through some of his unfriendlier bits.

FTP

FTP (*file transfer protocol*) is the sturdy, ancient, and reliable way to shuttle files between two computers over a network. With Panther's FTP service turned on, other folks on the network can access your directories via FTP:

1. **Launch System Preferences.**

2. **Click the Sharing icon.** If necessary, click the Services button.

3. **Click the FTP Access option** (Figure 15-15).

4. **Establish a Connect.** To access this Mac via FTP, establish an FTP connection to the address given at the bottom of the Services setup window.

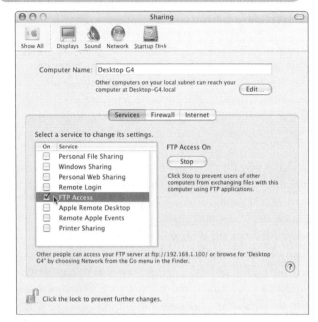

Figure 15-15
Turning on FTP access

Personal Web Services

One of the many benefits of Panther's Unix roots is the fact that Apple included Apache, the Unix-based iron-horse, super-atomic, kick-butt powerful Web server software that runs nearly every reliable and decent Web service on the planet. So with just a couple of mouse clicks, you can make your Mac a for-real Web server, serving content to any machine (Mac, PC, Linux, Commodore Amiga, whatever) on the local network that has a Web browser.

And here you immediately see the utility of Personal Web Services. It's handy for "broadcasting" local information — you can easily assemble a simple Web page with project status info, for instance — but the Big Win is that the Web is a concept with which the most inexperienced user is familiar and that every operating system supports.

So, for example, if you need to share a document with the entire office network, you can either explain to 300 people how File Sharing works, making sure you explain it one way to the Mac people and another way to the Windows people, and that when the Linux people tell you how

WHEN I WAS A YOUNG FTP WHIPPERSNAPPER.....

Oh, merciful Lord in Hamilton, Ontario, Canada...why would you want to open your Mac to FTP access?

Wait, actually it's a useful feature. Sometimes you are confronted with a problem of how to slurp a bunch of data between two unfriendly, dissimilar machines and FTP is just the only decent solution. The last time I opened my FTP services was when I desperately needed to load a bunch of spreadsheets from my desktop to an old Newton PDA. No modern software would interface the two, but I had a Newton FTP client and a wireless card for it. It took me all of 5 minutes, to get *some* sort of software solution running (there are still some diehards who keep the Newton alive, albeit in a "See? Did you *see?* Gramma twitched her left eyeball! I think she's finally coming out of that coma she dropped into 40 years ago!!!" sort of way).

But no kidding: FTP is sort of a crude solution from a security standpoint. FTP was created in a simpler time (there might have actually been Hobbits running around outside when it was first created) when security wasn't on everyone's mind. So, turn it on, do the thing you need to do, *then turn it off again.*

much better *they* could have handled it, you don't hit them terribly hard. Or you can simply turn on Web Sharing, create a simple HTML page that links to the document, and just tell people to point their browsers to the URL.

To turn on Personal Web Sharing:

1. **Create the Web pages you want to share.**

2. **Place the Web pages in the Sites folder in your home folder.**

3. **Launch System Preferences.**

4. **Click the Sharing icon.** The Sharing window appears. If necessary, click the Services button.

5. **Click the Personal Web Sharing option** (Figure 5-16).

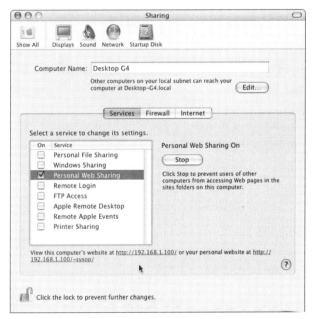

Figure 15-16
Turning on Personal Web Sharing

6. **Access your Web server.** To access your personal Web server, take the http address displayed at the bottom of the Services setup window and plug it into the address field of any Web browser.

Don't confuse Personal Web Sharing with the sort of service that you get from a real ISP to host a real, public Web site. This service is designed for light duty on a local network and little more. And like FTP, it leaves your Mac vulnerable to break-ins, so if you intend to leave Personal Web Sharing up all the time, hide your Mac behind a router on the network for safety's sake.

▼ **Note**

And if you didn't understand that last sentence, it's a sign that you shouldn't mess with it at *all*.

SHARE FOLDERS: A SHORTCUT

You know, you don't even have to learn HTML to benefit from Personal Web Sharing. Apache has a quirk or feature: Normally, when a browser accesses a URL, it automatically looks for and loads a file called index.html. That's the "top" page of the Web site. But if that index.html file doesn't exist, Apache sends back to the browser a directory of the Sites folder's contents, and you can download all those files by clicking them.

So, presto. It's the simplest possible way to share files with absolutely everyone on the network. Just toss the files into your Sites folder and turn on Web Sharing. Other users can download the files they want just by visiting the URL you give them and clicking the links that automatically pop up.

Remote Login

The good thing about Remote Login is that (unlike everything else we've been discussing here) it doesn't just allow you to move files around. Remote Login allows you to take complete control of your Mac from nearly any other computer on the network running the right sort of software. I mean, no kidding. You can move files around, delete stuff, launch apps, force apps to quit, turn basic services on and off...all through a text-based command line. It's hard to imagine a common problem to which Remote Login is the best solution, but it's easy to imagine a very *uncommon* problem to which it's the *only* solution.

LIKE TO LIVE ON THE EDGE? LEAVE REMOTE LOGIN OPEN

Leaving Remote Login open is one of the riskiest things you can do with your Mac. I recommend that before you turn it on, you go out and see a movie, preferably one of *The Lord of the Rings* movies or the restored edition of *Lawrence of Arabia* if it's playing nearby. First, because they're great movies, and second, because they're 3 hours long. If by the time you return to your home of office you still have even the foggiest idea of why the devil you wanted to turn on Remote Login in the first place, then go ahead. But don't say I didn't warn you.

I think I'm telling you about Remote Login for the same reasons that any responsible parent tells his children about fighting or drinking or sex with anybody at any time for any reason so long as I'm alive. I'm really sort of hoping you won't try it yourself until you're older, but if you do try it, you shouldn't stumble into trouble like an ignoramus.

For example, you're on a weeklong vacation, road-tripping across the country to find the perfect bowl of diner chili. Your phone rings. It's your sister, who's house-sitting. One of the reasons she agreed to water your cat and feed your plants all week was the fact that you have this great Macintosh G5, and she wants to spend the week playing with iMovie and GarageBand.

But she doesn't know the password. You *meant* to create an account for her before you left, but you forgot, and you don't want to give her the password to your own account. So, when you reach your next hotel, you plug your Power-Book into a phone line, launch the Terminal app, and run a command-line program called *ssh*. You log in to your home Macintosh just as though you were sitting behind the keyboard 900 miles away, and create a brand-new account that lets her log in to your G5 and start editing video.

Far-fetched? Yes. But a good example of what this service is good for.

The bad thing: *It allows you to take complete control of your Mac from nearly any other computer running on the network.* Remove the word "you" and substitute the word "A suitably clever and determined egg-sucking weasel intent on wreaking havoc," and you see the problem.

To turn on Remote Login:

1. **Launch System Preferences.**

2. **Click the Sharing icon.** If necessary, click the Services button.

3. **Click the Remote Login option** (Figure 5-17).

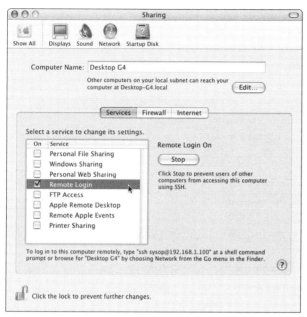

Figure 15-17
Turning on Remote Login

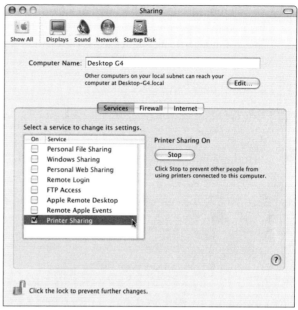

Figure 15-18
Turning on Printer Sharing

Printer Sharing

This option allows any Mac on your network to send print jobs to a printer connected to your Macintosh. For the sake of completeness, here's how to turn on printer sharing:

1. **Connect the printer to your computer.** Make sure that it is working properly.

2. **Launch System Preferences.**

3. **Click the Sharing icon.** If necessary, click the Services button.

4. **Click the Printer Sharing option** (Figure 5-18).

▼ Cross-Reference

For a more complete discussion of printing, see Chapter 10.

SHARING WITH WINDOWS USERS

In Chapter 9, you find out how easy it is to access Windows disk volumes that are available on your network. But turnabout is fair play. You can also allow Windows users to mount OS X volumes.

OS X provides Windows access with Samba, a Unix program. All you need to do to let Windows users access your computer is the following:

1. **Create a new account (as discussed in Chapter 2).** This is to allow access to your computer. Configure that account with the file/folder access you want Windows users to have.

2. **Launch System Preferences.**

3. **Click the Sharing icon.** If necessary, click the Services button.

4. **Click the Windows Sharing option** (Figure 15-19).

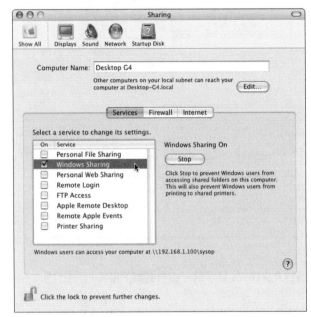

Figure 15-19
Turning on Windows Sharing

5. **Note the network address of your computer at the bottom of the window.** You may need to give this to Windows users.

In the best of all possible worlds, a Windows user can open Network Places and drill down through any subnets until your computer appears. A quick double-click on your

machine then displays a login dialog. After typing a correct user name and password, the portions of your files to which the Windows user has access appear on the Windows machine as if it were a local drive (Figure 15-20).

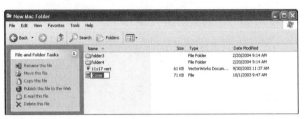

Figure 15-20
A Macintosh volume in a Windows window

Unfortunately, Windows's Network Places doesn't always display a new computer when it powers up. Sometimes waiting a while helps, but if the Windows user runs out of patience, he or she can add your computer manually:

1. **Open Network Places.**

2. **Double-click on Add a Network Place.** A wizard appears for typing the path to the server.

3. **Type the path to the server.**

4. **Type a display name for the server.** The wizard connects to the Macintosh.

Here I have to confess that even though my home office is a mix of Macs and a couple of Windows boxes, I rarely use Windows Sharing. I rarely have a need to swap files between the two platforms and besides, it's just *so* much simpler to either use Web Sharing or to just copy the file to my keychain drive and walk it over to the other machine.

I mean, don't get me wrong. I'm a geek, a big, honkin', major geek. Cut me and I bleed not red, but the nearest HTML-safe equivalent expressed in hexadecimal. But sometimes even *I* get fed up with some of the procedures that you have to crawl through to accomplish the simplest danged thing. SneakerNet isn't the fastest or slickest way of moving bits around, but it's nearly foolproof.

Except for that time when I stumbled over a 5-gallon bucket I'd been using to pour half-empty office Coke cans into, and the resulting sticky tidal wave took out a Dell tower PC.

On the bright side, after I knocked the bucket over, moving the file onto the gooey PC was no longer even necessary. Turned out to be quite a nice little time-saver, actually, because I was spending a hell of a lot of time maintaining that PC.

Shame about the cat, though.

16

I Loathe People! I Want to Secure My Mac!

In This Chapter

Physical Security • Passwords • Fostering Distrust Between You and Your Mac
Managing Passwords with the Keychain • Turning Off Unnecessary Services
Limiting Access with Firewalls • Protecting Files with FileVault
Deleting a File Securely • Backing Up! • Wireless Security

Yes, renowned philosopher B. B. King had it right when he sang "Ain't nobody loves me but my Mother...and she could be jivin', too." Trust nobody. People want to steal your PowerBook. Those who can't muster the energy to steal your tower Mac want to gain access to your data. Everybody wants the account numbers and passwords for your online banking accounts. At the last family wedding, your mother kept complimenting you on how good you look in that suit, but *that* was just a ruse to nudge you into quitting your Van Halen tribute band and taking an entry-management position at your uncle's plastics company.

The good news is that unless you have either (a) Congressional authority to second a launch of nuclear missiles (b) perhaps a beta of next year's edition of *John Madden Football*) it's unlikely that anyone is targeting you, specifically. The miscreants (weasels, reprobates, lizard scum) are just looking for unsecure machines in general and taking anything of value that they happen to find.

The even *better* news is that whether you're protecting your Mac on the analog plane (someone grabbing and running off with it) or the digital one (someone copying your financial info off your hard drive), you don't necessarily need to make your Mac bulletproof. You just need to discourage the casual interloper so much that they look for a less-vulnerable machine in the next room or at the next IP address along.

THERE BUT FOR THE GRACE OF WHATEVER, PART XXVII

Why be thankful that you're not a Windows user? Well, first and foremost, because the little chip that Microsoft implants next to your brainstem really gets uncomfortable when there's a drop in barometric pressure. But here and now I'm talking about the security aspect. Macs have a fraction of the Windows market and because those lizard scum want to attack the greatest number of machines with the least amount of effort, they're really not interested in thinking up ways to break into our hardware.

Our OS is inherently more secure than Windows XP, too, but in a sense a Mac is like the penthouse apartment on a twenty-story building with no elevator. It's just too much effort to get all the way up there, and there are plenty of other places to hit along the way.

PHYSICAL SECURITY

Let's start with the easy stuff: physical security. Although it doesn't strictly apply to OS X, you should consider what might happen if someone were to break into your home or office, or just happens to pass by an open door and spot a $2,000 computer that can easily be hidden under a jacket or carried to a car. Either individual could easily ruin your whole day. At best, you're out a couple of grand. At *worst* you have to worry about what that weasel might do with your financial info, your contact database, your personal photos, all of your correspondence.

(Did it just get cold in here? I thought I felt a chill.)

Short of installing an alarm system — not necessarily a bad idea but somewhat expensive — what can you do to stop a thief from grabbing your Mac? You can purchase a computer lockdown cable kit and use it. All Macs have a

provision for these things: You get a hard-to-cut-off tab that snaps into a ready-made port on your notebook or tower. It permanently fuses itself to the machine and provides a ring that a chain or a cable can pass through, locking the hardware down to the desk or a pipe in a nearby wall.

Granted, anyone with a strong pair of cutters can snap through the aircraft cable that usually comes with such kits, but it's good protection from crimes of opportunity. Remember, you don't have to have the most secure Mac in the world — just the most secure Mac in the room.

▼ Note

This is the classic "I didn't know how much I needed this until I owned it" accessory. If you can't imagine ever being so foolish as to leave your PowerBook unattended, can you imagine being so foolish as to let your battery run down 2 hours before a long flight, and having no alternative but to leave it in an unlocked office to recharge? It's just a good thing to have this thing sitting somewhere in your laptop bag.

PASSWORDS

Your Macintosh's first line of defense is its passwords. A password (sometimes also called a *passphrase*) keeps other people from logging in to your account and also ensures that only authorized users can perform actions — such as installing software — that change the configuration of your computer.

An effective password is easy to remember but hard to guess. If that sounds like a contradiction, don't worry; it isn't. One way to construct good passwords is to use two short, unrelated words connected by a special character. For example, green!toe is a pretty good password. Green and toe are unrelated words and the exclamation point between them means that an egg-sucking weasel can't use an automated password-guessing program that simply throws every word in the dictionary at it.

A METHOD TO PASSWORD MADNESS

Here, I'll give you my Super Top-Secret Golden Pathway To Choosing Passwords That Are Easy For You To Remember But Impossible For Others To Guess: Use "codebooks." Last week, I forgot the password to one of my servers. Well, I just pulled my battered old copy of *The Complete Directory To Prime-Time Network TV Shows 1946-Present* off the shelf. It's the book I always turn to when I eed to change this machine's password. I just kept flipping through it and trying any title that happened to leap out at me.

A few minutes later I had successfully logged on to my server (with the password "leg-work"; a 1-hour crime series that lasted four episodes on CBS in 1987. Starring Frances "Fargo" McDormand, interestingly enough). I quickly remembered that it was somewhere in the middle of the book, and as soon as I spotted Chief Marge in there, it all came back to me.

I can safely share my super-secret method with you. Why? Because I have nearly a thousand books in my home library alone, and even though I've told you what the codebook for this one server is, good luck guessing the right password. The book's 1,200 pages long and mentions about eight shows per page. Better get cracking.

Another good way to construct a password that is hard to crack is to replace letters with numbers. You could, for example, choose "replace" for your password and then use the number 3 instead of the letter "e": r3plac3. Now you have something you can remember but that is also very hard to guess.

And longer passwords are always better than shorter passwords. Don't forget about the threat of someone peeking over your shoulder as you type. If they see you type

K...I...T... they're 60 percent of the way to guessing that your password is "Kitty." If it's actually "kitchen-blender-filled-with-enough-tequila-and-ice-to-stun-an-elk," then they're probably not getting in.

Common wisdom says that you should change passwords frequently (every 60 to 90 days, for example). But there's a big drawback to doing that: It makes your password hard to remember. You'll either forget it, or you'll worry so much about forgetting that you'll do something regrettable like write it on the underside of your keyboard. You'll have to find a pivot point you're comfortable with. If you change your password every week, keep 'em short and simple. If you only change it once a year or so, make it long and brain-bangingly hard and make *bloody* sure no one ever sees it.

▼ Tip

There's an exception, though. Assuming that you are the only one who knows the password to log in to your OS X account, you should seriously consider writing it down, sealing it in an envelope, and storing it in a safe deposit box. If you are unable to access your computer for any reason, this ensures that some other person you authorize can do so. Or do you think you'll *never* wipe out on that stupid motorcycle you bought when you turned 40, and your spouse will never have a need for all of your family financial records in an emergency?

What *shouldn't* you do when choosing a password? Don't use the name of family, friends, pets, birthdays, anniversaries...or *anything* that someone else might know about you or be able to find out. If your cubicle is packed with Simpsons action figures, "Homer" is going to be one of their first five guesses, I guarantee you.

Don't recycle passwords, either. If an egg-sucking co-worker correctly guesses that your Mac's password is "warren-zevon," he's going to see if it'll work on your eBay account, your mail account, and anyplace else that occurs to him.

When you work with OSX, you encounter several types of passwords:

- **Administrator passwords:** An *administrator* is a user account that has the right to perform system modifications, including installing software, using System Preferences to change settings and preferences, managing user accounts, and so on. The OS X Installer creates an administrator account for you when you install the software. You can create others, but keep in mind that the fewer administrator passwords that exist, the lower the chance of one of them falling into the wrong hands.

▼ **Note**

You don't need to be logged in to an administrator account to perform actions that require administrator privileges. In fact, it is wiser not to be. (If you walk away from your computer and leave it logged in to an administrator account, anyone who uses the computer has access to the entire system.) Instead, OS X asks for an administrator password when you attempt to perform a restricted action from a user account. Once you supply an appropriate password, your restricted action can proceed.

- **User passwords:** A *user password* is the password to any user account without administrator privileges. This is what you use to log in to a user account.

- **Master password:** If you use FileVault (discussed later in this chapter) to encrypt the data in your personal folders, your computer needs a *master password* that can override the user password. The master password is a safety device that you use only when a user forgets his or her user password. An administrator sets the master password, which works for all accounts on the computer.

- **Application and Web site passwords:** As you work with programs, documents, databases, and Web sites, you'll accumulate a rather large collection of accounts and passwords. You can manage these with one of

Panther's handier features, the Keychain. Stay tuned for more info on that dealie because using the Keychain nudges the Macintosh Exprerience a few yards closer to Perfection.

FOSTERING DISTRUST BETWEEN YOU AND YOUR MAC

...And believe it or not, it's actually a *good* thing if your Mac occasionally looks at you with the jaundiced eye of one who's loved and been wronged in the past. Your user account name and your password are the chief line of defense keeping other folks from sitting behind your keyboard and accessing all of your information. At one end of the spectrum, Panther can simply start up and log you in without asking for any proof of identity; at the other end, it can become paranoid about the possibility of creeps, weasels, and ne'er-do-wells waiting for you to step out of your cubicle for a tacobagelwich, and then plopping their backsides into your chair easy-as-you-please

Which is right? Depends on the likelihood of creeps, weasels and ne'er-do-wells. Oh! And shifty-looking idlers. They're the worst.

Passwording startup

When you first install OS X, the Installer prompts you to create a single user account. If you are the only person using your Macintosh, then you can configure OS X to log in to that account automatically at system startup, without requiring you to supply a password. This works well if you aren't worried about someone restarting your Mac and gaining access to your account.

▼ **Note**

I'm sorry, but I need to interject. You're using the most stable and steady version of the Macintosh operating system ever created. Arguably, it's the most stable OS available *anywhere*, rarely requiring restarts. And yet you can't summon the 18 picocalories of energy required to tap seven or eight tiny keystrokes once or twice a week?

There's a *reason* why the U.S. has failed to bring home Olympic gold in Men's Singles Badminton, ladies and gentlemen; I'm just the only one with enough pride in this great nation to point it out.

But if more than one person uses your computer or if you want to secure the login – or if you can imagine a reality in which someone might, you know, be able to actually pick up your PowerBook and walk away with it – you should disable the automatic login:

1. **Launch the System Preferences application.**

2. **Click on the Accounts panel.**

3. **Click on the Account name at the top left of the window.** (See Figure 16-1.)

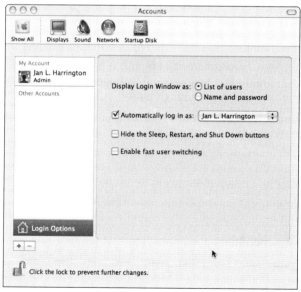

Figure 16-1
Disabling automatic login

4. **Click on Login Options at the bottom left of the window.**

5. **Remove the check from the "Automatically log in as:" check box.**

6. **Close System Preferences.**

Passwording sleep and the screen saver

Removing the automatic login isn't enough to protect your Mac from someone who walks up to your computer. You also need to prevent someone from waking up your computer when it is asleep or disabling the screen saver. When you require a password for wake up and the screen saver, you need to enter that password to wake up the computer or disable the screen saver and return to the normal display.

▼ **Note**

> Boy, is this important. How long would it take someone to jiggle your mouse to clear the screen saver, read whatever emails are open on your screen, and then reactivate the screen saver and beat a safe retreat? No time at all. How long would it take them to click into the Terminal, do a little Unix mojo to give themselves an account on your otherwise secure Mac, and then close the Terminal and leave your Mac the way you left it?
>
> Well, slightly longer. But still less time than it's taken you to nuke up a Cup-O-Noodles in the break room and take it back to your desk, anyway.

To require a password to wake from sleep or clear the screen saver:

1. **Launch the System Preferences application.**

2. **Click on the Security panel.**

3. **Place a check in the "Require password to wake this computer from sleep or screen saver" check box.** (See Figure 16-2.)

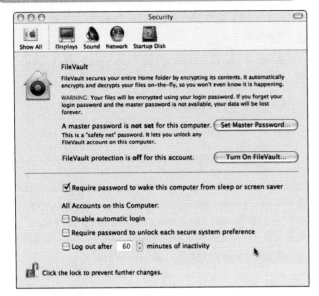

Figure 16-2
Requiring a sleep or screen saver password

4. **Close System Preferences.**

MANAGING PASSWORDS WITH THE KEYCHAIN

The big catch-22 of passwords is that if you exercise the basic rules of common sense, you'll wind up needing to remember a dozen different passwords of brain-mincing complexity. The third or fourth time you lost an hour of your time because you couldn't remember a simple email password like "aj8s7ssyu-aisj-blue" you'll probably change all of your passwords to the word "password" and move on with your life.

Well, Panther has anticipated your pain and given you a big chewable aspirin in the form of the Keychain. Using Keychains, Panther can automatically remember all of your passwords *for* you, and automatically type 'em in when they're needed.

The best thing about the Keychain is that it all happens automagically. The OS creates a system-wide Keychain for you by default and keeps it ready. When a so-called "Keychain-Aware" app (such as Safari, iChat, or X's built-in Mail app) asks you for a password for the first time, the app will give you the option of storing the password in your Keychain file as well (Figure 16-3).

Figure 16-3
Mail asks you if you'd like to store a password in your Keychain file

If you consent, then that's the last time the app will ever ask for it. Forevermore, it'll just grab it from your Keychain. And a Keychain-aware app or resource can store any sort of password in there. Access to Web sites, file servers, remote Macs, AirPort base stations...the Keychain can handle it all. It can even securely store personal info, like credit-card numbers or the security code to your alarm system.

Your Keychain is protected by its own password; by default, it's the same as your system password.

▼ **Note**

A password that allows access to all of your *other* passwords? Yikes. If ever there was a reason to invent a password like "jmichaelstraczynskiand-billsienkiewiczplayingxylophone," it's this.

When you log in to your Mac, the OS automatically unlocks your Keychain for you. Why not? By logging in, you've already proven that you are who you say you are. But if the Keychain remains open all the time, that's a Bad Thing. You're liable to take a 2-hour lunch break after all, and during that time the Keychain would allow anyone sitting at your desk to access anything you've passworded. Instead, it automatically locks itself if it hasn't been accessed recently — by default, it's 5 minutes. Any later than that and it won't do squat until you provide your Keychain password once again.

Still not sold on this whole Keychain concept? OK, try this on for size: Keychains are portable. Your desktop Mac automatically enters passwords for three dozen different servers, accounts, and Web sites. But then you grab your PowerBook and head for the airport, and 6 hours later you're in a Sheraton in Tulsa desperately trying to remember your email password, right? Wrong. Simply make a copy of your Keychain file — you find it in a folder named "Keychains" inside your "Library" folder — and put it on your PowerBook. It's still secure (it asks you for the Keychain password before unlocking itself) no worries there. But now your PowerBook can automagically access the same services as your desktop.

Creating Multiple Keychains

If you want, you can even have multiple Keychains on the same machine. This is handy when there's one set of passwords that everybody needs (access to the company file servers and the airport routers) but another set of passwords (email, iChat) that are specific to each user.

Using the Keychain Access application

Part of the glory and majesty of the Keychain is the fact that it works completely automatically. You don't have to configure it if you don't want to. If you *want to,* use the Keychain Access application to manage your Keychains.

1. **Open the OS X Applications folder on your hard disk.**

2. **Open the Utilities folder.**

3. **Launch Keychain Access.**

Placing Keychain Access on a menu bar

If you are going to make extensive use of Keychains, you can simplify launching Keychain Access by putting a Keychain menu on your menu bar (see Figure 16-4). To make the menu appear:

1. **Launch Keychain Access.**

2. **Select View — Show Status in Menu Bar.**

A Keychain icon will appear in the menu bar at the right. To remove the Keychain menu, repeat the preceding steps.

Figure 16-4
The Keychain menu

As you can see in Figure 16-5, the Keychain Access main window shows you a list of existing Keychains at the right. The items in the currently selected Keychain appear at the top of the main portion of the window.

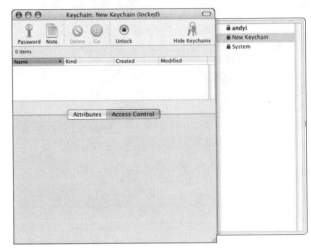

Figure 16-5
Keychain Access

When you click on an item in a Keychain, Keychain Access shows you either the item's attributes (Figure 16-6) or the item's access control list (Figure 16-7), the list of applications that can access the item's contents.

Creating new Keychains

You can either add new items to your default Keychain or create one or more additional Keychains. To create a new Keychain:

1. **Launch Keychain Access.**

2. **Choose File → New Keychain.**

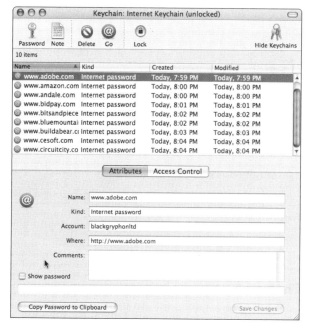

Figure 16-6
Keychain item attributes

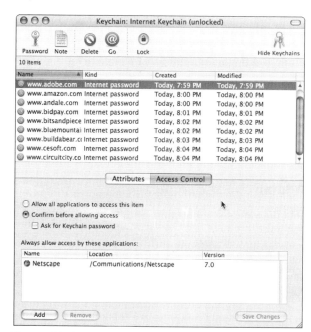

Figure 16-7
Keychain item access control

3. **Type a name for the new Keychain and click OK** (see Figure 16-8).

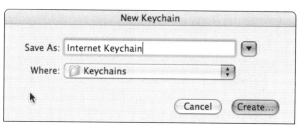

Figure 16-8
Naming a new Keychain

4. **Type a password for the new Keychain and click OK** (see Figure 16-9). The Keychain is now ready for use. To use it, select its name in the list of Keychains at the right of the Keychain Access main window.

Figure 16-9
Creating a password for a new Keychain

Manually adding items to a Keychain

The Mac OS adds items to your Keychain automatically, but you can do it manually as well. The process is slightly different depending on which type of item you are creating.

To create a password item:

1. **Launch Keychain Access.**

2. **Select the Keychain to which you want to add the password item.**

3. **Select File ➔ New Password Item.** The dialog in Figure 16-10 appears.

4. **Enter a name for the item.** The name of a password item is quite important. If you simply enter a name (for example, www.amazon.com), the Keychain assumes that you are describing an application program and gives you an Application item. However, if you enter a URL, the Keychain will give you an Internet item, which you need if the Keychain is going to interact correctly with Web browsers.

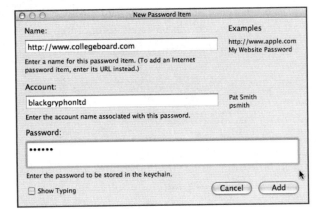

Figure 16-10
Creating a new password item

5. **Type your account name.**

6. **Type the account's password.**

By default, the password doesn't appear; you see bullets as you type it. However, if you want to see the text of the password, check the Show Typing check box, as in Figure 16-11. Keychain Access asks you to enter the Keychain's password. After you do that, you can see the password for this item only.

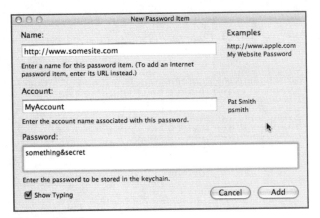

Figure 16-11
Viewing a password

Changing a Keychain item's name

The biggest problem to entering a URL as an item name is that the item appears in the Keychain as *www.somesite.com*, rather than with a meaningful name. You can fix that problem from the Access panel (Figure 16-7, which you saw earlier). To do so:

1. **Select the item in the list of Keychain items.**

2. **Click the Access button, if necessary.**

3. **Change the item's name.**

4. **Click Save Changes.**

Adding specific applications to the control list

Creating an item does not enable applications to use the item's information automatically. You need to add specific applications (in particular, Web browsers) to the item's Access Control list:

1. **Click the item in the list of Keychain items.**

2. **Click the Access Control button, if necessary.**

3. **Click the Add button.** A file selection window appears.

4. **Locate and select the application to which you want to give access.** Assuming that the application is Keychain aware, it can now access the account and password information stored in the Keychain without your intervention.

Storing secure information on a Keychain

As mentioned earlier, you can also use a Keychain to store various types of miscellaneous secure information. For example, you can store credit card numbers for credit cards that you use frequently when shopping at Web sites, software registration numbers, and so on. Such information is stored in a secure note. To create one:

1. **Launch Keychain Access,** if necessary.

2. **Select the Keychain to which you want to add the secure note.**

3. **Select File → New Secure Note.**

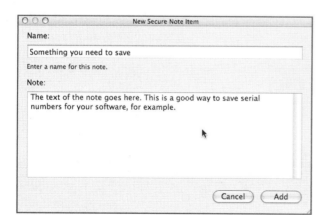

Figure 16-12
Creating a new secure note

4. **Type a name for the note.**

5. **Type the contents of the note and click OK.**

Using multiple Keychain files

Finally, you can have the Mac use more than one Keychain file:

1. **Launch Keychain Access, if necessary.**

2. **Select File → Add Keychain.**

3. **Navigate to the location of the Keychain file.** The Keychain file can be anywhere: on an external drive (like the aforementioned and not terribly amusing USB Keychain drive, or even somewhere on the network).

4. **Click on the file and click the "Open" button.**

The Keychain should now appear in Keychain Access's "Keychains" drawer (Figure 16-13), alongside any others that you've added to the default Keychain.

Figure 16-13
Creating a new secure note

▼ Note

Don't worry about multiple copies of your Keychain file floating around. Keychain Access doesn't copy the file into its own directory. It just remembers where it can find the file. Once you unplug the USB drive or disconnect from the server, *zip!* The Keychain disappears.

TURNING OFF UNNECESSARY SERVICES

Boy, has this chapter been a major downer or what? Okay, let me throw you a bone and offer a word of positive encouragement, atypical for a chapter on Security: If you're worried about some unauthorized weasel taking control of your Mac or accessing its files through your broadband or network connection, don't be. There are plenty of ways for the aforementioned mammal to do you and your data harm, but the sort of attack that makes the CBS Evening News isn't at all likely to affect any Mac users. Here we're talking about software that navigates through a network, twisting doorknobs and looking for unprotected ways to get inside your hardware. That's Windows stuff.

Still, even a shred of vulnerability isn't the same as no vulnerability. And if you have really sensitive corporate data on your drive, you'll want to take the extra step of closing and locking any entranceways that you're not likely to ever use, yourself. In Unix parlance, a *service* is an operating system program that provides support for a specific activity such as file sharing or printing, or serving Web pages. If these services can allow you and other happy and well-adjusted individuals to access your Mac, there's also the outside chance that they can inadvertently allow in those egg-sucking weasels as well.

For safety's sake, OS X leaves all those services off by default (see Figure 16-14). As a rule, you shouldn't leave them on unless you actually need regular access to them. So, if you find yourself in the Bizarro World and need to share files with Windows people, you can turn on your Mac's Windows File Sharing service temporarily, and then turn it off again when you're done:

1. **Launch the System Preferences application.**

2. **Click on the Sharing panel.** You should see the Services pane. If not, click the Services button.

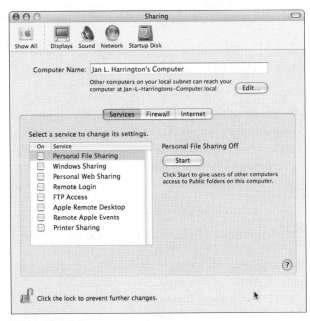

Figure 16-14
OS X services

WHY THE EGG FIXATION?

Why do I insist on describing these people as "egg-sucking weasels," "vile miscreants" and "menace to all good, freedom-loving peoples everywhere" instead of the word "hacker"? Because the word's been corrupted by the mainstream media. The canonical definition, courtesy of Eric Raymond's *New Hacker's Dictionary*: "A person who enjoys exploring the details of programmable systems and how to stretch their capabilities, as opposed to most users, who prefer to learn only the minimum necessary." Hackers are to be admired, appreciated, taken out for a shave and a hot meal. Crackers (the weasels) are to be nailed up inside a wooden packing crate and then left in some tropical jungle near the habitat of the only land mammal known to be (a) a predator and (b) handy with a prybar.

3. **Click on the name of the service.** Services are located there on the left side of the pane.

4. **Click on either its check box or the Start/Stop button in the adjoining panel.** This will start or stop the service, depending on whether or not it was already running when you clicked the button.

LIMITING ACCESS WITH FIREWALLS

Mac OS X's built-in firewall does much the same job as the Services tab: In broad terms, it prevents people from getting into your Mac through a network. The difference is in execution. The Services tabs simply lets you pull the plug on some of your Mac's networking features. The network firewall actively repels all attempts to access your Mac from the outside. Doesn't matter who or what wants to get access or for what reason. It ain't getting in.

▼ Note

You may occasionally encounter a reference to a firewall as a piece of hardware. In that case, the firewall software is running on a standalone piece of hardware that can be plugged into network hardware such as a router. It's a simple and largely foolproof way to protect a whole network as opposed to just one Mac.

To turn on the firewall:

1. **Launch the System Preferences application.**

2. **Click on the Sharing panel.**

3. **Click on the Firewall tab.** (See Figure 16-15.)

4. **Click Start.**

The firewall is like the bouncer at the door to a snooty club. There's only one way in and it's *through him*, and he's just shot you a glance from his peripheral vision that very effectively communicates that you are clearly *way* too big

a geek to be allowed into a supermodel-enriched environment like this one.

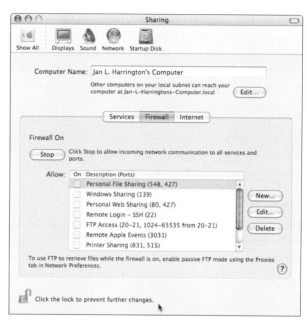

Figure 16-15
Enabling the OS X firewall

BUT ARE YOU LEADING A FIREWALL-EY LIFESTYLE?

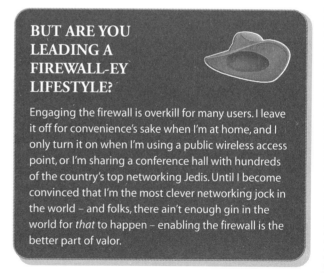

Engaging the firewall is overkill for many users. I leave it off for convenience's sake when I'm at home, and I only turn it on when I'm using a public wireless access point, or I'm sharing a conference hall with hundreds of the country's top networking Jedis. Until I become convinced that I'm the most clever networking jock in the world – and folks, there ain't enough gin in the world for *that* to happen – enabling the firewall is the better part of valor.

But, of course, it wouldn't be much of a party if he let *nobody* in. Remember, the real profit at a dance club is in beverage service, not the cover charge. So he has a little clipboard full of names with him. If you're on the list, you're straight through with a smile. Otherwise, he's prepared to deliver a cogent argument on the limitations of superstring theory in an Einsteinian universe, using your neck and nearby parking meter as visual aids.

Back to reality, or the version of it that Apple has created for us. In the Firewall tab, that scrolling list is the bouncer's clipboard. All the services that you've checked are allowed to access your Mac across a network. The hassle of having a firewall is that if the bouncer has never heard of your brand-new network gaming system (or any other unusual network software), it's not going to let its traffic through and your Mac becomes invisible to other gamers.

That's what the New and Edit are for. When you buy this sort of software, it comes with instructions on how to add it to your firewall's list of approved network traffic. The next time you want to pretend to be a disgraced former vice cop blowing up junior-high students 2,000 miles away who are pretending to be zombie alien commandos, the game will tell the firewall "I'm on the list, man," and it'll be waved straight on through.

PROTECTING FILES WITH FILEVAULT

Although you may spend between $1,500 and $3,000 for an iBook or PowerBook, the most valuable part of that computer may well be the data on your hard disk. If your laptop is stolen—and if it was asleep and unpassworded—the thief can wake up your computer and browse through your finances, company trade secrets, private memos, your Internet fanfic-in-progress about the cast of *McHale's Navy* gettin' it on with the cast of *The Love Boat,* and so on without a problem.

The solution is to encrypt your data files so that no one can read them without your encryption password. Data encryption is therefore the process of changing your readable files into something unreadable. Without the decryption key, your love letter to Tony Orlando is just random gibberish. OS X supplies encryption through its FileVault utility.

 Tip

Encrypting the data on your hard drive is cool beans. No question. But under some circumstances you might want to consider something simpler and even more secure: working from an external hard drive and physically locking it in a safe at the end of the day. There are some things that a weasel in the employ of the Russian Mafia can't accomplish from a networked computer in an apartment in Romania.

Encryption has both its good and bad points:

- **Encrypted files are unreadable by the casual thief or system cracker.** It takes considerable effort (and computing power) to crack the type of strong encryption that OS X uses.

- **You have to encrypt and decrypt the files.** Because you can't work with encrypted files, you must decrypt a file every time you want to use it. When you save the file, you must encrypt it again before it is written to disk. In general, this slows down processing.

- **Encrypting and decrypting files require a password.** FileVault uses your login password. In addition, when you turn on FileVault for the first time, you also create a master password that can you can use if you have forgotten your login password. However, if you happen to be an administrator user and you've forgotten both your login password *and* the system's master password, you're hosed. The encrypted data becomes unrecoverable.

- **To be truly effective, only one administrator should know the master password.** The problem with this strategy is that if that person is ill or leaves your organization, you may be stuck without anyone who knows that password. A solution is to have at least two people who know the master password, but the more people who know the master password, the easier it is to compromise your system.

FileVault encrypts everything in your home directory. You must therefore take care to store all sensitive documents in your home directory or one of its subdirectories.

To turn on FileVault:

1. **Launch System Preferences.**

2. **Click the Security icon.** The Security panel appears. (see Figure 16-16).

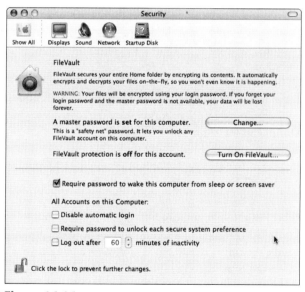

Figure 16-16
The FileVault management window

3. **Check the text in the button next to the master password section.** If it says Set Master Password, click the button. Otherwise, skip to Step 6.

4. **Type the new master password and a hint to help you remember it,** as in Figure 16-17.

5. **Click the Turn on FileVault button.** A stern warning appears (Figure 16-18). If you continue, you are logged out. When you log back in, FileVault encrypts the contents of your home folder. If you have a lot of data, then the initial encryption may take roughly the same amount of time it would take an adult Emperor penguin to complete the Boston Marathon, riding on another Emperor penguin's shoulders.

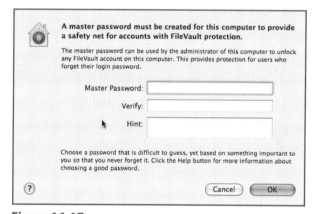

Figure 16-17
Setting the master password

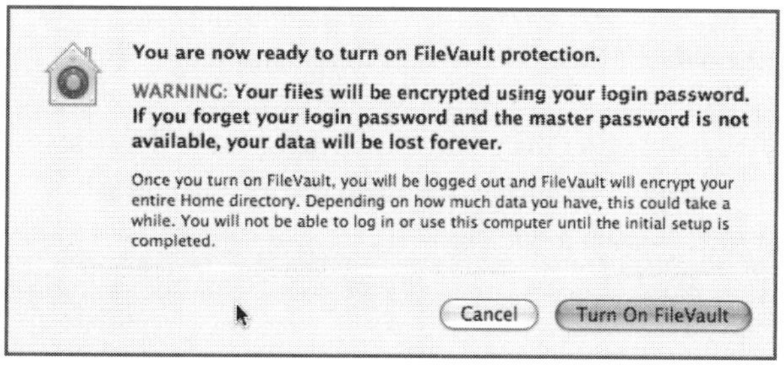

Figure 16-18
The FileVault warning

6. **If you set the master password already, click Turn on FileVault.** This initiates the encryption of your home folder.

To turn off FileVault:

1. **Launch System Preferences.**

2. **Click the Security icon.**

3. **Click the Turn Off FileVault button.**

DELETING A FILE SECURELY

When you want to delete a file or folder, you drag it to the Trash and then empty the Trash. The file or folder is gone, right? Wrong. The file or folder is inaccessible, but its contents remain on the disk until the space is used for something else.

Until the disk space is overwritten, special utilities can often recover a "deleted" file or folder. If you are the only person using your computer, then you probably don't care. If, however, your computer is shared—either at the keyboard over a network—or if you're about to give your old Mac away to a worthy relative, then you may want to obliterate files and folders completely.

To securely delete a file or folder:

1. **Move the files and folders you want to delete securely to the Trash.**

2. **Select Finder → Secure Empty Trash.**

OS X overwrites the space that the files and folders occupy with random characters, a process that takes longer than simply emptying the Trash.

BACKING UP!

A major part of an overall security scheme that is often overlooked is backup. Hard disks are very reliable, but they do have mechanical parts that can malfunction, and malfunction more easily than just about any other part of your computer. Even if your hard disk is alive and well, you can also suffer from file corruption caused by unexpected software crashes and glitches. Your best protection is a good, clean backup copy.

▼ **Note**

And every time I'm about to take off on a business trip, I reflect upon the fact that I am an imperfect vessel and I have failed to live a pure and chaste life. And then when the blood returns to my face, I perform an immediate backup. If my PowerBook gets stolen, well, that's too bad but I'm confident that with legs like these, I can make another $2,000 in no time. But what about the manuscripts and data?

Backing up your data can be as simple or as brain-bangingly difficult as you want. The only limit is your ambition.

If you're shiftless and lazy, you can just pop a CD-R into your drive once a week or so and copy the contents of your Documents folder onto it.

If you're even slightly ambitious or paranoid, you should buy a "real" backup program. Apple Backup comes free with your .Mac account and it's quick, clean, and feature-riffic. But the gold standard for both Mac and Windows is Dantz Development's *Retrospect* (www.dantz.com). It can handle the entire backup process for you, running at your command or at scheduled intervals. It can back up whole drives or just selected folders. It can *restore* whole drives or selected folders; you can even tell it "turn back the surly hands of time and make my drive the way it was three backups ago," and without even pausing to say "Yes, Master," Retrospect makes it happen.

MARKING YOUR TERRITORY

Which brings up a point: You hedge your bets wonderfully by pollinating the world with your system backups. I hid a 10-gigbyte hard drive inside the suspended ceiling of a pal's basement. He had no idea it was there until a pipe burst in my office and caused my Mac and all of its peripherals and data to start making their own gravy. Thank Heavens I kept a backup in another house!

Flexibility is indeed the name of the game. Backing up your data is only effective if you do it regularly, and a good piece of software like Retrospect stays out of your way. Before long, you'll work out a scheme that works for you. Me, I back up my entire drive once a week and my various project folders get backed up several times a day.

You'll also need to think about what sort of storage media you're going to use for backups.

- **Burnable CDs and DVDs** are cheap and plentiful. They're also slow and have limited capacity; back up a whole 40-gig drive on these and you swap discs so much that you'll start seeing the dang things dancing around your head while you sleep. Plus, you can't really reuse them. At some point, you're going to have to safely destroy these discs before tossing them out in the garbage. Still, they're handy for quick backups of single folders.

- **External hard drives** are a compelling modern option. You can purchase standalone FireWire drives for less than a dollar a gigabyte, which means that $200 buys you a backup drive, its media (i.e., the mechanism inside), and enough space for three complete backups of your entire hard drive. It's rocket-fast

and best of all, if your internal drive is toast, you can boot from it. The only caveat is to resist the temptation to leave it connected to your Mac. If you do, when the slings and arrows of outrageous fortune (or a big fire) strike down your internal drive, it'll probably take out your backup as well.

- **Tape drives** are the classic targets for backups, and are still the medium-of-choice for network administrators. Each tape holds a boatload of data and each one costs less than a Big Mac with large fries and a Coke. The drive itself is a killer, though, and the huge expense tends to scare most individual users off.

- **Network backups** are a possibility, too, and now that more and more homes and small offices are going wireless, this sort of backup becomes more and more practical. One Mac (with a big honkin' hard drive) contacts each of your Macs late at night and stores a backup of their contents locally. It's slow, but you're asleep in bed anyway so it really doesn't matter. It does have a big drawback: Unlike tapes, discs, or even an external hard drive, this specific kind of network backup can't be carried out of the building. So again, unless an exceptionally thoughtful sort of tornado hits your office, a disaster that destroys your local hard drive could also take out your one backup. Backing up to your iDisk, or to a remote machine, gives you a little added protection.

WIRELESS SECURITY

"Wireless security"—some security professionals will tell you that such a phrase is an oxymoron, that there is no such thing. Why? Because wireless signals, as they are defined in the original WiFi (Wireless Fidelity) standard are not secure. Wireless transmissions can be easily intercepted and their content cracked. And let's not forget the "war drivers" who case neighborhoods with antennas made from Pringle's cans and wire coat hangers, looking for any network signals that might be passing through walls onto the street. If a war driver can pick up your network's signal, he can insert his laptop into your network and piggyback onto your Internet connection.

To make sense of all this, you need to understand a bit about WiFi and its variations. The Institute of Electrical and Electronics Engineers, better known as the IEEE (or "eye-triple-E"), developed the original "wireless Ethernet" standard. Subgroups of the IEEE are responsible for an entire range of network hardware standards, including wired and wireless media. The wireless Ethernet standard is known as 802.11.

The first AirPort hardware that Apple released adhered to the 802.11b standard, which supports transmissions of up to 11Mpbs at a maximum range of 150 feet. Although 802.11b equipment is easy to install and use, it is not particularly secure. It is subject to war driving (and war walking and war flying, depending on the miscreant's mode of transportation). It is also vulnerable to

- **Wireless sniffing:** A system cracker can insert a "packet sniffer" into the network and capture copies of the traffic passing on the network. He can then examine the contents of the packet at his leisure.

- **Hijacking:** A system cracker can insert packets into a network. These false packets can cause a computer to believe that it is communicating with a trusted computer, when instead it is communicating with a cracker who is attempting to steal information.

- **Inserting of base stations:** A system cracker can place an unauthorized base station into the network. If the unauthorized based station has a stronger signal than the legitimate base station, it can divert network traffic to the system cracker's equipment.

Probably the biggest security hole in the 802.11b standard is the Server Set ID (SSID). This is a password or pass phrase that a computer uses to identify the base station with which it communicates. Each base station has a single SSID that all computers use. When you purchase a base station, the manufacturer gives it a default SSID that is the same for all base stations manufactured by the company. System crackers know these default SSIDs, and attempt to use them to access a base station. If the default has been changed, then a dictionary attack — the system cracker tries every word in a dictionary — can often penetrate the base station's new password.

Doesn't 802.11b use encryption? Shouldn't the company encrypt the SSID to make it harder to obtain? Certainly. It's known as Wired Equivalency Privacy (WEP). But here's the problem: 802.11b encrypts data packets, but doesn't encrypt the SSID. It travels across the wireless network as plain text, making it very easy to intercept.

What can you do to protect an 802.11b network? Not a great deal. WEP's 40-bit encryption key is better than nothing to protect your data, but given the computing power of current desktop machines, a competent system cracker can break the key in a reasonable amount of time. The good news is that like so many facets of network security, your network doesn't need to be bulletproof. It just needs to be better than the base station a couple of yards farther down the street. Unless they have a specific target in mind, breaking WEP is too much trouble, given that there's usually a totally unlocked base station only a few minutes away.

Plus, do keep in mind that when you're using a secure Web site — for example to do some online banking — the browser applies kick-butt encryption on your data before it goes out over the network. So long as the URL starts with https:// you're pretty safe.

AND PORN RAINED DOWN FROM THE HEAVENS

You want an example that will frighten, amuse, and disgust you all at the same time? Let me tell you about MacHack, a compact but very fulfilling annual conference for Macintosh power developers. On the last night of the conference everybody packs into the hotel ballroom to show off any nifty new apps they wrote during the week. One year, somebody showed off a very special networking app. It sniffed the air for wireless network traffic, looking for snippets that represented requests for JPEGs from Web servers. The app would then make its *own* request, and add the picture to the increasingly complicated patchwork of graphics on the Mac's screen.

Naturally, the moment he finished explaining the basic concept, 500 geeks flipped open their PowerBooks and giddily began accessing the most...the...well, let's just say they started hitting Web sites that they knew to be graphics-intensive. And ladies and gentlemen, the ballroom's 15-by-20-foot projection screen exploded. The air turned mauve. An angel with a flaming sword stepped ominously out from the catering area, clearly intent on proving that there's no testament like the Old Testament, but he himself was so creeped out by the rapidly morphing image that he just sort of coughed and made an excuse about having left the lights to his Bonneville on.

Depending on your ISP, it's also possible to use a secure connection to your mailserver. Special protocols supported by Mail and other email clients encrypt passwords and data before they transmit, so if your ISP's mailserver supports those protocols as well, there's no reason to worry.

▼ Note

Naturally, there's *always* reason to worry. Did you know that a recent research study suggests that our bodies' fundamental cellular morphology is "allergic" (for lack of a better word) to the element Nitrogen? The single most prevalent element in Earth's atmosphere? That ought to cheer you up vis-à-vis the relative threat of weak, 40-bit wireless security.

If you have the original AirPort base station, consider carefully what you send over that wireless network. Avoid using it for sensitive information, be it business or personal.

The alternative is to use Apple's AirPort Extreme, which adheres to the 802.11g standard. Adopted in early 2003, 802.11g is both faster (54Mpbs at up to 59 feet) and more secure than 802.11b:

- **AirPort Extreme includes a built-in firewall.** In fact, this device acts much like a router in a wired network because it can accept a wired broadband Internet connection and a wired Ethernet connection. It also implements DHCP to hide internal IP addresses from the Internet.

- **AirPort Extreme implements 128-bit WEP encryption keys.** This is compared to the the 40-bit keys that 802.11b employs. These longer keys make encryption keys almost impossible to crack with anything short of a supercomputer.

- **You can control the amount of power with which AirPort signals transmit.** By lowering the power, you restrict the range of the signal, making it much more difficult for a system cracker to insert any equipment into the network. It also means that apartment-dwellers can dial down the signal so that it's strong enough to punch into your two bedrooms but not into the apartment across the hall.

Note

802.11g devices are compatible with 802.11b devices. However, when 802.11b devices communicate with an 802.11g base station, encryption is reduced to the 802.11b standard. Therefore, although you can use standard AirPort cards with AirPort Extreme base stations, you won't get the benefit of the added security that 802.11g brings.

Modern base stations have been upgraded to use a brand-*new* encryption standard, meant to address all the holes of WEP. The new standard's called WPA, or Wi-Fi Protected Access.

Whether you're using 802.11b (original AirPort) or 802.11g (AirPort Extreme), make absolutely sure that you've configured it to encrypt its signal. When you join the network, it should ask you for either a WEP or WPA password.

Encrypting the signal also restricts AirPort access to those people who know the base station's password. That sound you just heard was the sound of freeloaders driving on past your house and on towards your neighbor's.

YOUR MOTHER IS PROBABLY AT LEAST MODERATELY FOND OF YOU, ACTUALLY

In retrospect, it's possible that when I suggested that your mother had formed a relationship with you based on deceit and betrayal to best suit her own selfish ends, I may have over-played my hand. A bit. I mean, you know her better than I do, I suppose.

Still, the whole point of this chapter is that the weasels are out there. Fortunately, Batman had them pegged right from Page Three of his original comic: "Criminals are a cowardly, superstitious lot." Yes, they can do a lot of damage, but for the most part their tactics are predictable. They're not looking for challenges; they're looking for users who either don't know or don't care about fundamental security.

In a world without weapons, a single ugly bartender wielding a board with a nail through it can become king.

PART II

The Technical Bits

Automating with AppleScript

In This Chapter

One thing sets the Macintosh Power Users apart from the rest: their use of AppleScript. (And Unix. But AppleScript is a lot easier to use and a lot more practical and a lot more fun.)

Oh, and Macintosh-themed body modifications as well. I have a friend who carves the Apple logo into his hair for every Macworld Expo, and I can also testify that there are more Apple and Mac OS-themed tattoos to be found at that show than liquor-themed tattoos at a *Jerry Springer* taping. But again, AppleScript is a lot more practical than a tattoo or a piercing, it'll disappoint your parents a whole lot less, and it's a lot more fun than having needles pierce your skin hundreds of time a second.

The difference is people who gets things done in minutes, and people who get things done in hours; people whose Macs are naturally efficient and organized, and people with files scattered all over the place; people whose Macs do things that border on the sorcerous, and people whose Macs do more or less no more than what they did when they were first taken out of the box.

AppleScript — Mac OS X's built-in system-wide resource for automating routine processes and writing simple software — is the difference between *a* Mac and *your* Mac. AppleScript helps to build strong bodies nine different ways. If it were a person, it'd return its library books on time and donate blood regularly.

I am, as you may guess, a rather enthusiastic evangelist of AppleScript. I only have your interests at heart, though. When you learn AppleScript, you take your first step into a larger and more exciting world.

MEET APPLESCRIPT

The term "writing software" is instantly intimidating to any sensible user. You didn't lay out two grand to have the wonderful opportunity to spend weeks building your own apps. That's why you support the (sometimes) fine work of the Microsoft Corporation, after all.

Still, there are plenty of things you do with your Mac that involve just repeating a simple task over and over and over again. That's fine when you're working for The Man and you get paid for a full day whether you actually think or not. But when the goal is to finish a task as quickly and efficiently as possible, you wish there were a way to harness your computer's endless capacity to shut up and do what its told, no matter how dull.

NIKE DIPLOMACY

If you don't want to deface George and Abraham, at least slap some Sal stickers on a few lockers or something. If you walk into a typical Apple product manager's office and ask how influential Sal is in ensuring that AppleScript remains an important and critical part of the Macintosh experience, the manager will silently clear a few papers from the desk and point to a pattern of deep smudges in the wood. You see, there once was a time when this manager's product supported AppleScript in only the most basic, lame-o way, and this surface was pristine and unmarred. Then Sal burst in and kept jumping up and down on the person's desk until they agreed to improve things.

I'll give you a real-life example, torn from the pages of history itself. In the furious final weeks of producing this very book, it was discovered that each of its hundreds of illustrations had been named improperly. The six-digit code that began each filename was the *wrong* six-digit code. Do you have *any* idea how long it takes to rename hundreds of files by hand?

Well, neither do I. I wrote an AppleScript that told the Finder to process each file and change each filename individually. Days and days of tedious effort instead became an hour of watching *The Shield* on my TiVO downstairs, and then wondering if the script had finished its work, and then coming back up and discovering that it had finished the task before the second commercial break.

But AppleScript isn't a standalone app or a utility. It's a fundamental part of Panther's architecture, just as intimate as the mechanism that prints files or draws windows and menus. It's a superhighway that allows every piece of software running on your Mac — including the OS itself — to interact with each other and work together. If AppleScript causes the Mail app to check for new mail, it doesn't do anything so unsophisticated as send a mouse click to the Mailbox menu's Get New Mail item. It actually communicates with the code lurking *inside* Mail.

▼ **Note**

So AppleScript is like the general contractor on a big home-remodel project. It can do things on its own without having to control other applications at all, but in everyday use its typical function is to hand tasks off to specialists, make sure they have what they need to get the job done, and make sure that all these individual tasks are done in the specified sequence without any errors.

What makes AppleScript so gosh-darned super?

I would like to think that at this point, the mere fact that I'm slobberingly enthusiastic about something should be reason enough for you to march straight into your child's public school, tear down all those pictures of losers like George Washington and Abraham Lincoln, and replace them all with shots of Sal Soghoian and Chris Espinosa, Apple's Iron Man and Captain America of AppleScript, respectively.

Some of you might have been skipping around the book and haven't developed the sense of blind, robotic faith in me that causes everybody else to acquire that slightly glazed look of contentment and buried individuality that's resulted in so much comment around the post office recently. So here's what makes AppleScript so special:

- **You can control every Mac OS X app through AppleScript to one extent or another.** (But more on this later). It's a fundamental system resource.

- **It's powerful and flexible enough that it can do most anything.** Calculate the volume of a cone? Sure. Take 40 documents from your local drive; download 20 more from eight other people scattered all over the world; assemble all this content into a 100-page, full-color report; transmit this report to a shop for printing, binding and delivery; and email digital copies to four department heads? A tad more ambitious, surely, but well within AppleScript's capabilities.

- **Writing AppleScript is a basic skill that you can exploit elsewhere.** Not only can you use AppleScript in simple automation projects, but also, if you ever get the itch to start writing software for real, most of the popular Macintosh development systems (REALbasic,

Revolution, Apple's XCode system) can use your AppleScripts without any additional conversion or transmogrification. So, if you've spent a month gradually turning a three-line convenience script into a sophisticated productivity solution, you're probably about 80 percent of the way to turning it into a rock-solid commercial app.

▼ **Note**

But hey! Don't simply *assume* that you can't build a rock-solid commercial app solely using AppleScript! XCode, Apple's free, standardized environment for developing professional, high-complexity apps, fully supports AppleScript. There's an entire environment called AppleScript Studio that's there specifically to help you build for-real apps using nothing but AppleScript. Ain't no glass ceiling *here*.

- **With most programming languages, the code you write is as simple to read and understand as one of those customizable message signs that still sits outside the gas station 7 years after the owner lost the last vowel in the set.** No programming language is trivial to learn, but anybody can read a working script and get an immediate sense of what it does and how.

▼ **Note**

Just to leave you suitably agog, let's say you wanted your AppleScript to make a list of every file in a chosen folder whose file type is JPEG Image. What would the AppleScript for that be? Here it is:

every file in (choose folder) whose file type is "JPEG Image."

If *that* doesn't leave you agog, then your agogulator is long overdue for its scheduled periodic maintenance.

But is there anything about AppleScript that will make me want to drop my mouse, stomp outside, and go chuck rocks at birds?

I'm glad I ended that last section on a high note because in the interests of fairness I need to point out that

- **Application support of AppleScript is spotty.** Making sure that AppleScripted instructions control an application is the responsibility of the app's developers...and frankly, many of them feel that they have enough on their hands ensuring that their new fuzzy-logic search-and-replace routine doesn't have the ability to one day become self-aware and lead all the machines in an uprising that will result in Humanity becoming a slave race mining selenium and tungsten under the emotionless, unpitying steel heels of emotionless overlords. So, some apps (particularly those published by Apple itself) support AppleScript with all the zealotry of a member of alt.nerd.obsessive who's just read a public message claiming that the *USS Enterprise* could probably beat the *Millennium Falcon* in a battle. But others only support the four bare minimum AppleScript commands mandated by Apple: run, open a document, print a document, and quit.

- **The documentation really stinks.** Apple doesn't do enough to provide users with AppleScript tutorials. And because every application supports AppleScript in its own individual way, the fact that you've mastered the AppleScript skill of creating a new document in TextEdit doesn't necessarily mean you've picked up any of the skills you need to create a new outgoing email in Mail.

- **Debugging stinks, too.** At least in places. In plush, cushy development systems like REALbasic, when you make a mistake with your code, the system clearly flags it, clearly and specifically explains the

nature of the problem, and might even suggest a solution. AppleScript tells you "TextEdit got an error: NSCannotCreateScriptCommandError" and you should feel lucky it doesn't toss a derisive "*Duh!*" at you before hopping back on its skateboard and zipping away.

- **AppleScript's easygoing approach to English and syntax can often be a double-edged sword.** With a language like C or even Basic, the code has either been written correctly (the way that causes your project to build and run successfully) or incorrectly (the way that results in your computer doing nothing except repeatedly reminding you of what a dipwad you are, until you finally rewrite your code The Correct Way). In AppleScript, there are often several ways to achieve the same results. This is great because programmers can develop a style that makes the most sense to them, personally — but if you're trying to learn AppleScript by looking at other people's scripts, it can give you fits. You have to enter some parts of the script verbatim. Other parts are a matter of personal preference. Your mission, Mr. Phelps, is to learn to distinguish between the two.

▼ Note

For example, early on, the language's architects realized that without the word *the*, the line "set the title of the window to 'Utopia Limited'" reads like it's being spoken by Frankenstein's monster. People don't *like* Frankenstein's monster — misunderstood, yes, but come on, the dude's done some nasty stuff — so they decided that *the* is optional in a script. AppleScript will just *bloop* right over it.

USING SCRIPTS

"I'm sold," you're saying. "I'll take a dozen in assorted flavors." So how do you use AppleScript in my day-to-day life of home, work, and worship?

You can get started by using AppleScripts that have been thoughtfully written for you by Apple and by other users. You'll find a folder named AppleScript inside your Applications folder. It contains lots of useful sample scripts, along with documentation and a couple of scripting utilities.

Tip

If you want to see what some *non*-Apple employees have been doing with AppleScript, skip ahead to the end of this chapter, wherein I list a number of online scripting resources. Many of them have enormous hoards of useful scripts available for free download.

There are three different kinds of script files. You can see what their Finder icons look like in Figure 17-1.

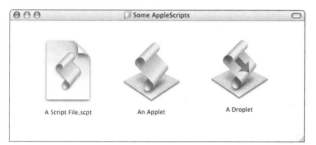

Figure 17-1
Script files, applets, and droplets: The three faces of AppleScript

- **Script files** are akin to AppleScript documents. You use this format for scripts that you're still tweaking because, while you can run them by double-clicking them, they can't run unless the Script Editor application is running as well.

- **Applets** are the standard, useful form of script. The AppleScript code has been saved as a Macintosh application — albeit one without a slick Macintosh user interface — so this script can run all by itself without any assistance from Script Editor.

- **Droplets** are a special form of applet. You can run them by double-clicking, but you can also drag and drop a file or a folder of files onto them. Doing this runs the droplet and tells it, "Whatever it is that you do, I want you to do it to all of *these* files."

Applets and droplets are examples of *compiled scripts*. That is, for the purposes of speed and flexibility, the plain-text AppleScript instructions have been transmogrified into something considerably closer to the hobo's stew of numbers and addresses that a CPU is used to working with. You can still open them in Script Editor and edit their AppleScript code — unless the author decided to keep the code under wraps — but they'll run considerably faster than plain old Script files.

Launching scripts yourself

You can place applets and droplets anywhere you'd place an application. Keep 'em in the Dock, where you can easily launch them; put them on the Desktop or in the toolbar of your Finder windows so you can drag files and folders onto 'em; and like any other app, you can even have Panther launch them every time your Mac starts up by setting them as Startup items.

Panther gives you another way of running scripts: the Scripts menu. This is a menulet that you can install in your menu bar by double-clicking the Install Script Menu app found in your AppleScript folder. The Scripts menu looks like Figure 17-2.

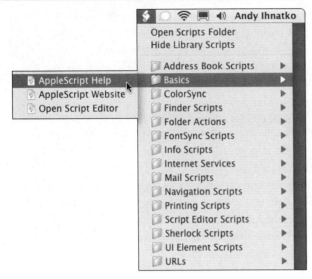

Figure 17-2
The Scripts menu

The Scripts menu

By default, the Scripts menu comes populated with the dozens and dozens of utility scripts that were placed on your hard drive when you installed Panther. Take a minute or two to walk through all those submenus and see what's there. There are some real gems to be found, including a whole collection of scripts that apply modifications to a whole series of filenames in the Finder.

The Scripts menu is populated from two sources: the Scripts folders located in your Home directory's personal Library folder, and your Mac's system-wide Library folder. Just drag in any applet, droplet, or script file. Scripts in your personal folder are yours and yours alone; any scripts you put in the system-wide folder become available to any user. The scripts pop into the menu immediately (Figure 17-3) and sink to the bottom of the list.

If you don't give a toss for any of those utility scripts, just select Hide Library Scripts and the menu only shows your personal stash.

Figure 17-3
A few custom scripts in the Scripts menu

Attaching scripts to Mail rules

A great many apps (including many of Panther's built-in apps) take advantage of AppleScript to increase their flexibility and power. The folks who wrote the Mail app, for example, couldn't possibly have thought of *everything* that *everybody* would *ever* want to do with Mail. Even if they did, they all work in California. It's usually way too nice outside to stay cooped up inside bashing out code all day.

Mail can be scripted like any other Mac app, but it also can run scripts as part of its automatic mail filtering system (Figure 17-4).

I've written a script that takes a specified message, converts it to text, and then installs it in my iPod's Notes folder so I can read it while I'm sitting in my doctor's office waiting for my weekly injection of sheep collagen. By attaching this script to a Mail rule, any time Mail receives an email from the Tony Danza Fanscene Message Board that I belong to, it's automatically slurped onto the iPod.

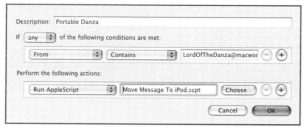

Figure 17-4
A Mail filter rule that triggers an AppleScript

That's just a single example of an app that can run an AppleScript automatically whenever a certain condition is met. They're all over the place. Go to System Preferences and click on the CDs & DVDs panel. It lets you dictate what Panther should do whenever a disc is inserted. There are obvious things you'd want to do when you insert a disc of a certain type (audio CDs are opened in iTunes, photo CDs get handed off to iPhoto), but you can also tell Panther to run an AppleScript. That's handy for customizing Panther's response. I wish iTunes could display editorial information about a CD, as other players can. If it bugs me *that* much, I can write a script that opens the disc in iTunes, gets the name of the album, and then opens a Google page on it.

It's just another way of turning Just Any Mac into a Mac that's specifically been dialed into your personal needs and preferences.

LET'S SEE AOL'S MAIL APP DO *THIS*

I've just reread the example about the script I wrote to place mail on my iPod. It's possible that you might come away thinking I'm not the harbinger of intense, brooding super-cool that even would provoke comment among Sean Penn or Johnny Depp. So I will confess that the Mail script I *really* wrote is one that takes advantage of both Mail's scripting features and that of an app called XTension (www.shed.com). This app works with cheap, home-automation hardware and allows the Mac to both turn lights and appliances on and off and accept input from motion and temperature sensors.

Because I live the life of the sensitive artiste (and, again, I have that whole brooding thing going on), I often leave the office for a few hours to breathe a little fresh air. Depending on what I've got cooking, I may or may not check my email immediately when I get back, which can have serious repercussions if something important has come in when I had no idea that anything important might be coming in.

So here's what I did: I got my disco strobe light (it was a gift. *It was a gift.*) out of the closet, plugged it into a home-automation box, and wrote a three-line AppleScript for XTension so that any app could turn it on. I attached this script to a Mail rule so that the strobe activates whenever an email arrives from one of my editors, and voilà! when I pull into the driveway and see through the windows that there's a full-on rave in progress in my office, I head straight upstairs and check my mail. Or, admittedly, I pull back out of the driveway again and hope that my assistant (either one of the two goldfish; doesn't matter) handles it. Either way, attaching scripts to mail actions is a useful feature.

Attaching scripts to folders

One of AppleScript's ginchiest features, Folder Actions, went away temporarily during the transition to Mac OS X, but now it's back. Just as Mail can run a script whenever a Mail rule senses that a specific condition has been met, Folder Actions allows you to attach a script to a specific folder and have it run whenever any or all of the following things happen:

- The folder is opened.
- The folder is closed.
- An item is added.
- An item is removed.
- The folder's window is moved or resized.

And here I encourage you to just lean back in your chair — get out of bed first and move to your desk if need be because I like the visual of someone leaning back with hands folded behind their head, staring thoughtfully at the ceiling; work with me here — and consider the implications of this. This is why AppleScript skills elevate you into a Power User. For example, why bother to manually organize your Documents folder? Attach a script to the folder that leaps into action whenever a new item is added and moves it into the proper subfolder automagically.

But that's *productive*. Brrrrr! How about something stupid. Get a load of Figure 17-5.

There was a folder on my office's publicly used Mac that my visitors were *told* not to mess with, but they insisted on messing with it all the same. I had to write a whole bunch of scripts and attach them to the folder to prevent folks from creating problems, but in the end, I was unsatisfied with having AppleScript just throw up a little error message politely asking them not to do that again.

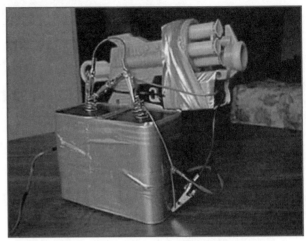

Figure 17-5
AppleScript applies a corrective action

So I bought a repeating-action suction-cup gun at the toy store, fitted it with the door-lock actuator from an old car, gave it 12 volts of battery power, and wired it into a little interface box that allows a Mac to interact with electronics. And yes, the box is AppleScriptable.

The first time a visitor tried to monkey with the folder, he got a polite warning. The second time he received three darts to the back of the head fired from concealment behind a potted plant placed there for that specific purpose.

I haven't worked as a system administrator in quite some time. I think it's because I was just so dashed effective at my job that I set an impossibly high standard for others to follow. Plus, I kept stealing photocopiers, and if I'd known that was the boss's daughter, I sure wouldn't have encouraged her to drop out of law school and start a pottery business. Hindsight is 20-20, you know.

You can attach a script to a folder through the folder's contextual menu. Folder Actions is a system-wide service that's disabled by default, so your first job is to turn it on. Control+click the folder to open its contextual menu and select Enable Folder Actions from the bottom of the list.

Note

I admit that Apple could have chosen a more logical mechanism for turning that feature on. Enable Folder Actions doesn't just affect this one folder; conceivably, it affects every single folder that has actions associated with it. If you've already assigned actions to a half-dozen folders, doing this will cause all of those scripts to become live, so to speak. Apple really ought to have put this into System Preferences instead.

Select the folder's contextual menu a second time and you'll notice that a few new items have been added (Figure 17-6).

Selecting Attach a Folder Action opens a standard Choose File dialog. You can select any script anywhere on your hard drive, but by default, it points to Scripts ➡ Folder Action Scripts located in your Mac's system-wide Library folder. There, you'll find a number of useful built-ins. Select add – new item alert.scpt.

Tip

If you want to create a Folder Action Script that's available to all users of this Mac and not just to you, be sure to copy it into the default folder.

This script is a useful thing to attach to your Drop Box. Every time someone on the network puts a file in your Drop Box, the script activates and alerts you (Figure 17-7).

Figure 17-6
Setting up Folder Actions via a contextual menu

Figure 17-7
Hail, Folder Actions! For now I know that Lenny has sent me the file he promised.

You can attach multiple scripts to a folder. Removing scripts is just as straightforward: Activate the folder's contextual menu, go to Remove a Folder Action, and select the script from the submenu.

Apple, which loves you and only wants what's *best* for you and your siblings, has also provided you with the Folder Actions Setup utility (Figure 17-8).

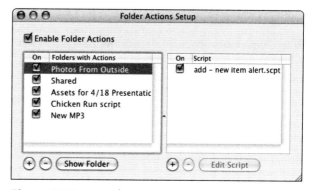

Figure 17-8
The Folder Actions setup utility

As you add more and more scripts to more and more folders, a management utility like this becomes more and more necessary. At a glance, it shows you which folders have scripts attached to them, and allows you to temporarily disable or enable them with a handy click.

BECOME A BIG PICTURE MAN

And here I say Thank The Great Gor Of Ranxeron-9. I'm what you'd call a Power User, which means that I've customized my Mac's operations to such an extent that I barely have half an idea of what's going on three-quarters of the time. I kept *losing* files in my Pictures folder once. It turned out that I had attached a script a week earlier to automatically process hundreds of photos that were coming in across the network, and I'd forgotten to turn that script off when I was done.

I choose to see this as a sign of my power and prestige. Do you think Donald Trump has half a clue what goes on inside his offices? Of course not. We're Big Picture men, too busy steering empires — his: an international real-estate and entertainment conglomerate; mine: a dual-processor G4 tower with "Babylon 5" stickers on it — to waste time on trivial details.

CREATING YOUR OWN SCRIPTS

When Apple first announced AppleScript back in 1993, it was truly going to be the miracle of the Zeppelin age. Not only was every Mac application going to be scriptable, but there were going to be three different increasingly ambitious *levels* of scriptability:

- **Scriptable.** Users can write AppleScripts that exploit this app's features. Sounds good, but how about

- **Recordable.** Users don't even *have* to write any Apple-Scripts. They can run the Script Editor application, create a new script file, click a Record button, and then go back to the app and perform whatever action he or she would like to automate. Return to Script Editor, click Stop, and hey-presto! An AppleScript to repeat that same action magically appears! But don't order *yet!* Because *some* apps are also

- **Attachable.** Wish you could change some of your apps' fundamental behaviors? Wouldn't it be useful if every time you pressed ⌘+S in your word processor, it would only save the file *after* giving it a quick scan to make sure you weren't using more than two of George Carlin's Seven Dirty Words in the church newsletter? Well, you no longer need to hit the bottle because you can customize an Attachable application into such an unholy perversion of what its creators intended that even the professionals who groom teacup poodles would point and say, "Dude...*too far!*"

Oh, what a Xanadu that would be! But Apple was only setting us up for heartbreak. Scripting features are determined by the app's developers, and very few companies are truly committed to AppleScript.

Recordable apps and attachable apps don't exist. "Don't *exist?*" you huff, racing to your mail client to roundly jump up and down on my head for making such a baldly incorrect statement and to provide me with a long list of apps that are *too* recordable and attachable, thank you very *much*.

But yeah, as a *practical* matter, they don't exist. Recordable apps are rare, and attachable apps are rarer. Even when you *do* joyously happen upon one in the wild, throw it in a bag, and haul it back to the States in hopes that you can get it to breed, you'll ultimately be disappointed with what it can do. Only *some* functions can be recorded, and only a *few* menu options are attachable.

As for basic scriptability, nearly every app supports at least four basic AppleScript commands:

- **Run.** Launches the app.

- **Open.** Opens an item, typically a document file.

- **Print.** Prints an item, again, typically a document.

- **Quit.** Fold. Pack it in. Give up hope. Take your ball and go home. You know...*Quit.*

RECORDABLE APPLE-SCRIPTS: NICE WORK IF YOU CAN GET IT

Why are there so few recordable and attachable apps available? Because AppleScript never won the grass-roots support that it deserved. To the point of view of the app's developers, anyone who's savvy enough to want to record a script is probably savvy enough to write one on his or her own. So why waste time adding recordability?

They sort of have a point, though maybe it's a self-fulfilling one. I don't count on an app being record-able, so I just go ahead and write my scripts from scratch. The only time I take advantage of an app's recordability is when I'm writing a larger script. I'll record the desired action first and use that as a starting point for the "real" script.

Anything above and beyond that is up to the ambition and commitment of the developer. It's a crapshoot of delight and disappointment. It's the *good* apps that keep you committed to AppleScript. Some apps are so script-happy that it almost seems like a waste to work with the user interface at all.

▼ **Note**

This includes most of Apple's own apps. I recently finished ripping every single CD I've ever bought in my life into a single iTunes library. I think I've spent more time writing scripts to manipulate the library and analyze my music tastes than I've spent listening to it.

Script Editor

Script Editor is the app you use to record scripts, edit existing ones, write brand-new scripts of your own, and crack open your applications to see just how scriptable

they are. You find it inside your AppleScript folder, which awaits you inside Applications. Figure 17-9 shows you a typical script-editing window.

This is Script Editor's entire interface, or near enough. Apart from Saves, Opens, and Prints, you'll never touch the menu bar at all. Here, give it a shot:

1. **Create a new script by pressing ⌘+N.** Alternatively, you can click File → New.

2. **Type the following code into the editing window:**

```
say "Greetings, Professor Falken."
delay 1
say "How about a nice game of chess?"
```

3. **Click the Run button.**

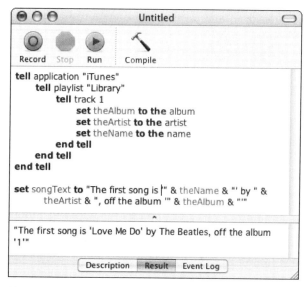

Figure 17-9
The Script Editor, with a simple script up on the lift so we can finally do something about those brake pads

There you go; you're now a programmer. I bet your skin's half a shade paler already.

If you were watching the window carefully you noticed that the Stop button enabled itself while your script was running. Clicking that sucker terminates the script in mid-run — a very useful feature when the script that you *thought* you told to look through your entire hard drive for Microsoft Word documents and copy duplicates onto a blank CD and then burn it, actually winds up emailing those boudoir photos you had done at the mall to everyone in your 1,100-person Address Book.

▼ Note

Which ordinarily wouldn't happen. AppleScript doesn't make mistakes like that. But if there's one thing more powerful than AppleScript, it's Karmic Justice. Yes, *you*, the lady in the pink raincoat I encountered outside Blockbuster this morning. That was *my parking space* and you knew it. Well, who's laughing *now*?

As you start to work with longer and more complicated scripts, you'll probably start making regular use of the Compile button. Essentially, it double-checks your spelling and grammar. If something you've typed doesn't make sense as AppleScript, it flags it for you and does its best to explain what the problem is. If everything's flawless, it reformats the script with fancy nested indents and type styles, like you saw in Figure 17-9.

Underneath the code section of the window exists a little pane of information. It can display three different things, depending on which of those three tabs underneath it has been clicked:

- **Description.** It's a good idea to describe your script and what it does. You're going to start writing a *lot* of scripts (No, really, I've paid a large man $30 to come over to your house and beat the snot out of you if you don't. So, I mean, time's a-wasting), and without attaching notes to these things, it becomes really easy to forget why you bothered to write this particular script in the first place.

- **Result.** That's a debugging tool. When a script runs to the very end, the results of the last operation it performed are displayed in the Result tab. You can see an example in Figure 17-9. The last thing this script did was build a sentence out of the information it retrieved from iTunes. Thus, this sentence winds up in the Result pane.

▼ Tip

I talk the big talk when it comes to AppleScript, but my arrogance ends when I sit down at the editing window. I have taken the wise words of Rabbi Norm Abram and kept them close to my heart: "Measure twice, cut once." Or in this case, "Don't try to debug a new snippet of code by inserting it inside a ten-page script and hoping for the best; write it separately, keep modifying until the Result is what you predicted and hoped it would be, and *then* trust it to work properly as part of the larger project." If the Result tab were a woman and I were a married man of considerably greater means, I'd be buying it a condo and visiting it on the side.

- **Event Log.** An even more sophisticated debugging resource. At the root of a gas engine is combustion. At the root of national-level politics is unresolved childhood inadequacy issues. And at the root of all Mac software are events. These are the molecules of what goes on behind the scenes — the actual activities that software has to carry out to make things happen. Script Editor can maintain an Event Log that keeps track of everything your script did during execution and what the immediate result was, step by step by step.

With the current version of Script Editor, it's impossible to stop the script in mid-run to see if the line "**set** theArtist **to the** artist" evaluated properly. But if I click the Event Log, I can see that this line of script returned the text The Beatles, just as it should have.

It's an essential tool when you need to learn precisely *where* a script went off the rails. You can fine-tune the behavior of the Event Log through the History tab of Script Editor's preferences.

Ah, yes, we seem to have overlooked the Record button. Well, let's just clear that out of the way so we can move on.

Recording scripts

Like I said earlier, recording scripts can be a hit-or-miss proposition. There's no way to tell whether or not an app is recordable — or exactly how useful its recording features are — until you give it a whirl.

Let's toss in a ringer for our example: the Finder. It's eminently recordable and as an environment for mind-numbing, repetitive behavior it gives secondary education a real run for its money.

I often organize my windows in a specific way that lets me reorganize my hard drive's clutter quickly. *Regardez-vous* Figure 17-10.

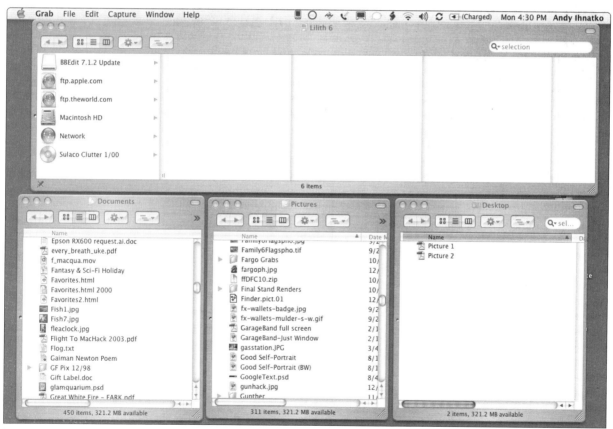

Figure 17-10

What my Finder screen looks like when I'm trying to beat poor, defensive Chaos into Order with a motorcycle chain

It's a master column view of the whole hard drive up top, and three windows of subfolders arranged on the bottom. But it's a pain to create and arrange these windows manually, so I'm going to record a script that does it for me.

1. **Create a new script file in Script Editor by pressing ⌘+N.** Alternatively, you can click File ➜ New.

2. **Click the Record button.** The Stop button activates.

3. **Click over to the Finder.** Create those four windows, click in them until they're displaying the folders I want to examine, and change their views to the styles I want (one set to Columns and the rest set to Lists).

4. **Click back into Script Editor when the windows are just the way I like them.** Notice that the script window is now jam-freakin'-*packed* with script.

5. **Click the Stop button.** The final result is what you see in Figure 17-11.

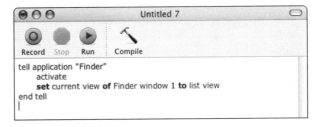

Figure 17-11

A successful recorded AppleScript

Woo-hoo! Just imagine having to type all that in yourself! Recording scripts *rules!!!*

▼ Note
Correspondent carefully extends pinky and index finger while curling ring and middle finger under thumb; resulting hand-sign is then proudly lofted into the air to create an overall motif of horns customarily seen in traditional representations of Satan, and thus signifying one's allegiance to same.

Not so fast, Skeezix. Why don't you try something even simpler, like recording all the steps of using the Finder to connect to an FTP server? Go ahead. I'll wait here.

Uh-huh. You wound up with something like Figure 17-12, didn't you?

```
tell application "Finder"
    activate
    set current view of Finder window 1 to list view
end tell
```

Figure 17-12

A stinky recorded AppleScript

The only thing it actually recorded was that thing at the very end, when you finished logging in to the FTP server and you changed the window's view from Icon to List. See what I mean? Spotty and unpredictable. Recording scripts isn't *totally* useless, but once you've picked up some scripting skills, you'll practically never use it.

Well, the Finder window thing went well at any rate. I might want to actually use that script later. Which dovetails us nicely into...

Saving scripts

Saving a script has a couple of quirks, compared to saving document files in other applications. No big surprise...in a sense, you're building software here, so you have to decide how this new software is going to be deployed, you know? Figure 17-13 shows Script Editor's standard Save dialog.

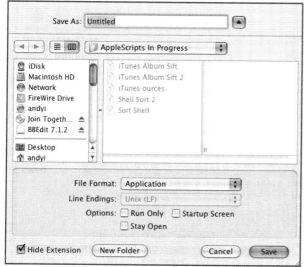

Figure 17-13
Script Editor's Save options

The file format options are as follows:

- **Application.** The most *useful* form for your finished script. It'll run whether or not Script Editor is present, and it can run as a drag-and-drop utility if you've scripted it properly.

- **Script.** If you're still working on your script — or if you're coauthoring it with another scripter — you might want to save it as a Script file instead. It's slower and not quite as versatile as an application, but it's a little easier for a scripter to work with.

- **Text.** It's a file containing nothing but words. No formatting, no other data at all. Useful for publishing purposes and when you need to read your script on an OS that doesn't support AppleScript (like a PDA or a Windows notebook).

You also have three options available to you:

- **Run Only.** Normally, a saved script, even one that winds up as an Application, can be opened in Script Editor and modified. If you want to protect your code from tampering or theft, click this option.

- **Startup Screen.** Sure, *you* know what this script does and know how to use it. But will everybody else? Clicking this option will take the text you wrote in the Description tab of the script window and package it as a startup screen that appears whenever the script is run.

- **Stay Open.** Scripts normally run once and then quit. Checking this box causes the script to stay open and active. There's a special kind of AppleScript code called an idle handler that takes advantage of this. If it's *incredibly important* that iTunes is always up and running (it has to be available to serve music to all the other Macs in your house, let's say), you can write a script that checks every 10 minutes to relaunch it if it doesn't appear to be in the list of running apps.

Give the script a name, click Save, and you're golden.

 Tip

Remember, if you want this script to appear in the Scripts menu, save it in Library ➔ Scripts ➔ inside your user folder. If you want the script to appear in the Scripts menu of all of this Mac's users, save it in the system wide Library folder (click on your hard drive's icon in the Finder to see it).

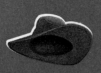

THESE AREN'T THE DROIDS YOU'RE LOOKING FOR; MOVE ALONG

It's been a long day. I barely had lunch. All day long, the FedEx and UPS delivery people and the mailman have wondered why I've been so brusque with them instead of engaging in the usual 20 minutes of neighborhood gossip, play-by-plays of recent surgeries, et cetera. I mean, I haven't been shirking off and I haven't sandbagged a *single thing* in all my years of working on this book.

So can we *please* just pretend you never saw those two bundle options? Trust me, you don't need to know how to use them. A *bundle* is a special format that lets you enclose files and resources along with the script. Like, if your script normally takes about 8 minutes to complete its task, maybe you want to have it play *American Pie* to keep the user entertained while waiting. If you save the script as a bundled application, you can stick the MP3 file right inside the app, so everything's in one nice, convenient package.

Examining AppleScript dictionaries

Script Editor has another function on top of building, debugging, running, and saving scripts: It lets you examine an application's *scripting dictionary* to learn how it can be controlled via AppleScript.

As I pointed out earlier, the strength or the weakness of an app's scripting support is up to the developer. Any functions or capabilities that are specific to the app have to be *provided* by the app. And they also have to provide AppleScript programmers with documentation explaining what these app-specific functions and data types are.

The word *documentation* has to be used loosely. The developers write up a list of data types the app can recognize and deal with and a list of functions the app can perform, and make this list available to you, eager young space cadet, within the application itself in the form of a scripting dictionary.

▼ Note

I will begrudgingly admit that many developers provide you with online scripting documentation, and there's often a whole page of sample AppleScripts on their Web sites. All the same, keep your expectations low. The scripting dictionary is the only thing you can absolutely count on, and a scripting dictionary helps you understand AppleScript about as much as an English dictionary helps you to understand the lyrics to "Louie, Louie."

WHEN THE SCRIPTING DICTIONARY LETS YOU DOWN

If you were hoping to find a certain command, but the dictionary broke your heart, that doesn't necessarily mean that you can't script it. Panther brought with it a new AppleScript feature called *GUI Scripting*. It's a system by which a script can send keystrokes and mouse clicks to an app and manipulate its user interface the same way a user can.

So while iChat's scripting dictionary doesn't let you do something as esoteric as changing your online chat icon, you can do it by having GUI Scripting select the right menu and then click the right button in the right window. I used this feature to turn my chat icon into a live webcam; every minute, my iSight video camera takes a new picture of me and updates my chat icon with it.

There are plenty of privacy issues associated with webcams, but at 32 x 32 pixels, I think I can scratch more or less whatever I want with impunity.

Script Editor can open and read these dictionaries. Just click Open Dictionary within Script Editor's File menu. Script Editor presents a list of all installed apps. Pick an app, and you'll see what additional features and functions it brings to the AppleScript family (see Figure 17-14).

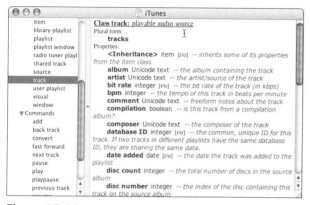

Figure 17-14
iTunes' scripting dictionary, laid bare

A dictionary is organized into *Classes* and *Commands*. Classes are a sophisticated construct of modern computer science, but the word thingamabob just about covers it. This list contains all of the thingamabobs that this app has been specially trained to deal with. In iTunes' case, you've got playlists, tracks, music sources, equalizer presets...all those things that Microsoft Excel's programmers were too lazy to teach *their* apps about.

Then you've got yer commands: **play** starts playback, **next track** skips to the next track, and so forth. In the end, reading through an app's scripting dictionary is useful to the extent that it'll give you a sense of the app's capabilities. I want to write an iTunes script that does something to my music library on an album-by-album basis. Can I ask iTunes for a specific album, or do I have to find and gather together all of the album's individual tracks myself? I look through iTunes scripting dictionary. Dang, it looks like there's no built-in way to process albums, so I'll have to write that feature myself.

LEARNING APPLESCRIPT: RESOURCES

Time and space prevent me from including a full primer on the AppleScript language. (And when I say time and space, I, of course, mean money. This is simple Einsteinian physics, people. Einstein said that time and space were merely vibrational manifestations of matter, and to me, nothing matters more than money. Slip me another three bucks and I'll be all over this whole Primer thing but otherwise, nothin' doing.) So instead, I'll steer you toward other resources. The best way to learn AppleScript is to examine a script that (a) already exists, and (b) works. Over time, you'll wind up working your way through all of the sample scripts Apple left for you in the Scripts menu. Scroll around until you see a script that seems to do something interesting, open the Script file in Script Editor, and play with the code.

No kidding. I've written plenty of AppleScripts that use Mail to create and send an email, but the central nugget of that code is always the lines I found in one of Apple's samples from the Scripts menu. Remember, kids, it's only thievery *if* you feel guilty about it later on.

Joking, joking. Apple's scripts say explicitly that you're free to recycle these samples as you see fit. Plus, this is exactly what AppleScript's framers originally intended — learning by example.

You'll *absolutely* want to go back to wherever you tossed your Panther install discs and get out Disc 4, the Developer Tools CD. I can confirm for you that this disc contains hardcore supergeek resources and references so potent that even now, just reading about them causes calcium deposits to form around your neurons simply as a defensive measure. But on this disc lurks a complete set of AppleScript documentation and reference materials that'll help explain the basics of writing AppleScript all the way through the intermediaries.

Tip

If you can't find this disc or don't want to install it, most of the best bits are on Apple's Web site at www.apple.com/applescript/developers/. But you're going to want to be able to access this information without being tied to the Internet. Note that I didn't end that sentence with the term "trust me," though I could have. But I've already used it once, and Andy Ihnatko doesn't go around begging for respect. Do you hear me?

Some other places to go:

The AppleScript-Users mailing list (www.lists.apple.com/)

This is a public mailing list that's chock-full of seasoned scripting experts, newbies who've yet to write their first *tell* block, and everyone in between, all asking questions and swapping techniques. AppleScript is full of landmines that require either the sort of lateral thinking that leads to either madness, greatness, or the annual redesign of the federal tax code and only someone Who's Been There can explain how AppleScript works...and more importantly, why it sometimes doesn't.

Apple's Scriptable Applications page (www.apple.com/applescript/apps/)

Partly as a user resource and partly to sell people on the power of AppleScript, Apple maintains a Web page lifting all of the built-in Panther apps and iLife apps that support AppleScript, and embroiders each item with some sample scripts complete with explanations. When you want to start learning how to script Safari, this is your starting point.

MacScripter.net (www.macscripter.net/)

Hands-down the best AppleScript information and education resource outside of Apple. What the hey. Throw Apple in there, too. At this writing, MacScripter contains more than 1,300 sample scripts in every conceivable category for your benefit and edification. It attempts the impossible task of documenting every major Mac app's level of scriptability. There's a busy, busy, *busy* message board where newbie questions are always welcome; MacScripter has succeeded in building a real community.

Doug's AppleScripts for iTunes (www.malcolmadams.com/itunes/)

This site does one thing, but it does it with remorseless thoroughness: It's all about scripting Panther's music player. It's actually a fine place to focus your scripting skills as they flower. The downloadable scripts range from simple five-liners to ones whose scale and ambitions demand the use of the term Heroic.

SCRIPTUS ANNOTATUS

Still and all, I'll show you a very simple script to start you off. And, because you were one of the first 500 callers to take advantage of this incredible offer, I'll annotate some of the high points afterward.

For a free word processor, TextEdit is actually pretty slick. On top of all of its built-in features, it's Microsoft Word–compatible, so it's actually possible to use it as a serious productivity app. But I can't use any word processor that doesn't have a word-count feature. Adding one is easy as pie. Just create a new Script file containing the following code, and save it inside your Scripts folder:

```
tell application "TextEdit"
        set theText to the text of document 1
end tell

set theLength to the number of words in theText

display dialog "There are " & theLength & " words in the
text."
```

Running this script returns the number of words in the frontmost TextEdit document. It also gives me three opportunities for blathering on:

- **Tell...end Tell:** Reflect upon the fact that there are anywhere from dozens to hundreds of apps installed on your Mac. If you have something to say to just one of them, you can't just stand on your chair and shout "Hey, *you!*" So when you have something to say, you surround it with a tell block so that it doesn't get intercepted by the wrong app.

  In this script, the only thing we need TextEdit for is to get the text of the document (document 1...aka, the document whose window is in front of every other TextEdit window). So that's the only line you put inside the tell block. That's not always completely necessary. The rest of the script is part of the core AppleScript language and *should* work anywhere. But it's sloppy to put more inside a tell block than you absolutely must. It's *more* than sloppy...it can often have unpredictable results. For instance, I *could* have put this line inside the tell block:

  ```
  set theLength to the number of words in
  theText of document 1
  ```

  ...and I wouldn't have needed the line of script that comes after it. It would have run just fine, but it returns an incorrect result. When AppleScript counts the number of words *outside* of the tell block, everything is both hunky and dory.

- **set...to** is how you load up a container ("theText," in this case) with data. When AppleScript encounters

this statement, it evaluates everything that comes after "to" (be it a mathematical calculation, an operation to retrieve information [like we're doing here], or the result of another operation). I don't have to bother declaring "theText" ahead of time, or telling AppleScript that it's supposed to contain text. AppleScript figures out that stuff dynamically.

▼ **Note**

If you've taken an introductory course in programming, a *container* is what you think of as a variable. Oh, and subroutines? They're called *handlers*.

- **display dialog** generates a standard Macintosh dialog with the contents you specify. For simplicity's sake, we're using the plain-vanilla, ready-to-wear dialog. It has text, plus OK and Cancel buttons. AppleScript lets you customize these pretty thoroughly. Because the dialog is just giving us some information, there's really no need for a Cancel button, for example. Go to the Scripts menu and look at the dialog samples under the Script Editor Scripts menu. "display dialog" generates its own results, too. If I made the line "set someContainerName to display dialog (etc.)," someContainerName would hold the name of the button that the user clicked.

▼ **Note**

But AppleScript's built-in dialog functions are pretty limited. They can't get a whole lot of information from the user and they can't display a whole lot in return. When you absolutely, positively need something more ambitious, it's time to look into AppleScript Studio.

And we're saving ourselves a step by building the dialog's text on the fly. The ampersands are your signal to AppleScript that you'd like all those items schmooshed together into one string of text.

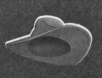

CHECK YOUR TELLS BEFORE BEGINNING THE HUMAN SACRIFICES

Often, when a script *just isn't working* and I'm so frustrated that I'm willing to sacrifice a living creature to the Cloven-Hooved One to make it work (a moth, maybe — let's not lose our heads here), I just tighten up my tell blocks and the problem magically disappears. Just something to keep in mind before you consider offing an intern to get a project finished.

When you're stuck with me as a dinner guest, there are three topics you don't want to introduce: The JFK assassination (Oswald did it and he acted alone; for bonus points, let me run down the 12 most popular conspiracy theories and why they're utterly baloneyous), the Apollo program (yes, I was born 30 or 40 years too late, but I'm still convinced that if I do a few pushups I might make it as a backup LEM pilot on Apollo 18), and AppleScript.

I'm as enthusiastic about AppleScript as I am about my favorite books and movies. You've never experienced this thing? Oh, sit down, you poor, poor man or woman; your whole life has been a mere prelude to seeing *The Stunt Man* or reading *The Code of the Woosters* for the first time.

AppleScript is *exactly* what's right about computers in general and the Mac in particular. There are some scripting-ish solutions for Windows, but no other platform brings such a level of power to such a low level of user expertise. AppleScript means never having to say, "I *wish* I could do this on my Mac."

18

Unix...Alas, the Name Is Its Only Funny Part

In This Chapter

The Brass Tacks • The Command Line: Meet the Shell circa 1983
Your First Commands: Listing and Launching Files • Look! It Does Tricks, Too!

The Unix operating system has been an important and recurring off-screen presence throughout this book, much as it is in Panther itself. If you were a kid during the Seventies, Unix is to Mac OS X as Charlie was to *Charlie's Angels*. If you were a kid during the Eighties, it's like Norm Peterson's wife Vera in *Cheers*; during the Nineties, Niles Crane's wife Maris in *Frasier;* and 2000, Karen Walker's husband Stan in *Will and Grace*. And if you're one of those people whose main motivation for meeting new people is to have a brand-new chance to tell someone "No, I don't *watch* television...and let me tell you *why*...," then I suppose the "I went to college for two semesters and I desperately need for everyone to know it" comparisons would be to Godot in *Waiting for Godot* or Harry Lime in *The Third Man*, provided, of course, that we overlook the fact that Lime does indeed turn up in the final reel. Hey, I'm willing to overlook the fact that you haven't missed a single episode of *Fear Factor* in 3 years. Meet me halfway, here.

That is, even if you never see Unix or interact with it directly, it's always there behind the scenes, making things happen. And the beauty of Panther is that, yep, you can use your Mac for years without ever interacting with Unix directly. Not unless you *want* to, of course.

Well, this chapter is designed to make you *want* to. There's a lot of power tied up in Unix and every Mac user should take a look under the hood and see what's there. You'll leave with a better understanding of your Macintosh, you'll learn a few tricks that'll come in handy, and perhaps the next time it looks like your date is about to tell you about how to increase system performance by looking for stalled processes, you won't set the tablecloth on fire as a distractionary tactic and then run away.

 Note

Yes, Janice Hallidow of Northampton, Massachusetts, I remember and it *still* stings.

THE BRASS TACKS

First thing is, you pronounce it "YOO-nix." — not tee-hee tee-hee tee-hee! It's like – hee hee hee! – that, you know, *other* word!

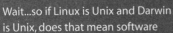

ANTI-SOCIAL DARWINISM

Wait...so if Linux is Unix and Darwin is Unix, does that mean software written for Linux will run on my Mac? Alas, it ain't that simple. It's like how folks in Boston and folks in Atlanta both speak English, but if I were to go to a diner down South and ask for ice cream with jimmies, with a frappe to drink and my, that's a *wicked* hat you've got on, pally...well, confusion may occur.

But! All Unixes are similar enough that (a) they network to each other as easily as chips and salsa, (b) they use the same commands, and (c) it's not terribly difficult for a programmer to take an app written for one Linux and make it work with Panther.

(And, Jimmies are chocolate sprinkles, a Frappe is a milkshake, "wicked" is a term of extreme approval, and "pally" is what you call someone whose name you never caught. Okay, we're out of time for today. Tonight, I want you all to read the chapter on How to Pronounce "Leominster" and what to do when your car enters a rotary. Class dismissed.)

Unix isn't one single commercial operating system, like Panther and Windows are. On a rough basis, it's more like a *specification* for an operating system that many, many different companies and organizations have implemented — which means that there are plenty of different implementations. You may have heard of an open-source OS called Linux. That's a flavor of Unix. Mac OS X's flavor of Unix is called "Darwin."

THE COMMAND LINE: MEET THE SHELL, CIRCA 1983

At the root of every flavor of Unix is the *command line*. No menus, no windows, no 3D-animated figures of Don Knotts tap-dancing onto your screen and singing the date and time. You type text commands at the prompt, and Unix responds in the form of plain, monospaced text.

You interact with the command line through Panther's Terminal app, which you can find lurking inside the Utilities subfolder of your Applications folder. Here's what you see when you launch Terminal (Figure 18-1).

```
● ● ●          Terminal — tcsh — 80x24
Last login: Tue Mar 23 04:02:16 on ttyp4
Welcome to Darwin!
[Bobbendrae:~] andyi%  █
```

**Figure 18-1
The Terminal window**

Yup, that's all you get. Behold, the glory of the *shell*, which is how you refer to a Unix command-line environment. The Shell is actually a piece of Unix software for taking the commands you type and giving them to the OS. The shell program built into Panther is called *bash*. There are others: csh, tsch, ksh, zsh...all have certain creature comforts that make it a little less painful to work with commands that can be twice as long as Prince Charles' full royal title.

As a Human with no special interest or training, you'll never become concerned with the differences. But professional Unix system administrators put as much thought, passion, and venom into their personal choice as any two slightly drunk bar patrons would into a discussion of whether a duck could beat a chicken in a fight.

All you need to know is that terminal presents this interface to you in a standard Macintosh window, so you've got scroll bars (oooh!) and can resize the thing (aaaah!); but on the whole, welcome back to The State of the Art in User Interface, circa 1983.

▼ Note

A year before the Macintosh came out, Dexy's Midnight Runners charted 80 spots higher than Eric Clapton in the Billboard Annual 100, and George Lucas announced that he wouldn't be making any more *Star Wars* movies, ever. You just *knew* that something good *had* to be coming up, just to restore humanity's faith in a compassionate and loving God...

The last line of text in Figure 18-1 is the actual command line:

- **Bobbendrae:** The name of the Macintosh in use.

- **~:** The name of the directory the user happens to be sitting in at the moment. In Unix, the tilde is shorthand for the user's home directory. In Macintosh-speak, the home directory is that directory with your name on it inside the folder named Users.

- **andyi:** The account under which I've logged in. Because I logged in already, back when I started my Mac, there's no need for me to prove who I am any more and the command line recognizes me instantly.

- **%:** The actual prompt. *That's all I can tell you right now, Sparky. You got a command for me?*

YOUR FIRST COMMANDS: LISTING AND LAUNCHING FILES

There's a command for everything in Unix, and a Unix wizard needs to know every last one of 'em. You, on the other hand, just need to know a couple of basic commands so you can play around a bit.

Type ls at the prompt and hit Return. The Terminal window fills with text like this:

```
[Bobbendrae:~] andyi% ls
Applications              Music
Dancin' Dave.pict        Pictures
Desktop                  Public
Documents                Send Registration
Downloads                Sites
Green Monster Bkdrop (PICT)   Temporary Items
Junkyard Wars.pict       Z'ha'Dum.mp3
Library                  columbo.pict
Movies
[Bobbendrae:~] andyi%
```

The ls command is short for list and lists the contents of a directory. Yes, when interacting with your Mac through the shell, that is what your Home folder looks like. In the Finder, it looks like this (Figure 18-2):

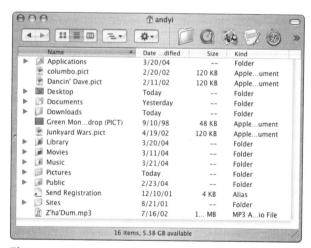

Figure 18-2
A Finder view of the same Unix file listing

If you look at the command line, you see that you still haven't left the home directory. Let's move inside a folder, shall we? The command to navigate inside a folder is...it's...

No, wait. We have no way of knowing which of these items is a file and which is a folder. We need to tell ls to give us more information. Most Unix commands have plenty of options available to them, usually by typing a dash and then a letter after you type the command. Try typing this:

```
ls -F
```

...and then hit Return. Here's what you wind up with:

```
[Bobbendrae:~] andyi% ls -F
Applications/              Music/
Dancin' Dave.pict          Pictures/
Desktop/                   Public/
Documents/                 Send Registration@
Downloads/                 Sites/
Green Monster Bkdrop (PICT)*  Temporary Items/
Junkyard Wars.pict         Z'ha'Dum.mp3*
Library/                   columbo.pict
Movies/
[Bobbendrae:~] andyi%
```

That's better. Every item that's a folder is followed by a slash. *Now* we can use the cd command to change to a different Directory. Let's go to the Movies folder:

```
[Bobbendrae:~] andyi% cd Movies/

[Bobbendrae:~/Movies] andyi% ls -F
 Nick Baseball/       TPIR XMas/           jedidad2.mov
 Nick Baseball.mov    Triumph Clones.mov   letterman bruce/
"Glory Days".mov      TVShows/
Koppel Letterman.mov  jedi dad/
[Bobbendrae:~/Movies] andyi%
```

Why a slash? Because that's how Unix delineates the path through a nest of folders. For example, to move inside the Demos folder, you can navigate to Movies and then do another cd command to get inside the folder. Or you can do it all on one command by typing the full path from the home directory to the folder: cd /Movies/TVShows.

"cd/Movies/TVShows". If there is a folder inside that and a movie inside *that*, the full path to the movie becomes /Movies/TVShows/Dynasty/JoanCollinsCatfight.mov.

 Tip

Incidentally, if you ever want to confirm where you are, type pwd and press Return. Unix spits out the path to your current location.

Notice that when you moved into another directory, the contents of the command line changed to show you your new location.

You're thrilled, I can tell. The delight in your eyes zaps onto this page and the glee is so potent that it's pierced the very veil of space and time and I'm feeling it right now, several months in the past, as I write this. You were hoping that after spending $2,000 on a new computer, you'd wind up spending a lot of time looking at monospaced, unformatted text and typing commands that would only make sense if you started hitting yourself in the head a lot harder than you've been doing for the last 3 minutes. Okay, why don't you take a break and watch a movie. You can tell that jedidad is a QuickTime movie because of its .mov extension. Every Mac file has a filename extension that tells what sort of file it is. The Macintosh graphical interface hides this from you in the Finder, but look, in case it hasn't gotten through to you yet, you ain't in Kansas any more, Dorothy.

The open command is the equivalent of double-clicking on a file in the Finder. It launches the file, opening its default application first if necessary:

```
[Bobbendrae:~] andyi% open jedidad2.mov
```

And thank God, you're finally looking at graphics and listening to sound and looking at a *real* app with a *real* graphical user interface!

If you're scowling because you were unable to open diddley-squat on your own Mac — or even if diddley-squat was *precisely* what you could open — you must have tried to type in a filename that had a space in it. The Finder's happy to deal with spaces in filenames. Unix ain't. You have to precede all filename spaces with backslashes. Unix will puke all over a command like

```
open Triumph Clones.mov
```

But it can handle the file perfectly well if you type it in as

```
open Triumph\ Clones.mov
```

▼ Note

I know we're in a retro, 1983, Reagan-era Thou Shalt Not Drag-and-Drop a Single Bloody Thing sort of mood in this chapter, but if you drag a file or a folder into the Terminal window, Panther is nice enough to put the file's full name and path onto the command line for you at the cursor. It's a real lifesaver; as you get deeper and deeper into nested folders, the act of correctly typing a pathname becomes less like a necessary procedure and more like some sort of fraternity hazing stunt, the sort of thing that killed a pledge at another campus in 1997 and forced the Dean to close the chapter down.

Let's go back to the Home folder. Whoops. In the Finder, just click the Back button in the window toolbar. In Unix, there's no Back button, but two periods side by side achieve the same effect:

```
[Bobbendrae:~/Movies] andyi% cd ..
[Bobbendrae:~] andyi%
```

This takes us back to the Home folder because Home was just one backward step away. To teleport straight to Home from anywhere in the hierarchy, use a tilde:

```
[Bobbendrae:~/Movies] andyi% cd ~
```

The tilde always represents your Home folder.

So, have you started learning Unix yet? Barely. I want to say that by navigating through your directories and opening a few files, you've taken the Pontiac Unix for a quick drive around the block, but in truth you've moved just beyond shifting over to the driver's seat and grabbing the wheel and making "Brrrrmmm...*brrrrmmmmmm!*" noises while your Dad's in the 7-11 buying smokes.

Why, I haven't even told you the simple, easy-to-remember command that deletes every single file off your hard drive in an instant. No warnings or nothing. Just *phhht*...there goes your whole hard drive. I bet you could almost type it accidentally. You probably ought to know what that command is. So if you value the data on your hard drive, place $15,000 in clean, unmarked $10 bills in a brown bag with a red ribbon and leave it taped behind the basin of the third sink from the men's room door at Boston's South Station train terminal.

Very droll, Ihnatko...move on. See, Panther's shell sort of assumes that if you *know* about the Terminal app and you're actually motivated to *type* commands that it can understand, well, then you *must* know what you're doing. So it'll allow you to do the most destructive things and make the sort of mistakes that will cause you to turn the air purple around you with the force of your sheer desire to Wish-So-Hard-That-Magically-What-Just-Happened-Wouldn't-Have-Happened. So you need to tread with extreme caution. When you type Unix commands, make sure you're typing them in correctly; and when you go and learn Unix on your own, don't assume that you can simply Undo a mistake.

 Tip

Unix helps you out a little, in the form of extensive online help. Type man followed by a space and any command, and Unix displays the full online manual for that command. It scrolls on for page after page after page until you beg it to stop. And while reading Unix documentation, Unix interprets pressing Control+Z as your begging it to stop.

LOOK! IT DOES TRICKS, TOO!

True, you're still a Unix neophyte, but there are still a few commands and tricks you can use that'll leave you convinced that a little knowledge can be a useful thing. Just double-check your typing on all of these commands before you press Return and remember, capitalization counts.

How long has my Mac been running?

You want incontrovertible, tangible evidence of how stable Panther is? Use the uptime command:

```
[Bobbendrae:~/Documents] andyi% uptime
```

Unix returns the following:

```
 7:21  up 14 days, 17:21, 3 users, load averages: 1.89 1.49
1.37
```

This tells me that it's been more than 2 weeks and 17 hours since the last time I restarted my PowerBook (Lilith 6). There are musicians that move from MTV to

CourtTV more slowly than my old Mac went from Startup to System Crash under Mac OS 9.

As for the information that follows the uptime, it's giving you some data on how hard the CPU is working.

 Note

If you're interested in that info, try the top command. This command is like the Activity Monitor application in your Utilities folder. It throws up a constantly updated status board listing all of the bits of software currently running on your Mac and what sort of demands each one makes on your system. Except it does it in ASCII text in the Terminal window instead of in a nice, clean, GUI-like Activity Monitor.

If I'd have written top as a separate Trick, its title would have been "How Can I Fill The Terminal Window With A Suffocating Morass Of Inscrutable Data?"

How do I empty the Trash when the Finder's being all snitty about it?

It's one of the most *annoying* conversations you can possibly have with a Mac:

"Empty the Trash."

"Can't."

"Why not?"

"Apparently, there's a file in there that's in use by another piece of software."

"Oh. Sorry, I didn't know that. Which file is it?"

"Ain't telling."

"C'mon, tell me."

"Nope. *Nuh*-uh."

"And just how in the name of Cher's sainted wigmaker
do you expect me to properly *close* the problem file if
you won't tell me which one it is? Or which piece of
software refuses to let it go?"

"We never *talk* any more. Do you know that this is the
longest conversation we've had in 9 days, 7 hours, 34
minutes, and 28.9 seconds? Maybe — hey, just *maybe* —
if I could get your nose out of the CNN.com sports page
for a few minutes every morning, this relationship
wouldn't be headed straight to /dev/null!"

At which point you make dark noises about how a 20-inch
flat-screen iMac isn't an easy object to hurl out a window,
but that you think you could just manage it.

The best way to handle this problem is to shut down the
Mac, and then try to empty the Trash immediately after
you restart. But sometimes you don't have time to do that,
and sometimes it doesn't even work.

If you feel you have no choice, type the following:

```
sudo chflags nouchg ~/.Trash/*
```

Translating this from left to right, you're saying, "Temporarily give me Godlike powers to do absolutely anything
I want to on this machine, even if I'm about to do something dangerous, deadly, and instantly regrettable; change
the flags associated with a file; the specific flag I want to
change is its unchangeable flag, which, if set to yes, means
that the file can never be deleted...please set it to no; and
do that to every file in the Trash."

You should now be able to empty the Trash as usual.

How do I make a catalogue listing every file on my hard drive?

The ls command has a nice little option that tells it to
list not only every file in the current directory, but every
file in every folder in the current directory, and every file
in *those* folders...and so on and so on. Navigate to your
Home folder (cd ~) and type this command:

```
ls -FR
```

Good. But the result is thousands of lines long and it all
just whips through the Terminal window. Well, Unix gives
you a simple way to redirect the output of any command
so that its results sploosh straight into a text file instead of
the Terminal window:

```
ls -FR > allmyfiles.txt
```

The file allmyfiles.txt will appear in your Home
folder and you can open it in TextEdit or any other word
processor.

On what day of the week was my grandmother born?

The command `cal` generates a calendar representing any month or year you specify. If your gramma was born on December 8, 1932, type "cal 12 1932" and you'll get this:

```
    December 1932
 S  M Tu  W Th  F  S
             1  2  3
 4  5  6  7  8  9 10
11 12 13 14 15 16 17
18 19 20 21 22 23 24
25 26 27 28 29 30 31
```

So it turns out that the old girl was born on a Thursday. If you omit the month, it'll generate a calendar for the whole year. Type `cal` all on its own and it'll spit out one for the current year.

 Note

I use this command a lot when I create Web pages. It gives me plain, correctly formatted text of the current month and I can easily embroider the dates with hyperlinks to monthly events. (Truth be told, I actually wrote an AppleScript that has `cal` generate the calendar and then does all the embroidery automatically; but here, near the end of this chapter on command usage, I am refreshed by the cool breeze of heads spinning around me, so I probably ought to dial it down a notch.)

My boss won't let me have a DVD player in my office. Can I still watch the greatest movie ever made?

Abso-tively. Just use this command (the results are shown in Figure 18-3):

```
telnet towel.blinkenlights.nl
```

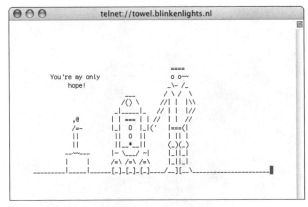

Figure 18-3
Even at stick-figure resolution and no sound, *Star Wars* is still freakin' *Star Wars*

All through this chapter, you've been typing commands to hunks of software located on your Mac, which responded to you putting text in the Terminal window. Telnet makes that happen with software located on other computers (even one located in the Netherlands, like this one). When Telnet opens the connection, that remote computer automatically starts a piece of software that plays *Star Wars Episode 4: A New Hope* through your Terminal window, all in glorious animated ASCII text.

I want to point out that I'm now walking-slash-jogging 4 miles at a stretch three or four times a week. Hate it with a passion, too. I've bought books about running in which the authors ooze on and on and *on* about the glorious mind-body-spirit connection and the freedom that comes with movement and the meditative effects of the rhythm of your footsteps and the high you get when the endorphins kick in. Well, I've done a half-marathon, folks. The only high I got through the whole process was through the fumes of the various lotions, oils, unguents, and liniments that I had to apply every day for a whole week afterward just to keep the sobbing to a sort of dignified ebb. It's no mystery that these folks could write so rhapsodically about running. *They were sitting in a nice, comfortable chair in a nice warm house with a donut and a big glass of Yoo-Hoo next to the keyboard.*

Although I really don't get the reasons why this is so important, I go out and do it. Why? Because people tell me it's a good idea. And...

To be honest, I think I've lost my grasp on where I was going with this. I think the point was that Unix seems like the exact opposite of what Mac users signed up for — actually, it's the opposite of what *anyone* using a computer after 1990 has a right to expect — but if you never open Panther's Terminal window and start seeing what Unix can do for you, your Macintosh experience will be forever incomplete. Your first successful Unix command is your first step into a larger and more wonderful world.

In truth, though, it's probably more important to me that I complain about having to go out and exercise in a couple of hours. I've tried snarking to my goldfish as I lace up my running shoes, but it's a deeply unsatisfying experience. I mean, I can tell already that you're not as judgmental as they are.

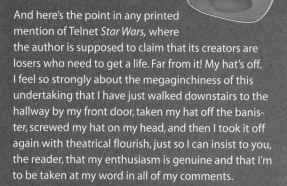

TELNET *STAR WARS* ENDORSEMENT

And here's the point in any printed mention of Telnet *Star Wars*, where the author is supposed to claim that its creators are losers who need to get a life. Far from it! My hat's off. I feel so strongly about the megaginchiness of this undertaking that I have just walked downstairs to the hallway by my front door, taken my hat off the banister, screwed my hat on my head, and then I took it off again with theatrical flourish, just so I can insist to you, the reader, that my enthusiasm is genuine and that I'm to be taken at my word in all of my comments.

Incidentally, this is probably the one and only time you should ever use Telnet. There are times when you might indeed want to talk to or even control another computer through your Terminal window, but you should use a command called ssh instead. It's safer and more secure from prying eyes.

PART III

Bonus Material

19

Twenty Questions from My Aunt Estelle

I'll be up front: I don't actually have an Aunt Estelle. I have 30 of them. No, 50. Certainly not more than 80. Hang on, let me just click over and check for new mail...

Okay, as of 2:12 a.m. today, I have a little more than 90 Aunt Estelles. I'm terribly fond of them all, even if I was unable to get them to see the wisdom of pooling all their resources together and buying me just one spectacular gift from the whole lot of them every Christmas. As it was, I was the only kid in my middle school who wore a brand-new pair of socks and underwear every day, and the only freshman in my college dorm who didn't know how to do laundry.

Actually "Aunt Estelle" is the name I give to first-time Mac owners — in the case of actual aunts, they're sometimes even first-time computer owners — who email or phone me with questions. Usually the questioner begins by explaining her connection to me. "I go to the same salon as your mother's friend, Alice, and my hairdresser mentioned my problem to her, and then Alice suggested to *him* that I call you and ask why my computer keeps turning itself off." Which just goes to show that everybody on this planet is connected to everybody else. So if you've been arrested for reckless driving in some country backwater and you can't raise $1,000 bail, you probably just haven't been working the phones right.

And I *do* like hearing from Aunt Estelles, (a) because I believe in the Brotherhood of Man and all that; (b) because if I blow these people off, there's a better than 50 percent chance that it'll get back to my Mom; and (c) they usually ask questions that I've never considered before. I completed basic training a long time ago, and I've forgotten what it's like to be confronted by all this for the first time.

MY OWN KEVIN BACON INDEX

Incidentally, Kevin Bacon was in *Mystic River*, directed by Clint Eastwood; Eastwood was in *Unforgiven* with Gene Hackman; Hackman was in *The Birdcage* with Nathan Lane; Lane was in *Ironweed* with me (as an extra). So if you're playing The Kevin Bacon Game and you're one of my Aunt Estelles, your personal KB index is the number of steps to me, plus three. And it *would* have been plus one, except I had to cancel my extra commitment to *Mystic River* to keep a deadline.

I also think about my own ineptitude when it comes to cars. I know that you're supposed to put oil in. There's a metal stick-thingy that tells you how much oil is in there already. Good. But is it *bad* when you add that one bottle too many, and the level goes beyond the Full mark? That *can't* be bad, right?

There's an answer to this question, but just try finding it. The world is full of experts who passionately discuss whether the Lowen 410 intake pair cuts more HWBs than the Model 90 that came stock with the car, and how that affects line torque at low RPMs. But go to an online message forum and ask, "Why would I want a car with a manual transmission instead of an automatic?" and the only suggestions you get are to go out and work on your butterfly collection. As if a swallowtail is puddling *anywhere* in the Northeast at this time of year!

So, I'm always pleased to help out co-workers of my sister's mother-in-law and all my other Aunt Estelles. It's the right thing to do. And if I get into heaven, it'll be a late-buzzer squeaker and I'll be glad I walked in there with these extra karma points in my back pocket.

You may think I'm kidding, but the following are all actual questions selected from the past 2 months of incoming email expressly for this chapter. You might want to stick a bus transfer or something on this page to bookmark it. If word gets around that you know something about Macs, you'll start acquiring Aunt Estelles of your own.

I'm thinking about buying (my first Mac, a replacement for my old Mac). Should I do it now or wait for something new to come out?

Yeah, that's a poser. It's an incontrovertible fact that the moment you buy a new computer, the company either drops its prices or comes out with a brand-new model that has all of the old one's features, except it's faster, has a bigger hard drive, and has a built-in Easy Bake Oven. That's one of the reasons why the Treasury Department redesigned the $20 bill. Computer manufacturers got sick and tired of having to *guess* about this all the time, so each piece of U.S. currency has a tiny chip that senses when a major CPU purchase is being made, and can wirelessly transmit that info to a central server.

▼ Note

...Along with the comment that those shoes are *so* last season, that your handbag is a knock-off, and that you seem to be the only woman on *earth* who doesn't know that your husband's been sleeping around. See? And you thought it was one of your *girlfriends* who started all that gossip about you.

There's some advice that will come in handy, though:

- **Encourage that Upgrade:** If you have a friend who seems to be unhappy with his current Mac and due for some karmic retribution, talk him into upgrading. Once he's taken delivery, it'll trigger Apple's release of the next and greatest, which is when you should head for your nearest Apple Store.

- **Check the Rumor Mill:** Apple has an official policy of not commenting on unreleased products, and it's been a long time since it clamped down on unofficial leaks. But Mac rumor sites often manage to piece together the facts on what's Apple will release and when. So, if you're seriously worried about buying an Edsel one week before the Thunderbirds roll into showrooms, spend a little time poking around on www.macosrumors.com. Mind you, there's a reason why rumors are called rumors. It's all baloney until you see it at store.apple.com. For more about online resources, see Chapter 20.

▼ **Note**

Just because everyone was right about your shoes and the handbag and all those nights your husband had to work late is no reason to blindly believe that Apple will introduce a tortilla-shaped PowerBook in November.

- **Look at Your Calendar:** Apple usually introduces the *big* new stuff at predictable spots during the calendar year: The first half of January (Macworld Expo/San Francisco, which is the biggest annual user-oriented Mac event); late May/early June (the World Wide Developers' Conference, in which Apple announces its plans to the folks who design third-party software and hardware); September-ish and October-ish, when Apple might be motivated to drop a price or two in anticipation of the holiday buying season. So, if you're thinking about buying a new PowerBook in December, it's probably worthwhile to wait until January.

- **Is Steve Jobs Delivering a Keynote Address?:** The other tip off is usually when Apple announces that Steve Jobs is delivering a keynote somewhere. Visit

www.apple.com and look through the scrolling headlines. They like to give Daddy something shiny to show off.

- **Is Apple dropping prices?:** When Apple suddenly drops prices on a specific product, it's usually because it intends to replace it soon and doesn't want to get stuck with lots of inventory. So, think about whether you'd much rather have the old PowerBook at a $300 savings or if you'd rather have a higher-performing PowerBook for the old price.

Finally, realize that staying ahead of the curve is a mug's game. If you keep holding off until The Next Great Thing comes out, you're going to be using that 512K Macintosh for a long, *long* time. Apple's *always* working on something better, and it never designs and markets a new product with the goal of not making its existing customers intensely envious. After all, it was tried with the Apple III. And did it ever make an Apple IV? I rest my case.

The Software Update app keeps popping up and suggesting that I download some software upgrades. Do I really need all this stuff?

1) No, you don't. 2) Yes, you do.

Clicking the button to add "support for Sun's Java VM 1.4.2 API" and it's not going to benefit society to the same extent that the last iMovie update did— you know, the one that refused to save any project file if its subject matter was a child's birthday and the video lasted longer than 6 minutes? But 3 months from now when you visit the Charles Rocket fan site, instead of a set of animated navigation buttons, you may see a generic icon of a steaming cup of coffee indicating that your computer couldn't execute the embedded Java object.

All of these updates take up so little room on your hard drive. And when Apple releases one, it's usually because there's a smoldering puddle of white and clear acrylic and chromed metal where someone's iMac once was with the culprit being a subtle problem with the keyboard driver. If you find the Software Update pop-ups intrusive, go to System Preferences, select Software Update, and click the pop-up menu so that it can check for updates on a monthly basis instead of daily or weekly.

 Note

One exception to the rule: When Apple releases a major OS update — for example, 10.3.3 becomes 10.3.5 — you want to hold off for a week before you install it. If it contains a major, show-stopping bug (not unheard of), Apple will release 10.3.*six* toot sweet, and you'll be happy you weren't one of the users who innocently plugged in a LamabadaWare USB keyboard and caused all the data on the hard drive to be transmogrified into ASCII happy faces.

I've been told that I need to buy an antivirus program, but I can't find one for my Mac!

Not to worry. Worrying about viruses (and Trojan horses and worms and all other forms of nasty software that secretly installs itself inside your operating system and exploits and shares the data and resources of your computer) on a Mac is like worrying about drive-by shootings in Rutland, Vermont, or deft nuance in an Adam Sandler performance.

At this writing, Mac OS X viruses are unheard of. They just don't exist. Praise the inherent security of the Unix operating system. Praise Panther's specific enhancement to what was inherited from Unix. Mostly, thank the fact that virus programmers are lazy, good-for-nothing blankety-blanks who know that a Mac-specific virus only infects one-thirtieth as many machines as one for Windows.

Symantec (www.symantec.com) *does* sell an antivirus product for Macs. It's chief purpose is to scan your email for incoming Windows viruses. Those things can't infect a Mac, but if you're kind enough to forward those emails to a Windows person, congratulations...you've just helped to spread the virus. And aren't Windows users punished *enough*?

How do I turn it *off*? I can't find a switch anywhere!

That's because a Macintosh is a sophisticated, multi-user, multitasking, journalled operating system and not a toaster oven. So, if you were to suddenly cut the power when your Mac is desperate for you to *not* cut the power, bad things happen. Files get corrupted. Hard drives become unbootable. The dead rise from their graves and begin to walk the Earth, seeking to feast upon the brains of all those who wronged them in life. (Note: I read that last one at macosrumors.com. Grain of salt. Good excuse not to go about wronging people in life all the same, however.)

There is indeed a power key, but pressing it merely tells your Mac that you want it to go bye-bye now, and that it should do everything it needs to do in order to safely turn itself off. You can achieve the same thing by going to the Apple menu and selecting Shut Down.

 Note

If for some (unholy) reason you *want* to just cut the power immediately, terminate with extreme prejudice, live life on the edge without the sanitary complications of getting something pierced, etc., hold the Power key down for a few seconds. And don't say I didn't warn you when the mouldering corpse of your third-grade teacher crashes through your front window, pins you to the floor with surprising speed and power, and demands to know where your report on the solar system is.

It's also possible that you don't even *want* to turn it off. A Mac (like most modern computers) has some pretty advanced power-management features. If you select Sleep instead of Shut Down, Panther turns off every component that draws lots of power, like the display and the hard drive. The Mac becomes dark and inert and draws just enough power to snap straight back to life again when you tap the keyboard. Unless you're paranoid about power usage, haven't Shut Down in recent memory, or are about to leave the house for a long, long time, it's better to just Sleep it.

Cross-Reference

For more about starting and shutting down your Mac, see Chapter 2. If you're experiencing problems with your Mac, check out Chapter 21.

Every time I open a Web page, my Mac tries to dial the phone to connect to the Internet instead of just using my wireless connection. Is something broken?

Maybe. Panther's networking has a feature called *multi-homing*. It means that deciding on a method of connecting to the Internet is your Mac's problem, not yours. Go to System Preferences ➜ Network, and select Network Port Configurations from the Show pop-up menu (Figure 19-1):

This is a list of all the different ways your Mac knows how to connect to the network. When your Mac needs to connect, it tries each of these methods in that specific order, from top to bottom. The Mac shown in Figure 19-1 looks for a wireless AirPort connection first. Then, it looks at the FireWire port. Eventually, it dials the modem to see if *that* works.

You can change this order just by clicking and dragging items and rearranging them. Figure 19-1 makes sense for my specific setup. I always have AirPort available at the

office. Sometimes I use FireWire networking. The rest really doesn't matter, but I want to make sure my Mac doesn't start doing obnoxious things (like tying up my phone line) when it doesn't need to.

Figure 19-1
Setting the order of succession in Internet connections

So, if Internal Modem is higher on your list than AirPort, click and drag Airport to the top. There's your problem.

If that *isn't* it, then either you've turned AirPort off (turn it on using the AirPort menulet), or you haven't configured your AirPort properly and your Mac can't find it. Run the AirPort Setup Assistant again.

How do I download my email from America Online?

You, er, run America Online? Nearly every email service on the planet uses a universally accepted public standard for downloading email (POP or IMAP). *Except* AOL. Panther's built-in Mail app isn't compatible with AOL and neither are any others. I think when you log on and the "You've Got Mail!" announcement barks out in the sort of voice that is otherwise used to convince you to buy a three-year extended warranty on a $120 TV set, you should get the idea that you're not exactly in an environment in which users are worshipped, y'know?

I don't have enough places to plug in stuff.

Congratulations! Unfortunately, you are not alone. In fact, millions of people have only enough RAM, storage, processing power, and peripherals to adequately address their needs. The problem is "adequate" just ain't enough here in the new millennium.

It's easy to run out of places to plug in USB and FireWire devices. Many devices are *daisy-chainable*, meaning that they plug into one of the Mac's ports but they have ports of their own into which you can plug additional devices. Your Apple keyboard, for example, has two USB plugs at either end. At some point in your long, strange trip you'll probably wind up buying one or two *hubs*. Hubs are sort of like those power strips that act as colorful fire hazards. Plug a hub into your Mac and you can now plug four or

GET A NICE BLUE TAN

I really am proud of you for outgrowing your USB and FireWire ports. But for the record, when you run out of ports, well, that's when you should go out and buy a second (third, fourth) Mac for the office. A hub only costs you $20 or $30, but think about the money you'll save on tanning booths. I spend most of my day sitting here surrounded by some seven or eight monitors, and every blue-skinned geek I meet compliments me on my healthy, bluish-green tone.

six devices into the hub. Hubs are available for both USB and FireWire devices.

Where's the Eject button on the CD drive?!?

Don't got one. It's a similar deal as with the power switch. If the CD (or DVD) drive had a button that caused it to spit out the disc, you might spit it out before your Mac is done with it. It's a stability issue. To eject a disc, give your Mac a proper "Mother, may I?" first. Either click the Eject button found next to the disc's name in the Finder, or push the Eject key on your keyboard. Panther will close down all of the disc's files and otherwise ensure that spitting out the disc will not be referred to as "The exact moment when my entire life took a dramatic turn worthy of either a Russian novel or an episode of *Falcon Crest*."

I'm totally lost. Where are my files?

One of the few real downsides to being a multi-user OS is that you're not necessarily the king or queen of this Mac's world. Under Mac OS 9, the entire contents of your Mac's hard drive were yours. And Windows XP hides away anything that it feels you have no need to see. Result: You go to save a file, you try to navigate to a new folder...and after 20 or 30 seconds you don't see any of your familiar folders and you have no idea where they went.

In addition to your own personal directory, your hard drive contains directories for all of this Mac's other users; directories for the Mac OS X operating system *and* MacOS 9; directories for shared folders; directories for code libraries; well, I can sense that I've done my job and reminded you of how confusing this all is, so I'll stop here.

This is one of many areas in life in which you can reap great rewards by pretending that the whole world revolves around you and that anything outside of your own little world is of absolutely no importance to you whatsoever.

EJECT COMMANDS, CANDLEPIN BOWLING, AND OTHER CULTURAL TRAUMAS

Using the OS to eject CDs, rather than some eject button located on the drive *has* to be one of the toughest concepts for former Windows users to grasp. Neither way is necessarily better than the other, but it seems to resonate with our genetic programming somehow and taps into the same system that tells us that a tribe that makes fire with a stick and a bone instead of with a rock and some leaves has such a fundamentally warped outlook on our shared environment that their utter annihilation is absolutely essential to our tribe's survival.

The only modern-day analogue is when someone from New England tries to explain candlepin bowling to an outsider, and he gets to the part about how the pin-setting machine intentionally leaves fallen pins in the alley. I still have little shards of green glass in my scalp from that bar fight.

"Your" world is completely encapsulated inside your Home folder (Figure 19-2).

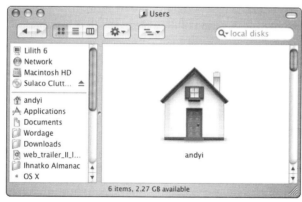

Figure 19-2
The Home Folder: Your personal fortress of solitude

Whether you're in the Finder or in a standard Open File/Save File dialog, clicking the little house with your name next to it navigates you straight toward your personal files and apps.

When are you going to get a haircut?

I'm happy with my ponytail, thanks.

What sort of recordable discs should I buy for my Mac?

If you mean "What kind?," then you should buy CD-Rs for audio CDs and for data discs that you only intend to write to once, and CD-RWs if you're creating a data disc and you want to erase and replace all of its contents from time to time. DVDs are a lot more complicated because there are so many different kinds.

At this writing, the only burnable DVD drives that Apple ships are SuperDrives, which use DVD-R discs. Not to be confused with DVD+R or DVD-RW or DVD-RAM or anything else.

If you mean "What *speed?*" then you've raised a somewhat sticky question. When you go into an office-supply superstore, you're confronted with spindles of blank discs boasting speeds all the way to 32X. 1X is the speed at which you can play an audio CD from start to finish, so you can burn an 8X disc in roughly one-eighth of an hour.

The problem is that, once again we get into mutually assured destruction. Disc burners are dirt-cheap, and the only way a manufacturer can gain any advantage in the marketplace is to rush faster drives onto shelves. But with every speed increase comes a new set of physical specs for the discs, which means that a spindle of 32X discs may or may not work in a drive that's only rated for 8x speed.

DVD STANDARDS: LET'S LOBBY FOR SOME TECH DÉTENTE!

Why are there so many different kinds of DVDs? Because all the different drive manufacturers were pretty desperate to start selling burnable DVDs to consumers. Normally, they don't start turning the things out until they've all gotten together and chosen *one* standard that everyone can support, but when one manufacturer bolted off to be first to the marketplace, everyone else took off behind him. Thus demonstrating that maybe the Cold War had actually been a pretty clever scheme. With *one* system of global annihilation, nobody had any motivation to get ahead of anybody else. Oh, if only tech companies could work with each other as well as the U.S. and the Soviet Union did during the 1960s and '70s!

Making things even more complicated, Apple's disc drivers are aware of these problems and try for maximum compatibility. So, if you try to use a 4X DVD-R with a Super-Drive that only works at slower speed, iDVD burns the disc just fine...but at 1X speed. So whatever the price difference was between the 1X and 4X discs, you might as well have given it to *charity* for all the good it did you.

Your best bet is to head on over to www.apple.com, click the Hardware tab, and look at the tech sheet for your specific model of Mac. If you look at the sheet for the 20" iMac, for example, it promises that 32x CDs work just fine with it. When in doubt, buy slower discs.

Finally, if you mean "Which *brand* of disc should I buy?," most stores sell the generic discs shrink-wrapped into huge, 100-disc cylinders and sold so cheap that if you manage to find a rebate coupon online, you might actually *make* money buying one. Then there are the nice, name-brand discs that come in their own individual jewel cases.

There's no handy rule of thumb regarding which brand is the best or even if the generics are necessarily not as reliable as the name brands. You can pretty much trust that if a disc (a) burns successfully with no errors, and (b) you store it in an environment free from light, dust, and scratches, one is as good as the other.

Still, I tend to keep both generics *and* name brands in the office. The generics are for stuff I burn for fun and things I'm sending to friends. But when I'm archiving photos or backing up data, I use the name brands. Mechanically, they are a bit more rugged, and the fact that each one is stamped with the name of a big-time manufacturer means — naturally — that the company has to be worried about lawsuits. So, they're certainly going to do anything they can to ensure that they've been properly certified.

I forgot my login password.

Not a problem. If you're sharing this Mac with other people, find someone who (a) has an Administrator account, and (b) wasn't so foolish as to select "S00opER_!_! PHR333aKQUE928" as a login password. He or she has the power to change your password to something that's easier for you to remember and isn't a humiliating reference to a Rick James song.

If you're the lone wolf of the plains, dig out your Panther install discs. Reboot from Disc 1 (stick it in the drive and select Restart, pressing C on your keyboard). There's an item in the Panther Installer's menu for resetting the system password.

 Note

This is why you desperately need to keep this disc from falling into the wrong hands, assuming of course that you lead such a lifestyle of way-hey-hey excitement and thrills that someone might conceivably want to gain access to your Mac and take a look at your upcoming Rotisserie League hockey draft picks.

Can I send mail to people who don't have Macs?

Yup. Internet email is based upon a long-standing, well-documented, and free open standard, so you can read any email sent from any computer just fine on any other computer. Mail.app goes this one further: When you send a file attachment, it automatically uses more than one method to prepare it for its journey. So whether a Mac or a PC receives the file the recipient's mail program can decode it properly.

My PowerBook (or iBook or iPod) battery won't hold a full charge.

Stinks, doesn't it? Lilith 6, my current PowerBook, can only last about 45 minutes on battery, as opposed to nearly 3 *hours* when it was new. It's all due to the chemistry of modern batteries. They're going to wear out *eventually*, and the symptom of age is reduced capacity.

If you want to prolong the useful life of your battery, always give it a full charge after you use it. Doesn't matter if you only used it for 15 or 20 minutes. The most damaging thing you can do is run your PowerBook all the way down to its low-battery warning and then charge it back up again.

▼ Tip

One of the best investments you can make is a second power adapter. If you're constantly taking your PowerBook down to the living room to answer email while watching CourtTV, leave one plugged in next to the sofa and the daily routine won't have the slightest impact on your battery. A new PowerBook battery costs about $150. A new adapter costs about $60. No contest. Learn from my mistakes: When I fly from Boston to San Francisco, I have to spend those 6 hours *reading,* for God's sake.

It's just that I was talking with your mother the other day, and she kept saying how *nice* you would look with short hair.

Well, I just prefer to wear it long.

Why is my Mac so *slow* all of a sudden?

You probably just need to restart it. When Panther's performance drops down to the sort of speed that would cause a snail to cross over into oncoming traffic and blow past it while honking its horn and flipping it the bird, it's usually because over the past X days or weeks of nonstop operation the system's need for memory has just kept growing and growing.

Panther, like all Unixes, relies on a system of virtual memory. Your Mac might have 512MB of actual RAM, but if you open so many applications that the OS needs more, it treats disk space as though it were memory, shuttling information between drive and RAM as needed. Normally, this scheme works great. If some of the software you're running is slightly defective, it leads to torpor (Learned that word in second grade and have used it about once a week ever since. Thank you, Mrs. Bellisamo!).

When a program no longer needs a hunk of memory, it's *supposed* to tell Panther that it's okay to free that hunk up for other purposes. If it doesn't, it just keeps calling for more and more hunks, which means that Panther has to use more and more virtual memory, which ultimately means that your Mac can't figure out what 62 divided by 0 is without having to access the hard drive.

▼ Note

Web browsers are *particularly* notorious offenders. A dozen Safari windows often means having to wait an extra couple of seconds every time I click a link. I don't need to restart my Mac all that often, but I usually wind up restarting Safari at least once every couple of days.

Thus, you're probably going to want to restart your Mac once a week. Keeps things healthy. All of Panther's memory is set back to 0, and you have a nice, fast, clean slate.

If these slowdowns are happening a *lot* though, you might want to think about reinstalling Panther (see Chapter 2). It's possible that a critical part of the OS has gotten thrashed sometime in the year or so you've been using it. Internally, a simple one-step process for getting a piece of system information becomes the extended director's cut of Abbott and Costello's *Who's on First?* routine as one bit of software goes through endlessly protracted and patient discussions with a defective part of the OS to make this happen.

▼ Note

This, incidentally, is true of every single OS I use. It's not just a Mac OS X problem. Over the years, I've become convinced that if there's just one simple tip for keeping computers healthy, it's to reinstall the OS from scratch once a year. It's like spring cleaning.

That said, I never seem to encounter these slowdowns on my Windows XP machines. It's one of the few things I prefer about Windows. The only other advantage is that you really don't feel sad or guilty after you wield your keyboard like a broadsword and beat the crap out of a Windows machine.

How about if you kept the long hair, but just cut it short up front?

Then I'd have a freakin' *mullet*. As a geek, doesn't society judge me harshly *enough* without my actively feeding the fire by getting a Billy Ray Cyrus haircut?!?

Thomas Jefferson had a ponytail. Paul Revere had a ponytail. Mozart wore a ponytail made out of *real pony hair*. Why can't you get behind me on this?

I think this software Installer is stuck. It started off okay but the little progress thermometer hasn't budged an inch in a long time.

Hmm. That's a possibility. But whether you're installing a single application or the entire OS, there are procedures involved that can take a long, long time to complete. That progress indicator doesn't mark the amount of *time* the process takes; it moves forward the Installer completes each *task*. So, if the Installer program has to do 30 things and the last one is Convert every document on this 30GB hard drive to Mandarin Pig Latin and then back again, well, that extra one-thirtieth is going to take a while.

Here's what I do. If the progress indicator seems stuck, I move my mouse pointer so that its point is parked right at the thermometer's current position. That gives me a fixed, known landmark with which to compare the bar's movement. Then I go off and read monster comics or whatever for a while. If I come back and I see that the progress bar has advanced a few pixels, then I don't worry.

You don't want to interrupt an installation while it's in progress. There are easier ways to render your Mac inoperable, but it involves vodka and an open flame. If I have to, I'll leave a Mac running overnight rather than force a restart.

I keep trying to print, but nothing comes out! And I'm not getting any error messages!

That's because as far as your word processor and Panther are concerned, the printing system is working just fine. There's no direct connection between an app and a printer. The app hands the job off to Panther's print manager, which hangs on to the job until the printer's ready to handle it.

It's great from the perspective that you can print 170 pages of documents and then go off and watch a movie while the print manager acts as traffic cop. There's *supposed* to be enough communication between the entities that if something goes wrong, you'll learn about it, but the error-reporting system isn't perfect. So, while the manager is waiting patiently, the user is sometimes left wondering just what in the name of shampoo-and-conditioner-in-one is going on.

If you've been left wondering just what in the name of shampoo-and-conditioner-in-one is going on, go to the Dock. If it's working on a print job, the printer's icon should appear there; clicking it brings up a list detailing what it's working on (Figure 19-3):

Well, just *great*. There's an error and I didn't find out about it until I went looking for it. Ninety-nine times out of 100 — I checked; hey, I'm a professional — you can get things moving again by deleting any pending print jobs (select them in the list, and then click the Delete button), and then walking over to your printer and turning the power off and then on again.

It's also possible that at some point you clicked the Stop Jobs button, which tells the print manager to accept print jobs but not to actually print them until someone starts the print queue again. But you said that there was no error message when you printed. Panther is supposed to warn you about that before accepting the print job.

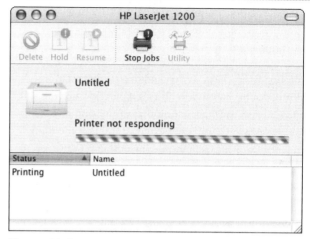

Figure 19-3
Uh-oh, here's why nothing's coming out of the printer

I'm *supposed* to be able to access my network from nearly a football field away through my wireless AirPort base station. I'm lucky to make it from the rec room to the bedroom!

Well, it's your own damned fault. *Don't* give me that look, either; *you're* the one who insisted on getting a brick and natural-stone treatment for the north wall of the living room. I *told* you that if you just painted the wall a reflective white, you'd save $6,000, and only *half* of that savings would cover the cost of a wall-sized projector that hooks right up to your Mac.

Not only is that so-called grown-up wall treatment expensive, it also blocks radio signals. If you imagine the AirPort as a big light bulb that throws off radio signals, no computer in that wall's shadow can connect.

That's just one problem of getting a base station to work properly. Every wall between you and the base degrades the signal. Everything pumping out RF (like a TV or a cordless phone) can cause interference. Metal shelving can screw things up, too.

Two things to try. First, just try rotating the base station 90 degrees along various axes. It's a simple trick, but the difference between a base station that sits flat and one that hangs vertically on a wall can be dramatic. The same thing often works for your computers. Obviously, you can't use a PowerBook while hanging upside down, but you can rotate your chair so that you're facing the southern wall instead of the eastern one.

You can also try adding an external antenna to the base station. AirPort Extreme base stations have external antenna connectors built in; the standard base station requires a little warranty-voiding surgery. The chief benefit of buying and installing an external antenna is directionality. Normally, the base is like a bare light bulb, spreading its signal in all directions. An external antenna helps you focus its output where you need it. But don't expect miracles.

What if you get it cut, and if you don't *like* it, you just grow it back?

Give my best to Dad, Mom. Talk to you next week, okay?

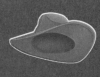

THE TRIALS AND TRIBULATIONS OF GETTING A GOOD WIRELESS SIGNAL

If you have a titanium PowerBook G4, just try to accept that this world is a vale of tears and that mankind is born to suffer. The G4 was one of the first Macs to have AirPort antennas built in, and, boy, did Apple make some poor choices. First, it located the antennas at the bottom half of the machine under your wrists, where they're almost certain to be covered up by something. Secondly, titanium isn't very transparent to radio waves, so the end result is that the PowerBook G4 is about as stealthy as an F117A fighter, which is to say, not very.

On later PowerBooks and iBooks, Apple moved the antennas to the top of the screen. I bought my new PowerBook for lots of reasons. Chiefly, there was no room for any more stickers on the old one, but the one feature I appreciated the most was the fact that for the first time in 2 years, I could actually access my home wireless network from the comfy chair.

20

Drop the Book and Come Out Peacefully: Online Resources

Here, let me seed you with some of my favorite Macintosh-oriented Web sites. If you add these URLs to your regular rotation, you'll be as plugged in and well informed as even the most beloved, respected, and egotistical Macintosh pundit.

NEWS

MacCentral (www.maccentral.com/)

MacCentral is the online news presence of *Macworld* magazine. It's updated with ferocious and tenacious frequency and has the broadest range of coverage. It's a great first-click-of-the-morning; in one collection of headlines you find news about products, partnerships, Apple as a company, future strategies, and links to outside news stories that aren't directly Mac-related but are likely to influence the Macintosh Experience in the weeks and months to come.

MacObserver (www.macobserver.com/)

Like MacCentral, this is a new site, but if it covers breaking stories with less intensity, it makes up for it with a stable of columnists and commentators (including yours truly), and tips and techniques.

MacOS Rumors (www.macosrumors.com/)

This is a fun site, so long as you make sure your eyes keep flickering to that URL — *Mac Rumors*. This isn't a news site. This is gossip and scuttlebutt about future Apple hardware and software releases and the anticipated moves of Mac-related companies. Oftentimes, the rumors on this site prove to be right on the money. Oftentimes, you wonder if the software used to post new items shouldn't be hooked up to a Breathalyzer or something to make sure such obvious rubbish isn't posted again. But this site is always an illuminating read.

FEATURES AND PRODUCT REVIEWS

Macworld (www.macworld.com/) and MacAddict (www.macaddict.com)

The two most important magazines on the newsstand also have two of the most important Mac-related sites on the Web. Timely news isn't their forte; they produce material on monthly deadlines, not hourly ones, so if yours truly is ever arrested for breaking into an amusement park while wearing a firefighter's helmet and the bottom half of the Philly Phanatic costume, you won't read it *there* (not for a few weeks, anyway — and don't judge me; you just don't know what love is).

But they have the production resources of a full magazine staff, which means that they have extended product reviews, detailed how-to articles, and highly professional content from top to bottom.

TidBITS (www.tidbits.com/)

TidBITS is that most unusual of beasts: an online-only publication that fights in the same weight class as the print magazines. Its reviews are reliable, its analysis always insightful, and it has a unique editorial voice and point of view.

HELP/COMMUNITY

Apple Service & Support (www.apple.com/support/)

I have no idea why Apple's online answer database isn't the number 1 link in everyone's Safari bookmarks file. It's unlikely that you're the first person to experience a specific problem or to be confused by the right way to install memory or customize the Dock. Here's where Apple gives you a searchable database of informative, step-by-step articles that cover the whole span of the Mac product line, going back to the Reagan administration.

Even if you're serene in your mastery of Macintosh knowledge, you should check this page regularly. Apple sometimes institutes warranty extensions of Mac hardware when it discovers an unusually prevalent problem — so this is the place where you find out that Apple's willing to swap your Mac's current power supply with a new-and-improved one if you ask.

MacInTouch (www.macintouch.com/)

MacInTouch was (along with TidBITS) one of the very first Mac-oriented electronic publications. In the past few years its focus has shifted slightly, taking it away from breaking news and into community discussions of new software and developments. That is, while MacInTouch duly reports on the release of a new public beta of iChat, the real reason why you click on the link is to read the MacInTouch community's debate on its pros and cons. When you install a system update and you start to have problems, this is the place to read about other users' experiences.

Slashdot (http://apple.slashdot.org/)

Slashdot is a lot of things (news site, message board, merchandise mart), but I think any smart definition of what it is begins and ends with the phrase, "Slashdot is so...*itself*." Its Apple subsection contains some of the most passionate and informed (and occasionally confusing above all) discussion about what's going on in the Mac world. Bonus: The Web site's software rates the karma (aka, trustworthiness, respectability, civility) of the person posting the message, so each post comes with an indication of how much credibility you can attach to it.

MacSlash (www.macslash.org/) brings much of Slashdot's vibe with less of its intimidation.

MacFixIt (www.macfixit.com/)

This site is a real lifesaver. It focuses on one concept: problem-solution. If items start disappearing from your Dock for no reason, there's probably a report up on MacFixIt that explains the cause of the problem and how to fix it. The only downside is that it's a pay site. New items are free, but searching through MacFixIt's handy archives is going to cost you.

SOFTWARE

VersionTracker (www.versiontracker.com/) and MacUpdate (www.MacUpdate.com/)

Some of the best Mac software is available as downloadable shareware or freeware. I have a hard time choosing between these two as my favorite Macintosh download site. They both diligently assemble a wide range of apps. Both offer a simple, searchable database. On both sites, every file is backed up by user ratings and comments, so

you can steer yourself straight to the best iPod utility of the 12 available for downloading. And both are nice enough to list all of the latest software right on the top page. It's always worthwhile to check in from time-to-time just to see what's new, and, better yet, to discover a great app that (a) You've never heard of and (b) would never have found on your own.

In the end, it's unimportant to rate one of them as the winner; between them you have the capability to totally choke your ISP's bandwidth with downloads.

Apple Mac OS X Downloads (www.apple.com/downloads/macosx/)

Apple has its own download area for Mac OS X shareware and freeware. The library isn't nearly as extensive as MacUpdate's or VersionTracker's, but it has a more professional, catalogue-ish appearance that I find appealing. You won't find anything edgy here, but what's here is prime material.

SHOP

DealMac (www.dealmac.com/)

I'm not going to recommend any one store to you. Instead, I'll recommend DealMac, the site that always steers you toward the best bargains. It knows every one-day price drop, every coupon code, every rebate, and sometimes its news items are so compelling that you can't bear *not* to buy products. The online vendor keyed in the wrong price... *plus* there's a $30 rebate, *plus* there's a coupon code for 20 percent off any purchase and a free shipping promotion that ends on the 27th, for a total savings of 60 percent. See? I can tell that you're *already* getting out your Visa card, and you don't even know what the product is!

DealMac is especially handy when the item you're shopping for has volatile prices that change day-to-day. If you're in the market for a gigabyte of RAM, just stay tuned to Deal-Mac (or sign up for keyword-based email alerts). When the price is (quote) "The lowest we've ever seen on memory modules of this capacity" you know it's time to bite.

ANDY IHNATKO'S COLOSSAL WASTE OF BANDWIDTH (WWW.ANDYI.COM/)

A Web site and blog that truly live up to the name.

21

Troubleshooting by the Seat of Your Pants

Macs are wonderfully stable and reliable, particularly when they run Panther. But the only way to ensure that your Mac never experiences any slowdowns or random crashes or other signs of petulance is to (1) carefully install Panther on a compatible machine, following Apple's guidelines and instructions precisely, and then (2) shut down the Mac and never use it again. Apple doesn't *tell* you that in the ads. I've written letters. I'm just as mad about it as you are.

Ideally, when your Mac starts acting funny, you would have a very experienced and knowledgeable friend or relative in your address book. You'd explain the problem and he or she'd walk you through some diagnostics and then tell you how to fix it.

 Tip

Incidentally, consider making a friend of a very experienced and knowledgeable Macintosh user. They're easy and affordable to maintain, sleep on any absorbent shredded bedding, and you can find their food supplements in any establishment where you're allowed to speak into a fiberglass cartoon character from the comfort of your car.

Not everybody's quite so lucky, though. For your benefit, here's the standard ladder of things to try when your Mac acts up on you and you have no clue why.

This isn't a step-by-step list. It's just a batch of techniques that often tend to solve the problem, and they're arranged so that the procedures that are easiest to perform, require the least amount of your time, and carry the lowest amount of risk appear nearest the top. Numbers One through Three can be accompanied with a shrug of the shoulders and a cheerful muttering of "Why not? *The Simpsons* is a rerun."

By the time you get to the bottom, you should wipe perspiration (real or imagined) from your brow, silently ask yourself if you have any right to play God, and then breathe deeply and move forward. You're building character, only *this* time you didn't have to spend 3 hours behind your dad's push-mower to acquire it.

DO NOTHING

And, yes, that is indeed a serious and solid piece of advice. When your Mac grinds to a halt and *appears* to lock up, if the screen seems to update in odd ways, or if weird ghostly images of menus and windows cut in and out briefly, as if drawn by a contractor who's already been paid for this job and isn't interested in making things look *good*, it's possible that nothing's wrong that the Mac can't fix on its own once it gets the chance.

Your Mac has to do a lot of behind-the-scenes bookkeeping to keep the OS and all of its applications running smoothly. Sometimes these bookkeeping chores get a little backlogged, and it tries to do far too much all at once. This doesn't cause any *damage*, mind you, but it means that Panther might temporarily act slow, ugly, and clumsy until it completes all the items on its to-do list.

So take this as an opportunity to go off and get a Coke. You have a couple of chicken fingers left over from last night's takeout. Heat 'em up and enjoy. Give your Mac some Alone Time. Let it have a good cry; maybe give it a copy of *Beaches* or *Miss Firecracker* to watch. By the time you sit back down at the keyboard, the torpor might be a thing of the past.

This, incidentally, is one reason why it's a good idea to have Panther display the current time within your menu bar (go to System Preferences, click Date & Time, click the Clock preference tab, and click Show the date and time.) So long as 2:31 p.m. becomes 2:32 p.m. becomes 2:33 p.m., I'm willing to wait a problem out. However, when the clock is frozen, that's usually the sign of a more serious problem.

"DO NOTHING" WORKED FOR APOLLO 11

"When in doubt, first, do nothing" was one of the most important rules that NASA's mission controllers developed during the early days of the space program. The lunar module's landing radar kept freezing up and giving cryptic error codes during Apollo 11's descent to the lunar surface. They didn't know exactly what the problem was, so they let the computer sort things out: perfect landing. Apollo 12 got hit by lightning *twice* during launch, throwing entire systems offline. They did nothing until the ship reached orbit and discovered that the system could easily reset itself.

And as a taxpayer, the computers on board Apollo were the most expensive computers you've ever owned. So if it worked for them…

QUIT PEACEFULLY

If a complete lack of effort on your part accomplishes nothing, then quit the app that's acting up. It's possible that you can't access the menus, but press ⌘+Q anyway (the system software that drives the keyboard almost never slows down or crashes). And *then* walk away and get yourself another drink.

Admittedly, Quitting Peacefully isn't likely to work if Doing Nothing has already failed. But it's like when the police say, "Drop the weapon and lay facedown on the ground" to the man with the gun, the bags of charred money, and the face full of dye that he got when he walked out past the bank's doorway. The next step is pretty inevitable, but it's also rather extreme and you'd like to be able to explain to people that you tried to do the peaceful and polite thing first.

THE WISDOM OF IHNATKO

I don't know what idiot looked at the Ten Warning Signs of Alcoholism and snuck in the phrase, "Do you ever drink alone or when you're depressed?" I'm sure that this is something that alcoholics do, but this also describes what a system manager is doing and feeling when a computer is suddenly acting all petulant on him for no apparent reason.

So don't worry about it. Go down to the kitchen and get yourself another beer. So long as you're not driving, or singing "Radar Love" so loud that it disturbs the other tenants.

▼ **Note**

But this tip actually *does* work well with Web browsers. These apps just have a fundamental nature to run more slowly the longer you've been using them. When Safari takes more time to do a Google search than it'd take me to visit a professor of literature at his home and *ask* him the title of the play-within-a-play in *Hamlet*, I quit and relaunch it. And suddenly, it is once again the snappy, sprightly browser I used to know.

FORCE QUIT

You want to try to Quit peacefully before force quitting because taking the latter action on a running app (even a troubled one, an app that never benefited from the many advantages that you or I took for granted growing up; in a word, an app that was never held closely and told, "You are *loved*") can cause problems later on.

What problems? At minimum, you can *count* on losing any unsaved changes in the app's open documents. At worst, an unseen but important file that Panther or the

app uses for internal bookkeeping won't close properly — or may become corrupted — leading only to additional instability to the app and possibly even the OS at some future date.

▼ **Note**

Reader: *You, too, are loved*. I'm sorry it's taken me more than 20 chapters to say that, but I usually keep my emotions pretty wrapped up. I guess I've just been a damned, prideful fool.

FREE UP SPACE ON YOUR HARD DRIVE

Panther is based on Unix, and if Unix has a need for additional memory, it grabs some chunks of unused space on your hard drive and treats it as virtual memory. Which makes it very, very important that you not fill your drive to capacity. Apps may refuse to launch, and the ones that are running may run as slow as Slow Bob Slowley of Slowdon, last-place finisher of the World's Slowest Slow Person competition, who runs as if he is waist-deep in pancake batter.

▼ **Tip**

Yeah, I know. It's not your fault. Clutter is just plain attracted to your hard drive. The Omni Group (www.omnigroup.com) has a really nifty little utility that I use all the time. OmniDiskSweeper can scan your drive and highlight all its biggest space hogs. If you pay the $15 shareware fee, you can delete 'em with the click of a button. Don't worry; it warns you before you delete anything that Panther needs.

The first time I ran ODS, it instantly and painlessly freed up 3GB from my PowerBook's 20GB drive. Seems that months and months earlier, I'd tested a device that lets you tune in TV signals and record them on your Mac. Plumb forgot that I had 3 hours of TV shows on that drive.

As a general rule, I like to keep 10 percent of my hard drive free. I *prefer* to keep it at 20 percent.

SHUT DOWN AND RESTART

Shutting down your Mac is, of course, the super-atomic-wedgie version of quitting a running app and restarting it. All of the benefits of restarting an app now apply to every last component of the OS. It's like getting a good night's sleep, or just taking the license plate and the stereo from your car and abandoning the car right there on the highway. You emerged refreshed. There's a sense of renewal and getting a fresh start.

Proving that on this wretched hunk of rock upon which I've been stranded for lo these past 6 centuries, there is absolutely no *good* thing that doesn't have a bad side. The fact that Mac OS X is so much more stable than all previous editions of the Mac OS means that while you *can* keep it running for weeks and months without a crash, you probably wouldn't want to.

Until OS X, developers never had an opportunity to test their apps to see how they held up after weeks or even just days of runtime. Somewhere by Day Two, the user would cause a system crash (clearly ignoring Apple Technical Library Document #29283: Do not look at menu bar funny (09/19/93v12)), and have to restart the Mac.

Under OS X, tiny bugs — hitherto undetectable — quietly build in strength over the course of days until eventually they cause huge problems. And sadly, some of these microbugs are in Panther itself. So it's just good policy to shut down and restart your Mac once a week whether it needs it or not.

And I *do* mean Shut Down, not simply ticking Restart. A Shut Down does a more complete job of clearing out all of the old aches and irks and starting everything fresh.

YET ANOTHER APOLLO REFERENCE

Ahhhh! Another opportunity to make an Apollo reference. NASA had a similar experience with the Apollo command module. When Apollo 13 had its in-flight explosion and it had to coast back to Earth without power, its trajectory kept drifting too low and needed to be corrected. It turns out that one of the components in the craft had a design flaw that caused it to leak gasses in flight. It affected every Apollo ever built, but this was the first time it had ever made its presence known. Normally, the thrust of its rocket engines nullified the effect times about 1 million.

It's an interesting part of space history, and it also means that the slip-cased library edition of Apollo mission logs for which I paid $140 is now tax-deductible. And don't think I don't appreciate your reading this.

Incidentally, this is why I don't usually give out tips on how to quit and restart the Finder or the Dock, two items that can cause odd problems if they get bugged up. There are ways to do that, but my advice is to just do a Shut Down and Restart. Any problem that's caused the Finder to require a restart has probably corrupted other running apps and drivers, too. Best to shut them all down and let God (that is, the Boot Manager) sort it out.

RESTART AND ZAP THE PRAM

⌘+Option+P+R is so ingrained upon the consciousness of the Mac community that I'm surprised that the sequence of keys hasn't appeared on a line of bracelets and jewelry yet. COPR is the patron saint of, "I don't know why my Mac is acting up, and now I'll try some things at random."

Pressing those keys during startup causes a *tiny* speck of battery-backed RAM to clear itself. Why does this sometimes solve mysterious problems? Because this is the Mac's Parameter RAM, and it stores a few very basic settings that must be maintained even if the machine is powered off and *left* off. Among this info is the name and location of the drive off of which this Mac is supposed to boot. If some sort of bizarre malfunction causes your Mac's PRAM to become jam-packed with aerosol cheese, it can cause a problem that will persist from restart to restart.

This technique is nondestructive, and the only reason why it's so far down on the list is because it's a big pain to close all of your apps and documents and perform a Restart. And it's not like it always (or even *often*) solves the problem; it's just that it doesn't take too long to perform and you know it won't make things any *worse*.

RESTART IN SAFE BOOT MODE

Still not working, eh? Hmm. Maybe the last time you installed a piece of software or, better yet, the drivers for a new piece of hardware, the Installer program introduced a snippet of software that causes Panther to spin its head like a top and cover that priest by the side of the bed in pea soup.

Restart the Mac and press the Shift key. This restarts Panther in Safe Mode; that is, during the startup process only Panther's standard, bare-bones, must-have components are loaded. If your Mac suddenly becomes a happy and laughing little girl, you know that there's *something* inside your System Directory that's mucking things up.

Safe Boot also automatically runs a Unix disk utility called FSCK. So if the problem is a munged hard drive and it's an easy fix, you'll be sitting on velvet by the end of the (very, very long) boot process.

If it's a problem with Panther, the situation probably has just gotten a little more serious. You might want to jump straight down to the section "Reinstall Panther." Or...well, if I say "your ac-May ight-may be oken-bray," it'll magically cause it to happen, I won't say it in open text.).

Tip

A similar trick: Log on as a different user. It's faster than Safe Boot because Panther won't perform an FSCK, but it still gives you an answer to the question, "Is the problem with Panther, or is it a problem with something in my account?"

For this reason, it's an excellent idea to create a separate user account named Trouble or some such. Don't use this account for *anything* other than troubleshooting; you want to keep this account's contents as plain vanilla and unblemished as possible.

SHUT DOWN, UNPLUG ALL CABLES, AND RESTART

Take a deep breath.

Take another.

Close the door and pull down the curtains.

Take a third deep breath.

Okay. Now, check the back of your Mac. It's possible — I'm not saying this is *it*, I'm merely tabling the possibility — that the reason your keyboard is dead is because its USB cable has somehow come unplugged. And not, as you so loudly theorized, because your Mac is "a worthless unreliable piece of trash that somehow can just plain *sense* when you've got a big project deadline coming up and cause a system failure at the *worst possible moment*!!!!!!!!!"

This is one of the most common sources of utterly bizarre, unpredictable, and irreproducible problems. If a FireWire cable works itself *partly* loose, your hard drive may stop working. And it might even cause Panther to kernel-panic; it keeps trying to read the FireWire port, but it's jinked in just such a way that the wrong connector on the Mac's interface is grounded for just a millisecond, and then — boom.

MACGYVER, WHAT ARE YOU DOING?

The most embarrassing (and thus most influential) story comes from a memorable week I spent shooting a DVD with three of the Mac community's top experts. Our Airport base station stopped connecting to the Internet at absolutely the worst possible time. Sometimes we could find Web sites, sometimes the Internet disappeared entirely, and sometimes we could get a connection, but it was a horribly slow one. So, Person A started working on the theory that the base station didn't receive a firmware update; Person B thought that one of the Macs on the network might have been flooding the gateway with bad packets; Person C thought that the office's ISP had noticed our heavy use of the Internet and was capping our access; whereas I started working out ways we could access the Internet without using the router at all.

Only after an hour of fruitless four-man effort did these Incredible Mac Experts think to check the cable plugged into the base station. And, um, it turned out that the little plastic locking–tab thingy that keeps the cable firmly connected to the base station had broken off.

I jammed the toothpick from my Swiss army knife into the connector, and it locked it in place. Presto, everything worked fine after that. Since then, I never go hunting for a unicorn when the more likely suspect is a common brown horse with a cracked USB connector sticking out of its ear.

Thus, this is a good time for you to unplug absolutely everything except for the keyboard, mouse, and monitor, and restart. If the problem goes away, you know you have a bad connection somewhere.

It's also a good opportunity to make sure your cables are undamaged and in good condition. I was having a nightmare of a problem getting my new USB scanner to work. Finally, I looked for the weakest, cheapest-looking cable in my whole setup and replaced it with a nice, thick one. Presto: $10 spent at OfficeMax cut through a problem that gave me fits for hours.

One more question: Did you install new memory just before Panther started treating you like that bass player who's just started dating your 19-year-old daughter? It's possible that you have a bad memory module or that you zorched it with static electricity during installation. Try removing it and restarting. If you had the module installed professionally, take your Mac back to the shop that did the work.

REBOOT OFF A CD AND RUN DISK UTILITY

Get out Disc 1 from your Panther installation set. It contains a bootable copy of Panther. Stick it in your drive, restart, and press C while your Mac boots.

This causes a two-pronged effect. Now, you're not using your hard drive's installed copy of Panther at all. If your Mac magically runs happy, fast, and stable, you can at least be relieved to know that it's not a hardware problem and can (likely) be easily fixed.

The second prong of this procedure is the fact that Disc 1 also contains a copy of the Disk Utility application. Disk Utility (click Applications ➜ Utilities) can work two different kinds of mojo on a hard drive. Clicking the Repair Disk button scans your boot drive (or any other drive you specify), examines its data structures for abnormalities, and fixes them.

It also has that Repair Permissions button. Clicking the button causes the utility to examine *every single one of Panther's system files* and to make sure that its Unix permissions flags are properly set. A system file may just be 2K in size and contain seemingly unimportant profile info, but if Panther expects to read and write this file, and it *can't* because Unix thinks this file is locked and unchangeable, all sorts of unpredictable trouble can ensue.

Performing both these functions can take an awfully long time. That's why this advice is low on the list. In truth, you actually *want* to run Disk Utility and Repair Permissions on a regular basis (once or twice a month; it builds strong bodies nine different ways), but your Mac may be tied up with this for an hour or more.

While we're on the subject of booting off a CD and running a disk utility, give some thought to buying a copy of Alsoft's DiskWarrior. Disk Utility slaps at corrupted hard-drive directories, but DiskWarrior is downright antisocial about them. It's far more sophisticated and can fix a far greater range of problems. If your Mac won't start up at all,

you can boot right off the DiskWarrior CD and run the utility directly. And like Disk Utility, running DiskWarrior regularly keeps healthy drives smiling.

At this writing, DiskWarrior 3 is $79. Dirt-cheap compared to the cost of setting broken bones in your hand and patching a hole in the wall if your drive goes south three hours before deadline.

REINSTALL

Well, team, things are looking pretty freakin' bleak right now. You've eliminated nearly every possibility but two: something, somewhere, somehow inside Panther has become corrupted, corroded, malcontented, malformed, sticky, shiftless, demotivated, devolved, demonized, hypnotized...somethin' ain't right.

It is now time to drop the A-bomb: Shut down, reboot off Panther Install Disc 1, run the Panther Install program, and perform a clean, new installation of the operating system (selecting the Archive and Install option; see Chapter 2 for details.).

Time-consuming? Whoah, Nelly, yes. Say goodbye to possibly a whole evening's worth of working with *Tony Hawk Pro Skater 4* and other productivity apps. Destructive? Mmmmaybe. You shouldn't lose any of the contents of your home folder, but it's possible that you'll lose some of your old settings files and will have to tweak System Preferences setting all over again.

I'm a bit conflicted as to how best to paint this option: a scorched-earth approach of destroying your entire existing Panther system directory and sticking something else in its place? It sounds like something Dirty Harry would do in *Dirty Harry*, or what Sylvester Stallone will do to his management team if he winds up in just one more direct-to-video release. It just isn't orderly.

And yet I sit here, fortifying myself with another sip from my bottle of Coke, and finally typing, "Completely wiping out your old OS and replacing it with a brand-new copy once or twice a year is actually very, very good advice."

It's not the *big* bugs and tics I fear. My word processor starts crashing on me, I fix it, I move on. It's the little, undetectable, unfixable, *incremental* problems that I worry about. Modern operating systems are so complex these days that they can indeed suffer a condition akin to termite damage. One *little*, nearly anonymous system file gets corrupted. And then a code library that uses that file screws up and messes up another file. And those two files cause four more bits of code to mess up; on and on, like the first-act finale of a Gilbert & Sullivan operetta until there's barely a Panther component that is working up to spec.

That's when weird things start going wrong with your Mac. It's not enough to render your Mac useless, but it's enough to become an enormous pain. And the root cause of the problem is so far in the past that you will never, *ever* root it out, not even with a Cadbury caramel egg for bait and the force of a federal court order.

▼ **Note**

Witness the problem I'm having with the PowerBook that I'm using to write this chapter with right now. It can't run any Installers. I wanted to install that cool screen-capture utility I mentioned back in Chapter 12. No dice. Snapz Pro's installer quits unexpectedly. Software Update tells me that I have more that 100MB of Panther and iApp upgrades waiting to be downloaded and installed. I have as much chance of installing them as I have of getting Kate Winslet all to myself in a coat-check room for 10 minutes.

Sometimes things go wrong with Panther, and the *simplest and most effective* way to solve them is to just shrug your shoulders and start anew with a fresh copy of the OS. Mind you, it's not a trivial exercise. If you have any *major* projects going, it's best to finish them before doing a Panther reinstall.

But I prefer to think of this procedure as a spring-cleaning and not as tenting and bug-bombing your whole house.

CONVINCE YOURSELF THAT YOU NEEDED A NEW MAC ANYWAY

Well, maybe you don't want to be *that* morbid about it. But if nothing has fixed or alleviated your Mac's pain, you've reached the practical limits of what I can do for you, given that all I know about you and your Mac is that you seem to own one and you were nice enough to buy my book.

You've probably *heard* about the Genius Bars located inside every Apple Store. They're a great resource. Even if your Mac is out of warranty, the consultants behind the counter will stay with you for an hour trying to work out your problem. And if they come up blank, they've got a red phone — seriously, a dramatically spot-lit red phone — behind the counter that immediately connects them to even bigger brains sitting back at Apple.

Earlier on, I made mention of the fact that I sometimes need to use more than one Mac at a time. I have plenty of 'em here in the office and in storage. And every time I feel like I want to gloat about how much more *elevated* Macs are, how much more *reliable* and *easy to maintain* — I really like it when people get so frustrated with me that they rip a fire extinguisher off a nearby wall and tap me in the base of the skull with it — well, I think about all the times when the simplest, most uncomplicated act required me to go to three different machines before I found a unit that was in 100 percent operational spec.

We can be proud of our iMacs and G5s and Panther, but you can't lose sight of the fact that a Mac is a Mac, but it's also a *computer.* And the reason why God inserted computers into our lives is because He can no longer cause frogs and snakes to rain down on our heads for fear of a massive PeTA sit-down protest that would make it impossible to get any work done in Heaven until He issued a statement or something.

22

One Final Lesson

You've had a pretty productive time of it, I reckon. You've patiently plowed through 21 chapters of this book, and for that, I thank you. It wasn't easy going, I know; a Macintosh is probably the easiest computer there is to use and maintain, but there are still fundamental things about any computing experience that make you wonder if there isn't some sort of alien race whose spaceships run on impatience and disorientation, and the Earth is nothing more than the Exxon of this sector of the galaxy. I mean, take a look through a Mac or a Windows machine's full font library. You're not telling me that all those symbols were designed for people with mere binocular vision.

I also admit that, at times, your reading experience must have been like taking a cab ride through any major Italian city — lots of adrenaline and lots of worried glances and lots of desperately clinging to the thought that the driver is, apparently, a *professional,* and he *must* know what he's doing. Otherwise, he'd have been dead long before his Bonfat SL hopped the curb by the airport and he started tossing your luggage into the trunk and onto the hood.

You're nearing the end of our journey of Macintosh knowledge, but you're not *at* the end. Not just yet. There is still one final lesson to complete: You *must equal me in single combat.* Pick that light saber up off the floor and don't ask questions because my attack commences in 5 seconds. I swear this to you, young Jedi, you shall return to your home village either in glory or in pieces. Only your actions over the next 7 hours will tell the tale. Sorry. Got away from myself, there. I get so few opportunities for macho posturing that I rarely know when it's inappropriate. Forget it ever happened.

What I meant to say was that before I let you go, I need to stress to you the extreme importance of maintaining an air of impenetrable purple glowing arrogance at all times. It's a fundamental part of the Macintosh Experience. Author Tom Clancy used to adapt an old saying favored among fighter pilots: "Never ask a man what kind of computer he uses. If he has a Mac, he'll tell you. And if he doesn't...why embarrass him?"

Brilliant stuff. Really brings the point home. It's only the first of many anti-everything-else jokes you'll pick up during your first few months of Mac ownership. And if you're an old hand at this, repeating these old standards only keeps them fresh in your mind, like the Boy Scout Oath.

BEGRUDGINGLY ACKNOWLEDGING OTHER OPERATING SYSTEMS

At previous points in this book, I might have said conciliatory or even positive things about Windows and Linux. Disregard them. I wrote it when one of the boys from Legal was wandering through my part of the office, trying to mooch a Hot Pocket off of someone. It's all junk. Why would anyone *want* to use a Windows machine? The GUI totally lacks elegance, subtlety, or nuance; and every time I launch a Windows app, I'm increasingly convinced that most authors of Windows software are more interested in meeting a Hobbit one day than one of these *users* that they keep reading about on the Web.

And don't get me going on the hardware. I am a geek of admirable ecumenicism: I embrace technologies of all faiths and followings. I have three Windows machines in my home office and receive all kinds of Windows hardware in the mail every week. A recent peripheral is a typical case. I opened the box and the hardware inside was so tightly sealed in red and yellow warning tape that I wondered if the delivery guy didn't make some sort of mistake, and instead of a new network adapter, it was actually a Smallpox-N-Anthrax Party Pack from the Martha Stewart catalogue that Mrs. Pocatelli from next door ordered.

I knew what the warning text would say but I read it anyway. "STOP!" it ordered. "DO NOT CONNECT THIS DEVICE until AFTER you have installed the PROVIDED SOFTWARE!"

See, Windows is supposed to be plug and play. You plug in a device, Windows automatically knows what it is, and then it makes whatever additions or changes to itself that are required to make the new hardware work. The problem is that sometimes Windows gets it totally wrong and all it *actually* accomplishes is to make additions and changes to itself that ensure that this new hardware will never, *ever* work. So it's absolutely vital that you install the *manufacturer's* software before Windows can get its mitts on it.

Things like that just don't happen with Macs. I still remember the astonished looks I received from some of my Windows-only pals when I came into their office with my PowerBook recently. They wanted copies of a couple of my files and while they argued over where they could scare up a blank CD-R to copy them onto, I simply opened the lid, joined their wireless network, found their office's five file servers, and deposited the files into their shared folders. All with just a few mouse-clicks.

One of them looked like he was about to cry. "I bought a new notebook a month ago," he finally told me. "What you just did in 30 seconds cost me a week of phone calls to tech support."

Being a beacon of human kindness, I, of course, sympathized with him. "Apple just released a major update to the Mac OS that makes most of its networking work automagically." I explained. "I'm sure Microsoft will have this sort of thing in its next release of Windows," But even here, I was arrogant. Had I exhaled with just a *little* more force, he would have sensed that my unspoken suffix was "...in 2006, which is the latest slip date to the next big Windows update."

THE BETTER PART OF VALOR

It's important to be arrogant, you see, but it's even more important to manage a Windows user's reactions carefully. You want to keep them angry enough that they eventually wind up buying a new computer, but *not* so angry that the reason why they need a new one is because they beat you in the head with the old one. Remember: A jaw that's held shut with titanium wire can't spread the Gospel of Macintosh. And you can't be a vain blowhard with only *yourself* as an audience.

What about Linux? Good OS; some fantastic software. Comparing Linux to Mac OS is a lot like comparing a vintage muscle car to a brand-new, mid-priced SUV. There are potent arguments to be made that the former has more power and provides an attractive hands-on driving experience. But when I want to go to the store for some peanut M&M's, I hop in *my* car and go. Linux people have to pour some additive into their gas tank, replace the header they took off earlier in the day, crank the ignition while listening to make sure the number three cylinder is firing right...I mean, there are times when you want to be a Power User, and then there are times when you just want to buy some candy and maybe see if the new *People* magazine is in yet.

But in the end, the only time I've ever envied a Windows user was when something went wrong with my Mac and it let me down at *exactly* the worst time and I was frustrated and angry and in need of release. If I had thrown my Macintosh through the wall, I would have probably felt really bad about it later.

▼ Tip

Still, Mac users are cautioned about using arrogance against Linux users. Their usual (and quite effective) defense is for one of them to trap you in a headlock while the other one pummels you about the upper body with endless technical trivia about his or her system's superior performance, using names, specifications, and benchmark data on Window managers and networking standards and all sorts of things that no Mac user ever could or would need to care about. You're *supposed* to embarrass yourself by attempting to respond to this battery of data directly. If you find yourself in this situation, however, your best bet is to wait for the speaker to finish, allow for a 2-second pause, and then say, "And *this* makes you happy, then?" This usually leaves the speaker stumped. At which point, you waggle your sack of M&M's in their faces tauntingly and then drive off, leaving them to do whatever it is they need to do to unlock their car. I think it involves executing a sudo command and then running a Perl script.

THE GREAT SURVIVAL MECHANISM

Privately (*privately*) I concede that the Macintosh operating system is the product of mortal and fallible human beings and that the Panther Golden Master CD was not ejected fully formed from Zeus's forehead, like the formula Classic Coke was. On the day when I'm called up to testify in front of a Congressional subcommittee (have you been watching C-SPAN these days? One day it'll be *your* turn, too), I will tell the fair and honest truth: Users should take inventory of what they want and expect from computers and software, acquiring as much experience as they can. Then finally they should buy whatever hardware and software makes the most sense for them, be it a Mac, a Windows box, or a cantaloupe with a USB keyboard jammed into the pulp and the outline of a screen hastily marked on the skin.

Privately — and here's a big secret that you can only learn if you make it to the *very* end of a Mac book — arrogance always has been and always will be essential to the Mac's long-term survival.

Survival? The thing would never have even been *created* without the warm, womb-like embrace of serene arrogance! There were two wildly popular computers back in the early 1980s: the Apple II line and the IBM PC. Apple *owned* the rights to the Apple II. They could have evolved it in *any* direction they wanted, or incorporated *any* of their technologies into a new product.

They did not. Apple chose to enter the market with a computer that would have zero percent market share. They would run zero percent of the world's software, interact with zero percent of its hardware. Including the photographer who plugged it in and turned it on for the publicity photos, the original Mac 128 had an active user base of about 129. Apple succeeded thanks to the arrogant and unshiftable belief that this was a computer and an OS that *needed* to exist and which couldn't *possibly* fail to catch on.

And, well, whaddya know? Apple was right on both counts.

Over the past 20 years, arrogance has gotten us through the lean times and the fat times. Apple and the Mac's few but fierce early users didn't care that its one word processor could only handle ten pages of text before running out of memory: *I'm right, you're wrong, come back when you fully appreciate that fact and I'll happily teach you how to use this machine.* The Mac became a success and arrogance led Apple to new expressions of ego, and nigh-invulnerability to outside opinions: Apple created the Newton MessagePad, the world's first PDA. It would die a deathly death, but even in failure Apple gets credit for showing the industry that handheld pen-based computers were a Good Idea and had a bright future.

My belief in the viability of the company isn't based on arrogance. It's based on numbers. Others point to the Mac's slim market share, but I point to the company's consistent profits and the fact that folks who want to use Macs find that a Macintosh is exactly the sort of computer they want to use — and Apple is the only company making them.

Ironically, the only time the future of the company really *was* in danger was when humble, calm people, who made decisions based on facts instead of personal emotions, ran the company. These were the Dark Times, when Apple finally decided to cave into the conventional (read: idiotic) wisdom that the only way the company could continue was to license the operating system to work on third-party hardware, as Microsoft had done. Boy, did *that* backfire. The idea was that the licensees would make affordable, dirt-cheap Macs (an area that Apple never excelled at), and leave the high-performance workstation market to Apple. Instead, companies like PowerComputing rushed to place the hottest chips in the newest Macs and Apple was making the most of its money off those high-margin workstations, so they wound up bleeding Apple dry.

The management had effectively taken the batteries out of Apple's once-mighty Infinite Arrogance Generator. Now, it put them back in, only backward, with the effect of sucking the Apple campus bone-dry of every last wisp of confidence that could be found.

A NEW ERA AT APPLE

And then, Steve Jobs reclaimed a leadership role. Apple came back twice as arrogant and insufferable as it ever was, thanks to his infusion of confident, sandalwood-scented ego and his immediate directives. Clones: All licensing agreements are now null and void. Newton: It's finally starting to gain traction in the marketplace, but we're a

Mac company and it's not a Mac so it's gotta go. We're going to build a *new* Macintosh and its most apparent feature will be that it's molded out of the same translucent colored plastic as a Battleship board game. We think you users will get by just fine without a floppy drive, too. Why? Don't ask dumb questions.

It was the iMac, and it set the whole industry on fire. Other PC manufacturers are lucky to have *some* sort of detectible influence upon their specific, limited sector of the technology industry. The iMac was so influential that even George Foreman freaking *grills* started coming out in iMac colors. Most importantly, this expression of arrogance, this renewal of the idea that this computer was *so* good that it couldn't *possibly* fail, and who cares what the market research does or does not say, renewed the public's grudging confidence in Apple; and rumors of a takeover or buyout, which was once accepted by the mainstream press as an inevitability, rang dumber and dumber as the months rolled on.

Which brings us full circle to Mac OS X. Just when the Mac got back on its feet, it was announced that Apple was jettisoning the OS they'd been building and improving since 1984 and would be replacing it with something completely new: Unix. Possibly the most un-Mac-like operating system there is, unless you can come up with one that can only be operated using pen-like styluses jammed into your nostrils.

Did Apple waffle? No. It arrogantly insisted that *this* was the way it was going to be. Did users consider abandoning the Mac? Oh, *hell* no. They had their doubts about Unix, and demanded that X live up to their expectations; but they were arrogantly confident that anything had to be more pleasant to use than Windows, even an OS that required that you stick the stylus in another location entirely.

FINDING YOUR OWN INNER MACINTOSH BLOWHARD

Arrogance — for lack of a better word and to pinch a line from one of Charlie Sheen's best films and one of Martin Sheen's worst — is good. Why? Because when we speak of arrogance as Mac users, we're not talking about being closed to alternative ideas and being contemptful of people who think differently. I mean, we actually put that last phrase on posters and tee shirts and billboards.

Our arrogance is what allows us to commit to new ideas, committing to them wholly and completely. Once a new idea has earned our respect, our arrogance allows us to see past the Now of Mac OS X 10.0, an OS with practically zero commercial apps that was barely functional enough to print a document. Our arrogance allows us to see what 10.1 and 10.2 and 10.3 would be like — operating systems that find and connect to networks automatically, use next-generation graphics rendering to create a truly beautiful user experience, and pack enough horsepower to become the OS of one of the five most powerful supercomputers on the planet.

So our arrogance is a survival mechanism. Reflect upon the fine example and the plain-spoken common sense exhibited by contestants on TV's *Fear Factor*. They believe that they *can* drink a milkshake containing brains, eyeballs, spleens, and something the show's producers spotted leaking out of a rusty drum by the side of a highway. Result: They *do*. Success is success.

Don't restrict your arrogance to the privacy of your home, either. Go to the electronics megastore and try to help out the people trying out the latest Windows hardware. "You're here because you need to replace broken, incapacitated, or obsolete gear," you might say, provided the shopper is a lot smaller than you and you know for a fact that this isn't a part of the country with a conceal-carry handgun law. "But

LEADING WITH CHARACTER

What is in a name? Even here, we see the superiority of Apple over Microsoft. Both create consumer products by sticking a letter of the alphabet in front of a common word, but Apple chooses "i" as if to suggest *it's all about you, the user. We're always thinking about you first, even when it comes to typing the names of our music players.* Whereas when Microsoft thinks of consumers they think "X" as in "unknown" or "X" as in "deleted." Or possibly "X" as in "kiss." I've seen Microsoft executives; selectively that would indeed be a positive enticement but you really don't want to leave that sort of thing to random chance.

I'm here because the speed and power of my iMac got me out of the office shortly after lunchtime!"

When the IT people who support the computers in your company insist that they can't add Macs to the network, or that a necessary feature, application, or service isn't compatible with Mac OS, refuse to believe them. "You're not telling me that it's impossible," you should say in an email, cc'ing it to the head of the company. "You're telling me that either you *don't know how* or *you don't want to be bothered.*" And just to be extra helpful, head on over to Monster.com and headhunt for a couple of new IT people on behalf of your (overworked and underappreciated) Human Resources department.

There *is* one claim to Windows superiority that's hard to challenge. Most of the greatest games do indeed come out for the Macintosh later than the Windows editions, if at all. But when confronted by this, you should note that for less than half the cost of the custom video card a Windows user needs to buy in order to play games at cinematic quality, you went out and bought an Xbox.

If you're a more peaceful sort of person who dislikes direct confrontation, you may opt to simply wait until the Windows bigot foolishly leaves his car unattended and then let nature and an easy-to-use plasma cutter (rentable at attractive daily rates from any contractor's depot) make your argument for you.

Finally, remember that just because you're as absolutely and arrogantly intractable regarding your beliefs as the Windows user is about his or hers, *that doesn't make you a bigot.* Only people who are *wrong* and who *disagree* with you are bigots.

History will prove us right. Arrogance was the right way to go with the original Mac, it was the right way to go with the iMac, and it's the right way to go with Mac OS X and beyond. We're the winners. We cannot fail. *We shall prevail.*

Now, granted, this also happens to be the last thing that the Big Brother guy said in Apple's *1984* commercial, just before he got taken out by the blond, lateral-thinking decathlete with the sledgehammer. But with a properly egotistical attitude, you can spin that positively. Remember: Big Brother was a PC guy.

Index

0-7645-6794-2

0-7645-6796-9

There's only one Andy Ihnatko...

0-7645-6797-7

0-7645-7322-5

. . . but fortunately, there's more than one book!
Each loaded with valuable information, color, anecdotes, tidbits, and Andy's distinctive style.